Flaming?

Flaming?

The Peculiar Theopolitics of Fire and Desire in Black Male Gospel Performance

ALISHA LOLA JONES

To the people of Church of the Heavenly Rest: Make great impact!

Rev. Dr. Alisha L. Jones

OXFORD
UNIVERSITY PRESS

OXFORD
UNIVERSITY PRESS

Oxford University Press is a department of the University of Oxford. It furthers
the University's objective of excellence in research, scholarship, and education
by publishing worldwide. Oxford is a registered trade mark of Oxford University
Press in the UK and certain other countries.

Published in the United States of America by Oxford University Press
198 Madison Avenue, New York, NY 10016, United States of America.

Library of Congress Cataloging-in-Publication Data
Names: Jones, Alisha Lola, author.
Title: Flaming? : the peculiar theopolitics of fire and desire in black
male gospel performance / Alisha Lola Jones.
Description: New York : Oxford University Press, 2020. |
Includes bibliographical references and index. |
Identifiers: LCCN 2019044915 (print) | LCCN 2019044916 (ebook) |
ISBN 9780190065416 (hardback) | ISBN 9780190065423 (paperback) |
ISBN 9780190065447 (epub) | ISBN 9780190065454 (Online)
Subjects: LCSH: Gospel music—History and criticism. |
African American male singers. | African Americans—Sexual behavior. |
Sex role in music. Classification: LCC ML3187 .J63 2020 (print) | LCC ML3187 (ebook) |
DDC 782.25/40811—dc23
LC record available at https://lccn.loc.gov/2019044915
LC ebook record available at https://lccn.loc.gov/2019044916

3 5 7 9 8 6 4

Paperback printed by Marquis, Canada
Hardback printed by Bridgeport National Bindery, Inc., United States of America

Contents

Acknowledgments   vii

Setting the Atmosphere: An Introduction   1

1. "I Am Delivert!": The Pentecostal Altar Call and Vocalizing Black
   Men's Testimonies of Deliverance from Homosexuality   36

2. "Men Don't Sing Soprano": Black Countertenors and Gendered
   Sound in the Sermonic Selection   70

3. Pole Dancing for Jesus: Pentecostal Religious Pluralism and the
   Bodily Performance of Sexual Ambiguity in Liturgical Dance   87

4. "Peculiar 'Til I D.I.E.": War Cries and Undignified Praise in Gospel
   Go-Go Music   115

5. "Wired": (De)Coding Tonéx's Unapologetic Queer Body Theology   149

6. Ritualizing the Unspoken: Memory, Separation, and the Rhetorical
   Art of Silence   172

7. Church Realness: The Performance of Discretionary Devices and
   Heteropresentation in the House of God   198

8. "Preaching to the Choir and Being Played": An Altar Call   218

Appendices   227
Notes   239
Glossary   277
Bibliography   287
Index   309

Acknowledgments

Since the third grade, I have dreamed of being a researcher and educator. My parents and faith community have supported my vision, even when the path I took was into new, brave, and unkind worlds. First and foremost, I would like to thank them for their support. As I write these acknowledgments, we are dealing with a deafening silence as we mourn the loss of my natural and spiritual father, conversation partner, promoter, multi-media trailblazer, and "wisdom friend" Rev. Dr. Alvin Augustus Jones. To my fearless mother Rev. Dr. Martha Butler Jones, thank you for being vigilant about my academic and artistic formation, despite the various structural barriers that arose. My brilliant sister Rev. Angela Marie Jones has made me smile, kept me grounded, and celebrated with me during this process. Thank you to my fine partner Rev. Calvin Taylor Skinner for holding me up as I neared the finish line. I appreciate your insight, patience, and compassion when I needed it the most. To the members of my home church International Kingdom Church in Bowie, MD, I am grateful for your consistent prayerful support and presence namely Lisa Lynch, Elaine and Jimmy Grant, Paula Christopher, Margo Reed, Angela Telesford, Dozier Johnson, Gemma Louis, and Deborah Williams.

The University of Chicago music department faculty undoubtedly sharpened me as an ethnomusicologist while I conducted the dissertation research that is the foundation for this book. My dissertation committee, Philip V. Bohlman, Travis A. Jackson, Robert Kendrick, and Emilie M. Townes, dean of Vanderbilt Divinity School, was the best collection of conversation partners during my research. I must convey what an honor it has been to work with my dissertation committee chair Melvin L. Butler. He is a superlative mentor who has demonstrated rigorous research and equally brilliant musicianship, sincere collegiality, precise instruction, and engaged guidance in a manner I aspire to resemble. I also thank my graduate school peers for challenging me as a scholar.

I received support from two Fund for Theological Education fellowships, Swift Dissertation Fellowship, Andrew W. Mellon Dissertation Fellowship; the Joint Residential Fellowship from the University of Chicago's Center for the Study of Race, Politics, and Culture and the Center for the Study of Gender and Sexuality; a Martin Marty Junior Fellowship; and a Franke Institute for the Humanities Affiliated Fellowship. I thank the numerous colleagues and institutions who have invited me to present my research in progress.

My colleagues in the Department of Folklore and Ethnomusicology and throughout the campus at Indiana University (Bloomington) have been instrumental in making sure that I complete this book project. I am fortunate to converse every day with countless undergraduate and graduate students whose questions and insights have sharpened my conceptual frameworks.

I thank the manuscript reviewers for their careful examination of my book and their productive recommendations that have made this research richer. Specifically, I would like to acknowledge my editor Suzanne Ryan and the many members of her staff at Oxford University Press, including Leslie Johnson, Richa Jobin, and Andrew Maillet. I would like to express my deepest gratitude to colleagues and students who were willing to closely read and converse about my research namely Lauren Eldridge Stewart, Kimberly Peeler-Ringer, John Orduña, and Allie Martin.

Fascinating people inspired this research, several of whom are cited in this book. Thank you for allowing me to observe you and I hope that people will be stretched by your work. To borrow from a song of ascent Psalms 126:1, I am truly "like she who dreamed" of completing a research project that I think engages with both the academy and the community. Now, more than ever, I look forward to a life dedicated to loving God with my mind, and sharing the fruits of that discovery in a contribution to the body of literature in music research.

Setting the Atmosphere

An Introduction

> God don't need no matches, He's fire all by Himself.
> —Reverend James Moore, *Live with the*
> *Mississippi Mass Choir* (1990)

"Being able to quickly find the address of God" was multi-Grammy award and Stellar[1] award-winning gospel music producer Donald Lawrence's way of describing the most prized musical competency in music ministry at the 2017 Hawkins Music and Arts Conference in Chicago. Within historically African American Pentecostal worship, a minister's capability to get to God instantly and usher God's presence into worship seamlessly is referred to in the vernacular as "setting the atmosphere." To achieve this contact with God, ministers teach believers to seek God first and all men will be drawn unto God (John 12:32) and by extension, the assembly of believers. Setting the atmosphere requires a form of self-giving, where they prepare congregants to be receptive to the move of the Spirit through ministers' skillful interplay of message and music. Vocal music ministers in particular use the body aesthetically and sonically to stimulate and inflame transcendence among participants.[2] In effect, worship leaders are to be exemplary God chasers and catchers.[3] They tap into the Pentecostal and gospel music[4] traditions to "take people there," that is, to happiness, to joy, to love-making, to heaven in sensually and sexually conservative religious spaces. Gospel singing in particular is at once understood as worshipful, erotic, and sensual activity for both performers and listeners in which fire and desire are ignited through the process of encountering God—the One described in the Bible as a "consuming fire" (Deuteronomy 4:24; Hebrews 12:29). However, setting the atmosphere is more than collectively experiencing the performative qualities of a worship leader's spiritual fire. The *telos* of setting the atmosphere is to fulfill participants' expectations to have a tangible encounter with God during the worship experience.

Countless followers of Jewish and Judeo-Christian faiths have described their ritual approaches to[5] and encounters with God and sightings of celestial

Flaming? Alisha Lola Jones, Oxford University Press (2020). © Oxford University Press.
DOI: 10.1093/oso/9780190065416.001.0001

beings[6] throughout the ages using imagery,[7] signifiers,[8] and sensations of fire;[9] however, the entire body of literature on fire symbolism in Christianity is out of the scope of this work. One core Pentecostal Christian account in the New Testament centers on the spiritually symbolic significance of fire established on the Day of Pentecost following Jesus Christ's resurrection from the dead. Pentecostalism is marked specifically by the belief in speaking in other tongues (*glossolalia*) as the Holy Spirit gives believers the ability and the interpretation of those unknown tongues (*xenoglossy*) by someone in the midst. The events are recounted in Acts:

> On the day of Pentecost all the believers were meeting together in one place. Suddenly, there was a sound from heaven like the roaring of a mighty wind-storm, and it filled the house where they were sitting. Then, what looked like flames or tongues of fire appeared and settled on each of them. And everyone present was filled with the Holy Spirit and began speaking in other languages, as the Holy Spirit gave them this ability.[10]

The miraculous in this tradition is animated by metaphoric and real fire that is sounded and heard in a lingual, articulated, and envoiced manner, a sign that the Comforter has come to remain among those who await the return of Jesus Christ the messiah. Moreover, it is precisely the sense of audiation, that is, hearing as both a spiritual and cultural practice that begs for more examination in how we interpret the move of the Spirit.

Assumptions About Gender Expression

Setting the atmosphere is also a theological, aesthetic, economic, and political enterprise during which participants negotiate style, sociocultural bias, and spiritual familiarity. And, unfortunately, regular churchgoers are watching the enterprise fail, symbolized by the decline in men's church attendance. Now, church leaders are trying to fill the void by reinventing their worship service formats and programming throughout the week. As Christian believers investigate what may be repelling men, some have arrived at conclusions along gendered and musical lines attributing feminization[11] of the church spaces with the loss of "the masculine spirit" as indicated in the following excerpt:

> The feminization of the church . . .
> Why its music, messages, and ministries are driving men away.
> The next time you go to church

> Ask yourself, why do churches today look more like the women's department of a store than a battalion of men poised to kick demons away? Churches today have become very dainty. Hanging out in church for most men seems immasculine [sic]. The lack of men within the church, both in a numeric and leadership sense, has crippled our churches. How do we regain the masculine spirit in our worship? Men in the pulpit draws [sic] men. Have the worship and the music leader use weighty worship music . . . Let the young men accept the masculine task of the patriarch.[12]

The opening of Reginald Williamson's antagonistic workshop PowerPoint was presented in response to what he called "a great discussion in the 21st century," which posited a contradiction to what ministers say should be leaders' emphasis as worship is engineered. Instead of focusing on seeking God, Williamson is concerned with attaining a male-dominant vision of men in worship who are poised to engage in battle, as he puts it. To draw primarily men and then their households to church, Williamson proposes focusing on what cisgender heterosexual men like. He maintains that the prevalence of "feminine" elements and ambience in the black Christian landscape dissuades men's church attendance and spiritual flourishing—and Williamson is not alone in this position. In his controversial misogynoir[13] message "I'm My Enemies' Worst Nightmare" (aka "These Hoes Ain't Loyal"[14]), Dr. Jamal Bryant preached that the churches were feminized through the participants' gravitation toward emoting, and in contrast, US Muslim mosques[15] are more attractive to African American men because those entities cater to men's reasoning as thinkers.[16] Bryant's views are a femme-, trans-, and homoantagonistic sample of popular discourses with which I have been accosted as a woman in pulpit and music ministry that are meant to keep women in their place and elevate cisgender, heteropresenting men.[17] However, there are still other spectators who would retort that despite Williamson and others' statements, images and sounds of black male participation in Christian worship life abound on the sanctuary platform and television programming.

Gospel enthusiasts like myself may not find occasion to do critical analysis of the predominantly male images and social interactions that are ever-present in the pulpit and on the platform in African American churches and in multimedia gospel music presentations. This omission is due in part to cultural anxieties around critiquing the fact that black men are absent in certain parts of society. Representations of African American male religious and civil rights leaders have been a fixture in the media for more than a century; however, I have found that the pervasive imagery of black men in church leadership that is presently disseminated through the media conceals their underrepresentation in the African American church experience. To be more specific, those images deflect attention from the black male underrepresentation phenomenon in the church pews.

Scholars in men's studies, religion, rhetoric, performance studies, sociology have researched a decline in black men's participation in African American Christian worship experiences across denominations in which charismatic expression is permitted. Religion researchers have found that church leaders are incorporating male-centered teachings such as Muscular Christianity into the sermons and music of the worship, especially in African American churches.[18] In message and music, Muscular Christianity preachers and teachers advocate for an imagined, monolithic, and elusive black masculinity to re-establish men as "rightful" leaders in churches and homes. This strategy to use Muscular Christian content seeks to rectify the perceived underdevelopment of strong male identities. Church leaders also advocate for men's extracurricular involvement in developing boys who do not display signs of feminine masculinity or exhibit the potential to be sexually queer. These faith leaders maintain that men's active presence in church stimulates men's participation in households, while the leaders overlook solutions for the historical, socioeconomic issues that contribute to men's absence in the home such as un- and underemployment and mass incarceration in the United States. Moreover, a culturally relevant focus on African American men's issues such as disproportionate youth victimization, police brutality, resident vigilantism, myriad trauma, and heavy grief is deficient in popular Muscular Christianity teachings.

Nevertheless, Williamson's and others' observations regarding male absenteeism in black churches are partially true, but his argument and analysis are ill-informed. He does not account for or consider that men are pursuing private devotion, religious pluralism, other faith practices, or nonreligious lifestyles. Even though I take exception to several points made in Williamson's presentation, I also take the popularity of his perspective seriously and consider two issues that Williamson asserts that are deterrents to men's attraction to church: women's advancement in church leadership and men exploring symbolically same-gender intimacy with God.

While these oppositional teachings are attractive and familiar to some believers, recapturing a mythical past, there are countless men and women who are turned off by the male-dominant social order and anti-matriarch perceptions that male-centered theologies reinscribe. Such theologies cast women's gender equality and advancement in church leadership as an impediment to men's ability to worship. Socioculturally, black women are the backbone of "the black church."[19] And while women represent over 60 percent of the financial contributors, laborers, and laypeople in historically African American Protestant congregations,[20] they are severely underrepresented in the paid, decision-making roles of church leadership. The majority of these women—single mothers, teenagers, widows, and the elderly—are exploited as laypeople, especially in music ministry roles. And yet they serve as maternal pedagogues who are endowed assumedly with mother wit and musical acumen.[21] They are disproportionately entrusted with providing religious, social, and cultural training in their domestic and ecclesiastic participation with no or comparatively little compensation—a sharp decline from the gendered role of women music educators of yesteryear.

In the heteropatriarchal organization of church leadership, the male-dominated roles of music minister, instrumentalist, and choir director are presumed to be paid participants in the social order. The apprenticeships and compensation are increasingly reserved for men. This privileging of men's employment in music ministry is a key sociocultural strategy in a US economy in which black men are the most under-/unemployed. Music ministry is also an admired, culturally relevant alternative to other illicit streams of income. Even though historically women served in those musical roles as educators, directors, and instrumentalists, there has been a sharp decline in apprenticeships for young women into salaried/waged music ministry leadership roles. They are over-represented and encouraged to pursue participation in vocal music ministry, which is the least compensated area of worship leadership (read: professional volunteership) in black churches. And yet they are required to exhibit the same level of professional dependability and musical skill as the instrumentalists.

Musically, Williamson is not alone in his observation of the lyrical content and harmonic textures of the popular music. He asserts that the music and lyrics are "too soft and romantic to appeal to men" in a manner that implies Jesus is their boyfriend, praising his beauty and tenderness. He wrote further that the music is "geared toward women's desires for safety, security, and *harmonious relationships*" (emphasis mine). Insider musicians such as Bishop Yvette Flunder have joked that with lyrical adjustments of pronouns, the "Jesus is my boyfriend" repertoire[22] could easily be love songs because of the amorous feelings they convey to a male God that is formed as the object of deep desire.[23] The convertibility of the songs becomes even more apparent when men sing. For believers who subscribe to a heteropatriarchal social structure, a man singing to a male God—a God whose Spirit is described as indwelling or entering into the believer, no less—is an aural and visual distraction when they consider possible queer meaning. Furthermore, "Jesus is my boyfriend" repertoire becomes a means through which men publicly perform permissible same-gender desire (to a male God) within conservative theological settings, while escaping the chastisement for explicitly same-gender intimacy with men.

In the popular imagination of socially conservative African American congregants, conventional gender identity is an "oppositional state of being that bifurcates a spectrum of traits into masculine and feminine poles."[24] Men are to distance themselves from traits associated with women's domains. As I have followed narratives of paranoia about men assuming a posture of worship in the church space designated for women, I noted insiders' use of terms such as "flaming" and "effeminate" to ridicule men whose musical performance of gender and sexuality registers as feminine or queer. I have written elsewhere, in my 2016 essay "Are All The Choir Directors Gay?: Black Men's Sexuality and Identity in Gospel Performance," about what forms of feminine masculinity (i.e., effeminate and flaming) registers as for people in these networks:

> There are cultural and religious tensions that surround men's display of femininity in worship. A man's vocalized and embodied display of feminine attributes is a contested and ridiculed gospel performance practice. Among respondents in my research, men's gender nonconformity in attire, mannerisms, and vocal styles can readily be interpreted as signals for sexual nonconformity. In these informal exchanges, men who are gender nonconforming or have same-gender desire are often presumed to be one and the same, which is not the case.[25]

These essentialized sentiments about black male gender expression are the basis for the case studies in this book examining performance of and against the flamboyant choir director stereotype, reacting to that typecast as an aural-visual shorthand for the performance of queer possibility.

More to the point, when I asked men about reasons they have stopped going to church, they have expressed that chief among the deterrents to their regular participation in worship is the lack of diverse models of masculinity, which seems to validate the aforementioned suspicions that Williamson posits.[26] They characterize popular models in a binary of church masculinity consisting of either the archetypal virile, alpha-male preacher[27] or the effeminate, subordinate choir director/singer. The preacher and the music minister qua choir director/singer are seen as the paradigmatic facilitators of the worship. The former is imagined as a philanderer or pulpit pimp,[28] and the latter is presumed to be "flaming" and on the "down low." There is admittedly plenty of evidence to support those accusations of artistic manipulation through word and music, but I resist the urge to reduce preacher and singer attributes solely to their sexual prowess and gender expression.

Both archetypal male professionals in worship leadership—the preacher and the choir director/singer—are commonly itinerant personalities, given to mobile labor and access to expansive social networks. Preachers and singers overlap in their contributory roles during liturgical moments of African American worship music and rhetorics (i.e., speech, attire, gesture). I add that there is the coveted role of the multigifted preacher-musician, seamlessly flowing between musical and rhetorical performances during worship. Numerous men embody the preacher-singer, preacher-instrumentalist, instrumentalist-singer, and preacher-singer-instrumentalist roles. In addition, there is little speculative discussion among gospel participants about other less performative or focal male archetypes—ministry adjutants, audio/sound engineers, security guards, and trustees—that transcend the preacher/vocal musician binary of masculinity discourse. Given the centrality of music to African American religious and quotidian life, I am drawn to the stereotypes of male musicians and the assumptions made about their identity that influence gospel music patronage, reception, and dissemination. Due to queer men's social access to both women and men's private lives, men who share the imagined feminine domain of the choir loft and vocal worship leadership are threatening because they are poised to be double agents conceivably divulging the extent to which women and queer men are being financially and sexually exploited in the heteropatriarchal leadership structure of the church.

The men's aforewritten description of male worship leader archetypes is almost consistent with W. E. B. Dubois's male-centered construction of the essential features of black religiosity in "Of the Faith of the Fathers" from his 1903 seminal work *The Souls of Black Folk,* which includes the preacher, the music, and the third component he calls "the frenzy."

> Those who have not thus witnessed the frenzy of a Negro revival in the untouched backwoods of the South can but dimly realize the religious feeling of the slave; as described, such scenes appear grotesque and funny, but as seen they are awful. Three things characterized this religion of the slave,—the Preacher, the Music, and the Frenzy. The Preacher is the most unique personality developed by the Negro on American soil. A leader, a politician, an orator, a "boss," an intriguer, an idealist,—all these he is, and ever, too, the centre of a group of men, now twenty, now a thousand in number. The combination of a certain adroitness with deep-seated earnestness, of tact with consummate ability, gave him his preeminence, and helps him maintain it. The type, of course, varies according to time and place, from the West Indies in the sixteenth century to New England in the nineteenth, and from the Mississippi bottoms to cities like New Orleans or New York.
>
> The Music of Negro religion is that plaintive rhythmic melody, with its touching minor cadences, which, despite caricature and defilement, still remains the most original and beautiful expression of human life and longing yet born on American soil. Sprung from the African forests, where its counterpart can still be heard, it was adapted, changed, and intensified by the tragic soul-life of the slave, until, under the stress of law and whip, it became the one true expression of a people's sorrow, despair, and hope.
>
> Finally the Frenzy of "Shouting," when the Spirit of the Lord passed by, and, seizing the devotee, made him mad with supernatural joy, was the last essential of Negro religion and the one more devoutly believed in than all the rest. It varied in expression from the silent rapt countenance or the low murmur

and moan to the mad abandon of physical fervor,—the stamping, shrieking, and shouting, the rushing to and fro and wild waving of arms, the weeping and laughing, the vision and the trance. All this is nothing new in the world, but old as religion, as Delphi and Endor. And so firm a hold did it have on the Negro, that many generations firmly believed that without this visible manifestation of the God there could be no true communion with the Invisible.

Like Williamson, DuBois is concerned about attracting large masses of black men to worship and promotes a particular musical aesthetic throughout the book. Despite the aforementioned interdisciplinary exploration of black men's worship, there has not been research that analyzes the extent to which male musicians encounter the Spirit, and negotiate "this visible manifestation of the God there could be no true communion with the Invisible." And in what ways does this encounter with the Invisible, reveal something about their performance of interiority and identity that withstands or confirms gospel participants' long-held cultural and theological perceptions about the sundry dimensions of men's participation in worship?

Flaming?: The Peculiar Theopolitics of Fire and Desire in Black Male Gospel Performance intervenes into this crisis of black male participation by examining the striking aural-visual performances of gender expression and sexuality as the Spirit moves upon vocalists' bodies. By following the discourse surrounding the "flaming" choir director stereotype, I investigate the extent to which men's unique approaches to music-making are met with spectators' derision and queries about the extent to which their worship generates queer connotations. Participants are essentially guided by what constitutes a practice of the adage "where there is smoke, there is fire." If there are rumors about a man's sexual behavior or if he demonstrates queer potential, then it is so. This perception is tied to the biblical notion that believers are to stay away from the appearance of activity and affiliations that are regarded as evil (I Thessalonians 5:22). As such, derision and interrogation are the real deterrents to black men's public worship participation. Instead of dismissing same-gender meanings in the performances, this research evaluates multisensory, same-gender, or queer possibilities with an emphasis on the denotations perceived through listening to and viewing of aural-visual moments.

I conceive of flaming as fourfold: First, "flaming" is a popular depreciatory vernacular term describing men who present a noticeable feminine masculinity that is assumed to be a sign of their queer potential. Second, "flaming" is my shorthand for the instances during demonstrative Pentecostal worship, in which the Holy Spirit or Holy Ghost moves about the person(s), indwells the body, animates the person(s) through speaking in tongues "as the Spirit gives utterance," satiates the body, and peculiarizes the participant through spiritual encounters, in a manner that believers have characterized as "fire shut up in my bones"—an adaptation of Jeremiah 20:9.[29] In essence, flaming is the moment where spiritual fire and bodily desires are stirred and erupt in perceptible, outward, and/or public displays. Third, the term "flaming" signifies on imagery of divine purification, refinement (tried through the fire to come out as pure gold), and judgment with hellfire and brimstone. For instance, to account of the African-derived continuum between religious and the nonreligious, "flaming" may refer to human homophobic assault by fire that reverberates throughout the African diaspora in (non-)religious songs. This repertoire is aired on urban black radio stations such as the homoantagonistic Jamaican dancehall songs "Mr. Chi Chi Man" by T.O.K. or "Boom Bye Bye" by Buju Banton.[30] Lastly, "flaming" is a site of queer power reversal in which the accusations that were used to condemn people who are anointed and happen to be homosexual are reclaimed and found to be of no consequence. The accusations themselves are impotent, flimsy, and susceptible to go up in flames when confronted with the scrutinized musician's musical competence as a worship leader readily able to take people into the presence of God.

I observe another tangible hindrance in the sense that historically black Pentecostal congregations and gospel networks are unfamiliar with myriad expressions and formations of identity, especially when the spirit moves participants. Men whose masculine style of worship is seen and heard as transgressing conventional gender expressions and heterosexuality become a sociocultural aberration and political provocation, despite evidence that these musicians are used by God to convert souls and change lives locally and throughout the world. To transgress conventional gender expression and heterosexual presentation is a theological and political act in Pentecostalism.

Flaming examines the rituals and social interactions of African American unmarried or unpartnered men who use gospel music-making as a means of worshiping God and performing gendered identities in and beyond Christian contexts. Strikingly, these unmarried men are skilled at expressing their affection toward God, while rarely sharing their desires to be married or sire children.[31] I argue that these men wield and interweave a variety of multivalent sonic and visual cues, including vocal style, gesture, attire, and homiletics, to position themselves along a spectrum of gender identities. These multisensory enactments empower artists (i.e., "peculiar people") to demonstrate modes of "competence" that affirm their fitness to minister through speech and song. In charismatic Christian biblical interpretation and usage, peculiarity refers to those who are spiritually "set apart," "sanctified," or "consecrated" for God's purposes. While keeping alive this conventional meaning, I also use the term to index gender and sexual difference as articulated by African American men central to this project.

To be sure, to position oneself as peculiar, sanctified, consecrated, and/or set apart is a theopolitical act that is at once a form of agency in the world and conformity to Pentecostal believers' collective values of standing out. I expand on Anthony Bogues (2003), Corey D. B. Walker (2005), and Melvin L. Butler's use of "theopolitics of knowledge." In his "critical understanding" of Bogues, Walker asserts "theopolitics of knowledge" is

> the *always ready* trace of theological within the global flows of knowledge that circulate throughout the particular legitimated political, economic, social, and intellectual spheres in the modern Western world. In this scenario, the theological is a critical heuristic device that suggests, among other things, a systematic and logically rigorous account of the theoretical frameworks that contain certain necessary claims and commitments grounded on an absolute discourse symbolized by the significant signifier "God." Moreover, this conceptual device acknowledges that particular transcendental foundations guarantee modern universal claims to rational knowledge, which, in turn are utilized in cognitive frameworks and argumentative structures to secure claims to legitimate and legitimating forms of knowledge.[32]

My use of theopolitics is phenomenological shorthand for the attestations of experienced vitality and negotiation of the contested, intimate, glocal dynamics of spirit-filled/spirited worship that is performed in the sanctuary of the local assembly and possibly streamed into the global imagined community through the Internet.

Signifyin'[33] on the mood music hit "Fire and Desire" from the *Street Songs* (1981) album recorded by Rick James and Teena Marie, the "fire and desire" included in the title of this book alludes to the eros illustrated in the classic song and connects that eros to sensuo-sexual iconicity—erotic resemblances—that occurs within charged worship. The almost indecipherable, overwhelming, emotional-physical encounter with an animating, transformational, powerful, persuasive love; the kind of love that takes a hold of you and reveals a spiritual magnetism that conflicts at once with what is believed to be appropriate, timely, and morally right for the body. This book extends my research on the pleasure vocalists themselves may derive, concurrently maintaining Christian piety while providing forms of musical healing for others.[34] Expanding on the work of musicologists of gender and sexuality Suzanne Cusick, Susan McClary, and Philip Brett, I unlay the ways in which gospel singing is experienced as erotic and sensual for non-heterosexual, single believers, both performers and listeners. I uncover the insight we gain about the pleasure drawn from the auditory and bodily dimensions of gospel music-making. As a result, I assert sexual abstinence teachings obscure the imperceptible forms of sensual, romantic, and sexual exploration occurring in gospel music participation.[35]

Parting from the concept of sexual identity being tethered only to reproduction, I take up Suzanne Cusick's consideration of the circulation of physical pleasure through music. In doing so, she contends that "musician" just might be a precise way to qualify my gospel music informant's sexuality, sexual orientation, and/or sexual behavior: "For some of us, it might be that the most intense and important way we express or enact identity through circulation of physical pleasure is in musical activity, and that our 'sexual identity' might be musician more than it is 'lesbian,' 'gay,' or 'straight.'"[36] Additionally, I assert that there is much in common between the transcendence sought in worship and the euphoria found in sexual climax—and it is these commonalities that reveal the extent to which the unutterable nuances of spiritual encounters have yet to be unraveled when it comes to the homomusicoerotics of worship that is spirit-filled. By "homomusicoerotics," I refer to the erotics brought about when one encounters the sounds vocally emitted or instrumentally and rhetorically made by one of the same gender. Homomusicoerotics—and even homosonoerotics to account for soundscapes—is especially fraught in the heteropatriarchal and predictably homophobic historically black Pentecostal churches and venues where gospel music is performed.

My strategy to ascertain the aural-visual dynamics of rituals and social interactions is to examine the tropes that are distributed in popular black church discourse, especially through television shows, musicals, and YouTube videos. This book makes an intervention by offering a multifaceted structure for interpreting meaning in black male sacred music "performances" in Pentecostal settings with the following spheres of meaning: identity, aesthetics, gendered and sexualized symbols, and performance competency. The identity sphere encompasses self-identification, divine endorsement that includes notions of anointing and call, intracultural status, and postcolonial, intercultural perceptions. The aesthetics sphere accounts for the incorporation of dance, drum, and song into the African-derived performances. The sphere of gendered/sexualized symbols accounts for the extent to which space, roles, functions, and people are coded with meaning based on further assumptions and ignorances about the performer. The performance competency sphere elucidates the commonly valued and scrutinized skillsets of worship leadership and black sacred music-making.

Observing the overrepresentation of gay men in musical participation, performance theorist E. Patrick Johnson confirms, "One of the most enduring stereotypes in the black church, for instance, and one not peculiar to the South, is that of the flamboyant choir director, musician, or soloist" (184). Johnson's interlocutor named Freddie conjectured that gay men may flock to the choir because the choir robe resembles a dress. Others have speculated that gay men are drawn to the choir because they are "naturally," "creative," "artistic," or "talented." Johnson adds two other reasons for this over abundance of queer participation:

First, participation in the church choir provides a way to adhere to the religiosity of southern culture but also build a sense of community within what can sometimes be a hostile space. This is one instance in which seemingly repressive sacred space actually affords a vehicle for the expression of sexual desire. Second, as some of the men suggest, the choir provides a medium to express one's sexuality through the theatricality already built into the church service. Freddie's joke is an example—an example that hits close to home.[37]

Flamboyant choir director humor abounds in popular gospel musical discourse. For example, "He's sweet, I know," is a punch line based on a song made popular by gospel music icon Mahalia Jackson. I have heard gospel music fans commonly say that refrain as a way of observing and discreetly calling men "flamboyant" whose self-presentation exudes an aura of queerness. With regard to comedic sketches, a widely distributed portrayal is delivered in the "Choir Audition" webisode of gospel comedienne Lexi's *The Holy Ghost Enforcers*. The auditions are facilitated by an emcee whose style of dress and manner of speech resembles a stereotypical composite of the eye-catching choir director persona. In every episode, the reoccurring character Antwan aka 'Twan, played by DW Bass, wears some variation of lip gloss, a big rainbow bowtie, and a Louis Vuitton hobo bag, all of which register as visual markers of a man's queer potential in African American culture.[38] Using fluid hand and neck gestures and mouth popping, the emcee begins the auditions with a traditional greeting that abounds with gendered double entendre in his remarks.[39] 'Twan performs the customary script that marks him as an insider familiar with what is expected when people within black church culture address the congregation. In addition, he is adorned with symbols that hold queer connotation for gospel insiders but never does he self-identify explicitly as homosexual. 'Twan's articles of clothing, manner of speech, and physical location within the sanctuary in that webisode induces the paradigmatic representation of the "don't ask, don't tell" social contract about queer identity concealment that persists in black religiosity.

To analyze the stereotype in the 'Choir Audition" episode, I consult communication and gender and sexuality studies. Continuing the analysis of gender and sexuality scholars Philip Brian Harper and C. Riley Snorton, I posit in "Are All the Choir Directors Gay?" that the "don't ask, don't tell" social contract is fueled by black masculine anxieties that have been transferred from broader US society into black churches through rumors and speculation.[40]

Conversations and folklore surrounding the rumored pervasiveness of queer sexuality and gender expression in black churches bolsters the Black masculine anxieties about male gospel performance. Snorton's assessment takes into account specifically male choir leadership, whereby the male vocal worship leader "could almost be considered a trope in narratives about queer sexuality and the black church . . . as proverbial ur-text of queer sexual rumors."[41]

One of the most popular musical figures is the flamboyant choir director, a trope highlighting the ways in which gospel music is an aural-visual performance art—the choir loft space and choir director role—a site for scrutinizing musicians' sexual orientation and gender expression.

Further, Snorton asserts that in addition to the male choir director's capacity as an "arranger" or organizer of music performance, "his location—typically placed behind and elevated above the pulpit makes him a focal point of surveillance."[42]

Choir directors' worship leadership competency includes their aptitude to attract and vie for observers' gaze and listening within heteropatriarchal socio-cultural spheres. This skill set simultaneously draws both scrutiny and anxiety about their potential queer duplicitousness. And choir directors' ability to capture both the male and female gaze is lucrative. Men are typically the senior pastor, the decision-makers for hiring personnel in the historically black Pentecostal congregations. Women are likely in the congregation and the largest demographic who purchase music as a commodity through album, ticket, and paraphernalia sales. Within references to these men as cultural symbols, I observe that musicians use flamboyance in the following ways: to model interiority and demonstrativeness as worship leaders; to prompt other musicians, preachers, and congregants; to perform aesthetic values; to create aural-visual commodities for patrons; and to reinforce gendered roles in black church patriarchy in which feminine masculine or queer men are ridiculed. Doubts about a man's "straight" sexual orientation surface from observing his embodied musical performance, and jokes circulate about "gracious," "prancing," "colorful," "flamboyant," or "flaming" gospel singers and choir directors; however, vocal musicians are not the only men with queer potential, desire, and behavior.[43]

What Prompted This Research?

The inspirations for the research queries probed in this book *Flaming?* stem from two pivotal encounters with black men involved in gospel music industry programming and performance who challenged the essentialist portrayals of vocal masculinity as an impresario and a unapologetically gay vocal musician. Their narratives demonstrate the urgency of more in-depth ethnomusicological study. One of these moments is the posthumous "outing" of Eric Torian, which

served as an impetus for my consideration of male subjectivity in gospel performance. Pioneering impresario Eric Torain (1963–2002) was the executive
director for gospel music programming at the Washington Performing Arts
Society (formerly WPAS; now WPA), which offered performance opportunities annually through the Children of the Gospel choir (COTG) to about five
hundred youths. Each season participants were afforded the opportunity to
perform with composers and musicians such as Evelyn Simpson-Currenton,
Richard Smallwood, Joyce Garrett, Nolan Williams, Thomas Tyler Dixon, Ned
Lewis, Walt Whitman, Stephanie Mills, Daryl Coley, and Vicki Winans. In the
gospel music industry, Torain was one of several cultural intermediaries for the
Washington, DC metropolitan area gospel concerts, making sure that various
artists were able to perform and get radio play.[44]

In a public arts education response to youth victimization due to the 1990s
crack cocaine epidemic in Washington, DC, Torain created an alternative musical space in which his charges, including my sister and me, repeatedly and de-
claratively sang our rendition of the Mississippi Children's Choir's "(Yes,) There is
Hope!" from the *Children of the King* (1992) album.[45] He was one of several public
figures who heeded a call for men to take a more active role in youth mentorship
and prevent the youth victimization, devastating the nation's capital. Long after
I participated, I cherished my COTG experiences performing with various lumi-
naries and dignitaries and traveling the world. A few years after I graduated from
the choral program, I was blindsided by the following *Washington Post* obituary
that I received in my Oberlin campus email:

> Eric Torain, 39, who introduced gospel music into the annual program schedule
> of the staid Washington Performing Arts Society and founded its acclaimed
> Men, Women and Children of the Gospel Mass Choirs, died June 12 at a hos-
> pital in Greensboro, NC. The former District resident had AIDS.[46]

This public revelation of Torain's AIDS status as the cause of death seemed, at
that time, like a statement about his identity. Consequent to the publicity surrounding Torain's death, there were conversations about gender and sexuality
in Washington, DC among the young people whose lives he affected, many of
whom would not otherwise have talked about the AIDS pandemic.

Among black Christians in the early 2000s, it was assumed that men who died
of complications due to diabetes used that term as code for HIV/AIDS. If they
died of HIV/AIDS, they were assumed to be involved in sexual relationships
with other men. HIV/AIDS was a "gay disease." Those who succumbed to the
virus were, consequently, denied pastoral eulogies, and their families were not
allowed the convenience of discretion about the manner in which the disease
might have been contracted. Indeed, there have been constant rumors that

some legendary gospel figures, such as the Rev. James Cleveland (1931–1991), had died of AIDS and were "closeted" gay men. Regardless, Rev. Cleveland was still widely feted and patronized long after his death. According to black religion scholar Stacy Boyd, "That Cleveland may have been gay and may have died from AIDS does not deter industry leaders from describing him as the king of gospel and does not prevent people from singing and 'shouting' to his music."[47] His narrative is an iconic example of the contradictions—musical consumption despite queer sexual orientation suspicions—that persist in heteronormative African American Christian religiosity and gospel music industry.

The other pivotal moment was when Tonéx, a well-known recording artist in gospel music circles, unapologetically came out as a gay man. Shortly after embarking upon doctoral study at the University of Chicago in 2007, I asked questions about a gospel artist named Anthony C. Williams, also known as Tonéx. I have had conversations with numerous informants who point out that he embodies tensions highly characteristic of gospel music pop culture. They commented on the peculiarity of his attire, hair, and choreography. Over the years, these conversations have revealed an apparent lack of familiarity with the unmarked spectrum of gender and sexual identities in black Christian communities. Some onlookers have even expressed bewilderment at the spelling of his name Tonéx, along with his sudden change in 2010 to B.Slade, both of which feature a silent "x" at the end.[48] The signifiers that Tonéx incorporated into his performances and recordings prompted observers to question whether or not he is gay.

Before I began researching black men's performance of sexuality and expression of gender, I assumed that Tonéx was merely trying to convey his heterogeneous stylistic range as a performer and that it was not an intentional expression of his sexuality. I knew that Tonéx had, on several occasions, preached sermons rebuking gay men for their overt display of sexual identity. For example, in the late 1990s, at what I will call "Mt. Sinai Church" in Washington, DC, Tonéx preached about men's need for "deliverance" and for God to change them. News of his ministerial chastisement of the congregation spread like wildfire because of the cognitive dissonance that it cultivated among believers, many of whom had deduced from his androgynous gender performance a "closeted" queer sexual orientation but could or would not prove that it was true. Rumors also circulated about how Tonéx's actions were consistent with discreetly gay preachers' parroting of homophobic sermon styles, a shared survival mechanism that is a public performance to deflect from the detection of their queer sexual preferences.[49]

When he eventually let the public into his truth, disclosing that he was gay in 2009, I became curious about Tonéx's performance of gender and sexuality as he shifted into social life as an openly gay man with the new stage name B.Slade. During my interview with him in 2011, B.Slade claimed that other gospel musicians have publicly depicted queer influenced performances, featuring gestures from black and Latino gay ball culture during major gospel awards shows; however, these artists performed in code, displaying competence in a kind of musical queerness without explicitly disclosing their lives as gay men to outsiders of that scene. They protected their private lives in order to remain members in their faith community.

Since 2007, B.Slade's career has represented part of a process to identify spaces for the important full disclosure of performers' identities in gospel music. As Tonéx attests and Eric Torain demonstrated, black queer men are significant contributors to the gospel music industry. And many of these queer men are still not comfortable revealing who they are to their brothers and sisters in Christ to the point that some men die suffering with both physical disfigurement and spiritual trauma. Through the gospel music industry, Eric Torain facilitated a black male presence for hundreds of fatherless children during a crisis of youth victimization in Washington, DC. His gospel music progeny are among some of the most sought-after musicians and scholars. B.Slade's contribution to gospel music discourse exemplifies a subversive black Pentecostal masculinity that is openly negotiating queerness. My reflection on Eric Torain's impact and ethnographic work on Tonéx have led me to probe larger questions that have been percolating for years, juxtaposing the decline in black men's public worship practices with their contributions to gendered gospel performance in African American Christian faith communities.

As such, the notion of disclosing queer sexual desire and history is traditionally communicated by those who are associated with music ministry, after they have claimed to no longer have sex with other men. Male vocal musicians have become the highly scrutinized worship leaders within black churches, evaluated for the ways in which the aural-visual features of their musical performance reveal their queer potential. In the research to follow, I seek to provide the tools for dissecting the contentious sociocultural nature of the flamboyant choir director stereotype and gospel audiences' negative reception of their performances. To do so, I provide a brief genealogy of gospel figures whose narratives signaled a shift in discussions about queer sexuality.

A Brief Genealogy of Gospel Musician's Queer Sexual History Discourse

I connect Eric Torain and B.Slade to a rise in black Christian men's self-disclosure of their queer sexual history, since the 1980s and well into the turn of the twenty-first century. Notable musicians have been scrutinized for the queer meanings they generate through their testimonies, discretion, and style. Also, there have been numerous events that have fueled the flaming choir director stereotype as a trope for queer possibility. As the HIV/AIDS pandemic swept through the United States in the 1980s, the virus was associated with the sexual activity of men who have sex with men. Consequently, people's sexual behavior was brought into the public sphere, especially into historically black Pentecostal churches that disapproved of same-sex relationships. I do observe a correlation between vocal musicians' (probably preemptive) self-disclosure and anxieties surrounding the wages of sin being brought about through HIV/AIDS-related death. Christian believers who were infected with HIV/AIDS through various forms of sexual intercourse, blood transfusion, or intravenous drug use feared the stigma that was overwhelmingly associated with the disease. However, black Christian believers were not on the forefront of getting education about the virus or how to serve those who were affected or infected by the disease. Countless believers died in shame; however, it has been musicians' disclosure of their private lives over the last thirty-five years that has brought to the fore the anxiety of "the black church" about sexuality and queerness.

Prominent transgender disco performer Sylvester James contracted the virus and returned to his Pentecostal Christian roots to cope with his condition.[50] Visibly sick, James sought spiritual counsel from Bishop Walter Hawkins and Pastor Yvette Flunder at the Love Fellowship Center in San Francisco until his dying breath. Bishop Hawkins and Rev. Flunder faced chastisement from Pentecostal believers for their support of James. Anti-gay sermons decrying "sissies" became increasingly popular. James's demise became a troubling signifier of what happens should a person fully embrace their queer identity. For years since then, rumors have spread about musicians who died of blood-related or undisclosed diseases. Speculation about the true cause of their passing has overshadowed the power of their legacy. One of the most famous cases in gospel music is the posthumous accusation that Rev. James Cleveland, the founder of the Gospel Music Workshop of America, died of complications from HIV in 1991.

At the apex of the HIV/AIDS pandemic, Rev. Daryl Coley became the first gospel music artist to self-identify as delivered from homosexuality in a 1995 interview with *Gospel Today* editor Teresa Hairston in the article "Daryl Coley: The California-Born Gospel Singer Overcoming Homosexuality and Diabetes." Through the framing of his self-disclosure, Coley's sexual history was likened to a malady, thus reinscribing the stigma that hovers around his identity. Over the last twenty years other vocalists have made similar disclosures. Among them, recording artist Rev. Donnie McClurkin from Long Island is the most popular spokesman to have identified as delivered from homosexuality (2000). Conversely, rarely do preachers divulge that they have queer sexual history.

Likewise, I have noticed that homosexuality becomes a hot topic following well-publicized sex scandals involving prominent religious leaders. For instance, the September 2010 allegations against the "hypermasculine,"[51] homophobic, and heteropresenting Bishop Eddie Long, who faced accusations of sexually inappropriate behavior with minors, fueled contextual discussions of homosexuality. Long was senior pastor of New Birth Missionary Baptist Church in Atlanta, a major site for conferences, live recordings, and concerts in gospel music. His ministry was responsible for mentoring and launching the careers of several ministry gifts such as Dr. Jamal Bryant, "the Prince of Praise" Byron Cage, "the Gospel Luther" Darwin Hobbs, comedian Pastor John Gray just to name some. He allegedly used lavish gifts and trips to coax his "spiritual sons"[52] in the congregation into sexual impropriety.[53] Long later stated during his streamed service,

> I have never in my life portrayed myself as a perfect man. But I am not the man that is being portrayed on the television. That's not me. That is not me. By the counsel of my lawyers, they have advised me not to try this case in the media. It still has to be tried in the court of justice. And to be honest, I think that is the only place I can get justice. I feel like David against Goliath but I got five rocks, and I haven't thrown one yet.[54]

Various observers remarked about the irony and perhaps Freudian slip of Bishop Long likening himself to David in relation to the allegations. Davidic imagery saturates gospel music and Pentecostal rhetoric, habitually without critical analysis of his performance of gender identity. Although David was heteropresenting in his relationship with Bathsheba,[55] queer theologians and Hebrew Bible scholars have also interpreted him as having a discreet same-gender romantic relationship with Jonathan, if not *overly* homosocial and homoerotic.[56]

The allegations against Bishop Long looked like the illicit and clandestine intimacies that are explored in the homosocial networks of male-dominant church leadership structures. Such intimacies prompt me to interrogate the ways in which predominantly male leadership ranks are maintained, offering further incentives than solidifying fraternal bonds or adhering to a biblical prohibition against female leadership. There are other veiled purposes at play in these structures. I contend that these structures also conceal the Christianized form of what French theorist Jacques Derrida described as phallogocentrism that is preserved in rhetorical and musical spaces for men's same-gender social, romantic, sensual, erotic, and sexual exploits, and of course, self-pleasure.[57]

Reading, Performing, and Constructing Peculiarity

Men are serving congregations in the pews, pulpit, and musicians' pit in various capacities, they contribute to the musical life of the congregation through participatory performance. There is no demarcation between the congregants and worship leaders in ushering the presence of God in corporate worship. Throughout African American religious narratives, one finds musical representations of several predominantly male church roles such as deacons lining out hymns[58] and instrumentalists offering a sermonic selection. "Sermonic selection" refers to the liturgical placement (not an actual genre) of special music or featured music that is performed as a segue into the sermon to set the tone for the message. Traditionally, sermonic selections are intended to set the atmosphere by relating to the message that will be preached through planned or improvised presentation. Consistent with traditional presentations of masculinity, male ushers' militant and close-to-the-body gesture constitute a performative aspect of worship. Unfortunately, though, music ministry participants and spectators distinguish those models of masculinity from the plethora of discourses generated about men who participate in music performances that display their potentially queer identity. What is at stake is that a musician's display of queer potential is scrutinized as a symptom of a spiritual struggle that will contaminate the worship experience. The social anxieties that I observe around men's display of queer potential prompt my interrogation of the perceptions about gender and sexuality that are distributed through teachings derived from male-focused ideologies such as Muscular Christianity.

Through a progression of transcongregational case studies, I observe the ways in which African American men traverse tightly knit social networks to negotiate their identities through and beyond the worship experience. Coded and read as either hypermasculine, queer, or sexually ambiguous, peculiar gospel performances are often a locus of nuanced protest, facilitating a critique of heteronormative theology, while affording African American men opportunities for greater visibility in and access to leadership. This research thus examines the performative mechanisms through which black men acquire an aura of sexual ambiguity, exhibit an ostensible absence of sexual preference, and thereby gain social and ritual prestige in gospel music circles. By attending to the needs of fellow artists, clergy, and congregations, musicians also gain the discretion of those in positions of power who derive pleasure from their musical services and enforce a don't ask, don't tell arrangement. Same-sex relationships among men constitute an open secret that is carefully guarded by those who elect to remain silent in the face of traditional theology, but musically performed by those compelled to worship "in Spirit and in truth." Voluminous African American gospel fans infer a connection between a musician's gendered performance and a "lifestyle" assumed to lie outside the boundaries of traditional Christian morality. How does gospel music-making allow black men to construct alternative masculinity or manhood, even as audiences selectively "read" queerness into their sounds and gestures?

Although women play an important role in shaping these narratives as patrons and professional personnel, I have found that conversations about gender and sexuality in black gospel music center on the sexual orientation and gender expression of men. "Homosexuality" is discussed almost solely as a men's issue and in terms of men's inadequacy or effeminacy that manifests during demonstrative moments in worship. However, there are a few cisgender Pentecostal women musician narratives of queerness: openly self-identified "same-gender loving" women (Bishop Yvette Flunder and Lynette Hawkins), formerly lesbian (Rev. Dr. Juanita Bynum), and virgin lesbian (Dejuaii Pace), but they haven't posed a threat to the power structures in the tradition.[59] Church of God in Christ (COGIC)-raised Yvette Flunder and Shirley Miller, her partner from the famed gospel artist family the Hawkins, have been public about their relationship. Now a bishop in the Fellowship of Affirming Churches that she founded, Flunder has been a pastor to black gay men and male allies who have been ousted from black churches due to their beliefs. On the heels of her very public divorce from Bishop Thomas Weeks III, COGIC-raised preacher and recording artist Juanita Bynum confessed during a 2012 radio interview, "I've been there and I've done it all. I did the drugs, I've been with men, I've been with women. All of it."[60]

Flunder, Hawkins, and Bynum have all fashioned platforms for themselves as pastoring-preaching women in exile from the COGIC church, which does not promote the ascension of women to senior posts in church leadership. Recording artist Dejuaii Pace of the legendary Pace family is a vocalist whose livelihood was tied to music ministry with her sisters. In 2011 she revealed to the public that she was addicted to food, and that she was a virgin and a lesbian on the television show *Iyanla, Fix My Life* that aired on the Oprah Winfrey Network (OWN). She had disclosed her identity to her family a few years prior and that she had been doing the personal work connecting her food addiction to her repressed sexuality.[61] After the initial news cycle when these stories were released, there hasn't been much focus on that detail of her life other than the occasional jokes about her masculine energy or speculations about her heterosexual marriageability. Throughout this research, I refer to the men's ethnic identity and racial/phenotypic attributes with the terms "African American" and "black" respectively, unless otherwise designated in a citation or conventional term usage. I will refer to some of the men as "homosexual," "gay," "queer," and "same-gender loving" (SGL).[62] Each term conveys the social position of the men with whom I have spoken, and I try to privilege in my writing the ways in which my subjects and informants self-identify. While a great number of the men refer to themselves as homosexual or gay, there are some men, especially young adult activists, who draw a distinction between being gay[63] and same-gender loving in their self-identification. A vast majority of my conversation partners have expressed a preference for being referred to by same-gender loving or SGL. I do my best to distinguish between the terms "homosexual," "gay," "SGL," and so on when appropriate, and to assign the proper terms to the proper persons throughout this text. There is also a glossary included for definitions of other unique terminology in this book.

I approach this topic with a great deal of caution, in part because I sense that my research could be the only encounter that a lot of readers of this book will have with gospel music. Moreover, my consultants have expressed a belief that the sexual ambiguity of church performers and the outing of popular artists negatively effect the evangelical "witness" of gospel music. Keenly aware of the politics of my work and its potential influence on perceptions of religion, race, and gender within both the "black church" and the academy, I wish to avoid reinscribing stereotypical notions of black church culture and of black men as always deceptive and/or on the "down low." Musicologist Robert Walser has articulated a similar concern with regard to writing about class and gender issues in heavy metal music:

> Critics of popular music must take care to acknowledge the politics of their work: while it is imperative to be critical, to avoid bland enthusiasm or dispassionate positivism, analyses of popular culture must also be empathetically drawn if they are to register accurately the contradictions and subtleties of popular practices. Otherwise, they too easily serve as mandates for elitist condemnation and oppression.[64]

There are countless contradictions and subtleties that manifest in popular African American Christian and gospel music practices. I want to emphasize that African American Christianity is diverse and complex, as are other spiritual traditions. This project is an empowering opportunity to offer a more nuanced representation of black Christian men and their music-making. And it is also empowering for me, as a black female scholar who is sympathetic to womanist and black feminist issues, a positionality to which I now turn.

Positionality, Identity, Experience, and Multisited Ethnography

My experiences with Eric Torain and Tonéx heightened my awareness of how I am positioned in relation to this project. As an African American heterosexual, cisgender female/femme, ethnomusicologist, theologian, music minister, conservatory-trained vocal musician, men's studies scholar, and peculiar Pentecostal believer, I embrace a number of insider-outsider identities that provide me with a unique set of vantage points.[65] Throughout my ethnography I was asked, "Why are you interested in researching men?" This question is a threefold signifier to me that my study of men is a contested realm of inquiry for women to enter, is assumed to be a man's domain, and has been a locus for outing and betrayal. Citing literary scholar Nancy K. Miller, African American literature and culture scholar Michael Awkward noted decades ago that it has become a trend to "get personal" in ethnographic writing, such that

> the question, "How does your work reflect the politics of your (racial/gendered/sexual) positionality?" may have overtaken the inquiry, "What is your theoretical approach?" as the most popular conversational gambit at conferences and other sites of professional interaction. Indeed, we might say that sincere responses to the injunction, "Critic, position thyself," are seen by many as among the most effectively moral and significant gestures of our current age, protecting us from among other sins, fictions of critical objectivity that marred previous interpretive regimes.[66]

I am especially concerned with the uniqueness of where I stand and how my (racial/gendered/sexual/social/cultural) positionality intersects with my research. I recognize that these identities have afforded me experiences that encompass a wide variety of exposures, biases, assumptions, and curiosities. Yet I am also profoundly aware of both the social boundaries that fieldworkers have to navigate, and also the prejudices and restrictions that I continue to encounter as a black woman engaged in critical inquiry concerning black men.

Around the time I started inquiry into discourse about black men's performance of identity, womanist and black feminist researchers were responding to the glaring omission in analyzing masculinities. In her groundbreaking text *Sexuality and the Black Church: A Womanist Perspective* (1999), then-Howard University Divinity School professor Kelly Brown Douglas reflected on seminarians remarks about homosexuality when she taught, comments that I know quite well, variations of which I have written about elsewhere:

> I can love the sinner, but not the sin.
>
> Homosexuality is an abomination.
>
> To be gay goes against nature.
>
> If we were supposed to be homosexual, God would have created Adam and Steve, not Adam and Eve.
>
> I don't mind gay people, but why do they have to be so vocal and pushy about their rights?
>
> Homosexuality is a White thing.
>
> Africa did not have homosexuals before European went there.
>
> Homosexuality is detrimental to the Black family.[67]

Such commentary is baffling and is misrepresentative of the members who have constituted our communities for years. Queer people have *always* been with us, as loving, active, and creative participants in our communities. Prompted by insight from her friend and theological colleague Renee Hill made about womanists' neglect of the topic of sexuality in religious studies, Brown Douglas pursued research on sexuality discourses in black churches. Hill wrote:

> Christian womanists have failed to recognize heterosexism and homophobia as points of resistance that need to be resisted if all Black women (straight, lesbian, and bisexual) are to have liberation and sense of their own power. Some women have avoided the issue of sexuality and sexual orientation by being selective in appropriating parts of [Alice] Walker's definition of womanism. This tendency to be selective implies that IT is possible TO be selective about who deserves liberation and visibility.[68]

That selectivity of the definition also erases the lesbian knowledge of its author that is infused into the profundity of its fabric. Like Brown Douglas, I have been challenged to think deeply about this omission and contribute to the body of literature from a womanist and black feminist perspective in solidarity with lesbian women.

As I pass through interdenominational, gospel performance settings, I am attuned to constructions of male privilege that are based upon fundamentalist biblical interpretations restricting the extent to which women can be "used by God" as church leaders.[69] For an African American woman, particularly one who is also a Pentecostal minister, to think, speak, and write critically about black men in these spaces is, in many respects, a transgressive act. I see my interrogation as transgressive because it confronts "the assumption that women are peripheral and secondary historical objects of church and community life— the others."[70] And thus my inquiry into the nature of how male-dominant ranks engage music, a deeply womanist realm of aesthetics and spirituality, becoming what Alice Walker refers to as "womanish"—a radically bodacious subjective critique of patriarchal black church systems.[71]

The notion of peculiarity has been a useful concept for analyzing the ways in which men's performance evokes questions and scrutiny along gender lines that also engages discourse on women's contributions in African American charismatic churches. Previously, women have also been researched as "peculiar" in their contribution to Pentecostal worship, specifically in the Oneness Pentecostal tradition that is described in English scholar Elaine Lawless's *God's Peculiar People: Women's Voices and Folk Tradition in a Pentecostal Church* (1988). As is true of Pentecostal congregations,

Not only do women attend these churches, but they participate in the services in greater numbers and with more intensity, because this religious arena is approved as a forum for free participation in emotional religious response and ecstasy. Because historically women in this country have not had many such forums available to them, it is understandable that where their participation is condoned they take full advantage of the opportunity to speak and to perform.[72]

I appropriate the term "peculiar" to articulate the ways in which my identities are held as binaries in tension and even contradiction with each other. Citing the work of African American studies scholar Daphne Brooks, religion scholar Ashon Crawley coined the neologism "spatial genitals" that he adapted in response to gender studies scholar Anne Fausto-Sterling's "cultural genitals" to describe the scrutiny in the traditional Pentecostal imagination as black women negotiate their bodies within gendered leadership hierarchies in performative realms like pulpit ministry. It refers to the

gendered interpolations of *space* based on the binary sex system (male/female). Bodies in specific locations are read through spatial genitals and are understood to concede, contest or contaminate social relationships based on their reflection within the space. Put simply, based on biological constructions of bodies (i.e., "sex"), subjectivities are inculcated (i.e., "gender") with acceptable gestures, stylizations of body, conversation.[73]

I have also observed that there are spaces in churches that are imagined to be for feminine and masculine participation. The pulpit and music pit for instrumentalists are perceived as the masculine and/or heteroperformative domains. The congregation and the choir loft are fashioned as the feminine and/or queer domains. This construction is presumed to the extent that I have heard the comment, "Of course, you would research gay men because women and gay men are always together in music ministry." That statement suggests to me the perceived shared feminine interests and spaces of women and gay or feminine-presenting men. When women and even feminine-presenting men move beyond designated feminine spaces, there is a disruption of the social order in Pentecostal church settings. This disruption of social order is rooted in misogynistic views that are furthered in unchallenged male-centered theologies. "Black women's bodies in Pentecostal pulpits literally shift and reestablish borders, are oppositional forces to the very idea of the iconographic status of masculinity."[74] I add that feminine-presenting and queer men shift and reestablish borders in Pentecostal frameworks as well. Women and queer men "developed a means to move more freely and to be culturally at 'odds,' to turn the tables on normativity and to employ their own bodies as canvasses of dissent in popular performance culture."[75] They both, women and queer men, are also sacrificial as they submit their discursive bodies to serve in African American worship settings in which church leadership finds a peculiar pleasure in their exclusion, oppression, and placation. Crawley writes further:

> Queer theory illumines the discussion about the shifting nature and instability of identity . . . It is a process of recognizing, reckoning, recovering, reconciling and refashioning oneself or group from the ruptures of the past. As such, I postulate that both the pulpit and women's performance on the shifting pulpit are indeed queer.[76]

I agree with Crawley that as a woman, my performance on the shifting pulpit either in word or worship is queer. It is indeed peculiar to deviate from the social script of deference to heteropatriarchal leadership and to undo pulpit rhetorics (musical, gestural, etc.) that are injurious to marginalized congregants. Through the dissemination of my music research as an author and practitioner, I endeavor to make marginalized believers' words and actions easier to perceive and comprehend.

Nonetheless, I have struggled to find the safe, sacred space to express in familiar language the aspects in which my perspectives theologically diverge from the community that called me into ministry. I am ordained by a community that upholds conservative beliefs about gender and sexuality to which I no longer fully subscribe. For example, some church leaders in similar communities support economies that consume music by men who are silent about their progressive sexuality (i.e., nonabstinent single, nonmonogamous, or queer) in order to maintain their livelihood. I perceive this as an exploitation of gay male musicians' talents. It is an economy in which believers feel entitled to presumed queer men's competence in ushering them into "meaningful" worship, while denouncing the queer sexual identity of the music-makers. As one informant posited at a Chicago worship service in 2011, "It is unfair that churchgoers and pastors celebrate musical sounds but only if silence about their sexuality is maintained." The gay musicians maintain silence because if their patrons knew explicitly that they are gay, they could be dropped from their music industry labels for violating moral clauses and/or from their ministerial posts. According to entertainment attorney Renee Cooper, morality clauses are standard in contracts and "basically prohibit certain personal behavior that may have a disparaging effect on the other party to the agreement." Cooper explained further, "Thus, a morality clause in a gospel recording agreement won't differ much from one that is part of a secular agreement."[77] In lieu of public battles around breaking morality regulations, gay musicians eschew conventional rhetoric and rely on their competence as music ministers to demonstrate the modes in which they are used by God to lead people into worship. As one informant stated, "I can show you better than I can tell you." Another musician said to me while we listened to a famous Chicago artist whom fans have presumed to be gay, "How can a person argue that they do not feel the presence of God when they hear this song?" Such "meaningful worship leadership" competence that engages the auditory senses to facilitate transcendence contests any doubts regarding their ability to be used by God. How is it that gospel music patrons do not perceive the sexual difference of gay musicians? Moreover, the fact is that patrons have both consciously and unwittingly navigated the identity difference as they consume the music but will not advocate for full incorporation of musicians who are sexually different. For me, this sort of arrangement is an unethical contradiction between moral codes and integrity among church leaders.

The impression that a man's sexual orientation, gender expression, or display of queer potential negatively impacts his effectiveness in ministry falters in the face of all available evidence. For years, musicians have had discourse about the prevalence of gay musicians within their ranks. I have had conversations with musicians, in which they admit that spiritual attacks and moral struggles are the flawed nature of the call to ministry: "Congregations secretly want their pastors to be a womanizer and their music minister to be gay."[78] In other words, necessary for the performance of their roles, pastors are supposed to be virile and music ministers are supposed to be "soft." Both identities are held to be problematic but necessary for performance of their roles within the worship experience. The musicians reveal contradictions that reinscribe heteronormative and misogynistic constructions of manhood. Musicians' observations about the unspeakable nature of the call to ministry simultaneously depict the "manliness" ascribed to the pulpit, even as their musical participation is thought to be queer(ing).

In both transcongregational fieldwork and everyday life, I draw on and problematize my own relationship to the communities in which restrictive traditions are embraced, while using multisited ethnography to examine the circulation of cultural perceptions about the manners with and venues in which African American men worship. Following anthropologist George E. Marcus (1995), I acknowledge that cultural logics about black men worshipping are produced during live and virtual African American Christian worship experiences and thus, I followed the connections, associations, and putative relationships[79] surrounding these men. I embarked upon multisite ethnography by "following the conflict"[80] encircling the peculiar or contested performances of African American male identity that challenged conventional notions of gender, class, race, and theological conformity. As I participant-observed in Washington, DC and Chicago, I found that my local transcongregational ethnography was very much a microcosm of a broader national discourse about African American male

Christian identity across denominations that welcome charismatic expressions through gospel music.

Scholars in anthropology have noted the challenges of multisited ethnography such that it poses a threat to what Clifford Geertz (1973) called "thick description" of the sites, gaining access to informants, and learning the languages for each site. Cindy Horst (2009) offers, nevertheless, that through multisited ethnography another aspect of thick description emerges with an attention to the networks, relations, and flows within systems. I was able to gain access to my informants largely through introductions from other informants. I also had to immerse myself into learning the regional and popular vernacular that is used by same-gender loving believers so that I might interpret the myriad, discreet communication techniques about black male identity. Finally, I adopted a multidisciplinary approach to my analysis of the cultural meanings that included research from religious studies, men's studies, philosophy, dance, cinema, gender studies, rhetoric, and homiletics.

In my fieldwork from winter 2008 to 2014, I attended events associated with gospel music performance and worship services in Washington, DC and Chicago. I conversed initially about my research with musician colleagues, with whom I already had a good rapport. I found that a dialogic approach allowed me to develop trust among the gatekeepers within these circles. Then they recommended other musicians who would also be interested in sharing their stories. The dialogue approach anthropologist D. Soyini Madison outlines "keeps the meanings between and the conversations with the researcher and others open and ongoing."[81] While dialogue fulfilled my research obligations to complete the research, it worked out forms of symbolic reconciliation and communication between my consultants and myself. In the very act of research, I initiated and modeled an ethic of care, which is an integral part of my scholarly and spiritual epistemology. I am influenced by feminist Patricia Hill Collins's concept of an ethic of care that "prioritizes my individual expressiveness, together with a respect for emotions and a capacity and commitment to empathy."[82] I conveyed to my consultants my capacity for sensitivity, discretion, and confidentiality. In conversations with them, I used vocabulary that was much more inclusive than that used by others in the circles in which I did my research. My rapport with new consultants was established through introductions by trusted friends and with my assurance of anonymity for those who shared with me their personal stories. Consequently, sometimes dialogue generated impromptu group conversations about shared experiences within gospel performance. As I developed relationships through musical labor and creative exchange, we built and shared our experiences within the black gospel tradition.

This data relies primarily on the research methods of ethnographic fieldwork, consisting of interviews and participant observation centered on performances of black churches and concert halls in Chicago and the Washington, DC metro-politan areas. These are sites where I both attended events and worked as an itin-erant preacher and music minister—a ministerial status that provides me with cross-denominational mobility and access. The members of these congregations express a variety of perspectives on black men's sexuality, while developing preferences and skills sets informed by both local and virtual exchanges. I chose these two cities as ethnographic sites because of the positions that they share within the popular American imagination of black men worshipping, as places black men sojourn in order to attain "proper manhood ideals," socioec-onomic status, and political prominence. Though other "chocolate cities" such as New York, New Orleans, Atlanta, and Detroit are sites for the attainment of proper manhood ideals, Chicago and Washington, DC have a particular saliency in the US imagination as sites for analyzing the politics of black men's demon-stration and mobilization. Stacy Boyd observes, for example, how "the media has focused the American imagination on the large congregations of emotion-ally expressive men who gather in Washington, DC in sports arenas and at the increasing number of men's conferences around the world."[83] Both Washington, DC and Chicago signify the behaviors in which African Americans' freedoms are expressed through their collective visibility and geographic movement in predominantly black cities.[84]

Black men's collective movement, visibility, and music in the public squares of Chicago and Washington, DC are attached to a long legacy of law, surveil-lance, anxiety,[85] censorship, and power struggle. Chicago and Washington, DC also represent sites that have been marked by "black on black violence"[86] and black male absenteeism narratives. Chicago is the city in which then-Senator Barack Obama delivered a 2008 Father's Day speech at the Apostolic Church of God, calling for a reversal of black men's absenteeism in home and church. Black feminists have critiqued these gatherings, according to political scientist Melissa Victoria Harris-Lacewell (2006),[87] as reinscribing sexism, homophobia, and classism as these men-centered gatherings seek to dismantle racial and socioec-onomic injustices. Black feminist bell hooks (1995) has offered the critique that the male leaders of these men's events should promote the contributions of and continued partnership with women. My ethnographic work with participants will ground my assessment of the meanings that are generated in these public spaces, where black men are imagined to be menaces to society. With these landscapes in the horizon of black gospel performance, I observe the extent to which the politics of black men's willful presence, movement, and collective visi-bility are demonstrated and worked out in worship.

I completed local participatory ethnography in Washington, DC and Chicago in 2014, and investigated the methods in which the communities engage with news and social media discussions about popular national performers and events that sparked masculinity and manhood debates. During conversations with informants through 2019, I followed the musicians and performances in the news and social media that resonated with my informants and challenged the monolithic perceptions of masculine models of worship. Through this process I recognized how black religiosity is both existential and imagined. It is important that my assessment of the fields within the book project encompasses the tangible and intangible components of performance that are due in part to diasporic networks of religious groups that do not function in isolation and the layered, shared histories to which black men refer in order to conceive of a visible identity.

The churches I observed feature a deliberate incorporation of modern tools, symbols, and signifiers that cue participants to the community's cutting-edge access to the global world. Multimedia have been incorporated into the worship of African Americans since the early twentieth century. For this reason, I consider *technologies of communication*[88] as a dimension of my fieldwork, specifically the techniques in which men fashion their own worship spaces. Ethicist Jonathan Walton examines the platforms in which media such as race records in the 1920s, radio revivals, and broadcasts worship via streaming have long been a part of the African American worship experience providing a wider exposure for dynamic spiritual leaders.[89] Modern African American religiosity encompasses the use of broadcast television on networks such as The Word Network, Black Entertainment Television (BET), and Trinity Broadcasting Network (TBN). Preachers and performers also have disseminated their ministry efforts through other platforms such as YouTube.com, Vimeo.com, StreamingFaith.com, and assorted social media. Throughout this book, I feature some significant and emerging figures in gospel performance who engage multimedia such as Jungle Cat, Tonéx, and Donnie McClurkin to further illustrate black male performance visibility in the gospel music community.

Can Black Men Worship?

Yes, black men can and are worshipping, escalating their encounters with God in rhetorical, musical, bodily, and sociocultural languages they recognize. As I have mentioned in my 2016 article "Are All The Choir Directors Gay?," participants and scholars in religion have observed that there are two masculinities that are most visible within African American Christian worship traditions: the paradigmatic preacher and the vocal musician. Sociologist Michael Eric Dyson[90] has observed the reoccurrence of moments in worship, during which preachers who are presumably heterosexual deliver homophobic sermons. Preachers are both demonstrative and reoriented to a close-to-the-body stationary stance in the pulpit throughout their sermon delivery. They are then followed with musical performances by soloists and musicians whose manner of delivery is flamboyant, demonstrative, and presumed queer. The concept of flamboyance is a remarkable term in these settings that refers to demonstrative and ecstatic facility in cueing the choir and instrumentalists during performance. However, the Black gospel participant, regardless of sexual orientation, is expected to have charisma. Music Director at Clinton College Dr. Tony McNeill described flamboyance in a personal communication as "anything that draws attention to the person instead of the content of the message being conveyed. I do not associate [flamboyance] with being gay or straight. Most people when they hear that term do have an automatic association with being gay." Worship leader, voice professor, and countertenor Patrick Dailey similarly described flamboyance as "operating in the flesh" or being vain in performance. He said, "You should not draw attention to yourself. We were taught you draw attention to God."[91] There are a few ways in which scholars have interpreted the musicians' demonstrativeness. Ethnomusicologist Melvin L. Butler (2014) has observed that the demonstrative worship registers as the evocation of David from the Hebrew Bible as model for an undignified praise in which men make music and dance with all of their might before God. However, performance theorist E. Patrick Johnson (2011) attests to queer gospel music soloists' engagement of spectators through flamboyant or demonstrative performances. He reclaimed the term by describing flamboyance as "operating in the flesh" or being vain in *Sweet Tea* (2011). Both Butler and Johnson acknowledge that flamboyance is code for a performance of feminization or queerness.

At stake in discussions of demonstrative masculinity in worship is the struggle to interpret and reconcile theologically the gospel performer's display of queer potential at the height of worship within a heteronormative construct. Constantly participants interpret queer potential and self-identification as something from which believers must be delivered. While anxieties about male presentation of effeminacy or queerness are not the only impediments to men worshipping, those phobias are dominant themes in debates about black men's gospel performance. What are the conditions in which participants' anxieties around detecting femininity in men's performances shape the gospel music and worship aesthetic? In what ways does the privileging of heteropresenting male participation influence decision-makers' choices about musical productions, collaborations, and/or gender equity in the financial compensation? To what extent do self-identifying queer male performers have to negotiate their identity so that they preserve their livelihood in an industry that caters to a majority female fan base?

These two male roles—the preacher and the vocal musician—are performed in tension with each other in the worship setting, but they are not always opposing figures among each other in their private social lives. The preacher and the musician are expected to deliver biblical and social scripts that subscribe to literalist readings of scripture. For example, I have heard music ministers' stories in which preachers have been directly informed that their music minister is gay. Anthropologist William Hawkeswood's ethnography challenged these gender roles and the work they do in African American churches:

> They accept and benefit from the gay men's extraordinary participation; in some cases the only men who participate regularly as choristers, organists, and ushers are gay. Even some preachers are gay. But to keep the coffers replete, the preachers must address their congregation in the most religiously conservative manner possible.[92]

Hawkeswood writes further that nongay parishioners expect to hear Holy Bible-based sermons, as they are accustomed, even if this means that they must promote homophobic teachings. Since most of the participants are women who are single (including divorced, widowed, common law wives, lesbian, etc.), the homophobic sermons serve their presumed heterosexual interests as well. "Thus, the preacher and the church get the male participants; the women have non-threatening male companionship; and the gay men find a socially acceptable role in the Black community."[93] The social and theological fixation on black male representation and participation in churches reinforces this nonthreatening power structure and social appeasement.

When one takes a closer look at the symbolism at play in men's worship representation, the call for male participation in spiritual warfare is quite puzzling—a seemingly impossible task, really, when one considers the symbolic contradictions at work. Williamson and others' fixation on assembling men engaged in spiritual warfare, "poised to kick demons away," is ironic because of the ways in which black men's bodies have been regarded historically in the popular religious imagination as the embodiment of the demonic, due to negative stereotypes about their African-derived physical and spiritual attributes. Their performance of masculinity in worship and gospel music scenes in particular is an opportunity for the exploration of racialized, gendered, bodily, and spiritual intersectional dimensions of Christian practices that are remnants of postcolonialism. Theologian Dwight Hopkins's (2004) research on religion and eroticism establishes a genealogy for the popular depictions of black men's bodies as demonic or bestial, stemming from Eurocentric Christian traditions. To unpack the implications of such representations, he inspects two injurious, colonial theologies that have been bequeathed to black people from European colonizers who settled in the United States: a theology of antagonistic dualism and a theology of prudishism. Expanding on a quote from religion scholar Robert E. Hood, Hopkins writes:

"The church officially reinforced this entanglement of aesthetics, carnality, and negativity of Blackness at the fifth-century Council of Toledo." White religious men decided that Satan was a monster with a huge penis. Three centuries later, one finds a naked black Devil painted in Europe. Given this genealogy of their Christian European ancestors, it is not totally surprising that when European ethnic groups came to the U.S. and changed their identity in to "white" people (against Blacks), white Christianity and the broader U.S. civic religion (that is, white monopolization as a god-complex) enslaved African and African Americans.[94]

Then while engaging a theology of antagonistic dualism, Hopkins contends that white supremacist Christianity has required a bifurcation of the body and mind (or body and soul). To antagonistic dualism, he links a theology of prudishism rooted in self-denial Puritanism and conservative Victorianism. In his estimation, purity was equated with refraining from erotic contemplation, while Victorianism "upholds high culture and advanced civilization."[95] The adoption of these theologies was a means through which black Christians repudiated stereotypes that they were naturally "hypersexual" people.[96] These stereotypes are traced to images of demonized blackness that were constructed at the Council of Toledo in the fifth century: the religious concept of sexualized black beast body (cemented in a theology of antagonistic dualism and a theology of prudishism) did not fall from the sky. A historical legacy birthed it with white, European Christianity as a prime architect.[97] Black men's bodies have been tethered to negative perceptions that encumber spectators' and participants' assessment of their potential to worship with abandon. To navigate anxieties associated with the black male body, men have been socialized to deemphasize certain embodied expressions of worship and emphasize performing their interior disposition. Following historical representation of demons, exorcising the demonic from black men—those who are apprehended as demons (e.g., menace, thugs, brute, superpredator) themselves—is a remarkably futile effort proposed in modern deliverance rituals if we follow the logic.

My colloquies with clergy and lay people about the performance of gender and sexuality in gospel indicate that through stylized performances of masculinity, men are now initiating a revisioning of their worshipper identity that is both more bodily and spiritually oriented. They are thinking critically about what is required to draw near to God.

Men's worship is stylized as any other component of their image and presentation. Black male assertion of stylistic independence is, as philosopher Cornel West asserts, a "form of self-identification and resistance in a hostile culture . . . The prevailing cultural crisis of many Black men is the limited stylistic options of self-image and resistance in a culture obsessed with sex yet fearful of Black sexuality."[98] My work does not seek to advocate for a particular masculine style of worship; however, I do analyze black gospel music as a sonic "safe space" in heteropatriarchal constructs, a safe space that comprises a performative *home* for black men who appropriate gospelized musical styles to express ambiguously gendered social and musical identities. Furthermore, I suggest that these stylistic options both incorporate and oppose discussions about Christian machismo that have become hegemonic in black gospel music circles, whose members understand a white male God as normative, without the allowance of inclusive language and symbols. "African American men in particular and Black Christians in general must change the image of God from the great white patriarch to one more aligned and consistent with Black progressive masculinities."[99] A reconsideration of the racialized, gendered, and heteropatriarchal God imagery and symbolism disrupts the perceptions circulated through the oppositional masculinities paradigm—preacher and choir director—in African American worship experiences.

Building upon the work of Dwight Hopkins, English scholar Stacy C. Boyd's *Black Men Worshipping: Intersecting Anxieties of Race, Gender, and Christian Embodiment* (2011) addresses this preoccupation by exploring the anxieties associated with black male embodiment in worship and spectatorship, while worshipping in a racist, patriarchal Western context. He employs the term "Christian embodiment" to account for the "bodily manifestation of Christian ideology and the corporal implication associated with self-identification as a Christian."[100] Boyd's conceptualization of Christian embodiment is crucial for men's construction of manhood that finds meaning in their body as they relate to a crucified God. This suffering coupled with anxieties around the racial difference perceived in the hypersexualized black male body in a racist, patriarchal Western context distinguishes black Christian men's experience from white Christian men's experience of embodiment.

Chapter Descriptions

In historically black Pentecostal churches, the themes of male-centered theology, male underrepresentation in the pews, queer male overrepresentation in music ministry, and reception of flamboyant performances illuminate the dynamics of the performative choices that musicians make. The chapters are arranged to illustrate the components of black men's performance of identity in worship such as various configurations of masculinities, aura-visual meaning, style, liturgical moments, rhetorics, and performance practice that are contested in African American Christian gospel performance.

In the first four chapters, I analyze components of the aural-visual trope of the flamboyant choir director and vocal musicians through three features of music in the African Diaspora as set forth by musicologist Samuel A. Floyd Jr. (1995) with a focus on their gendered meaning: song through vocal music, dance, and drum accompaniment. In chapter 1, I construct a social genealogy of men's narratives of deliverance from homosexuality to study the ways in which such a designation functions socially in the gospel music industry. In chapter 2, I observe a black countertenor's embodiment of what I call "gendered sound" and the peculiar vocal qualities that are socioculturally perceived to signify a man's queer potential. In chapter 3, I dissect the sociocultural sensitivity about the extent to which men's dance or gesture in worship registers as queer by analyzing a case study of a man who worships God through pole dancing. Chapter 4 examines men's performances against the "softer," woman-like, "flamboyant" vocalist through research on a percussion heavy music from Washington, DC called gospel go-go. These first four chapters show that there are assumptions and restrictions about the kinds of sounds, gestures, and accompaniment textures that "masculine" black men can make to worship God. When musicians traverse those restrictions it is distracting to gospel spectators who subscribe to a heteronormative ideal.

After establishing the dynamics of the ways in which gospel audiences assess the aural-visual qualities of men's performance, the remaining chapters confront discussions on a self-identified musician's silence and self-disclosure of (ex-)gay men to exhibit the various facets of unspokenness. In chapter 5 I investigate a case study of Tonéx, a queer preacher-musician, who embodies a combination of the most popular stereotypes of African American men's worship—the preacher and the choir director/soloist/instrumentalist, while wielding multifarious rhetorics during his musical performance. Using Tonéx's case, I contest the portrayal of same-gender loving men as down low, secretive, deceptive, and always withholding information about who they are from their loved ones. In chapter 6, I embark upon a more in-depth exploration of the social and theological implications for male musicians like B.Slade (formerly Tonéx) who decide to resist conventional rhetorics by performing modes of unspokenness. While music scholars have researched the moments in which the musical rest is a facet of sound,[101] I offer that unspokenness is a prized aspect of African American orality and nonverbal communication. Unspokenness manages musical moments in the face of censorship and oppression, during worship experiences where queer potential is assessed and rebuked. In chapter 7, I examine ethnography of formerly gay gospel recording artist and pastor Donnie McClurkin's sermonizing as a performance of the heteropatriarchal scripts that manage gospel enthusiasts concerns about queer(ed) musicians' spiritual fitness and protecting the social order of church leadership.

In the epilogue, I reflect on my exploration of black men's performance of their gender and sexuality through gospel music and opportunities for social change. Gospel music constitutes, for many, a sonic safe space that provides one of the few places where performers are able to assert their agency in movement, taste, posture, confession, and community. I review some of the frequently asked questions that have been elicited while I have conducted my research. I also consider topics that I will research further. As black men articulate their identities in a multisensory manner, the development of an artist's persona is combined with the histories, culture, socialization and ignorance of observers. These are lenses through which observers process the musicians' symbols, signifiers, and silence within their performance. My hope is that *Flaming?* will create opportunities to blaze a trail of understanding and hope in these oft-isolated domains.

1

"I Am Delivert!"

The Pentecostal Altar Call and Vocalizing Black Men's Testimonies of Deliverance from Homosexuality

In July 2016, the gospel music community was abuzz with the announcement made on the Trinity Broadcasting Network that Stellar and Grammy award-winning Pastor Donnie McClurkin (née Donald Andrew McClurkin) was engaged to fellow Christian recording artist Nicole C. Mullen. After being pressured to comment on air about the nuptials, McClurkin apprehensively stated his intention to go to counseling before they got married. Despite the fact that McClurkin and Mullen had so much in common—including the facts that they were musicians, single parents, and abuse survivors (sexual and domestic respectively)—fans expressed skepticism about their prospective union.[1] In response to the public's questions, he clarified later via YouTube live stream that they were not engaged. They intended to go to pre-engagement counseling before he formally proposed marriage, a status about which he has expressed anxiety.[2]

One should note that in all of the dominant Christian conversations surrounding their engagement, the public did not consider that Mullen might prefer bi-sexual or feminine-masculine men (even though he has never publicly referred to himself as bi-sexual before his deliverance); be open to his sexual preferences that might include anal play and penetration; believes that she can change him through her womanly wiles; or that she might be bi-sexual or (ex-) lesbian herself. Or that they may have decided to make a business/brand/musical merger as international worship leaders. Such options can be financially and socially advantageous for both of them, given that they are single-parent ministers and it is in their interest to be perceived as living a holy life.

Countless ministers have forged various configurations of these marital arrangements to shore up their financial stability and social clout, which includes partaking in lavender marriages where one or both partners are queer. For example, on August 5, 2019, Prophet Larry Reid interviewed Prophet Tymel Thompson for his YouTube.com show *Larry Reid Live*. A seasoned faith leader, Reid tends to use his live streaming social media platforms to facilitate conversations about difficult topics in black churches. Thompson consented to interview in response

Flaming? Alisha Lola Jones, Oxford University Press (2020). © Oxford University Press.
DOI: 10.1093/oso/9780190065416.001.0001

to questions surrounding his relationship with his estranged wife and admitted that he was in a long term committed same-gender loving (SGL) relationship as a teenager before he married his third wife Prophet Sarafina Thompson.[3] When they started dating, Tymel Thompson was separated from his wife, a relationship overlap that is frowned upon in Pentecostal circles. Tymel and Sarafina began to minister together as itinerate prophets. In order for them to get expenses paid as a itinerate couple in ministry, they lied and presented themselves as married. As the relationship progressed, they discussed in relationship counseling that they both had a same-gender loving past. They agreed to meet each other's sexual needs, which included anal play for Tymel. Unfortunately, over the course of their marriage, Sarafina told people in their social networks that Tymel was gay out of spite without qualifying the rumor or disclosing her own sexual identity and history. The rumor alone stigmatized him and caused people to withdraw ministry invitations.

Prophet Tymel Thompson did not allow the rumor to persist. He is one of very few hetero-presenting ministers who has publicly without qualification talked about a past same-gender relationship. In his interview with Larry Reid, Prophet Tymel did not self-identify as delivered, but rather, he talked about how he negotiated his queer associated sexual preferences with the woman he loved. Frequently, when I present my research, married male attendees divulge the same narrative to me, a stranger, of having dated a man before they married a woman. I usually ask if their wives know. Only one man has confessed that his wife does know his sexual history with men. Christian believers have myriad histories, preferences, and tools for sexual pleasure. And often, a compulsory heterosexual lens does not provide us with the tools to presume or to ask the right questions.

In 2009, editor of *Gospel Today* magazine Dr. Teresa Hairston asked McClurkin, "Are you getting married?"

Marriage? I was supposed to get married twice. I let them both get away (I'll take the blame!) [he laughs]. I desire more than anything else to get married and have another child. I want that more than anything.

Hairston queried further, "If you have a desire to get married, what's the problem?"

The challenge is finding a wife out of a sea of women! When you get to a certain place, it's hard to trust that people want you and know you and love you for you. Also, it's hard to take my past and my hurt and now, at 50, move forward. Remember, I threw myself into God and gospel music; and made that my world, my everything my life; and now to come out of that cocoon—which was both beneficial and detrimental—it's hard. I've got to drum up all it takes to find a wife.[4]

On face value this line of questions and responses seems mundane, but it is not at all, because McClurkin self-disclosed in 2000 that he was delivered from homosexuality. So, when the news broke of his engagement, gospel music enthusiasts strained to untangle his anxiety from his sexual past as a man who self-identifies as delivered from homosexuality through Pentecostal belief and practices. While McClurkin has become the most popular spokesperson for deliverance from homosexuality, it is lesser known that Pastor Daryl Coley was the first in the gospel music industry to go public as delivered from homosexuality and recorded his interpretations of deliverance for the remainder of his career.

Extracting from the reception of musicians' deliverance testimonies since gospel artist Pastor Daryl Coley's self-disclosure as formerly gay, their accounts prompt communication about what constitutes deliverance. While expanding upon my previous research about stereotypes within gospel music networks that construe black male vocal participation as queer (2016), I explore the sonic qualities and functions of black men's simultaneous self-disclosure of their self-identified homosexuality and public renouncement of queerness through their deliverance testimonies to telescope in on what deliverance rituals accomplish for gospel musicians and their patrons. I use function to connote one of the four aspects of rituals and ritualizing as posited by performance theorist Richard Schechner to telescope in on what deliverance rituals accomplish for gospel musicians and their patrons.[5] From his list of seven functions of performance, I find that the probing of three features are at stake: to mark or change identity, to heal, and to deal with the sacred and/or the demonic.[6] In a culture where queer believers are habitually regulated to a "don't ask, don't tell" social agreement, the testimonies of men delivered from homosexuality conform to what feminist writer Adrienne Rich called compulsory heterosexuality (1960). While deploying ethnomusicological, phonological, linguistic, critical race, and gender studies analysis, I examine these delivered believers' coded and textured performances of orality in Pentecostal worship. My intention is not to confirm or dispute the men's claims, but rather to investigate the social contradictions spectators have noted. I conduct this research as an ordained Pentecostal pulpit and music minister in the Word of Faith, charismatic Christian tradition, who both respects and critically analyzes this music scene. Undoubtedly, I have witnessed and experienced various types of spiritual and physical deliverance; however, I have not facilitated rituals of deliverance from homosexuality or gender expression.

I begin by describing a popular use of the term "deliverance" to examine the tensions bolstered by circulating teachings derived from a tradition that is undergirded by thick, responsorial musical accompaniment, as in the Coley song when we hear "He Delivered Me." Launching from Coley's COGIC professional music context, I revisit the 2014 incident at the Church of God in Christ (COGIC) Convocation involving Andrew C. Caldwell that catapulted long-standing Pentecostal deliverance terminology into twenty-first-century popular culture. The 2014 COGIC case study exemplifies a typical scenario in which a preacher uses derision to prompt deliverance candidates. I connect Caldwell's testimony genealogically to popular vocalist McClurkin's testimony of deliverance from homosexuality that has come to serve as a template for the acceptable form of self-disclosure in Pentecostal discourses. Then I compare the incendiary sound bites from the controversial 2014 COGIC sermon to a female preacher, Pastor Kim Burrell's 2017 response to the Caldwell occasion as a common contested script that cues musical rituals of testimony. Lastly, I provide a few vocal musicians' perspectives that contest the efficacy of deliverance messages, refuting that homosexuality is a condition from which a person *must* be delivered or from which one *can* be delivered at all.

What Is Deliverance from Homosexuality?

A primary site where the multifarious theopolitics of fire and desire are parleyed—that is, one's carrying of both the spirit of God and their own natural affections respectively—is in the historically African American Pentecostal Christian ritual of deliverance from homosexuality in worship services.[7] "Deliverance" traditionally refers to a release from addictions (drugs, alcohol, food, and sex), physical ailments, and perceived spiritual afflictions such as diabetes, HIV/AIDs, or homosexuality.[8] While deliverance characterizes various types of healing through spiritual work, black gospel music fans overemphasize the term in a gendered and sexualized manner, referring to a man's "struggle" to resist homosexuality or their display of "flaming" or flamboyant gender expression and/or style through their public persona. Moreover, the notion of deliverance is performed predominantly through men's testimonies about becoming heterosexual with what they believe is God's help. In black Pentecostal Christian vernacular, giving a testimony or testifying refers to the oral tradition of publicly sharing intimate, favorable stories to amplify God's work in a person's life, with the objective of encouraging others in their Christian faith and prompting exuberant praise. Routinely supported by musical responses to sermons, public testimony is a key sign of defeating the powers of darkness by "the word of [one's] testimony."[9]

Through ministers' message and music, believers and attendees are either identified as candidates for or are persuaded to seek deliverance. Regularly during the altar call in public worship services, preachers rhetorically initiate and prompt the deliverance rituals,[10] and musicians provide the soundscape to induce and to seal the spiritual work the ministers seek to accomplish. In Pentecostal theological view, one's homosexuality (e.g., same-gender attraction, sensuality, sexual behavior) and nonconforming gender expression threatens the spiritual vitality of the ministers' service, as indicated by their ability or lack there of to set the atmosphere for worship, readily ushering in the presence of God.

The outcomes of these rituals are conspicuously commemorated in recordings by black male gospel vocalists in which they demonstrate evidence of God's approval; that is, speaking in tongues, changing lives, and facilitating communal encounters with God. Presenting oneself as convincingly heterosexual is a theological and political social maneuver. However, openly queer musicians counter that they can provide the very same evidence as those who report being delivered, and serve as music ministers in a manner that disproves such rituals even matter. Thus, at the very least the attributes and worship leadership potency of high male singers are consistently assessed for hints of queerness. And at the most, male gospel singers in general are surveilled for their potential to perform female gendered sound and movement; gravitate toward homosociality; seek God through prayer; and ultimately present a persuasive heterosexuality that condemns same-gender loving people to hell. They understand musicians' ability to present evidence of deliverance to be both a scripted tradition of spiritual witness and a skill set of competent performance that can be learned by anyone as a craft of survival and readily can be perceived and inspected by believers through vocal performance.

The Vocalized Sound of Deliverance

In 1995, Stellar and Grammy Award-nominated gospel vocalist Pastor Daryl Lynn Coley consented to an interview with *Gospel Today's* editor Teresa Hairston for an article titled "The California-Born Gospel Singer Overcoming Homosexuality and Diabetes." It is the earliest music industry account of a gospel vocalist claiming to no longer be homosexual through spiritual "deliverance." In the interview with Hairston, Coley described the sensuality and vulnerability that is required of skillful, gifted singers that could lead to situational sexuality:

> Artists in general are very sensitive people, who are very open . . . So there's not a "distinction" in feeling for people and for situations. The Enemy really makes himself prevalent in (sexual) situations and it takes the Lord to help

you overcome. We've got to deal with sexuality across the board. Not just the gay life. Sometimes we feel like (when) we get wrapped up in a person, (then) maybe the Lord will make allowances, but if it's not the way the Word says, it stems from unrighteousness. It's a spirit that's transferred throughout the whole thing. So you have to be very careful. Young men and young women are impressionable. There's a line we just have to teach our children to maintain. As a church, we preach against homosexuality, but we don't deal with the subtleness of the Enemy. How it can woo you and get you at your lowest point.

Two years prior to his self-disclosure, Coley released *He's Right on Time: Live in Los Angeles* album (1993), an album that explores the various ways in which God has shown up, particularly through the expressed attributes of and synonyms for the Holy Spirit. He was promoting "He Delivered Me," one of several songs in his catalogue that depicts a process of deliverance: prayer, self-discovery, self-disclosure or confession, liberation, and affirmation.[11] He believed that sharing his story was the most effective way to reach people.

> That would have never happened unless I had total trust in the Lord and spiritually stepped totally outside of Daryl and allowed God to step in. But there were so many people that came up to me and let me know, "Daryl, (your testimony) was a point of deliverance for me. It becomes a point of being transparent and trusting God." I still get approached, and still get the looks, but I know how to handle it and how to deal with it and not be offensive. How to maintain integrity.

The iconic song captures the exuberant musical testimony that one might encounter at the culmination of a persuasive Pentecostal sermon, followed by an upbeat "shout" accompaniment. In the narrative, Coley musically testifies that his deliverance from sin was induced by a "voice from heaven" and in return for his deliverance he will praise God (professionally) forever.[12] Then he ups the ante and proclaims God can fix the listener's problems that are more onerous, than say, the diabetes diagnosis he faced. God can heal incurable diseases such as the HIV/AIDs pandemic that had been ravaging the California bay area and artistic communities at the time, as he sings the succeeding lyrics:

> CHORUS
> I prayed to the Lord and He
> (He delivered me)
> I once was blind but now I see!
> (Yes, he delivered me!)
> He saved my soul from a burning hell.
> He healed my body so I can tell how

(how he) how he
(de-li-ver-ed me) delivered me.

VERSE ONE
I once was an outcast,
I was a sinner just like you;
One day I heard a voice from heaven say,
There is so much work to do (so much work to do),
then I took the Master's hand
and I joined the Christian band,
and now I praise His name forever
for He delivered me (yeah).

VERSE TWO
If you have a problem,
the doctor's thrown up his hands,
Jesus has got your healing
and He can do what no doctor can (no-o doctor can).
Don't worry about your problems,
just place it all in the Lord's hands,
for He is faithful and He promised
that He'll deliver you (yeah).

Known for his brassy tenor voice and Pentecostal, Afro-Latin jazz-inspired style,[13] the melodic contour begins noticeably set in Coley's lower, speaking range.[14] Just before the climax of Coley's sung testimony, the harmonic texture shifts from a major mode to minor mode in the bridge of the song, the semitones are emphasized in the melody, sonically accentuating the hellish tensions from which God has brought him. Coley attests, "He raised me, He saved me, He bought me, He taught me, He filled me, He thrilled me, He kept me..." Among the litany of ways in which God delivered him, Coley signifies on vocalized evidence by rolling the "r" (a.k.a. an alveolar voiced or pitched trill) in the word "thrilled," and thus, illustrating the resulting lingual animation of his deliverance—so powerful that it unties the tongue of a man who was once homosexual.[15]

According to Pentecostal belief, one who is in need of deliverance could not possibly provide evidence that the Spirit of God indwells them.[16] One's demonstration of infilling of the Holy Spirit is a criteria for authenticating one's spiritual vitality for setting the atmosphere in worship, as opposed to quenching the Spirit due to a lack of spiritual fervor. Thus, "thrilled" becomes a sonic multireferent for spiritual fire, vocal resonance, transformation, pleasure, the exoticism of Latin linguistics, and physical ability by demonstrating the dexterity of his articulators in a manner resembling speaking in tongues: the essential evidence that one is filled with the Holy Spirit in the Pentecostal tradition; thereby, verifying that they are transformed or are no longer "playin' church."[17]

Specifically, high voice male vocalists' overrepresentation in these public accounts of spiritual "healing" from homosexuality reinscribe the sonic stereotype within historically black Pentecostal churches that to be involved in vocal music ministry is a feminizing or queering act, situating men emblematically in the overlapping feminine domain of treble timbres. For some, Coley's narrative confirms the stereotype that men exhibit an affinity for feminine sonic domains through church music participation because he learned music from listening to his mother—a maternal pedagogy of oral transmission. "I remember," he recalled, "my mother doing her vocal exercises and me imitating her."[18]

Conversely, women's deliverance testimonies are unlikely to be distributed due in part to the sociocultural fixation on protecting established constructions of black masculinity to the exclusion of women's deliverance experience. In other words, if a woman were to deliver a deliverance narrative among Pentecostals it is not received as a remarkable, fixed change in sexual orientation.

My cursory analysis of Coley's vocalization as representing a sonic confirmation of heterosexual identity is a hearing situated in a compulsory heterosexual perspective. But what if we compared this initial heterosexually oriented hearing with a queer hearing of his music—that is, one privileging a same-gender loving person's observation and experience of deliverance possibility?

For some believers who conform to compulsory heterosexual constructs, the spiritual and vocalized "thrill" Coley found through deliverance ministry is the result of relinquishing queer appetite and behavior. And others, who examine the song with a queer listening, hear him as mining black and Latino Ballroom modes of performance in which signification—the use of multiple meanings—is common practice. For example, the phonetic and rhetorical devices performed in Coley's "He Delivered Me" are heard as double entendre, signifying on a celebration of same-gender intimacy and eroticism.[19] Concurrently tapping into Pentecostal vernacular, queer listeners hear and see the soloist in the song as being liberated from the self-loathing that deliverance rituals and homoantagonistic rhetorics are said to cultivate so much so that he speaks in tongues—and thus provides evidence that he has the Holy Ghost through sexual healing. For instance, in the footage of the live recording, Coley singularly enters stage right of the auditorium singing a vocable descant as an introduction to "The Comforter Has Come,"[20] deploying an aural-visual style evocative of the iconic R&B tenor balladeer and fellow diabetes patient Luther Vandross's[21] vocalized and sauntered entrance during the wildly popular 1987–1989 recorded performances that were captured on *Live in Wembley* (1991).[22] Like Coley, Vandross was known for his musical abilities as an arranger and background or session vocalist. Dressed in a bejeweled black suit like Vandross, Coley is dandy-adjacent and adorned much like female believers and various gospel performers such O'landa Draper and Dr. Bobby Jones[23] are observed to be in Pentecostal settings such as COGIC, where he flourished as an adult.[24] In fact, insiders have joked that COGIC is an acronym for "Church of Gays in Christ," describing the noticeably queer landscape and soundscape of attendees. The queer connotations of bejeweling are not lost on me, chiefly because beading clothes is a significant practice among women and femme-identified performers in the black and Latino gay Ballroom scenes. Similarly, both Coley and Vandross public personae have generated discourses, speculating about the nature of their sexual identity and the extent to which—to borrow from Vandross himself—they "loved the one they were with." For example, former colleagues have recounted the performance derived designations that they deployed for men who worked on their team as being queer euphemisms for their love interests: manager, sound engineer, background vocalist, personal assistant, and page turner. Coley in particular traveled with a sound engineer to engagements of various scales. One informant said to me that when Coley visited his church, the host directed the sound engineer to the sound booth, but "the sound engineer" did not seem to understand why he was being directed to the booth. They reside in a genealogy of aural-visually induced queer speculation.

Semantically, Coley supplements the conventional male gender pronoun "He"—a pronoun that is aurally interchangeable with expressions of same-gender intimacy—for a second person pronoun ("you") and the divine synonym "Deliverer." Additionally, the term "deliverance" is interpreted as a queer euphemism for sexual release, sexual healing, or orgasm. Thus, Coley's thrill sounds like an ecstatic confirmation of same-gender love, implying the simultaneous public and private scripts at play in this gospel narrative. He is the embodiment of two narratives in which believers daily aspire to exhibit spiritual vitality while negotiating scorned queer sexual desire in the public sphere. However, sometimes the publically performed "quarrels with the body," to borrow from sociologist Michael Eric Dyson, are not as artfully conveyed as in Coley's recording. Sometimes they are scrutinized and derided. The next section examines an instance in which the sonic and visual markers of a less convincing communal display of deliverance from homosexuality that unearths the sociocultural frictions when observed through the broader public's reception.

I Am Delivered

In November 2014, controversial video footage of the 107th annual COGIC Holy Convocation was disseminated throughout the United States media, exposing the tensions surrounding the (im)potency and peculiarity of musically accompanied deliverance sermons and rituals. COGIC is the largest historically black Pentecostal organization that has cultivated the most well-known gospel music artists including the Winans family, the Clark Sisters, Pastor Kim Burrell, Pastor Donnie McClurkin, and the Hawkins family. Spectators' grievances were concentrated on a sermon Reverend Earl Carter delivered against homosexuality and men's expression of femininity in music ministry on November 8, 2014, during which he declared,

> Because you are sensual. You want to feel like a girl. I wish God would give you a monthly of a girl . . . Since you wanna be a girl, God oughta put it all on you. Have you switching, put pumps on you. He [God] said since you don't believe me, I'm gonna turn you over to a reprobated [*sic*] mind . . . The homosexuality is the punishment. Your switching is the punishment. Your high heel shoes is the punishment. Your pocketbook and your lipstick is the punishment. Your tight pants is the punishment . . . And anybody that do such things—not only homosexuality . . . You are worthy of death.

Punctuating every spoken phrase of exhortation was a clamorous musical response from the band, complete with block chords played on the Hammond B3, incessantly struck cymbals, kick drum from the drum set, and plucked flourishes on the guitar.

There are several keywords interwoven throughout Carter's comments that are packed with meaning for Pentecostal Christians. "Sensual" was code for an imagined female domain of being sensitive, involuntarily exhibiting expressive qualities in the public sphere. To describe the punishment that stems from these unchecked expressive qualities, he lists fashion symbols typically associated with women that gender-nonconforming men had been displaying while attending the convocation.

Insider and outsider spectators noted the avalanche of misandry, homophobic, misogynistic, gynophobic, and transphobic imagery with which Carter communicated his message, pronouncing a painful, anatomical transposal on men who, in his estimation, act like women. Carter's exhortation was misandry/ misandnoir because he expressed disdain for musical, gender-nonconforming black men at the convocation with his use of the problematic term "sissies," likening them to girls. His appeal was homophobic because he unmanned queer men, exchanging the "manly" discharge of semen with women's discharge of blood, wishing upon them the continuous symbolic evidence of same-gender sexual penetration. Simultaneously, he communicated a true revulsion of men anally penetrating men that reinscribes the receiving body as the weaker vessel (ref. 1 Peter 3:7). Also, Carter's pronouncement registered misogyny in his gynophobic characterization of menstruation as cursed, reestablishing antiquated ideologies about women's bodily experiences of discharge as an affliction, a symbol of impurity,[25] and a symptom of God's punishment. Lastly, by conveying such a loathing for women's anatomy and the men who wear female coded attire, he imputes a transphobic sentiment upon men who identify with traits associated with women. In Carter's judgment, men exhibiting these attributes without repentance risk being turned over to a "reprobate mind" (ref. Romans 1:28 KJV). This means other believers may resolve that the men are wicked in character, leaving them to their own destructive devices.

At the climax of the service, immediately following Carter's sermon, Bishop Brandon Porter, the Jurisdictional Prelate of COGIC from Tennessee, facilitated an altar call for the thousands of attendees gathered. An altar call is a moment during worship services where attendees are invited through sermon, prayer, and song to the front of the gathering to acknowledge their transformational experience. The musical texture at that moment in the service was dense, filled with instrumental responses of strands of arpeggiated and "chopped" or struck block chords played on the electric organ and drum rolls. Andrew Caldwell went to the front and stood, facing the platform. This was his first time attending the convention. He had been fasting for days. He was weak and had spent the previous night in the prayer room praying for deliverance from his "effeminate ways." Speaking into the microphone, Porter said, "Break every yoke . . . He's delivering you now . . . [speaks in tongues]."[26] He pointed to Caldwell and asserted, "Whatever it is you need God to do . . . He just told you it is done right now. What did you come down here for?" The musical accompaniment stopped as Porter turned the microphone to Caldwell, whose response was "to be delivered more." Porter corrected him by saying, "To get delivered," as the organist responded by playing an instrumental flourish. Prompting Caldwell to elaborate, Porter asked, "Do you believe the Lord tonight has set you free?" "Yes, sir," Caldwell said. Porter said, "Turn around and tell those people . . . Tell them." Then Caldwell walked toward the assembly with mic in hand, exclaiming in a tenor register to the believers, "I'm not gay no more." Shifting from a tenor to a slightly lower speaking register, he growled, "I am delivered." Citing attributes evoked in Carter's sermon, he said further, "I don't like mens no more. I said I like women. Women, women, women, women . . . [he transitions to speaking in other tongues] I said women. I'm not gay. I will not date a men. I will not carry a purse. I will not put on a makeup."

After Caldwell gave his testimony, Bishop Porter placed money in his raised hand and requested others to encourage him, a cue that seemed to observers that Caldwell was paid off for his deliverance testimony. Was it staged? Who benefits from such a staging?

Decriers have observed that Caldwell has benefited financially from sharing his testimony by booking speaking engagements with Carter, the pastor who preached the contentious sermon before the altar call. Since that incident, Caldwell has admitted to monetizing his social media presence (his first check from Facebook was approximately $10,000) and church appearances. According to his Black Entertainment Network (BET) interview, he created an LLC, registered "Delivert," hired a management team, secured business partnerships with corporations including Delta airlines, and brands himself as a gospel comedian.[27] Some have even speculated about whether COGIC leadership planted Caldwell in the service to enliven COGIC teachings on sanctification through spiritual deliverance.

To whom and for whom was Caldwell delivering his testimony? Who were Caldwell's audiences? While Caldwell is not a gospel musician, this case study of the performative dimensions of his testimony provides insight into how the gradations of orality, which I describe as the continuum between speech and singing (2016), are performed and evaluated in black Pentecostal worship. As I mentioned earlier, Pentecostal believers deliver their testimony in a practice that is derived from the biblical passage Revelation 12:11a, in which one is believed to defeat the "accuser of the brethren"—interpreted as Satan—"by the blood of the Lamb [the Messiah] and by their testimony." But in this case, instead of being liberated by his self-disclosure and highlighting evidence of God's work in believers, Caldwell exchanged one sociocultural affliction for public ridicule, with the broader public's distribution and analysis of his testimony.

And yet in many ways, observers described Caldwell as performing a hoax; in other words he was viewed as being fully in control and getting attention he wanted, sanctioned or not, to attract future sexual partners and/or ventures. Such a ploy to capture the public eye through queer or "flaming" performance during the worship service, brings to mind an explanation provided by the performance theorist and black gay man E. Patrick Johnson's *Sweet Tea* (2011). For Johnson, the worship service is an intersectional site for the development of performed queer identity. As a male child soprano, he relished the opportunity to be a soloist, using the mic and his choir robe as a form of drag that contradicted the homoantagonistic proclamations in worship:

In my youth, I was one of several budding queens in the church, and we all learned very quickly—subconsciously or not—how to express and affirm our queerness without ever naming our sexuality. To riff off the title of a song by the gospel group the Clark Sisters, we knew that "to name it is to claim it." Thus, we used the choir as our sword and shield. In the children's choir, we baby church sissies would flame as bright as we wanted, and it was totally acceptable. For many years, the choir was my saving grace. The choir was where I felt free to express myself and where I felt appreciated. By the time I was twelve, I had quite a reputation for myself as "the little fat boy with the high butt and high voice that could sing." I was the only male soprano, and I could outsing any of the girls in the soprano section. I go the church to shoutin' every Sunday by singing solo originally sung by Yolanda Adams with the Southeastern Inspiration Choir out of Houston, Texas. The song is call "My Liberty"—how prophetic.

Grown folks marveled at, and some of my peers envied, my soaring melismas and general vocal theatrics. What I realize now, but didn't back then, I was a budding diva who was using the medium of gospel music to express not only my spirituality, but also my sexual and gender identity. I would catch the spirit at times, especially during my solos, and step down out of the choir stand and twirl down the aisle while my robe ballooned around by [sic] pudgy body—all the while holding a note and making sure that no one took the microphone out of my hand. The little queen in me was begging to show out, and I had a captive audience.

Johnson unlays the agential and empowering dynamics of choral participation and worship leadership as a soloist that resemble the same sort of work that is accomplished by Caldwell literally out-testifying, entering into the rhetorical domain of proclamation, while contesting what he utters through the congregation's experience of his presumably queer embodied presence. The testimony undoes the homoantagonistic proclamation, and thus causes the claims to the spiritual legitimacy of deliverance from homosexuality to fall apart. By doing so, he asserts that both the homoantagonistic sermon and the testimony of deliverance are more scripted and parroted than actualized.

News of Caldwell's testimony was so widespread that late-night television show host Jimmy Kimmel scrutinized the video, describing the event as "a miracle so miraculous, you have to see it to believe it. And even then, you might not." After Kimmel showed the footage to viewers, he jests, "His boyfriend is gonna be furious when he sees this clip."

Audio recordings and video footage of Caldwell's statement "I am delivered," the audio and the use of the term, spread quickly on the Internet as a performance signifyin(g) on the contradictions perceived in deliverance testimonies. The week immediately following the incident, musician Andre Forbes released a mixtape[28] featuring Caldwell's recorded testimony. His voice was looped, arranged in a spoken call-and-sung response with Andre Forbes's harmonized background vocals echoing, "I'm not gay no more." The intonation of Caldwell's spoken call-and-sung response displays his lower, forced, speaking vocal range.[29] It is a vocal style that various choir or group leaders use, tapping into preacher-vocalist aesthetics of a person gifted in seamlessly flowing between spoken and sung worship leadership. For example, Stellar and Grammy award-winning recording artists Reverend James Cleveland, Bishop Hezekiah Walker, and Kirk Franklin are popular preacher-vocalists known for their spoken "lead vocalist" style of gospel music with ensembles or choirs, emphasizing their oration over their singing ability. The song accompaniment style is reminiscent of 1990s gospel textures similar to those produced in Bishop Hezekiah Walker's "Jesus is My Help" (1997), combining rhythm section and synthesized instrumentation with high fidelity sound effects such as a crowd cheering or applauding.

Usually, the incorporation of the preacher-vocalist style merges two gendered and sexualized domains seamlessly within prized male worship leadership roles that accentuate orality: the male preacher is imagined as heterosexual and the male vocalist is imagined as queer until proven otherwise.[30] When done competently, the preacher-vocalist style manages congregants' perception of men's identity through a gamut of performance devices such as rhetorical delivery, lower vocal range, and "masculine" attire such as suits, declamatory gestures, and use of pulpit space in the worship. Essentially, male and female preacher-vocalists temper "feminizing" perceptions of singing with the sonic qualities associated with speaking.

"I am delivered" became a characterization of the peculiar ways in which some believers self-identify as delivered from homosexuality while displaying gender nonconformity and "wrestling" with same-gender desire despite their sexual orientation change testimony. These contradictions are rooted in heteropatriarchy, the pervasive tethering of one's sexual orientation to one's gender expression in black Pentecostal Christian discourses, as well as in other conservative Christian settings.[31] Homosexuality is stigmatized more than sexual indiscretions such as adultery and fornication. In his video response to the 2014 COGIC spectacle titled "Deliverance from Homosexuality?," COGIC-raised bishop Carlton Pearson said that black churches are reconsidering what they believe about homosexuality, including the "don't ask, don't tell" position in churches. Pearson then pointed out that the hypocrisy among those who administer deliverance is immensely heterosexist, favoring men in power:

> The double standard is becoming increasingly conspicuous or continually becoming conspicuous . . . There are district superintendents like the man who spoke. There are pastors and leaders, there are deacons and elders in churches who struggle with sexuality, homo- or hetero-, and they are not faithful in their marriages. And they struggle and wanna be [faithful]. Had the same altar call been made for people who need deliverance from adultery, I wonder how many would have come or deliverance from fornication.[32]

On the one hand, Caldwell's testimony confirmed that his previous queer gender expression and presentation of women-gendered attire, specifically purses and

makeup, correlated with his sexual identity. On the other hand, his pronunciation of "womens" also registered for listeners and observers as a caricature that
has been echoed throughout popular culture.[33]

Central to the public's contestation about his testimony was their struggle to
decipher the intelligibility and coherence of his utterance. As I alluded to in the
title of the chapter, viewers of his testimony footage pointed out that he had audible difficulty in saying words such as "delivered" with his transposed enunciation of the final alveolar consonant "t"—an emphasis phonetically indicating
a lingual occlusion or obstruction of air flow in the vocal tract. In addition, his
style of "speaking in other tongues" was also described as fake. The exaggerated
manner with which Caldwell delivered his testimony led people to speculate, apprehensively, about whether he was mentally stable or delivered fully owing to
the belief that one's sexual orientation can be detected through his or her speech
pattern, a notion that is held in various heteronormative contexts.[34]

Deploying a queer listening and viewing of his identity presentation, one
openly homosexual black male musician described Caldwell as exhibiting a
speech impediment that "he intentionally exaggerated" to perform a stereotype
of spoken queerness phonetically (i.e., a lisp and lingering final consonants).[35]
He added that such a rhetorical technique coupled with "effeminate" or feminine
masculine gesture is a lucrative gender expression in gospel settings. Further,
according to disabilities researcher Fiona A. Kumari Campbell, ableist bias in
deliverance assessment and practice promotes the view that impairment should
be "ameliorated, cured, or indeed eliminated. . . What remains unspeakable are
readings of the disabled body presenting life with impairment as an animating,
affirmative modality of subjectivity."[36] Several openly gay informants stated
Caldwell's style of talking was something other than vernacular speech. They
described him as "simply uneducated." Online observers created #delivert and
#womens Twitter hashtags, comedic sketches and social media memes.[37] They
even recorded musical interpretations parodying Caldwell's hyperpluralization
of nouns ("womens") and lack of subject-verb agreement. Unfortunately, the
public's assessment of his potential speech impairment revealed ableist bias in
popular debates surrounding what constitutes the qualities of successful spiritual
deliverance. Other viewers described Caldwell as "up to it" or his testimony as
a public performance of shenanigans in which he became the center of attention, captivating the virtual and present audiences through his performance of
parody, thus launching his trajectory as a celebrity.

COGIC leadership appeared to be in a bind that impeded legitimizing deliverance teachings. In response to the national attention that COGIC attracted,
the presiding bishop of the COGIC denomination, Bishop Charles E. Blake, distanced himself in the media from the tenor of Carter's sermon with a videotaped
scripted apology.[38] He outlined COGIC's love ethic and that they should uphold

biblical literalist teachings, while treating everyone with respect. Blake's apology was lukewarm, falling short in both explicitly affirming gay congregants and not condemning those who condemn gay COGIC congregants. Moreover, Blake's statement does not castigate Carter for preaching deliverance, but rather, denounced his use of indelicate rhetoric. This rhetorical move is key because it is well-known among Pentecostals that anti-gay sermons evoke the musical telos within Pentecostal worship—the shout—and thus prompt attendees to give even more. According to Kelefa Sanneh's 2010 interview in *The New Yorker* with Pentecostal minister and openly gay recording artist, Rev. Anthony C. Williams (a.k.a B.Slade and formerly Tonéx), "You can talk about a slut, a hussy, a heifer, a player, any other subject—you are not going to get the response you get when you start talking about fags, or gays . . . It's like a football game!" And yet heterosexual male preachers are not alone in preaching these strident sermons that encourage blood sport. Formerly gay and cisgender, hetero-presenting/sexual women also preach these types of sermons.

Caldwell is not the first self-identified delivered man to address the COGIC convocation about deliverance in a manner that evoked skepticism and ridicule from both Pentecostal Christian believers and outsiders. The succeeding section situates Caldwell's testimony style and content as being consistent with the long-held public script of deliverance that is performed during the COGIC convocation and other Pentecostal gospel music performances. Since the mid 1990s, African American male vocal musicians have explicitly responded to the gay-shaming sermons with musical performances of deliverance from homosexuality. Delivered vocal musicians such as Daryl Coley and Donnie McClurkin have spoken fondly of making music, characterizing it as a restorative outlet, a method for social bonding, and a tool for connecting with God. Next, I examine the most well-known African American male vocal musician's testimony of deliverance in which Donnie McClurkin reveals his gay history and pursuit of spiritual change. I observe that his self-identification of a delivered identity provides a testimony consistent with Pentecostal holiness doctrines, manages rumors, preempts him from being outed by others, and allows him to resume leading Pentecostal Christian believers into worship following his contrite disclosure.

The "I Am Delivered" Testimony Template

While there are undeniably heterosexual men who have recorded music about experiencing deliverance from an array of sin and temptation, the focus of this section is on preacher-singer Pastor Donnie McClurkin, the most popular artist with a testimony of deliverance. A notable moment for McClurkin was his extemporaneous testimony at the COGIC convocation in 2010. As he stepped forward to speak in the service, he raised an open hand toward the musicians, signaling them to stop the altar call music. McClurkin addressed the attendees in the wake of the artist formerly known as Tonéx's (a.k.a. B.Slade) 2009 interview on the Lexi Show of the Word network, in which he disclosed that he does not struggle with being gay. He is unapologetically gay. Tonéx's claim threatened the potency of McClurkin's testimony of sustained deliverance through a daily walk with God. McClurkin said, "They are covered by gifts and they are covered by music." To amplify his remarks, McClurkin suggested that the instrumental music/"the music" was an ambient distraction, sonically covering or entrancing the spiritual affliction of the queer and gender-nonconforming believers that he saw at various COGIC events such as the midnight musical. He argued that it was the music-making that allures and covers young people as they are drawn to musical participation through their exceptional gifts. McClurkin resolved that parents must be vigilant in protecting and guiding their children.

Deploying American studies scholar Roderick A. Ferguson's queer of color analysis,[39] I focus on McClurkin as a sample of the depictions of men who proclaim deliverance from homosexuality as a means of admitting same-sex desire, instantaneously claiming and distancing from their past through song and rhetoric, and inviting accountability/scrutiny going forward. During my research on accounts of men delivered from homosexuality, I have observed that his testimony is a template of common features within the canon of deliverance testimonies that are told in local congregations. In an effort to convey the depth of miraculous change that informs the music they perform, various gospel vocal musicians deploy "struggle"[40] language within their deliverance testimonies. Regrettably, the most ubiquitous testimonies of struggle with same-sex desire begin with incidents of inappropriate behavior such as molestation or incest enacted by people within "the church." Ironically, "the same Bible that is used against women, LGBTQ individuals and other marginalized identities is simultaneously used to shame survivors and privilege harm-doers," testifies child sexual assault survivor and religious studies scholar Ahmad Hayes-Greene.[41] Other characteristics of the testimonies are the accusation of clergy neglect of the victims of sexual misconduct,[42] the role of music-making and prayer in coping, and the submission to public deliverance rituals.

Tenor, songwriter, and pastor of Perfecting Faith Church in Freeport, NY, Donnie McClurkin's testimony of deliverance from homosexuality is the most popular story in the gospel music industry. He was one of several black male vocalists from the 1980s–2000s who rose to prominence as an itinerant worship leader, setting the atmosphere for white evangelical audiences: Morris Chapman, Larnelle Harris, Wintley Phipps, and Alvin Slaughter, to name some. The pretext for his account begins in incestuous, same-sex pedophilia that he believes introduced him to homosexuality, which, inopportunely, buttresses the problematic conflation of pedophilia with homosexuality. Central to McClurkin's testimony in his book *Eternal Victim, Eternal Victor*, is the ways in which music functioned as a form of escape from the same-sex sexual abuse and incest that he experienced on more than one occasion.[43] Unfortunately, McClurkin claims that there were male predators like his uncle and cousin in his church culture.[44] McClurkin maintains that a "seed" of homosexuality was planted in him through his sexual experience with a male authority figure in his family.

Gospel performers seldom share accounts of being born with same-gender desire, homosexual curiosity, sexual fluidity, or sexual questioning. Also, they do not talk about consensual situational sexuality as the result of incarceration, clergy submission arrangements, and other scenarios of intimate encounter. However, by traditionally disclosing homosexual experiences in relationship to physical or spiritual violation or being "turned out," their bodies become inscribed with pathological meaning. For example, while observing a feminine presenting man, a Pentecostal man said to me, "Clearly, something [sexual] has happened to him and God can heal him." He and other Pentecostals presume that feminine gender expression is not only demonstration of queer potential but also a physical remnant of queer sexual violation. Once these traits are identified, believers are to do spiritual work to uproot the spiritual challenges. Upon conforming to this ongoing process of spiritual work, McClurkin declared, "I AM DELIVERED."[45]

A year before penning the declaration "I am delivered" in his memoir, this global musical evangelist recorded songs consistent with COGIC Pentecostal theology that emphasized the Holy Spirit moving about him and the participants in his music ministry. McClurkin's "Caribbean Medley," from his *Live in London and More* (2000) album, is a mashup of Jamaican Calypso songs with the lyrics "Fiyah, Fiyah, Fiyah, Fiyah fall on me." A queer listening of this recording reveals the ways in which the protagonist welcomes the fire of the Holy Spirit, its process of purification, while not being consumed by the fire through the power of God. While that medley and that reprise in particular is fraught with Pentecostal evocation, one student at the University of Chicago who heard this song immediately connected McClurkin's (un)intentional use of Jamaican Calypso/Reggae inspiration as a palette for sonic subversion and queer shade, using that genre to assert his imperviousness to the hellfire to which he was once condemned without qualification or compassion due to his discrete homosexual identity. This is a powerful message of a potential weapon not prospering against queer men in the African or Caribbean diaspora, a social group who have been threatened with being burned by fire should they be found in homosexual acts in countries such as Jamaica.

Keeping in mind the "don't ask, don't tell" social arrangement in Pentecostal settings, McClurkin maneuvers through his personal history in fascinating

ways. Conspicuously consistent with the stereotypes of where one may detect a man's queer potential, his mode of homosexual socialization was based
in verbal communication. To explore sexual attraction to and overtures from
other men in heteronormative church settings, he wrote that he learned how to
be socially and culturally "bilingual"[46] in his communication with other men
in mixed company in order to keep his homosexual identity secret. Expanding
upon the DuBoisian double-consciousness,[47] performance theory and gender
studies offer modes of analysis that examine the black homosexual men's bi-
and multilingualism as sexual discretion, also known as the down low (the DL).
Former queer-of-color McClurkin's bilingualism was tailored as he navigated
the compulsory heterosexuality of gospel music and Pentecostal settings.[48]
While living as an African American homosexual man, McClurkin operated
in what communications studies scholar C. Riley Snorton calls in his research
on down low men a "glass closet," which is an analytical metaphor "to describe
how black sexualities are characterized by hypervisibility and confinement
and subject to regulation and surveillance."[49] This hypervisibility is conveyed
with the term flaming. Illuminating the mechanics of McClurkin's social bilingualism further, queer theorist José Esteban Munoz investigates black homosexual men's ways of knowing in compulsory heterosexual contexts. He
describes the unique language and recognition cultivated in black sexuality on
the DL:

> We are so used to white masculinity setting the standard for the closet. Now
> when we talk about it in relation to communities of color, it's not so much about
> the single man on a subway; it's about a network of men who recognize each
> other as DL, and they have this new concept or word to describe it that isn't the
> closet. It's a way of projecting out a bunch of likes and dislikes, a code of the way
> you experience the world in relationship to desire and sexuality.[50]

And thus McClurkin's mere disclosure of past homosexual coded communication and networks signifies breaking the fetters of queer silence—that is, deliverance from enforced duplicity in his religious life due to his same-gender desires
and sexuality.

One might argue that evidence of McClurkin's deliverance is his siring of a son
through sex with a woman outside of marriage.[51] While paternity is uncontested
proof that he has had sex with a woman, it is not adequate proof of the quality of
his sexual attraction to women in the court of black church opinion.[52] Despite
the fact that fornication is considered sin, his single parenthood has been han-
dled with kid gloves. Unfortunately, he has admitted that he has been an absentee
father, which reinscribes another anxiety in black communities associated with
black male leadership within families: the stigma of black male absenteeism in

homes and families. It is not lost on me that ironically at the 2010 COGIC convocation, he rebuked men for being absentee in their child's lives, citing fathers absenteeism as a contributing factor to queer sexual orientation:

> Where are the fathers that say, "I will not kill you. I will not condemn you but I will nurture you."
>
> And today, I am overwhelmed in this holy convocation because I see feminine men. And listen, do not applaud like it is a bash. It is because we failed. It is not their fault. It is not the children's fault. It is because we failed.
>
> We didn't father our children. We didn't cover our children. We didn't discern the seed and we didn't uproot it. We failed our boys. We failed our girls.[53]

His focus on fatherhood in his public talking points might be intended to assuage the urgent concern that he has not earnestly pursued a woman in order to conform to compulsory heterosexuality. His use of the word "seed" reinscribes the notion that sexual queerness and gender expression are embedded into people through "sexual perversion." His account does not include people who describe themselves as having never experienced sexual violation. Regrettably, his performance as a father is not surveilled as closely in the public eye as his marital status is, which evokes questions about the strategic nature of his true concern about parent's rearing their children properly.

Regardless of whether or not there is evidence of his sustained deliverance, Pentecostal gospel music fans monitor McClurkin's proclamation and presentation of heterosexual ideals in his performances. As both a performance and a survival strategy, McClurkin's testimony of deliverance is a form of disidentification that empowers him to reclaim the inherent status of hetero-presenting men in the heteropatriarchal leadership structure of gospel music networks and Pentecostal congregations. Performance theorist José Esteban Muñoz unlays disidentification as "descriptive of the survival strategies the minority subject practices in order to negotiate a phobic majoritarian public sphere that continuously elides or punishes the existence of subjects who do not conform to the phantasm of normative citizenship."[54] In this case, McClurkin embodies a multiminoritarian status: same-sex child abuse survivor, delivered from homosexuality, Pentecostal Christian believer, and African American man. Emphasizing the performing and theatricalizing of queerness in public, Muñoz points out that developing these modes of communication were necessary in the face of anxieties surrounding a rise in hate crimes, anti-gay legislation, and the HIV/AIDs pandemic. Following Muñoz, I assert that the testimonies of deliverance from homosexuality do a similar management of anxieties while simultaneously queering heterosexuality by using the process of deliverance to suggest a slippage in the notion of a fixed sexual orientation.

Since McClurkin is a gospel vocalist and preacher, his testimony is positioned to set the precedent for framing conversations around the prevalent pathological perception of men's homosexuality and feminine gender expression in historically black protestant congregations, especially in Pentecostal holiness churches that espouse a sanctified way of life. Situating homosexuality as a spiritual ailment, in his book McClurkin reinscribes gay male sexuality as a problem. Homosexual men are perceived as the symbolic embodiment of sexual deviance and sexual violation. Like McClurkin, delivered men recount their testimonies in the public square. However, there is a prevalence of sexual violation attributed to male ministers and male churchgoing family members. When men speak of deliverance, it is assumed that they became gay through a violation or coercion. By using the rhetorical domain of storytelling, the sexual violation assumption embedded in the dominant delivered from homosexuality testimony implicates the ministerial leadership as complicit in a system of violence and victim-shaming, rendering the male minister's chastisement of homosexual men impotent. Adding insult to injury, this is also a system that rejects the very people who were violated within it.

Here I would like to point out that little is made public about the inner workings of litigation and reprisals within Pentecostal church organizations.[55] There has been much speculation and rumor distributed about who might have been McClurkin's past partners, and that information falls out of the scope of this research. However, I find it more interesting to think about how such concealment preserves heteropatriarchal images and administers humiliation to the very person claiming deliverance. This discretion serves as a scapegoat self-designation akin to the ancient practice of lepers shouting "unclean, unclean" when they traveled in the public square. The attention they attracted and the simultaneous contact they repelled is similar to the public declaration of deliverance from homosexuality in that designating one's self as such in itself is a form of mortification, isolation, and deflection from identifying who the delivered individual's partner is. The designation places one's identity front and center before they are able to create new meaningful, intimate relationships with women sexually attracted to heterosexual men. Several women with whom I have broken bread have expressed that men's public self-disclosure of their queer sexual history is unattractive and queer. Several have intimated that they might handle a man's history of sexual questioning better if it remained between the two of them.

Despite conflicting feelings about the nature or validity of the delivered men's healing, women are redefining deliverance by acting as discrete surrogates, supporting gay men's liberation with their maternal leadership, marital/sexual partnership, and media engagement. As in the case of McClurkin, most testimonys emphasize "Mothers of the church"[56] as an embodied safe haven for men who are survivors of molestation, rape, and incest. In his narrative, the women are described as transmitting a form of maternal pedagogy, teaching and praying with him, and modeling authentic Christian living that though well-meaning was also problematic. Growing up, "older mothers in the church" were the ones who he trusted to teach him how to present himself in masculine ways as indicated by the range in which young men were supposed to sing and their style of stride.

> When we wanted to sing soprano, you'd hear them say things like, "Get some bass in your voice!!" or "Men don't sing soprano!" Sister Braizley would teach me how to walk. If you held your hand up in a feminine way, they'd hit your hand and tell you to "Put your hands at your side. Men don't hold their hands like that!"[57]

Even though their mentorship was well-meaning, some of it was misguided and traumatic, exemplifying and transferring internalized misogyny. Women who are in romantic relationships with men delivered from homosexuality may become sexual surrogates, helping the men to explore their sexuality and perhaps sire children. Also, through the work of journalists and broadcasters such as Teresa Hairston and Lexi, we find journalistic surrogacy. Women are recurrently mediators of men's stories in the press, giving voice to men who may otherwise be silenced or disparaged for their sexual past. Even though they may wrestle with internalizing misogynoir ideologies in their participation (i.e., shortage of eligible men for single black women who desire to be mothers), these women affirm delivered men's desire to do what is right in the eyes of God and the church.

Does the public declaration of newfound nonhomosexuality position the men for fruitful heterosexual relationships going forward? Or is the new identity a way of articulating one's professional sexual discretion or "fall guy"/scapegoat designation to other men? Is isolation, self-loathing, and asexuality the goal? For whom is the declaration, if the work was already accomplished by God?

If any of McClurkin's male partners were married to a woman, then his new public designation as delivered is a form of humiliation not unlike those who have been made to wear a metaphoric scarlet letter of adultery throughout history. Moreover, if their unidentified partner(s) are prominent or even a preacher, then the concealment of their identity protects the perceived strength of the heteropatriarchy. Constantly, the men tell their stories of abuse as adults, after the suspect has died, and rarely do they name the predator when divulging their terrifying secret. Although his self-disclosure to the public is commendable, McClurkin's transparency functions much like down low sexuality as gender studies scholar Jeffrey McCune characterizes the DL. McClurkin's disclosure is a means of making sense of his presumably past "sexual experiences with other men, without having to mark [himself] as queer,"[58] while concurrently concealing his intersectionality in forming social practices in the present and future.

Unfortunately, the nature of these self-disclosure customs confines the deliverance testimony to the public imagination, problematically relegating their accounts to rhetorical devices, instead of calling for Christian accountability and criminal justice: a missed opportunity to reform the cycle of abuse. In his 2006 book *Understanding Child Abuse,* psychiatrist Edward Rowan advocates for survivors to seek punishment for their abusers, but "the adversarial nature of the proceedings is not always a positive experience for survivors and may even lead to additional trauma."[59] Even after the men self-disclose their deliverance, the victims of sexual abuse bear the sociocultural stigma associated with exhibiting perceived traces of same-sex desire, history, and fellowship. Conversely, their accusations of sexual violation function as a form of scapegoating, chastening the reputation of the predominantly male church leadership ranks. Substantiated or not, their claims of unfinished justice are also a way of sharing the stigma of queerness by suggesting that any minister or member of the congregation has the potential to be queered (i.e., violated, sensual, expressive, aroused, and/or experiencing queer desire) and engage in a form of inappropriate or illicit same-sex sexual behavior.

McClurkin describes his road to deliverance as lifelong. His self-identification as a person delivered from homosexuality is one of several components that serve as evidence of spiritual transformation, and allows him to distance himself from social stigmatization. Another approach to supporting deliverance is to hate a person's *actions* as opposed to disliking the *doer* of the actions. This ideology misleading as it attempts to redirect the repulsion that believers may feel about people who subscribe to queer sexuality and/or gender expression; however, the actions are very much an inextricable component of the doer's bodily responsorial performance.

The next section examines the love-hate ideology toward queerness and the sociocultural dissonances that emerge when a female preaching gospel recording artist makes remarks similar to Porter's ill-famed exhortation during the 2014 COGIC Convocation.

Love the Sinner, Hate the Sin

> But Moses spoke to the Lord,
> "The Israelites have not listened to me;
> how then shall Pharaoh listen to me, poor speaker that
>   I am?" —Exodus 6:12 NRSV

When this poor lisping stammering tongue
Lies silent in the grave,
Then in a nobler sweeter song
I'll sing thy power to save.
—"There is a Fountain Filled with Blood" (1772), William Cowper

Tuning into deliverance candidates' lingual dexterity is key in understanding how Pentecostals regularly assess the need for deliverance. Within the Protestant Christian tradition, the biblical text Exodus 6:12 and "There is a Fountain Filled with Blood" are beloved texts that serve as a counternarrative to the possible spiritual meanings of a believer like Andrew Caldwell, who is "differently-abled"[60] with a "lisping, stammering tongue" described elsewhere as an impediment. Being a "poor speaker" like Moses may be interpreted as a messianic trait by which a leader is endowed, enhancing their humanity or even more, inducing their ongoing need for God's help in properly using their different abilities. Numerous famous gospel vocalists' iconic sounds feature audible lisps or have talked about their focus on speaking and enunciation: Pastor James Cleveland, Stellar and Grammy award-winning Rev. Richard Smallwood,[61] and Stellar and Grammy award-nominated Pastor Travis Greene who describes himself as a walking miracle. In fact in his testimony, Greene deploys deliverance language as he recounts being resurrected from the dead twice—once as a stillborn and then as a four year old—and the lessons he learned as a result. "God really had to deliver me from finding value in things, affirmation, pleasing people, and even with being impressed with people or wanting them to be impressed with me. He really extracted that from me, and then launched me to this level of success."[62] However, in gospel music settings one's lingual rigidity coupled with feminine gender expressions are predictably interpreted as a spiritual shortcoming, revealing one's queer potential. And countless times, I have observed people assess a performer's or believer's manner of speech and gender expression, deducing they are likely queer and that the configuration of their self-presentation is aural-visual proof they are spiritually afflicted.

Upon drawing the conclusion that they estimate the person is both queer and different-abled, I have heard them express contempt couched in compassionate language with the homoantagonistic phrase "Love the sinner, hate the sin." This phrase is theological shorthand for focusing on hating the deeds the person does, namely their identity presentation, and not the doer. "Our hatred is never directed toward that person . . . We are to look past [sic] the persons and see and hate the spirit that's caused these things to happen through the person," according to McClurkin.[63] The sin is enacted through external ("the spirit") and internal ("through the person") forces; however, the prevalence of verbal derision and public humiliation in the deliverance practices creates harmful experiences for those seeking deliverance. [64]

Gospel music is regularly performed in heteropatriarchal settings that uphold both the male preacher and the male vocal musician as the primary worship leadership roles.[65] While the male preacher is imagined to perform a symbolically heterosexual, masculine, and dominant gender expression, the male vocalist is stereotyped as performing symbolically queer sexual potential, feminine gender expression, and a subordinate position in worship leadership. In historically black Pentecostal churches, this imbalanced power dynamic is economic, intimate, and closely related to the senior pastor, being both the one who preaches and makes decisions about hiring musicians and other church personnel. This decision is based upon the satisfaction—pleasure, really—they derive from the employees' services.

I have witnessed innumerable deliverance rituals from pulpit and music ministry vantage points that target feminine-presenting men in ministry like Caldwell. They experience a misogynoir with which I am familiar, especially in the historically black Protestant denominations that prohibit women from ascending to the highest ranks of church leadership, but they are promised social elevation should they reject the attributes they share with women. These intraculturally circulated stereotypes fuel the congregation's policing of black men's sexual behavior and their public distancing from exhibitions of queer potential. As a result, women internalize and parrot these heteropatriarchal values as well as enacting configurations of misogynoir and misandnoir. Through homo-antagonistic sermons that resemble the remarks Rev. Carter delivered during the 2014 COGIC convocation, both men and women help to bolster this heteropatriarchal system. Pentecostal preachers launch critiques toward queer believers, sometimes using problematic designations to describe their sexuality and gender expression with queer misandnoir terms such as "sissy," "flamboyant," and "effeminate." English and Africana studies scholar Stacy C. Boyd wrote about incendiary remarks that Bishop Alfred A. Owens Jr. made using the term "sissy" at the 7,000-member Greater Mt. Calvary Holy Church in Washington, DC. On April 6, 2006, Bishop Owens requested that the heterosexual men meet him at the altar to discuss what constitutes "real men":

It takes a real man to confess Jesus as Lord and Savior. I'm not talking about no faggot or no sissy. I mean a real man who has made up their mind . . . Wait a minute! Let all the real men come on down here and take a bow. All the real men—I'm talking about the straight men.

Further, Owens told the straight men,

> Come on down here and walk around and praise God that you are straight. Thank that you are straight. Thank him that you're straight. All the straight men that's proud to be a Christian, that's proud to be a man of God. I'm proud of what God made me. Any proud men in the room?[66]

And with those words during the impromptu ritual enthroning hetero-presenting manhood, Owens ceremoniously reinscribed heteropatriarchal pride, while also reinscribing queer/femme devaluation. As Owens called for a moment of introspection and healing, his distracting use of the terms "faggot" and "sissy" spoil the moment for the queer believers who were under the sound of his voice. What could have been a redefining moment of real manhood was turned into a demeaning one for those who, for him, were diminished in their manhood because of their unconventional gender expression and sexual orientation. Additionally, vocal musicians internalize and replicate the same misogynistic scripts to elicit an ecstatic response in worship.

On December 29, 2016, deliverance rhetoric was again foisted into the public eye when COGIC-raised, sultry, alto and organ-playing gospel recording artist Pastor Kim Burrell preached a deliverance sermon that a congregant live streamed on social media from the Love and Liberty Fellowship International in Houston, Texas, where she is founder and senior minister.[67] In her ministry, Burrell performs in two sites of male dominance within Pentecostalism: the physical space of pulpit ministry, and the sonic space of treble timbres,[68] in which she vocally overlaps with tenors such as Daryl Coley. Her occupancy of these spacial and sonic domains of orality is key because male participants who share those sites are positioned for primacy in ecclesial and worship leadership. However, her womanhood limits her authority in Pentecostalism, so much so that homosexual and hetero-presenting men outrank her in sociocultural access as long as they do not identify themselves as queer.

In extemporaneous remarks that evening, she recounted how a pastor told her "don't mess with my sissies" when she preaches and then specified an interaction with a man who spoke to her in an "effeminate" manner, a resemblance to feminine behavior that she found off-putting. Then she admonished congregants to resist the "homosexual spirit" and "perverted" behavior, emphasizing, "If you play with it in 2017, you will die from it." Notably she referred to Caldwell, saying that his story makes a "mockery" of the church.

> Mr. "I Am Delivert" with all these different types of spirits . . . on Jimmy Kimmel . . . you see what the enemy is looking for? . . . The minute somebody comes out with a deaf and dumb spirit . . . a mute spirit . . . one that can't even

talk ... and that has a perverted spirit says that "I am delivert" ... You think the enemy isn't trying to make a mockery of the church?

Drawing from disabilities scholar Fiona A. Kumari Campbell (2008), activist Jade Perry detected that Burrell deploys homoantagonistic and ableist language that situated gender identity alongside disability and next to sin, much like Coley's interview. "[Kim] implies that both LGBTQI identities *as well as* disabled persons are inherently possessed by spirits / dealing with sin." Stemming from a Pentecostal holiness doctrinal constellation,[69] Carter and Burrell's sermons about the "homosexual spirit" are heteropatriarchal public scripts by which preachers conceive of same-sex desire as a demonic oppression that people may "deal" with, and from which believers should distance themselves. Unlike Carter, subsequent to the distribution of Burrell's sound bite, she faced what conservative gospel music fans viewed as an entertainment industry backlash. Within one week, Burrell's radio show program "Bridging the Gap with Kim Burrell" was cancelled. Lesbian talk show host Ellen DeGeneres uninvited Burrell from a scheduled January 5, 2017 appearance on her show with music producer Pharrell Williams for the *Hidden Figures* (2017) movie soundtrack who, we learn in his 2019 Winter *GQ* feature, grew up attending his mother's Pentecostal church in Virginia Beach.[70]

In response to Burrell's evocation of his (dis)abilities, Caldwell posted a video via social media on December 31, 2016, conveying that he was disappointed with Burrell, whose music he "supported for years." Caldwell divulged that her reference to him as "Mr. I am Delivert" and "deaf and dumb" stung.[71] Unwittingly, he confirmed being diagnosed as potentially retarded around seven years old and has dealt with a speech impediment, the attribute to which believers had pointed as undermining the potency of his deliverance claims. Both her initial remarks about an unidentified man's verbalized gender expression and Caldwell's speech illustrated the ways in which she and others detected men's need for deliverance by their vocal sound and pronunciation.[72] As the result of her negative remarks and others' scrutinizing the legitimacy of his testimony, he confirmed people's concern that he has in fact had suicidal ideations.

Additionally, Burrell deployed the homo-antagonistic phrase frequently deployed to situate men presumed to be homosexual by demonizing their sexual behavior: "love the sinner and hate the sin." Instead of making remarks based on either of the men's self-identification, she resorted to analyzing intangible markers such as the men's display of feminine gender expression to presume they have a sinful inclination. The projection of the believer as gay "without concrete supporting evidence (such as their self-identification) signals a conflation of men's sexuality with gender expression, which in actuality are two distinct aspects of identity. While sexual orientation references sexual partner preferences, gender expression is indicative of the socio-culturally developed male- or female-coded ways that individuals present their identity to the public."[73] On the surface, the statement "love the sinner" seems compassionate toward believers facing spiritual challenges generally. However, in the popular application of the statement toward queer men it is a homophobic and transphobic sentiment delivered under a theological guise. It is a sentiment that supports the logics by which believers derive pleasure from homosexual musicians' leadership via good, aesthetically pleasing behavior that is consumed, while deriding the same musicians for their same-gender sexuality and feminine gender expression.

In 2014, Deliverance from homosexuality dissenter, gay ally, gospel recording artist, and former COGIC bishop Carlton Pearson aired his disapproval of the patronizing love the sinner rhetoric coupled with the queer shaming language ("sissy" or "gay," "punk," "fag," and less often "dyke") that is used to coax people to submit to deliverance rituals, as evinced by the approaches Porter and Burrell administered. Pearson observes that the criteria for queer people to be accepted into Pentecostal Christian community are inequitable, not corresponding with the demands placed on heterosexual people who sexually transgress through adultery or fornication all the time.[74] Further, he averred that no one can change their sexuality but they can modify it, regardless of their orientation:

> It was made clear that night if you are a "sissy" or "gay," "punk," "fag"—all those comments that people apply toward gay men particularly, sometimes "dykes"— I've heard all that stuff. Horrible statements . . .
>
> You can come to the church if you get saved and delivered. You can't just be saved, forgiven of your sins. You've got to be delivered from your sexuality.
>
> You can no more be delivered from homosexuality than you can be delivered from heterosexuality or human sexuality.
>
> You don't get deliverance from human sexuality or being sexual beings.
>
> You can manage it, you can modify it, you can modulate it . . . You can abstain from acting out your sexuality.[75]

Because the stability of such deliverance practices is arduous to corroborate onlookers wondered what was the motive for Caldwell's testimony.

McClurkin's memoir corroborates this management arrangement in his description of leaders who proposition publicly identified gay men as "vultures." Vultures, as he puts it, are "predatory men that would soon attempt to take advantage of a broken boy and his confusion" that he encountered in the church; however, his account is troubling as he displays an internalized disdain toward queer men.

And there were brothers who seemingly befriended me under the guise of mentorship, only to reveal their desire and purpose to further the perversion and
increase the confusion. My world of security (the church) was invaded when
other broken men, in need of healing, made themselves known as predators.
Secret lives were revealed, and I was introduced to a deceptive underworld in
the church.

Singing on Sundays, after weekend rendezvous was commonplace. Seeing
other Christians in compromising places, yet faithfully, hypocritically and de-
ceptively at their posts in church as though nothing was wrong was typical.[76]

And as McClurkin recounts the private social arrangements, he illuminates the
multivalent nature of the "don't ask, don't tell" culture that Pearson mentioned
as well, in which shared private lives implicate observers as also questioning the
efficacy of deliverance.

This stigmatization of sexual behavior outside of the confines of the institution
of marriage has been instilled during and since the institution of slavocracy that
centered on slave owners manipulation of and benefitting from enslaved Africans'
sexual behavior. Here I note that Pearson makes an important tie from the sexual
dysfunction, anxiety, and stigmatization among fellow black Pentecostals to the
legacy of sexual assault and psychological warfare that European Americans
waged during the Atlantic Slave Trade. It is well documented that enslaved
women were raped and enslaved men were sodomized, among other sexual acts,
as a means of sexual gratification, siring, and dominance.[77] He asserts that to
have a conversation about deliverance and "sexual perversion" one must consider the role that US colonizers played in sexually violating enslaved Africans,
including:

It has been one of the most unspoken taboos in the gay and African American
communities . . . about sexual abuse of full-grown men, during the times of
slavery. When grown men who were humiliated and subjugated into some aspect of submission by allowing or performing sexual acts on white masters.
And it was humiliating. And in the culture, I remember my grandfather referring to that when I was in junior high school—I wasn't sure what he meant.
But it was an unspoken thing. The women of these men, the wives, sisters, and
mothers wouldn't even speak on it. It was never addressed but there was an innate deep seeded resentment over this whole conscious.[78]

During that period, American and European romantic racialists distributed
the notion that the Negro race was "the Lady of the Races," a more "effeminate,"[79]
or as George M. Frederickson wrote that scientific racist Alexander Kinmont
maintained, Negroes are "feminine and tenderminded" in comparison to white

people.[80] As such, the US concept of effeminacy was conceptualized as a racial and gender slur within the slave hierarchy, meant to characterize African subjugation. To use the term effeminacy is to verbally reinscribe the sexual dominance that thrived during chattel enslavement.

Among those violent sexual acts committed by European and American colonizers was the process of instantly and over time consuming black male bodies, the experience and witnessing of which was to break the spirits of those who beheld the atrocity causing them to submit to chattel slavery conditions to avoid that fate. This process of coercing Africans to submit to the slavocracy has profound implications for what it meant to convert and subsequently what it means to be delivered—that is, freed from the bonds of sexual humiliation, spiritual captivity, psychological terror, and physical brutality. The nadirs of white men's disturbing seasoning, dominance, and "breaking" of African men through rape and cannibalism during US slavery was the enactment of a pernicious double bind: coinciding same-gender envy with premium desire for black male flesh that cohered.

In addition to literal acts of eating, carving, and cooking flesh, European and American whites developed a culture of cannibalism wherein daily acts of violence, religious conversion, slave seasoning, and breaking and sexual brutality all fed into the master's appetite for African flesh and souls. Many historical texts on the subject of slavery describe the importance of the process of "seasoning" for breaking men and women and making them into docile "slaves." Elaborating on the culinary connotations of the word "seasoning" (season: "to heighten or improve the flavor of food by adding condiments, spices, herbs, or the like"). I link the physically brutal culture of seasoning to the parallel development of erotic appetites, tastes, and aesthetic longings for the black male.[81]

European and American white people's grotesque acts typified through cannibalizing African people confirmed how deeply entrenched the regard was of Africans as subhuman property, a dehumanizing claim that was legalized in the 1787 Three-Fifths Compromise to suppress enslaved Africans' votes.[82] Aiming to cultivate tractability in their enslaved Africans, enslavers deployed spiritual, social, cultural, and sexual forms of terror that have left an indelible imprint on the souls of black folks in the United States for generations.

Coveting black male flesh and enfleshment has been transferred from white men, internalized, and continues in how African American Pentecostal faith communities view and consume black male sexual possibilities through spiritual cannibalism insinuated as "deliverance." The culture of unspokenness that has developed in the face of gross duplicity—white cultural Victorianism and dualistic denial of traversing sexual boundaries—has infiltrated African American religious life, as we will discuss in more depth in chapter 6. Subsequently, the enslaved people were shamed and blamed for what was forcibly done to them under chattel slavery conditions. Pearson makes a persuasive argument positing that true deliverance from sexual repression; perversion and anxiety must include naming and uprooting the trauma of our colonial past.[83]

Also, Pearson connotes a distinction between what is said publicly (public script) and done privately (social contract),[84] and how speech may be used to deflect from or advertise queer possibility. While addressing the awkward task of determining if a homosexual believer is healed, Pearson said further,

> Now, the young man says he was delivered.
>   Well, with a gay person, you can't tell they are delivered, "healed" the way you can with a person who has a deaf ear and it pops open or a blind eye and it pops opens or with crooked limbs or they get out of a wheel chair—it's conspicuous that they are healed. But somebody who is saying they are delivered of their sexuality, gay or straight, how can you know that? That's supposed to be very private. We don't know when that man will have sex again or if he has since his testimony . . . Sometimes it happens after the service in one of the hotel rooms, sometimes with a leader.[85]

In this sense, "Love the sinner, hate the sin" is a disingenuous expression of deliverance that in its application reestablishes notions of surveillance, guilt, and blame particularly fixating on the involuntary ways in which queer(ed) believers vocally or bodily respond to the move of the Spirit and live in quotidian life. Inopportunely, one's self-disclosure as delivered from homosexuality, in the public sphere and in the assembly of the saints, positions them as a target for exploitation and scapegoating—a person who is consistently propositioned and blamed for navigating or avoiding same-gender advances because they are known for their queer potential. In the final section of this chapter, I highlight a few outspoken gospel musicians who redefine deliverance, declaring the harmful and inadequate application of deliverance teachings among gospel music enthusiasts.

Redefining Deliverance

Critics of deliverance from homosexuality have challenged the traditional notion of "delivered" that is deployed in Pentecostal holiness rituals, propositioning it refers to radical self-acceptance. For example, in the 2016 BET documentary *Holler if You Hear Me: Black and Gay in the Church,* COGIC-raised baritone music minister Charles Anthony Bryant proposes a different outcome of praying for deliverance. He claims that God can deliver believers from their way of thinking:

> I just knew that I would experience deliverance in the form of heterosexuality. I just knew that one day, not necessarily that I would wake up—but if I stayed true to the process God would reward me with heterosexuality. Never thinking that I would be delivered here [points to his temple] into a different way of thinking, knowing that my salvation is not compromised. Knowing that my walk with Christ is not compromised but, in fact, it is strengthened by me walking in my truth.[86]

Bryant provides an interpretation of deliverance that advocates for believers' liberation to be who God created them to be, just as they are, as same-gender loving people. Detaching homosexuality from being a threat to salvation, Bryant proposes a release from the anxieties that paralyze same-gender loving people from being truthful to themselves. The liberation for which he and others advocate includes freedom from the uncountable repressed modes of sexual expression that are even cultivated in Pentecostal teachings on heterosexual chastity.

For gay musician advocates, "delivered" is one's freedom to be authentic and truthful about their spiritual and bodily experiences—their spectrum of desires, exploration, questioning, histories, and tastes. One openly gay informant defined delivered by emphasizing freeing oneself from other people's opinion of them. While describing the complex humiliating and erotic connotations of deliverance rituals in worship, openly lesbian gospel musician Bishop Yvette Flunder observes the contradictions displayed in the spiritual healing practices and believers' quality of life. During a panel of the "Are the Gods Afraid of Black Sexuality?," a two-day interfaith conference at Columbia University's Center on African American Religion, Sexual Politics & Social Justice (CARSS) in New York City on October 24, 2014, Flunder reflected on the overrepresentation of discreet same-gender loving gospel composers and performers. She resolved that gospel music is gay music.[87]

Flunder's statement ironically confirms popular perceptions of queerness being associated with music ministry, while simultaneously challenging the perception that gospel music is the *cause* of a person's same-gender desire. On the contrary, she contends that God has endowed gospel musicians with extraordinary shamanistic attributes as mediators to the divine, making queer believers uniquely equipped to facilitate worship. Observing the contradictions musicians face, she said, "Essentially, we are told to deny or at least diminish our sexuality and forbidden to act on it and then we act on it like crazy." Flunder argues that this diminishment is especially contradictory for gospel musicians because of the mixture of sensuality, sexuality, and spirituality that characterizes worship and social life. Flunder explained further the sociocultural context for deliverance practices from a same-gender loving gospel musicians' perspective:

And a principle sexual subculture in the "African American church" is the same-sex or homoerotic culture, which is overrepresented in the gospel community. I've been singing gospel music for thirty plus years, and just about every really good song was either written by or performed by a same-gender loving person, whether they [publicly] identified as such or not. And the resulting psychosis that is caused by this dislocation manifests is major contributors to gospel musics, when they openly deny or diminish their sexual orientation; suggest that they have been *delivered* or set free . . . publicly and privately live a completely different life. These are people I know, that I am not here to vilify. I am simply here to say that the culture has produced this subculture and this subculture keeps people on essentially a treadmill of getting delivered and getting bound, and getting delivered and getting bound, and getting delivered and getting bound . . . Sexual oppression leads to sexual obsession. (emphasis mine)

Flunder's reiterated statement "Delivered and getting bound" was heard by queer attendees as a critique of McClurkin's contradictory public script that critics have said is illustrated through his 2000 hit recording "We Fall Down, But We Get Up." In the chorus, he sings three times, "We Fall Down, But We Get Up." And then he adds at the end of the stanza, "For a saint is just a sinner who fell down and got back up." His definition of saint is a sinner who commits to a cycle resembling the expansive form of the song and reoccurring practice of surveilled for traces of queerness. Flunder provides three main reasons for why gay gospel musicians participate in these deliverance testimonies and purposefully do not self-disclose their homosexuality: same-sex marriages are not supported; they anticipate a reduction in the impact of their ministry; and they fear loss of income from their gospel music patrons. Moreover, she conveyed her observation that as believers identify themselves as delivered from same-sex desire, they internalize the stigma of homosexuality, undertake self-loathing, and enact self-inflicted spiritual torture. Deeply rooted in her sense that fostering a proud same-gender loving identity is a matter of promoting integrity, she proposes that deliverance is through acceptance and conveyance of one's same-sex sensuality and sexuality. While gospel music performance is held as a means through which seekers are delivered, gospel musicians such as Flunder and Grammy award-winning musician B.Slade (formerly known as Tonéx) argue that the gospel music scene is a queering space—McClurkin's signal to stop the music during the 2010 COGIC convocation suggests it is too.

Their observations bring us full circle to the tremendous musical facility demonstrated in the Daryl Coley recording that in actuality conformed to the sociocultural parameters that manage anxieties surrounding men singing high and gesturing in a manner that resembles feminine attributes. The public's reception of the Andrew Caldwell footage evokes an examination of the sonic properties of deliverance practices and the tensions that emerge as men exhibit perceived traces of queerness, especially feminine attributes. Spectators and participants question and even mock the validity of the practices, since observations show that the traces of queerness remain and that believers are continuously in need of deliverance. For anxious homosexual gospel musicians, to disclose their identity in gospel music settings that emphasize Pentecostal holiness and compulsory heteronormativity is to enlist in a sociocultural blood sport within conservative black Christianity. Believers who self-identify as delivered from homosexuality negotiate the contradictions that spectators observed in the footage within healing practices that are supposed to liberate seekers; however, a significant amount of seekers and believers are shamed because of their history. And so to protect their coveted position as worship leaders readily able to access the presence of God, countless musicians choose not to disclose their queer or questioning history. With regard to highranking church leadership like Bishop Blake, church and faith leaders such as Rev. Larry Reid are becoming more conscious and vocal about the ways in which ministers' approaches are offensive. Although many gospel vocal musicians in particular have internalized stigmatization about queerness and promoted deliverance practices, artists such as McClurkin launch their own critiques of historically black Protestant contexts in subtle ways. Throughout the testimonies of delivered and openly gay gospel vocalists, pastors have been implicated in the perpetration and neglect of sexual abuse that has exposed countless impressionable youths to nonconsensual sex. Such accusations have prompted theologians to reconsider the ways in which believers, especially gospel musicians, talk about consent, sensuality, sexuality, and spirituality in Pentecostal and gospel music settings. The next three chapters look closely at the attributes that prompted scrutiny for the preponderance of the men I have interviewed: gendering of high-singing as feminine, gendering of gesture and dance, and contradictory reception of male musicians whose music is characterized by bass timbres, frequencies, and textures that are coded as masculine. These three succeeding case studies reveal the exception to the stereotypes and stigmas that have been circulated throughout the modern gospel music tradition.

2

"Men Don't Sing Soprano"

Black Countertenors and Gendered Sound in the Sermonic Selection

The summer before I enrolled in Oberlin College to study voice performance, I attended the Gospel Music Workshop of America (GMWA) in New Orleans for the first time in 1999. Founded by the great gospel composer Reverend James Cleveland, GMWA was known for attracting gospel music artists, industry execs, and amateurs to network, train, perform, and record repertoire.[1] As a production staff member for The Dream Network, my family's television network and production company, we were contracted to film the performances for the videos that would be purchased.[2] Every year the guild performed and recorded new works that were designated for children's choirs, women's choirs, men's and "combined" choirs. One evening when we were prepping to videotape the men's choir performance, a spectator approached me and suggested that I pay attention to the male sopranos during sound check. Adult male sopranos are not a common vocal classification in popular gospel music composition, performance, or radio airplay. The men sang their parts with robust sound and exuberant performance practice. They committed to their presentation. As I listened, I observed the spectator's nonverbal responses to the quality of their singing: facial expressions that registered to me as a mixture of awe, surprise, and cognitive dissonance. One hetero-presenting cameraman said loudly, "Are you kidding me? Male sopranos? I can't do this. You have got to be kidding me. Men do not sing soprano. Nope." He recoiled and waved his hand while walking out of the Ballroom. Another person remarked, "See. *This*—male sopranos . . . Men walking around in pink suits with long, acrylic nails—*this* is why people call GMWA, Gay Men Walking Around." Several connotations are at play in this statement. GMWA has long been a site for a spectrum of gender expression and throughout the years the annual gathering has been implicated along with various religious gatherings as a site for lascivious behavior or—to put it more bluntly—orgies. The cameraman's comment echoed how Donnie McClurkin heard the church mothers scorn men who sing soprano parts in chapter 1, the sociocultural epitome of sounding like women. I designate their ridicule as a practice of miseducation about gender expression reinscribed ironically through socioculturally maternal pedagogies.

Flaming? Alisha Lola Jones, Oxford University Press (2020). © Oxford University Press.
DOI: 10.1093/oso/9780190065416.001.0001

My response to the uncanny performance was not as passionate as the other spectator, largely because I was familiar with adult male soprano soloists, typically designated as countertenors, through my formal music training in European concert music. A few years prior to the GMWA conference I had encountered my first countertenor soloist in Halle, Germany, while performing at the invitation of the German government for the Handel Festival with the Duke Ellington School for the Arts show choir from Washington, DC under the direction of Samuel L. E. Bonds. I learned that countertenors are understood to produce a rare vocal sound, and they are able to traverse gendered domains in the roles they portrayed and the costumes they wore on the operatic stage. Traversing those gendered domains of vocal sound and attire was not a necessary statement about their identity. Subsequent to that rehearsal, I became attuned to the illegibility of men's gendered performance, specifically within the vocal domain of choral and solo performance. Eventually, I realized how important our production role was in capturing the musical life of the GMWA through video recordings of rehearsals and performances. This awareness began to shape the following question for me: What public arts interventions are made through televised broadcasts of unique black sacred music performances that challenge sonic and visual stereotypes of gender performance?

In 2011, when Patrick Dailey sang the solo in Nathan Carter's arrangement of "Some Day" at New Psalmist Baptist Church in Baltimore, it was the first countertenor performance to be broadcast on the African American Christian network, called The Word Network.[3] Based on Rev. Charles A. Tindley's (1851–1933) beloved 1916 hymn "Beams of Heaven (Some Day)," Carter's arrangement (2003) is set for SSAATTBB choir,[4] solo, and organ. The choir in Baltimore sang the first verse and refrain, after which a trio of female voices, as specified by Carter, sang the second verse and refrain. Finally, with "noble" posture comprising a lifted chest and arms held close to the body, Dailey sang the third verse and then ad libbed while the chorus repeated the refrain in the antiphonal or call and response manner that is central to gospel music styles. Notably, the third verse was set for a soloist, but Carter does not specify a gendered high-voice classification such as soprano or tenor.

While the absence of a soloist classification in the music is not remarkable, Carter's own preferences in performance practice are. Carter's omission of a specific vocal designation for the notated soloist part also suggests that the ideal soloist is anyone who can sing the part in a high *tessitura* (a comfortable singing range). The absence of a specific voice classification in the sheet music institutionalizes—that is, makes customary—a gender-inclusive and imaginative casting of the part. This casting flexibility overlaps African American vernacular practices that embrace fluidity between conventional vocal designations within the European-derived concert music composer's traditional prerogative and progressiveness in voicing rare singers. Further, to manage contentious cultural perceptions centering on men "singing high like a woman,"[5] the voicing flexibility helps contextualize African American operatic countertenors who lead worship in gospel settings.

Noticing the attention that Patrick Dailey's performance garnered, I first interviewed the Tennessee native in November 2011. Over the course of our ongoing conversations and subsequent collaborations, we discussed his performance practice choices and the issues he faces as a countertenor who performs in African American gospel contexts. According to Dailey, when Carter conducted this composition in concerts with his Morgan State University choir,[6] he generally featured countertenor Ernie Saunders as well as various soprano soloists. By programming high vocalists in a gender-inclusive manner within a historically black collegiate context, Carter provided his pupils with language and codes of conduct to present rare vocal designations to new audiences in live venues and multimedia platforms such as New Psalmist Baptist Church and The Word Network.

Dailey admitted that even in a twenty-first-century context, African-American countertenors are perceived as peculiar. "The fact of the matter is that you are already gonna present something—even if it is in the classical audience— you are already gonna present something to them that might be foreign to them already. You don't wanna turn them off at the very beginning."[7] As I considered Dailey's anxieties, the following questions emerged and form the foundation for this chapter: What assumptions about identity do gospel listeners bring to their encounters with high-singing male performances? What are the connections between the gospel audience's perceptions of a male singer's identity, body, vocal style, and range that make for positive reception of a countertenor's ministry? What are the interfaces in which the hegemonic perceptions of high-singing male soloists' identities are disputed or furthered as audiences decipher the countertenor's rare sound? And what are the techniques African-American countertenors deploy to challenge or confirm those assumptions?

Drawing on a case study of African-American countertenor Patrick Dailey and an ethnography of his live performance, this chapter is an ethnomusicological assessment of his social and theological navigation of the indistinguishable sexual and gendered vocal sound. African-American gospel singing challenges the gender binary framework that the American public expects of men as singing low and women as singing high. Public expectations can and do influence African-American vocalities. I focus on Dailey's aforementioned performance practices in Carter's "Some Day" at New Psalmist Baptist and at a symposium in Chicago as a means to highlight some of the complications that arise as sonically ambiguous presentations of gender intertwine and compete with long-standing heteronormative frameworks of gendered voice in gospel. I briefly review historical literature on countertenors and gender expression as a way of framing my discussion on the ways in which audiences may assess their performance competence. African-American gospel countertenors are situated in Western European opera's visual gender-bending traditions such as *en travesti* production—a practice in which men dress in conventionally women's clothing. Absent of visual cues of gender-bending displayed in opera, their vocal sound is an aesthetic and worshipful interruption of gendered gospel vocal music performance. I then analyze my interviews with Dailey to glean the choices he makes to demonstrate performance competence in African-American worship as a man who sings high. Dailey negotiates the tensions and intersections deftly between these dual processes of musical performance. He does so with an aspiration to deliver a presentation that is what he refers to as "anointed": music that is *from* and *for* God. Dailey's performance engages African-American audiences' various types of cultural familiarity to portray competency as a worship leader and trained artist.

Black Countertenor Sound

African-American countertenors with training as soloists in both Western art music and gospel music are unconventional, especially outside of historically black college and university (HBCU) contexts. Black vocalists are still underrepresented in predominantly white institutions. While the majority of black countertenors are trained at HBCUs, the countertenor *fach* (vocal specialization) is often socioculturally perceived in broader African-American contexts as queer, and the domain of nonblack musicians. Scholars have not yet explored the careers of African-American countertenors, or their approaches to participating in multiple cultural contexts such as gospel music settings. "Countertenor" is the vocal designation in Western classical music for men who are trained to "sing high," deploying a mature and comfortable vocal delivery such that uninitiated listeners are often unable to determine whether the sound is emanating from a male or female body. Their voices are designated as what Naomi André (2006) calls a "treble timbre," which means they perform music that matches the vocal range and quality of women contralti, mezzo-soprani, and boy soprani in the Western art music tradition.

Countertenors vocally transcend barriers of gender conformity, a phenomenon I understand as the musical ways that people consciously or subconsciously allow or adjust their vocalizations to fit society's expectations of how gendered bodies make sound. Sonically casted as submissive, they are sometimes assigned to sing women's operatic roles costumed in women's garments; however, they do not dress in women's attire while participating in church music ministry. The music ministers who employ countertenors also face challenges in choosing repertoire for them, particularly when those ministers do not have an established tradition or repertoire from which to draw.

At the Center for Black Music Research (CBMR) Symposium on Black Vocality in Chicago (October 2013), Patrick Dailey performed after I presented research on his broadcast performance at New Psalmist Baptist Church before scholars, black music enthusiasts, and church musicians. I asked participants who remarked on our joint lecture-performance whether they had previously heard a countertenor. Some attendees, specifically those who were familiar with men who sing high in Western art music, likened Dailey to the historic castrato depicted in the 1994 blockbuster film *Farinelli*. They drew a comparison in an effort to describe the similarity in Dailey's sound to Farinelli's portrayed sound. Participants were not sure why their ideas of countertenor and castrati sounds were similar to each other. Countertenors are not castrati, but they do share a similar vocal range and much of the same repertoire. The reference to Farinelli is a key sonic connection in that the castrato legacy exemplifies cultural and religious practices in which the Roman Catholic Church manipulated—and dare I say, violated—men's sexuality by castrating them for singing in service of the church. While extensive coverage of castrato scholarship is outside the scope of this chapter, I note the extent to which historical perceptions of castrati and the commoditization of gendered sound production in sacred music shed light on countertenors' reception today.

Uninitiated symposium participants conflated countertenors and castrati[8] largely because these singers register as queer, submissive, and unmanly to modern listeners today. This was evident in the remarks of participants at the CBMR symposium who said that they were unsure why countertenors and castrati sounded similar. I must note that while Farinelli, the Italian opera singer known as "the greatest castrato of all time," was played by an Italian actor in the 1994 film, his sound was a digitized high voice composite of an African American countertenor named Derek Lee Ragin and a Polish soprano, Ewa Malas-Godlewska. The manufactured Farinelli voice is a symbolic approximation of a historic aural soundscape, "an apt metaphor for the historical castrati whose voices were altered via their surgery and then greatly manipulated in the six to twelve years of vocal training in conservatories."[9] In examining the manufactured voice as a metaphor, I submit that the movie director Gérard Corbiau's use of a "virtual voice"[10] may be interpreted in four important ways. First, it inadvertently reinscribes, perhaps in the service of mass media expectations of sonic or vocal perfection, "classical music industry" discourses of black voices as inadequate instruments for Western art music performance. Second, the artificiality of the digitalized voice corresponds to the procedures by which some Western art music pedagogues, producers, directors, and conductors perceive and have written about the countertenor voice as a gimmick and artificially produced.

Third, the fact that some participants at the symposium confused a countertenor with a castrato, even one whose voice was digitally manipulated, suggests that people are unaware or misinformed of what constitutes countertenor and castrato designations and styles. And finally, in a sonic patriarchal construct, the composite voice symbolically imbues the woman's voice with the perceived superior male vocal qualities. To produce the composite voice of Farinelli as sung in the movie, performance required a symbolic merging of vocal categories via the sonic castration and whitening of an African American countertenor and the "manning up" of a European soprano as they digitally combined the voices to design a mixed racial and gendered representation of sound. With regard to my research, that peculiar racial and gendered digitalized mixture evokes queries regarding the male high-singing voice as an embodied symbol of gendered sound throughout global vocal music discourse.

The Representations and Symbolism of Male High-Singing in Music Research

Societies around the world have male high-singing traditions. I trace African American countertenors' lineage to the overlap of two singing sociocultural heritages: African-derived oral and European-derived concert music. Within both singing heritages, musicians and listeners cultivate gendered perceptions of vocal styles, repertoire, range, and characterizations of vocal sound. However, sociocultural tensions emerge as African American countertenors venture into formal training and performance in Western art music performance, while also maintaining their musical roots in the worship traditions of black congregations. In historically African American Protestant congregations, countertenors manage congregations' anxieties about the performance of masculinity, while in Western art music they navigate the racial and gender biases of casting in the predominantly white opera industry.

From African religious rites to African American gospel music, black men have used a spectrum of vocal qualities in vocal music performances. According to historical accounts chronicled by Francis A. Kemble, as men of African descent worked in the antebellum rural United States of America, white observers characterized them as singing with wide vocal range "rich, deep voices swelling out," male voices that seemed "oftener tenor than any other quality."[11] Citing Kemble, musicologist Eileen Southern described some of the men's style as *falsetto*[12] and their range as ascending to male soprano, as men's singing extended to what she called an "oftener tenor" quality and register.[13] With regard to gospel vocal ranges in particular, Southern observed a gendered performance of vocal registers, "male singers often emphasize their falsetto tones; female singers, their lower register tones."[14] Southern's research suggests that there is a conventionally gendered range for male and female singers—ranges that twentieth and twenty-first-century gospel artists have emotively expanded and varied. The lower vocal range has represented masculinity, virility, potency, hardness, and manliness. So much so that I found in my research that gospel baritones that their "low vocal designation is prized for its stimulating timbral qualities, suitable for setting the mood for worship the sanctuary and sex in the bedchamber."[15] Alternatively, the higher vocal range has represented femininity, effeminacy, impotency, softness, and unmanliness. In some of my interviews with men examining the stereotype that all male choir directors or vocal worship leaders are gay, the men derided male vocalists who "sing high like a woman."[16] Should listeners subscribe to an imagined fixity of gendered vocal range boundaries, African American men who "sing high" or sing in a higher register during gospel performance may be perceived as socioculturally queer, trespassing into a vocal domain designated for women. Visually, gospel choir directors tend to situate male vocalists toward the center of the choir. While other choral traditions confirm to this layout, the centering of male participants reinscribes the focus on the male presence and the sense that the directors' musical and sociocultural connection with men is literally and figuratively central.

Male high-singing has been featured in sacred performance throughout Europe since the middle of the sixteenth century. The Western preferences for high-singing male voices soaring above choirs in sacred compositions stemmed from an aesthetic of a metaphoric angelic and gender nonconforming sound. Such preferences for high-male singing in European music overlaps with the aesthetics found in African-derived music styles in the United States such as rhythm and blues (R&B) and African American quartet music. In fact, black men have pursued careers in opera and concert performance throughout the world since the nineteenth century.[17] However, the contributions of black high-singing male solo vocalists who have been trained in Western art music have not been explored extensively in ethnomusicological research.

The void in the literature is due in large part to racial and gendered biases to casting African American men in principal opera roles. Eileen Southern explained that historically, black "male singers generally found it more difficult to succeed in the concert world than did the prima donnas. For that reason, they were more likely to join ensembles, minstrel troupes in the nineteenth century, or touring concert companies."[18] African American operatic tenor and vocal pedagogue George Shirley adds, "Black American singers of opera have always been relatively few in number for reasons external to the race as well as internal. We remain minorities in the profession numerically and racially, which should certainly come as no surprise in an art form that appeals only to a minority of the majority in America!"[19] Even though there has been a disparity in casting

African American men, they have made significant contributions to contemporary concert and opera performance through their musical style, sound quality, performance in diverse venues, and social navigation.[20]

Carter's compositions are an intervention for the dilemma of barriers to entry into the opera and concert industries, providing African American soloists with the space to represent the performance practices of gospel and concert musics. He prompts them to do so in a manner that displays their multiple, musical consciousness in sacred music. Keeping in mind the melding of the African and European-derived heritages, the sonic symbolism of male high-singing evoked in Carter's compositional choices is multivalent. Carter's voicing of the treble timbres (female trio and high vocalist) in the "Some Day" composition resembles the type of personnel who were customarily chosen to embody symbolic transcendence in medieval to eighteenth-century Western church music repertoire. For the aristocracy of that time, treble timbre singers represented a sounded embodiment of divine power the heroic, the monarchy, the heavenly, the celestial, the otherworldly, and the "aesthetic of the marvelous."[21] Within medieval Western music traditions, high voices, regardless of gender, were privileged as sonic representations of culturally entrenched hierarchical values, dominance, and proximity to the heavenlies.[22] In fact, the heavenlies were imagined as a location where celestial beings were eternally young. Their vocal dominance also sonically illustrated passion, eroticism, and ecstasy.

The historical countertenor personae and their sound have been characterized in disproportionately anatomical, gendered, and angelic language in comparison to other vocal classifications. Writers have also signaled the complexity of conceptualizing gendered vocal sound quality by deploying anatomical metaphors with terms like "the Queen's Throat"[23] and "The Diva's Mouth."[24] Even in the gendered characterizations throughout the literature of countertenor sound, spectators and listeners remarked upon bodily queering of their orifice and larynx that produced the high range they sang. Like the participants at the CBMR Black Vocality symposium, the aforementioned authors also compare countertenor vocal sound to castrato sound as they examine the applicability of the metaphors to countertenors. Perhaps the similarity in the countertenor, castrato, and contralto sound and personae registers with twenty-first-century listeners in the same manner that it registered to nineteenth-century aristocracy as "hearing the past while simultaneously creating something new from the past."[25] Throughout the rest of this chapter, I will compare discourses around these vocal designations to account for the fluidity of gender that is represented in what Naomi André calls an "aural genealogy" of "treble timbres."[26]

The countertenor designation is an embodied negotiation between feminine sound and masculine vocal power,[27] a combination that has been characterized as "angelic" (François 1995), "The Heavenly Voice" (Pennacchi and

Scillitani 2012), or "The Supernatural Voice" (Ravens 2014). "Denaturalized, denied access to manhood and maturity, the castrati were said to have access to the heavens; theirs were the voices of angels."[28] The angelic characterization signals a long-standing Christianized *discordia concors* discourse that was conveyed through visual and performing arts representations of various classifications historically conflated with androgyny: hermaphrodite, intersex, third sex, transvestite, transsexual, and effeminate. Gender studies scholar Piotr Scholz researches the cultural history of the links between castrati and eunuchs, both of which embody the musical and social performance of gender ambiguity. He asserts that androgyny is the embrace of both sexes as symbolically united in a being.[29] The castrati's high vocal sound was a signifier of androgyny and sexual impotency. Moreover, one's embodiment of the androgynous was a cosmic symbolism of one's polar opposites uniting, and thereby achieving, the highly desirable goal of resemblance to the omnipotent God. In the article "Homosexuality's Closet," gender studies theorist David Halperin considered men's negotiation of "an angelic sound" with regard to renowned countertenor David Daniels as embodying the woman's soul: "The secret, inchoate transgendered condition evidenced by his paradoxical combination of masculine and feminine attributes, patterns of feeling, and personae."[30] Thus the sounded unification of polar opposites also conveys a potential autoeroticism in the male treble timbre sound, where there is a musical consummation between the feminine sound/soul that is enveloped by the masculine vocal power/body.

Despite the venerable tradition of men singing in a conventionally female register, skepticism around the countertenor vocal designation persists. I contend one must allow that any singer's exploration of his or her marketable sound is a process of selecting a comfortable vocal range and making choices for his or her vocal longevity. That subjective and collaborative selection process is both natural and relative to their vocal instrument and technique. For example, tenor and vocal pedagogue Richard Miller described the countertenor voice classification as a baritone who chooses to sing in his falsetto register in his early writings.[31] Miller's estimation of countertenor's vocal quality was to liken it to a vocal style, an heterosexist hearing of the vocal sound that closely resembles the antiquated perception that one chooses to be queer. Falsetto was traditionally considered in the Italianate school of thought as "una voce falsa" (a fake voice), a type of vocal trick. "Countertenors do not require the same amount of laryngeal muscle activity as the fully registered male voice."[32] He framed countertenor singing as a style rather than a vocal designation.[33] He later slightly adjusted his assessment in *The Structure of Singing: System and Art in Vocal Technique* (1996). Miller referred to countertenors as male falsettists in order to account for the similarities between the vocal designation and the style. "A performance phenomenon that must be dealt with in any serious consideration of contemporary singing is the male falsettists. The solo counter-tenor is here to stay. It is unrealistic for teachers of singing to regard him as a nonlegitimate [sic] performer. The counter-tenor should be taught, and he should be taught seriously."[34] In briefly addressing the countertenor as "a performance phenomenon," he reified their vocal illegitimacy among vocal pedagogues by not expanding on technique appropriate for the voice type, in the same way he wrote a pedagogy for the other vocal classifications. Like Richard Miller, countertenor and vocal pedagogue Peter Giles (1982; 1994) observed that high male vocalists have been perceived as men who imitate the female voice, who perform a gimmick, or as men whose singing is a vocal experiment. Even though countertenors have been not always taken seriously throughout history, their vocal designation is still deployed throughout operatic, art song, and sacred vocal music performance.

As African American countertenors move between the worlds of Western opera and gospel music, what kinds of choices do they make to demonstrate their performance competence as male trained singers who "sound like women"? In what ways do they also navigate their audience's expectations about the parameters for men's vocal sound qualities? To examine Dailey's sociocultural strategies of gendered sound in gospel music settings, I asked him about his performance choices as a formally trained opera singer who leads worship in African American Protestant churches. I now turn to a discussion of some of the strategies that he deploys to navigate the social and theological tensions that manifest as he sings in gospel music circles.

Social and Theological Tensions: Manliness and Performing Spiritual Competence

New Psalmist Baptist Church, the venue where Patrick Dailey made his television debut, is one of the largest churches in the Washington, DC–Baltimore area. The members of this predominantly African American congregation are socioeconomically diverse, ranging from working- to upper-middle class, encompassing various education levels. Dailey's performance at New Psalmist Baptist was broadcast on cable television on The Word Network ("Some Day" n.d.), whose programming features primarily preaching and gospel musical performances.[35] Such programming is popular among black preachers, musicians, and lay participants who regularly depend on television or streaming media to view worship services from around the world. Dailey's debut via The Word Network exemplifies the mutual influence between black religiosity and multimedia engagement. In his book Watch This!: The Ethics and Aesthetics of Black Televangelism (2009), ethicist Jonathan L. Walton describes the importance of considering participation in worship via multimedia outlets like televised services and live streaming as a part of modern religious practices. My inclusion of the television and Internet domains in my ethnomusicological research helps to account for the multiple narratives and media that are engrafted in globalized religious practice. In addition, the decision-makers in these platforms expose listeners and spectators to versatile music ministers and equip them with tools to properly receive them.

At the beginning of the service, Senior Pastor Bishop Walter Thomas pointed out that Morgan State University is noted for training black musicians such as the featured soloist for that morning's service, Patrick Dailey. Morgan State students and alumni worship at New Psalmist. In fact, Bishop Thomas, the conductor Fernando Allen, and Dailey are all proud heirs of the Morgan State University musical legacy championed by the late composer-arranger Dr. Nathan Mitchell Carter Jr. (1936–2004).

Morgan State students and alumni like Dailey perform a variety of repertoire on the concert stage and in church, a repertoire that includes anthems and praise and worship songs. Dailey led what is classified as a sermonic selection, which is a song that both precedes and sets the tone for the sermon. "I have asked the choir to sing this melody to remind us that one day we will all get home," Bishop Thomas said in his introduction during the service. "Brother Patrick Dailey, a tremendous singer, who God has blessed and I believe will have a glorious future in music, will sing this song."[36] By personally introducing the soloist Patrick Dailey, Thomas was an ally for the singer who performs what some visitors to the church and television viewers might have perceived as an unusual, even uncanny vocal performance. Thomas facilitated a pastoral and educational moment that guided uninitiated listeners unaccustomed to Dailey's countertenor vocal worship leadership.

When I interviewed Dailey in November 2011, he expressed his anxieties about the aural-visual qualities of his transdenominational vocal worship leadership, how he vocally and verbally presents himself, and the manner with which he uses his body in church performances to signify a conventional masculinity or sexuality. His strategies revealed that historically black Protestant audiences' receptiveness to countertenors' vocal performance is closely linked to the ways their sound is embodied. As a seasoned countertenor, Dailey knows his comportment will be heavily scrutinized. Dailey offered both spiritual and performance practices to guide the audience's reception of his voice within African American gospel contexts.

The performance venue context is key for Dailey's preparation. Even though he was apprehensive about making the distinction, Dailey shared with me that the congregation's education level and cultural exposure are crucial factors in the positive reception of his performance. He assesses the congregation's competence before agreeing to minister by gauging their familiarity with his vocal sound. Likewise, Dailey maintained that it is important for countertenors to assess the experience of the congregation's music director in selecting reper-toire for countertenors. Do they have a sense of the repertoire that is in his *fach*? In other words, do they know how to select music that is vocally comfortable and flattering for him? Are they willing to hire him to perform gospel selections that do not conflict with his vocal technique? Some music directors have requested, for example, that Dailey sing in a gospel tenor range, suggesting they perceived it to be in his "natural" or "fitting" (meaning manly) range.

"Can you sing *us*?" African American novices to Western art music often ask this of formally trained black singers who sing in gospel settings. Dailey shared this type of query was put to him, and I was also asked a similar question by youths several years ago when I was a guest artist in the Education Department of the Washington National Opera. Certain patrons will inquire "Can you sing us?" to assess whether the black vocalist is culturally competent in and still connected to African American singing styles. The singer, congregation, and director mutually gauge each other's cultural competence. Dailey understood this as a request to demonstrate his cultural accessibility by signifying on var-ious gospel vocal techniques such as singing melismas[37] that sonically evoke a skill perfected by contemporary gospel artists Kim Burrell or the Clark Sisters.

Using his transferable musical skills in his performance of "Some Day" at New Psalmist Baptist Church, Dailey's melismas—or the stylistic approach re-ferred to as "runs" in gospel music vernacular, during the reprise (a repeated passage of music—provided an ideal illustration of the ways gospel and opera overlap. Both operatic and gospel performance traditions utilize stylized me-lisma within the performance of efficacious singing. Musicologist Martha Feldman explained that in eighteenth-century *opera seria*, for example, en-chantment was achieved through various stylistic feats.[38] In the manner of a prima donna (the principal female singer in an opera) singing a signature ca-denza (a sung ornamented passage that is either written or improvised) in an aria of the bel canto (translated as beautiful singing) tradition, he utilized orna-mentation that alluded to traditional melisma, "runs" from the core gospel rep-ertoire. Dailey also demonstrated that he is aware of gospel repertoire and vocal delivery when he used a reprise. In effect, he "sings us." For example, competent gospel performers can respond to or interact with the congregation's enthused participatory cues or request to repeat a particular phrase in real-time consul-tation with the conductor or director and the accompanying instrumentalists. Since Dailey responded with that gospel performance competence, participants interpret his reprise as a musical response to the Spirit manifesting in the presentation.

Dailey also expressed that he performs "a neutrality" in his speaking register while he becomes acquainted with a congregation and their "competency" in terms of formal salutations. With new audiences, he spoke in a slightly lower register than his singing voice to establish an aural baseline, but not too low so as to avoid injury. When he demonstrated his adjustment to a lower range to me, I still detected an "oftener" soprano quality in his comfortable speaking register. Dailey often greets his audience with the salutation, "First giving honor to God who is the head of my life . . . " He used this verbal cue to signify an ideal black masculinity with a traditional "black church" salutation to the congregation that is a composite of protocol. Protocol, as demonstrated through salutations, is a prized dimension of African American Christian communication and hospitality, and a performative means through which he obtains an "ideal" southern black Christian manhood:

> Often when I get up in front of a new audience, I am very neutral. Like, if I am at church and they want me to sing an aria, I will say, [in a slightly lower register] "Praise the Lord everybody. I am Patrick Dailey. We are not going to be before you long. We are gonna sing this one aria for you and we will get out of the way."[39]

His protocol competency is signified with a salutation that starts in the manner of "First, giving honor to God" or "Praise the Lord, everybody." Dailey's demonstration of salutation literacy and performance of social familiarity is intended to convey to the audience that he is an insider and a competent worship leader as he introduces new repertoire and the vocal technique associated with countertenor performance. He maintained that taking such measures to frame his masculinity are vital for engaging those female and male patrons whom he maintains find performances of "soft" masculinity offensive.

As Dailey ministers in worship, he is also conscious of a congregation's simultaneous attraction to and speculation about the embodied nature of his gift. Like most black countertenors with whom I have spoken, Dailey frequently received questions about his gender expression and his sexual orientation after singing for new audiences. Listeners comment, "You sound like a woman." It is a frequent remark to which he and other countertenors have diverse reactions. This experience implies that considerations are still evoked about what his trained sound indicates about identity and his sexual preference. To ask it more bluntly: To whom does countertenor sound attractive?

Throughout history, enthusiasts attest that countertenor sound is attractive to both women and men—a parallel that resembles listeners' reception of castrati— especially those who are familiar with operatic roles that feature countertenors. As Halperin observed, although they are in the minority, there are certainly straight countertenors. However, there is something about the quality of sound and social meanings associated with the vocal facility that "seems to attract gay male singers—or to bring out a male singer's queer potential."[40] Despite the countertenor's queer "potential" being brought out, as Halperin put it, countertenors may also aurally evoke both envy and desire in women. Female listeners may experience what I connote as the latent or overt aural homoeroticism of countertenor same-gender sound or homosono production. At a University of California–Los Angeles voice studies conference after hearing my research on African American countertenors, one woman confided in me that she is attracted to countertenors more than any other vocal designation. "If I could have that voice! Their voices are such a turn on to me. If I could, I would only date countertenors. They are so hot."[41] She admitted that she was drawn to the countertenors' combination of the virtuosic, high voice, and the bravado they embodied on stage.[42]

However, the meme shown in Figure 2.1 from the social media handle @ChurchFunny illustrates some women's nonverbal communication, particularly facial expressions of cultural wariness, for men who sing high collectively in the gospel choir.

As I have written elsewhere, I observed that Dailey evoked the "black Baptist man" persona when performing in church and gospel performance settings. He indicated that when he is a soloist in African American churches, he "presents like a good Baptist man" by lowering his voice slightly and verbalizing a traditional salutation before he sings in order to deflect any questions about whether or not he is a homosexual. Dailey said, "I will say it like a good Baptist man who loves the Lord. I don't get up and say (in a higher register), 'Hey y'all he's so

Figure 2.1 The image is a meme that is illustrative of jokes based upon culturally common body language and non-verbal responses to sonic and gestural peculiarity that are widely distributed among gospel audiences.

worthy, chile.'[43] Mmmhmmm. No."[44] When I asked for clarification about his "good Baptist" persona, Dailey clarified that the persona description was a composite of heterosexist and patriarchal masculinity with whom he often interacted in traditional black church denominations and organizations. Inextricable from his verbal cues before his performances are the ways in which he uses his body to speak and sing to signal a good Baptist man's gender expression.

Embodied Countertenor Sound

In addition to sonically and verbally packaging his presentation so that African American audiences may be receptive to his performances, Dailey also uses his body to orient and manage their perceptions about his identity. He expressed particular anxiety about their search for effeminacy in his mannerisms. Traditionally, historically black Protestant congregations deplore effeminacy in black men, and become easily suspicious of mannerisms that fall outside of the heteronormative ideal. As the following interview excerpt suggests, there is a hegemonic gestural masculinity that Dailey believed he must perform in order to position himself for congregations' positive reception of his singing. Heterosexual-presenting men—regardless of their sexual preferences—are the ideal masculinity. He understood his conscious, gestural heteropresentation as a necessary device for him to be viewed as a competent and appropriate minister.[45] Patrick Dailey is also a formally trained dancer in ballet and modern genres. Dailey maintained that it was through dance training that he focused on his heroic, "masculine posture," comportment, and the ability to visually and musically partner with women in both dance and operatic performance.

ALISHA JONES: What do you mean by "present like a man"?

PATRICK DAILEY: There is Patrick and there is Patty. I guess Patty is the more fierce one but I am Patrick on that [audition] stage . . . For me, the presentation is masculine. It is me being myself because not only are you a black man. You are also a gay black man. All of your life you have to deal with being a black man. There is enough that we have fought for as a people. You can't turn people off. I have seen people sing and they wear the tightest H&M pants, they have the forearm going on, different color eyes, you know the contacts, foundation and powder on their face too—And you're a baritone.[46]

In Dailey's illustration, the performer's incompetence in persuasive gender presentation is heightened by the popular dissociation between men adorning themselves in feminine coded accessories and makeup with singing low, thereby conversely suggesting that men who sing high are assumed to be inclined to and associated with wearing (and preferring) women's fashion. Dailey claimed that black men face professional hassles when they do not physically present themselves in a manner consistent with hegemonic perceptions of ideal masculinity. Tenor and vocal pedagogue George Shirley remarked on the importance of a singer's professional ability to "look the part" and improve upon their stage deportment if it is wanting. He noted, "I will encourage acquisition of physical poise and grace of movement."[47] Dailey's heteronormative performance of masculinity as signified by training to be a competent dance partner prepared him to perform an ideal masculinity consistent with black social values of respectability.[48] He expressed that his goal is not to be a distraction. "Do not let your slip show," he said. In other words, do not use mannerisms that can be construed as effeminate. This statement illustrates that Dailey does not transfer the practice of performing *en travesti*[49] (in women's attire) into gospel presentations.

Patrick Dailey's social and theological negotiation of his countertenor sound exemplified the various sonic and visual scripts that a singer might enact across African-derived and European-derived cultural contexts. He adjusted his speaking range to a lower register to cue familiar masculinity for African American audiences with whom he is becoming acquainted. Dailey pursued a great deal of agency as he vetted new congregations and clients by making decisions about whether or not they are compatible musically. Dailey asserted his authority in deciding which engagements to accept. He allowed for opportunities to demonstrate his versatile music approach that merges African American gospel with Western art musics. While he exercised his musical discretion in selecting his engagements, Dailey also exhibited anxiety regarding his singing, gesturing, and speaking habits that might suggest queer potential in his identity.

While making a mark in sacred music history, Patrick Dailey's performance of Nathan M. Carter's arrangement of "Some Day" reveals the subtle ways Western art music conventions of classifying vocalists are utilized and revised in the interpretation of cross-cultural performance in African American churches. The sonic interpretations generated from the legacy of castrato performances furnish a point of reference for similar reception of the countertenor's vocal technique, sexuality, and gendered sound in historic Christian worship. And Dailey's work highlights the social and theological issues that countertenors may ponder to choose appropriate repertoire, vet receptive congregations, tailor their performance practice, and demonstrate their worship leader competency. Dailey adapted his musical performance of ideal masculine communication in order to demonstrate his competency as a transdenominational worship leader in African American churches. However, in examining Dailey's intersectionality, we find socioculturally diverse perceptions of what vocal range indicates about one's spirituality, sexual orientation, and attractiveness to their sonic and visual admirers. Undoubtedly, continued scholarly analysis of African American countertenors' contributions and experiences within multiple musical worlds will yield a well-rounded analysis of what it means for all African American musicians to finally find a home, *some day*, in both concert performance and worship leadership.

3

Pole Dancing for Jesus

Pentecostal Religious Pluralism and the Bodily Performance of Sexual Ambiguity in Liturgical Dance

"When the Spirit of the Lord moves upon my heart, I will dance like David danced"[1] is an oft-used expression in multifarious twenty-first-century African-American Christian churches, particularly those where improvised, peculiar physical responses to the Spirit exhibit the channeling of fire shut up in one's bones. Embodied musical worship conveys something significant about the embedded identity of the believer. In fact, it is quite normal for people in charismatic faith communities to say that "worship is an outward demonstration of an inward attitude." The music and movement imagery referenced in the Hebrew Bible or Old Testament narratives about the prolific psalmist David dancing spontaneously before the Lord (2 Samuel 6:14) when the Spirit of the Lord moves upon him provides support for charismatic faith communities with that mantra. This mantra about displaying one's spiritual interiority to the public points to the ways in which the meanings of gospel performance are understood to be both personal and mediated through the body, as Donnie McClurkin and Patrick Dailey have corroborated. This aural-visual philosophy about displaying one's interiority and personal spiritual devotion also reveals the grounds for gospel music fans' speculating about the quality of men's sexual proclivities based upon what they see and hear during performances. Fans observe certain gestures and mannerisms to situate choir directors, vocalists, and gospel music performers on a continuum of sexual orientation and gender identity ranging from "gracious" to "militant" forms of bodily responses.

Drawing on my ethnographic research of Jungle Cat's widely circulated, amateur "pole dancing for Jesus" performance footage, this chapter teases out the innumerable creative processes through which men's situating of identity takes place. My case study will center on Jungle Cat's creative processes at the intersection of his gender expression, social, cultural, sexual, sensual, and theological identities. Since Jungle Cat posted his video commemorating his longing for home on Resurrection Day in 2009, pole dancing has gained in popularity as a provocative expression of praise across geographic, racial, and gender boundaries that unearths the black masculine anxieties about bodily responses to the Holy Spirit. While several men post their expressions of unconventional praise

Flaming? Alisha Lola Jones, Oxford University Press (2020). © Oxford University Press.
DOI: 10.1093/oso/9780190065416.001.0001

dance styles online, Jungle Cat was the only African-American man at the time who "praise pole dances," as he calls it. He combined the symbolic meanings of the pole, with dance, and his pursuit of a deeper spiritual connection to God that engages religious pluralism. Jungle Cat's pursuit of a deeper connection with God is practiced largely in a ritual dimension of what I call a *gospelized mysticism*.[2] Jungle Cat worships God to recorded gospel music with ritual components[3] of private dancing, solitude, longing, and contemplation that absolve him from ecclesial, denominational, and organizational restrictions. While anxieties about black male identity also apply to more conventional forms of men's praise dance such as mime and step, pole dancing's erotic connotations elicit especially passionate responses from gospel music audiences.

In this chapter, I will consider Jungle Cat's background and the influence of his faith and love for God on his praise dance. I will then briefly look at the public's reception of his performance. I conclude with some of the social and theological tensions that manifest when men worship a God constructed as male. I argue that in the public's struggle to decipher the praise body language of the male pole dancer, conventional gospel music observers see this praise behind an aura of sexual ambiguity. Indeed, such worshipful performances are understood in a constellation of interpretations as the outward demonstration of an inward attitude. Analysis of a provocative praise pole dance to gospel music profoundly reveals events that are happening to a lesser degree in bodily gospel performance. His performance provides a fascinating specimen we may examine for masculinities constituted, queer identities performed, and symbols constructed in gospel music. Let us turn to Jungle Cat's first video recorded praise pole dance performance on Resurrection Sunday 2009 to decipher his body language.

The Performance

Jungle Cat chose to perform with the gospel ballad "I Need You To Survive" (2002).[4] Stellar and Grammy award-winning Bishop Hezekiah Walker's recording of this David Frazier piece begins with an instrumental introduction consisting of arpeggiated chords on piano and percussion accompaniment in the background.[5] Admittedly, as the music began I braced myself for a performance of irony highlighting the extent to which Walker's public narrative of not being homosexual may be contradicted by his vocal performance of supposed queer presentation.[6] To be certain, I do not dispute or confirm those rumors about Bishop Walker's sexual orientation; however, those rumors remain at work as we view Jungle Cat's worship and the humorous musical and bodily gestures anticipated in his performance. For example, Walker deploys both a baritone singing and speaking voice on stage and an "oftener tenor" speaking voice off stage, which suggests that baritone vocal timbral performance is perhaps more sonically acceptable for his gospel music public—a claim I have written about as the presumed heterosexual, unmarked range of male vocal performance in gospel.[7] That plus the fact that Walker is divorced from First Lady Monique Walker, who was his longtime collaborator, metaphorically fans the wildfire flames of spreading rumor. The rumors persist because of the noticeable silence surrounding the dissolution of their marriage, a discreet arrangement for male gospel musicians that has been read by the public as a signifier of homosexuality concealment. Such tensions can be observed in the silences following Bishop Walter Hawkins divorce from his spouse and musical partner First Lady Tramaine Hawkins and Rev. Daryl Coley's eventual divorce from First Lady Jenelle Coley. When questioned about their relationship dynamics I have heard several men confess, "I am not gay . . . I am just freaky" or "I am sensual and sensuality is not sexuality/sexual orientation." The artist formerly known as Tonéx attested that his sexual relationship with his former wife did not lead to the dissolutionment of this marriage. Their sex life was satisfying for him, and he acknowledges his realization of particular sensual and sexual preferences. Some may say "I am not gay, " and the allusion to their freakiness, sensuality, or sexual discretion is understood as a part of sociocultural game. Those phrases rhetorically detach them from the stigma of homosexuality, while leaving wiggle room to perform identity through other media.

As the choir of sopranos, altos, and tenors sing in unison with whispery vocals in the footage, the piano accompaniment recedes for a few bars, revealing the high hat pulse being played on the drum set. Soon, the piano reappears with chordal statements timed to reinforce the high hat pulse. While the song's overall structure is ABABCB, its greatest intensity lies in the C section. The recording's four iterations of this material feature unison vocals that are heightened by 4 semitone modulations. Wearing a hat, grayish A-line shirt, jeans, and Timberlands, Jungle Cat meanders to the pole erected in the center of what looks to be his dimly lit living room. His attire suggests a hard, urban black masculinity that signifies he has the potential for what sociologist Elijah Anderson calls "getting ignorant" that I explore further in chapter 4. His dreadlocks sway from side to side, as he limberly mounts the pole and swirls around it. Throughout the performance, he demonstrates his rudimentary pole tricks, as the following lyrics unfold:

> I need you, you need me.
> We're all a part of God's body.
> Stand with me, agree with me.
> We're all a part of God's body.
>
> It is his will that every need be supplied.
> You are important to me, I need you to survive. (2x)

> I pray for you, you pray for me.
> I love you, I need you to survive.
> I won't harm you with words from my mouth.
> I love you, I need you to survive. (Walker 2002)

The lyricist promotes closeness between humans as representing a fitting to-gether in God's body, alluding to Pauline teachings in the Holy Bible that refer to Jesus's body (Ephesians 4:16; 1 Corinthians 12:27). This song revises the met-aphoric texts about the body of Christ. It emphasizes connection to God and humans despite difference, which diverges with Pauline teachings elsewhere in the Holy Bible that encourage believers to distance themselves from those who are different (2 Corinthians 6:17). The lyrics, "I won't harm you with words from my mouth" is a restatement of the ethics found in the popular song "Order My Steps" (1994) by Glen Burleigh,[8] which instructs believers to exercise laryn-geal self-control as they "bridle [their] tongues" and "let [their] words edify." Interpreted more to the point, it is a cautionary repertoire about the pain suffered from uttering or spreading rumor, ridicule, and speculation. Some listeners expressed that the embodied ethical care and closeness conveyed with "I won't harm you with words of my mouth" is reminiscent of sensuousness and erotic suggestiveness that are found in the sacred text of Song of Solomon 1:2 (NIV), "Let him kiss me with the kisses of his mouth: for thy love is better than wine."

Nevertheless, Jungle Cat's gestures extend upward, in a direction that signi-fies reaching to God within African-American Christian praise dance choreog-raphy. By doing so, Jungle Cat extends the connection and nurtures closeness to God through an exploration of suffering and survival. Then, as he uses his limbs and entire body with the pole, he represents the horizontal axis of the cross. He asserts that God is not just above; God is a part of us all.

Constructions of Black Masculine Sacred Dance

There are particular social and cultural tensions in using non-religious dance styles such as pole dancing and symbols such as poles in conventional Christian worship contexts largely because of its heavily erotic inferences. Furthermore, queer dance styles of voguing, twirling, or tipping are also not openly welcomed and affirmed in gospel performance, unless, as suggested in the introduction, the dancing is exuberantly done without an announcement characterizing its origin or significance. Scholarly perspectives from music history, ethnomusi-cology, and black religious studies shed light on the social, cultural, and theo-logical constructions that shape reception of male liturgical movement in black worship. Musicologists have done well to research religious music-making of the antebellum period, during which time European Americans, who adhered to Victorian codes of respectability, considered enslaved Christians' sounds and the movements of black worship to be "heathenish" and profane.[9] The profane concept is a relatively recent notion in African-American religiosity. According to musicologist Samuel A. Floyd (1995), there were no distinctions between the sacred and the profane realms of life or between the spiritual and the material worlds in traditional African culture. Theomusicologist and popular culture scholar Yahya Jongintaba (1992), formerly Jon Michael Spencer, connects the introduction of the profane concept to African worship contexts from the era of Puritanism to the Second Great Awakening. In her work *The Music of Black Americans* (1997), musicologist Eileen Southern recounts the early conceptualization of music and movement that allowed for the early Christianized African-derived dance called the ring shout outside of formal (or denominationally sanctioned) African-American worship services. Regulations for "shouting" were very rigid and did not allow for the variety of dance expression that we might observe today, due to the sociocultural codes of the time.

> For the participants the shout was not under any circumstances to be construed as a dance, and strictly observed rules insured that the line between "shouting" and dancing was firmly drawn. Only songs of religious nature were sung, and the feet must never be crossed (as would happen in the dance). Among strict devotees, the feet must not even be lifted from the ground. Presumably, any song could function as a shout song or "running spiritual." In practice, however, the slaves preferred some songs to the exclusion of others, and a special body of these songs was developed among them.[10]

As a result of these regulations and beliefs about dancing, much of the preservation of older religious and nonreligious dance music repertoire was lost due to dance's association with damnation. "Most of the song collecting took place on plantations where slaves, having been converted to Christianity, came to regard dancing as sinful and no longer indulged in it."[11] Since the antebellum period, African-American Christians have revised their interpretation of the Hebrew Bible/Old Testament text. Indeed, black gospel participants have adapted their gestures and approaches to imagery that celebrates David as an iconic figure in demonstrative praise and worship to God.

The incorporation of pole dancing into worship evokes similar considerations about the appropriateness of the profane gestural connotations (mostly sexual and erotic meanings) associated with this dance tradition. Recognizing that religious and nonreligious realms were not distinguishable in the foundations of African worship, what are the characteristics of how dance is perceived now? Jungle Cat's pole dance has been referred to as a liturgical dance or praise dance; however,

I wonder if a liturgical classification properly fits this solo and private practice. According to liturgical dance practitioner Denita Hedgeman, contemporary liturgical dance today broadly "means to dance during public worship in the Christian Church. The word 'liturgical,' comes from the root word 'liturgy'. Liturgy is defined as a Eucharistic rite . . . A liturgical dancer is one who expresses his or her faith through movement ministry in a public worship setting. The goal of this form is to have spiritual communion with God."[12] Liturgical dance scholar Karen Curry defines liturgical dance as "the decent and proper expression to God or from God (prophetic dance) through dance using music and choreography that attributes honor and glory to God. It is not enough to be a Christian and dance to any kind of music using any kind of choreography . . . This dance, in order to be pure and perfect praise, must from its origin come forth for the specific purpose of glorifying God."[13] Thus liturgical dance, as set forth by liturgical dance pioneer and Christian education scholar Kathleen S. Turner in her forthcoming book *And We Shall Learn Through the Dance: Liturgical Dance as Religious Education*: "is expressive and imaginative movement that is used both inside and outside of worship that creatively educates and instructs Christians to comprehend the Holy Bible and their faith in the Trinity through the elements of space, time and design. Liturgical dance has a relationship with music, spoken word, and silence. For both the individual dancer and congregant, the church is identified as community through individual and mutual movement, and dance explorations that cultivate love, prayer, healing and reconciliation, while fostering Christian identity throughout the liturgical calendar. Because of its experiential properties non-Christians can be exposed to liturgical dance and be influenced by it."[14]

Therefore liturgical dance is not dance for dance's sake. Liturgical dancers are intended to dance for an audience of One while humans are permitted to observe the presentation. For these reasons and our purposes from henceforth, I will refer to Jungle Cat's performances as praise dance, which is also the term he used to characterize what he performed.

Ethnomusicologist Melvin L. Butler has noted that in present-day church and concert settings, some gospel performers aspire toward a David style of undignified worship in Pentecostal praise. Gospel recording artist Fred Hammond has produced songs, for example, recounting how David danced as a representation of his close relationship with God. As Butler states, "One of his most successful albums of the 1990s is entitled *The Spirit of David*,[15] in reference to David's character, his commitment to praise and worship, and repentant heart."[16] Conventional black Pentecostal or charismatic male worshippers regard David's display of "dancing before the Lord with all his might (2 Samuel 6:14)" as the exuberance to which they ought to aspire. The David style concentrates on the participant's sense of closeness to a monotheist construction of God, privileging God's presence and power over human's approval.

David as a model for masculine movement has been critiqued as a romantic aspiration by theologian and musician Cheryl Kirk-Duggan, in her chapter "Salome's Veiled Dance and David's Full Monty: A Womanist Reading on the Black Erotic in Blues, Rap, R&B and Gospel Blues."[17] Kirk-Duggan uses a womanist biblical interpretation of David dancing, to name it as "David's Full Monty." She argues that David's Full Monty[18] is a metaphor for the erotic that David consciously performed within God's gaze and for God's pleasure. David danced before God incorporating the aesthetics of his sensual, sexual body to demonstrate a vitality that simultaneously engaged the politics, pomp, and power of his social context. Kirk-Duggan's interpretation of movement offers a useful tool for considering erotic connotations of dancing before a God constructed as male.

Not only are there erotic connotations but also there is an exploration of sensuality involved. African-American studies and religion scholar and musician Ashon Crawley also writes about the complexity of sensual conveyance in public sacred space, stating that "the 'space' of the black Pentecostal tradition is multivocal: it is a space where the sensuousness of the black body finds meaning through the conferral of power and authority while, simultaneously and contradictorily, the space disciplines and polices particularly dangerous modes of power and authority of the agential self, through confusing and abusive discourse about sexuality."[19] A growing number of participants in this social media age choose to reserve their uninhibited praise for their home sanctuaries. Transferring corporate practice of kinesthetic knowledge to private devotion provides resources for men to confess their faults, be transparent, seek God, and experience God move in and through them. For example, because Jungle Cat transferred the practice to his home, YouTube viewers lose kinesthetic knowledge in translation as footage of his improvisational movement vocabulary is relocated to unchartered virtual realms of public reception by observers, who lack the shared knowledge of body language that would usually be cultivated in corporate embodied worship. And given our socio-cultural history in the US, one might presume that black men's public and private worship is always under real or imagined surveillance.

Kirk-Duggan and Crawley's explorations of the erotic and sensual in worshipful dance before God will inform my assessment of Jungle Cat's mysticism. I would like to deploy theologian Bernard McGinn's definition of mysticism as the "direct consciousness of the presence of God."[20] McGinn has observed that among the myriad Christian denominations and other world faiths, mysticism is a common ground experience.[21] Jungle Cat's story is an example of the personal nature of religious practice. As with many social groups, black religious practices are developed in conversation with religions of the world. Jungle Cat's homemade performance raises the questions: For whom (or to whom) is worship offered? And with what is it permissible to convey a man's deepest sentiments to God? The Internet is a virtual platform through which black men can negotiate

their spirituality, as they join their spirit and flesh through movement and embodiment in worship in languages they can recognize.

The mere suggestiveness of the phallic symbols and semantic associations
woven into Jungle Cat's performance (black man, dancing, privacy, God, Jesus,
pole, pole as a cross, praise, needs, survival, etc.) has caused this video of him
praise dancing to "I Need You to Survive" to be accessed online over 110,000
times. His performance contributes to an undoing of latent gendered paradigms
within liturgical dance.

Who Is Jungle Cat?

What insights into Jungle Cat's development of danced devotion in his home
give us an understanding about a male demonstration of intimacy with God?
Jungle Cat (whose given name is Tavon Hargett) describes himself as a sheltered
country boy from North Carolina who moved to Washington, DC for a change
of scenery. A librarian by day and a pole fitness instructor by night, his story is
that of cultivating a community of love and positivity. Hargett considers himself Apostolic Pentecostal—part of a network of churches that permit improvisa-
tory bodily responses to worship. He specifies his religious identity as spiritual,
nondenominational, and open to the wisdom of various faith traditions. Even
though Hargett concedes that he has been exposed to various faiths, he
maintains that he is most comfortable worshipping God on the pole to gospel
music accompaniment.

As Jungle Cat puts it, he is interested in perceiving God directly. As such, in
more ways than one, Jungle Cat is a mystic. By mystic, I mean he explores various
modes of transcendence to experience closeness with God. His performance to
the recording of "I Need You to Survive" is an example of his interpretation of
the mystical oneness conveyed in the song and the ways that oneness manifests
in one's bodily experience—both in isolation and with other believers—as he is
ritually grafted into God's body. While the term "mysticism" is not often used in
African-American Pentecostal worship, believers do participate in definitively
mystic practices. Psychologists of mysticism Jacob A. Belzen and Antoon Geels
have observed that in the intellectual dimension of mysticism literature mystics
strive to express their practice even when the mode of communication proves
inadequate.[22]

Since 2003, Hargett practiced *tantric celibacy* as a self-identified heterosexual
man. He is one of several charismatic and Pentecostal believers with whom
I have spoken who are exploring Tantra to expand their knowledge about sexual
education: the anatomy and its functions, the power of the erogenous zones,
nerve ending intensities, (in)voluntary behavior management, and the sensual

and sexual dimensions of pleasure for oneself and their partner. Numerous heterosexual Christian couples are seeking sex therapy by attending workshops on the ancient eastern tradition. Hargett asserts, "Tantra yoga seeks to find union with the Divine through the spiritual and divine use of sexuality. We seek to use sexual energy as a means of attaining self-mastery. Tantric yoga philosophy believes that one can achieve the same result through celibacy or sexual union." According to Tantra expert Elsbeth Meuth, "tantric celibacy" has several inferences of conscious celibacy, tantric sublimation, tantric self-love, or solo practice (autoeroticism).[23] Jungle Cat's self-identification, particularly as a tantric celibate heterosexual man, suggests he pursues self-pleasure as a dimension of his spiritual practices. He wrote in a follow-up email correspondence, "with enough of that energy stored and our hearts and minds clean and pure, it is much easier to perceive God directly." Self-pleasure is a vehicle through which Jungle Cat claims to achieve more "overall energy and health." However, among informants with whom I have spoken who practice Tantra, self-pleasure is understood as masturbation. Also, Jungle Cat has expressed familiarity with Circque du Soleil's performance of circus arts using the pole and the South Asian sport of *Mallakhamb*,[24] a practice where both men and women master using the pole in gymnastic feats.[25]

When Jungle Cat performed his first praise dance on Easter Sunday 2009 in his home, he recounts that it helped him to deal with his "church homesickness" of not celebrating Christ's resurrection from the dead. The aforementioned footage posted on YouTube.com was of a performance after one year of self-instruction. His use of the term "Easter Sunday" in lieu of the Christocentric "Resurrection Sunday" in the following excerpt from my interview with Jungle Cat conducted in May 2011 is his intentional way of alluding to the holiday's pagan derivation:

Alisha Jones (AJ): Why did you start doing praise pole dance?
Jungle Cat (JC): I will never forget my first praise dance. It was on Easter and I didn't feel like going to . . . I don't think I actually had like a church at that time. So it was Easter Sunday and I wanted to do something . . . but I didn't know what to do . . . .

I didn't want to just walk in, you know, in some random church. I wanted to have something to myself. So I put on some gospel music, like I always do. It just felt natural. It was no question. I never questioned it. I didn't have any reason to question it because I know how I worship. I was on the pole doing it . . . I didn't have any second thoughts. It was all genuine—I felt the presence of the Lord! Like it was just powerful for me. After I was done, I was in tears. I felt so good . . . And I posted it . . . So I just put it there so that I could look at it later and get encouraged by it. Because more people were encouraged I felt better about myself.

> Being a Christian is hard. It is hard for everybody . . . Just because someone says that it is wrong, don't mean it is. That is where they are coming from.

On St. Patrick's Day in 2008, Jungle Cat started teaching himself pole fitness. He claims that he had never seen stripping nor had he been to a strip club before he started teaching himself pole fitness. Hargett confesses that there were moments when he wanted to stop and give up but he recounts praying about his pole dance participation and still feels led to do it for God's glory.

Jungle Cat is an instructor affiliated with the American Pole Fitness Association. He asserts that his objective is to get more men into the sport so that women participants can have partners for pole tango and other duo styles. I attended a performance at the studio where he teaches. While he uses gospel music for his private praise pole dancing, he dances in his studio to R&B and pop musics. His participation in various popular dance forms does not diminish the significance of his sacred expression for indeed there is traditionally a continuum of religious and nonreligious expression. For instance, Hargett pole danced in July 2011 to gospel music accompaniment in a National Competition for the first time, using gospel artist Byron Cage's (aka "The Prince of Praise") rendition of "This Is The Air I Breathe" (Cage 2005).[26] In Jungle Cat's worship there is a unification of gender and race, of body and spirit; in a mystic realm that in a heteronormative construct defines closeness to God as symbolically more congruent for women to embody.

Misunderstood Body Language

Jungle Cat's use of Byron Cage's "This is the Air I Breathe" suggests that his Baptist and Pentecostal worship practice structures his modes of creatively expressing his spirituality through spontaneous movement to song. In Cage's cover of Michael W. Smith's Christian Contemporary music song, air is a representation of God's omniscience, a Holy Spirit that indwells the believer and seeker, a fresh wind. And it is precisely one's penetrative, enveloping experience of God as air that instrumentalizes the performer in simultaneously voluntary and involuntary ways. A God who is all of over him, keeping him alive.[27] In deciphering Jungle Cat's praise dance, spectators are privy to a gestural narration of personal communication and a substitution of corporate liturgical practice, a form of self-soothing in moments of church-home longing. His expressions of yearning disputes the view of absenteeism as an absolute indicator that men are deterred and disillusioned with practicing spiritual devotion. That assumption does not account for numerous migration scenarios in which men are committed believers who are unable to worship in their faith community where they hold membership.

Jungle Cat acknowledges that as he shares what is in his heart toward God, those unfamiliar with his improvisational movement vocabulary misunderstand him. In the coverage in the *Washington Post, Huffington Post,* and *New York Times,* Jungle Cat received his share of detractors and personal threats in video responses on his YouTube page. Their comments center on the reverence or irreverence of dancing for God using such an iconic image of female seduction, largely because of the mixing of sexualized symbols and signifiers. Waddie Grant, a writer from *GmagazineNow* who reposted the YouTube video of Jungle Cat, offered his impression about the video: "I could not stop laughing at the irony of a man pole dancing to a gospel song. Is this guy committing blasphemy? Let me know your thoughts." I was curious about Grant's suggestion that for some observers the combination of gospel music with an African American man using the pole to worship is sacrilegious. I took a cue from Grant's posted concerns and sought opportunities to engage African American men about their perception of Jungle Cat's worship practice.

In summer of 2013, I was invited to share my research in progress with African American male participants in a three-hour workshop for the African Methodist Episcopal worship conference. We explored popular footage of what some gospel participants have described as peculiar masculine worship or the stereotypical "flamboyant" choir director and the hyper-masculine[28] or "street credible" holy hip-hop performer. I asked for their impressions about the performances. We thought together about various perceptions of black male worship of which they were aware and what they imagined to be appropriate masculinity in worship.

The reactions were varied. A pastor expressed a lot of anxiety about observing other people dance or move their bodies in worship. He maintained that he did not want his wife to see him watching women dance in worship. The pastor also expressed discomfort around observing men shout. A male singer confessed that he explores his sensuality in worship. This small sample evinces the anxieties surrounding the observation of fully liberated and personalized worship.

During our time together, I showed them footage of Jungle Cat's worship. Although they did not express revulsion at his performance, it did prompt questions. The participants wondered, for example, about the extent to which his demonstration of physical fitness before God serves as a form of an outward showing of an inward attitude? Other participants were even more frank in their assessments, "Listen . . . What man really has a deep desire to pole dance? Like really? Is he straight? He is? [laughs] Mmmm . . . okay. [laughs] Alright." This response intimates that Jungle Cat is hetero-presenting in his verbal performance of identity. In assessing the worship workshop participants' questions about Jungle Cat's praise, I consider two of the reasons conveyed by observers for difficulty with and misunderstanding of his body language: 1) hegemonic heteronormative constructions of black masculine movement, 2) and the complex imagery of a man physically worshipping God. In my interview with Jungle Cat, he explains what initially drew him to pole fitness.

AJ: How did you get into pole dancing?
JC: Well, I fell into it actually . . . I didn't know what pole dancing was . . . I had heard that term, you know maybe in a joke—like you gonna be a pole dancer when you grow up, stuff like that. But I had never seen . . . I hadn't been to a strip club before my birthday—someone took me for my birthday this year though . . . I didn't know all these references people were making . . . Over the years, I have tried a whole lot of products . . . Everything I have seen on TV I've bought it . . .

The last infomercial that I bought something was . . . it's called the fluidity bar . . . And basically what a fluidity bar is . . . its like a portable ballet bar . . . and the work outs . . . what they were doing on TV . . . you can have a dancer's body . . . you can increase your flexibility like ballet dancers in the comfort of your own home . . . so I was like ok, I wanna do that . . . I am not that flexible . . . that is my hugest challenge . . . So I got that . . . And it was cool . . . really cool. I kind of, sort of noticed results . . . it wasn't like on TV. Of course, nothing ever is . . . So eventually, you know, that got pushed under the bed too and it stayed under the bed for a while and I was like I should pull this back out again . . . So, I pulled it back out. And one day I had this strange thought in my head. Like, you know . . . I wonder what kind of a workout could I get if this horizontal bar was vertical . . . And so I was like man it is probably no such thing as a vertical workout bar or whatever . . . but like me being the librarian that I am . . . yes, I am a librarian . . . [laughs]

I love researching stuff. I went to Google and I typed in "vertical dance" bar . . . I didn't think that I would get results . . . but the very first website was this site called verticaldance.com . . . I was like "Oooo, maybe this is something . . . "

So, you scroll down a little bit more. And you see a picture of someone doing some aerial pole dance move . . . it was probably something simple, like a butterfly or something . . . looking then you don't know what it is. It was breath taking . . . I don't know how to do that . . . and it is right beside another picture of some gymnast doing something. And it was like, "What is the difference you know between these 2 pictures?" And I was like nothing, as far as I am concerned. And underneath the 2 it said "nothing."

My very first actual, physical image of like pole was like work out, like art . . . skill and challenge. I didn't see it as anything dirty or exotic. From my first image that was all I had to go from. After I ordered my pole, right then and there. Well, the next time I got paid, I started looking on YouTube to look at the style and that I didn't see nothing dirty from it.

I must admit that when I shared Jungle Cat's encounter with pole fitness info-mercial demonstrations observers with whom I have spoken have questioned the veracity of his story. I acknowledge the unusual nature of his account and do not wish to dispute his claims. Some observers have questioned whether Jungle Cat is truly heterosexual. They express that his interest in working on his flex-ibility suggests his queer potential. One observer asked, "What straight black male athlete works on his flexibility?" Some have even speculated about the im-promptu nature of this performance, since he elected to turn on the camera and videotape his improvised worship.

From Jungle Cat's narrative, I have found it helpful to consider that the ques-tionable nature of his account, as sensed by my conversation partners, is his attempt to deflect social and theological suspicions about any behavior unbe-coming a believer in a hegemonic gospel masculinity. Believers are encouraged, for example, to abstain from the appearance of evil (1 Thessalonians 5:22) and the lust of the eyes and flesh (1 John 2:16). If Jungle Cat were to admit that his ini-tial encounter was through seeing live stripping or attending a strip club, such an admission would be a distraction to other believers. Those details would impede his proposal for appropriating pole symbolism and dismantle his campaign for lifting up the merits of pole fitness to culturally and theologically conservative groups. The strategy of feigning ignorance about pole dancing perhaps reveals that the practice is heavily laden with negative connotations. Jungle Cat's alleged willful obliviousness is his strategy to praise as he feels it and to advocate for pole dance (and dancers) to receive a clean slate. Feigning ignorance allows for spectators' further evaluation of the potential spirituality in his Christianized movement that would otherwise initially be presumed and dismissed as queer. Lastly, it is interesting to note that one of his biggest fans is his mother, which fosters an ethic of care in supporting his identity expression. According to Jungle Cat, at the moment when he doubted whether he should praise pole dance, his mother shared footage with her church in North Carolina. They commended Jungle Cat on achieving his fitness goals.

As I considered the men's worship workshop participants' commentary, I investigated further into the popular images of masculine movement in spe-cifically African American worship and encountered Jawanza Kunjufu's contro-versial *Adam! Where Are You?: Why Most Black Men Don't Go To Church* (1997). Drawn from his book conversations, Kunjufu offers workshops to empower black boys and men by answering questions. "What is your church doing to attract and keep adult Black males?" "What is your church doing to stop the schoolhouse to jailhouse pipeline?" "Do gangs & negative rappers have a greater influence on your youth than your church?"[29] In a similar vein as Reggie Williamson's presentation that I discussed in the introduction, Kunjufu interviewed men in Chicago to research the reasons they choose not to attend church, also known as the growth of black male absenteeism in the church. The men shared twenty-one reasons including its irrelevance, tithing requirements, Eurocentrism of the content, the length of the service time, required attire, queer sexuality, and streets/peer pressure to not participate. One of the interviewees' responses revealed common homophobic beliefs about music ministers' sexuality and manhood. Men involved in music ministry are perceived to be less manly because of the demonstrative nature of their musical movement. Kunjufu notes some extreme responses from the men with whom he conversed that constructed worship as a feminizing and queering activity.

> Several of the brothers said that the church is made up of women, elders, and sissies. You notice most of the brothers that play the organ or piano or sing in the choir, how they got their butt going up in the air. They love waving their open hand. No wonder they believe in turning the other cheek, they probably want to be kissed on it. They can't defend themselves ... One brother said, "That's why I let my girls go to church but not my boys. I want my boys to be like me. I want my boys to be strong. I want my boys to be macho. I don't want my boys crying ... I want my boys to be straight. I don't want my sons being taught by a homosexual teacher or being propositioned by one."[30]

Even though this account depicts some men's anxiety about interpreting other men's danced worship, Kunjufu does get warm, drawing closer to queer connotations that are generated in public worship. As I mentioned in Chapter 1, queered speech is one of several ways that one may advertise queer possibility, that is, susceptibility to queer intimacy. I would also add that advertisement of queer possibility occurs in myriad ways through one's public exhibition of competencies that display the performative possibility of bodily orifices, while animated in the sanctuary such as the facility of the larynx whilst singing or the agility of the buttocks/anus while shouting or dancing also signals one's bodily skill in transferrable excited corporeal states. The interviewee's comment "they believe in turning the other cheek" suggests that male dancing indicates passivity and masochism, the pleasure derived from pain. The men interviewed expressed such a disdain for the femininity of the church space that they would actively prevent their sons from attending church. The church space and social structure is imagined as queering to vulnerable boys. Only allowing daughters to attend actually advances the heteropatriarchal aims of this surveyed father. If only the daughters of the men interviewed are permitted to enter into the imagined predominantly female space, they will continue to practice the social order, through subscription to male church leadership over the female congregation. The men Kunjufu surveyed also expressed a dislike for men who exhibit open gestures and emotional vulnerability.

Some men saw churches as a threat with "sissified" musical spaces they perceive to be a magnet and harbor for men of either gay or ambiguous sexual orientation.[31] In their constructions of masculinity, men are not to be "soft," emotionally expressive, or move with grace as tenor George Shirley suggested, especially not while other men are spectators.

Similarly, in November 2019, footage of COGIC-raised Pastor John Hannah of New Life Covenant Church in Chicago was widely distributed in which he testified about how men are socialized to develop a feminine masculinity through the female homosociality of prayer, while preaching at the COGIC Convocation in St. Louis. In the Chicago area, he is well-known for 4 am prayer on Tuesdays, quarterly corporate prayer, and 24-hour prayer services with regular attendance of thousands. He has observed male participation in prayer or intercession ministry has come to be rare in the COGIC. Women are expected to carry the burden of communal prayer. For men who desire to pray, he argues that the inadvertent female homosociality fosters a feminine masculinity in male participants' gender expression or mannerisms – the same sort of prayer gathering Andrew Caldwell attended for a few days in 2014, before he testified he was delivered. Hannah showed a picture of himself on the screen of the convocation and recounted:

> I was in my early 20s. I was a single person and I sang in the choir. I didn't sing in the choir because I was a singer. I sang in the choir because I wanted to get close. I didn't sit in the back because I was taught that you gotta get close to the oil. But when I got in the choir I didn't know that God was gonna begin to expose me— teach me some other lessons. When I got in the choir, Dr. Mattie Moss [Clark] was over the choir. So, I was exposed to excellence. I was exposed to discipline. I was exposed to when the bar is raised, you don't bring it down for nobody. And don't go out half prepared. She would confront you and love you at the same time. So, she taught me not to settle. I would leave the choir sometimes and go up in the prayer room, where there was a light skinned woman named Mother Shaw. [Speaks in tongues] Her tongues her so cute. And I would sit in that prayer room and say, "God, I want the prayer oil." I need you to hear me, Church of God in Christ. The thing that scared me was that there were not a lot of men in the prayer room because we turn prayer over to women. Because we heard the scripture, "call for the wailing women." But when you send a boy into a room full of women and he wants her mantle, he also gets her mannerisms because there wasn't a man to release the mantle. So, you called him "a punk." You called him out of his name, when the only thing he wanted was the oil.

I sang in the choir because I wanted to get close to you all. [points to the clerical colleagues on the dais.] I didn't want your chain, I didn't want your suits, I didn't want you collar, I want your oil.

Hannah's polemic reinforced the misguided notion that feminine masculine gender expression is solely nurtured by being around women and to be avoided through socialization. When I facilitated a social justice workshop at Boston University in August 2015, some male workshop participants expressed disdain for "gracious" (code for feminine masculine) movement. "I asked a male cleric to explain what dancing 'with grace' means. He replied, 'I mean graceful like a woman. You know, the smoothness and fluidity in his hand gestures and his limp wrists.' When I countered with, 'Are women the only ones allowed to be graceful, smooth, or fluid?' He had difficulty formulating an answer."[32]

These stereotypes about bodily, musical participation illustrate the inner workings of the aural-visual assessment for gospel performance, framing how Jungle Cat's praise dance to gospel music performance functions as a deconstruction of the queer, demonstrative, gospel choir director trope. Unfortunately, choir directors are assumed to be men who in some way display a range of male femininity. When I asked my informants for national recording artist examples, they cited BET gospel television host Dr. Bobby Jones and choir directors Ricky Dillard and James Hall as examples of men who are highly demonstrative, performing the vocal and gestural stereotypes that register as feminine masculine or queer. For instance, Until 2017, Hall of New Jersey had not disputed or confirmed a queer sexual history or identity; however, he had been dating a woman. In June of that year, James Hall filed a lawsuit against Bishop Jeffrey Thomas alleging that Thomas stalked and harassed Hall after he declined the bishop's romantic advances. In the plaintiff's remarks about the case, he indicated that Thomas was jealous about attention Hall received from both male and female suitors, while caring for Thomas through his illness. Despite the fact that Thomas released photos that represent them as more than friends, Hall denies that they were ever lovers.[33] Consequently, the events that prompted Hall's lawsuit reinscribe the perception that the gospel genre makes musicians spiritually consumable to the public and that these musicians are to exercise sexual discretion in their private lives.

As I mentioned in the introduction, male gospel choir directors and vocal worship leaders are usually imagined as performing an aural-visual "open secret"—very animated, "soft," demonstrative, and "flamboyant" performers who will never divulge their true identity, while using their entire body to guide the choir and instrumentalists. The popular perception is that gospel choir directors are a focal point for surveillance and draw attention in the performance through music and gesture.[34] As illustrated through Hall's story, "flamboyant" Choir directors' ability to attract and to capture the congregational gaze arouses scrutiny or suspicions about their potential queer duplicity.

One of the A.M.E men's worship workshop participants told me, "It is just not cool for men to stare at other men, especially when they are worshipping God" (see also Burt 2007, 14). In his dance research on iconic black dancer Bill T. Jones, Gay Morris offers that these perceptions are based, for example, in a Victorian reading of male movement as being emblematic of a gay or ambiguous sexual orientation. In the United States context, there are other dimensions that influence the gaze upon black men's bodies. White supremacist logic, for instance, is a preoccupation with maintaining a social order in which people value the preservation of power structures that benefit people of European descent. In white supremacist power structures, black bodies are a contested site of meaning representing invisibility, criminalization, and sexual prowess, thereby ever warranting surveillance and policing. Further, Frantz Fanon argued in *Black Skin White Masks* (1967) that black men in particular are imagined as evil: something to fear, discipline, and relegate to marginalized places.

Some of the men Kunjufu interviewed believe that interactions with these demonstrative, musical men place impressionable boys and young men at risk, diminish their masculinity, and spiritually contaminate the worship.[35] A lot of men aspire toward Butler's aforementioned Davidic model of striving toward an undignified worship, nurturing a relationship with a God that is dissonant with a "closed" bodily worship, in which dancers focus on negotiating Christians observers' homophobic perceptions of what male praise should look like. Therefore within this heteropatriarchal vision of worship, men are perceived as queer, unmanly, or boyish if they are committed to a church or music ministry and move with open or "soft" gestures.

I would like to make clear that considerations about the relationship between dance, gesture, masculinity, and representations of faith are not peculiar to the contemporary Pentecostal African American experience. Masculinity literature in religion correspond to the strands of "muscular Christianity" teachings that reach back to at least the nineteenth century, and have been illustrated more recently in the Promise Keepers events of the 1990s. Charles Kingsley and Thomas Hughes disseminated the concept of muscular Christianity in Victorian England. Its thematic origins are in eighteenth-century notions that emphasized physical education as tantamount to moral education. The twentieth-century US version is much "more evangelical" and "more utilitarian and extrinsic in its attitude toward sport," according to Nick Watson.[36] Following Watson, C. Riley Snorton added, "The focus on the body is now seen as part of a divine mandate to physical cultivation, which both develops a proper appearance of masculinity and aids in the conversion of others."[37] Muscular Christianity proponents are concerned with the growing feminization of churches. To counteract the feminization, they advocate for men's involvement in developing masculine boys[38] who do not display male femininity.[39] At the very least, implicit in the muscular Christianity agenda are heteropatriarchal, misogynist, and homophobic models of family, community, and Christianity.

Jungle Cat's pole dancing revisits hegemonic masculinity in a manner that exposes how muscular Christianity is not diametrically opposed to men pole dancing. I observe that he revisits such "body language" to find ways of reappropriating gestures that complicate the masculine/feminine binary. I find it particularly fascinating to consider the emergence of such performances in the wake of recent crises such as the former gospel artist Tonéx's coming out as gay, where fans scrutinized his previous gestures, props, and appearance as performative aspects of his identity. Such perceptions of identity also prompt scrutiny of masculine representations in praise dance and musical gesture in contentious art forms like pole dancing.

Jungle Cat's male body is seen, in lieu of the presumed female body on the pole, in what performance studies scholar E. Patrick Johnson argues to be the queer gaze in heated worship. In a heteronormative construct, men are to view women and not other men. When Jungle Cat's private worship is made public through YouTube, he resembles Johnson's interpretation of writer James Baldwin's depiction of implied homoeroticism in the sensuality of Pentecostal worship in *Go Tell It on The Mountain*, in which John, the protagonist, explores his queer sexuality in the novel. Like John, Jungle Cat's "black body becomes eroticized when overcome by the Holy Ghost."[40] Johnson makes the connection between the ecstatic and orgasmic moments that are performed in worship and detects that within Spirit-induced sensuality there are referential resources intertwined with satisfaction—a mutual and corporate spiritual satisfaction that is shared with God in God's body (divine self-pleasure) and embodied by the dancer (human self-pleasure). This satisfaction informs possibilities within the pursuit of deeper connections with the divine.

In a reflection on what she calls the overrepresentation of sexual subcultures in the gospel music industry, openly lesbian Bishop Yvette Flunder gave the following excerpted remarks about the musical dynamics of sexuality and worship, during the "Are the Gods Afraid of Black Sexuality?" Conference at Columbia University October 24, 2014:

> Sensuality and sexuality permeate the African American worship experience. It is present in the spontaneity, the rhythm, the cadence, the dance, the music, the call and response and—what I call as a preacher and pastor for thirty-three years now, the cathartic climax at the end of the service. This connection to sensuality, sexuality, and spirituality in our African and Native American culture

exists but is often not celebrated in the Christian experience that is appreciated in the indigenous African and indigenous Native American faith.

Jungle Cat's performance moves in the view of worshipping men who would expect an enactment of this kind by women in the exotic dance and sex work industries. Those industries allow for the joining of the sexual, sensual, and spiritual that is not permitted in traditional African American Christian worship contexts.[41] Moreover, through that gaze, people experience dissonance because what they see is not typically read as Christian, let alone male or heterosexual. Thus the expectation of the viewer is not cultivated by the identity and meaning the dancer intends to perform. The tension emerges as observers gaze upon and interpret a queer performance in worship.

Looking Relations for the Black Male Body

Gospel music patrons assess performers by both their musical and gestural leadership, engaging participants hearing and sight. This assessment is rooted in the function and image of the paradigmatic dancing choir director. Whilst tapping into that visual iconicity and tradition reliant on the power of suggestions, Jungle Cat is one of several black men whose undignified praise is being distributed via the Internet for public examination. These men are dancing, using body language to repurpose gestural rhetoric and props that they used before they became committed Christians.[42]

A popular example is that of Bro. Franklin Owino Odhiambo, whose acrobatics that include winding, diving, and falling backward to the ground during church worship have drawn attention via YouTube.com.[43] Bro. Franklin recorded a video response about his demonstrative praise. According to Bro. Franklin, his praise is related to a testimony of overcoming mounting financial and physical hardships. Bro. Franklin's testimony has compelled him to praise with all of his might.[44] Such praise is conveyed through his skill as a former dancer and professional soccer player. Before I provided Bro. Franklin's testimony, people with whom I have spoken perceived his dancing to gospel music as silly antics. Another dancer is New Jersey based "Intercession Dancer" Caleb Brundidge, who performs praise dances with flags during church worship. A self-identified ex-gay man,[45] I notice that Brundidge's style of using flags in worship bares a striking resemblance to garment "twirl" techniques that are used in black and Latino gay ball and fashion runway culture.[46] Both men maintain that their dances are merely outward demonstrations of their inward attitude toward God.

Black men's dance performance is peculiar in that they embody a combination of race and gender that is invisible within United States' power structures. Male dance scholarship on performance visibility illuminates black men's negotiation of movement in gospel music performance. I found useful, for example, research pioneered by Laura Mulvey's theories of the gendered gaze in film. Those spectators socialized with codes of respectability have developed a framework, where men's dance, in general, has been interpreted as effeminate within Western heteronormative society. Male dancers are perceived to occupy the feminized space of the stage.[47] "To summarize this extremely briefly, in response to the spectator's gaze (and the presumption is that it enforces a dominant heterosexual male point of view) men in film look actively and thus avert objectification, while passivity allows women to be turned into eroticized spectacle."[48] All male dancers are rightly or wrongly presumed to be homosexual until they prove they are heterosexual. Such presumptions are rooted in the social practice that men are to gaze and women are to appear. Thus there is a disruption in power when men step into the "male gaze"[49] because in a heteronormative construct, a man viewing another man's movement is an erotic act. Further, a woman enacting an oppositional gaze of analysis and spectatorship of men's movement transcends the repressed gaze and is empowered[50] to inquire about the man's values and his identity. Consequently, viewing a man in motion causes a cognitive dissonance for those who discern a shift in social order.

Jungle Cat's performance disrupts the order of the heteropatriarchal gaze by submitting his inscripted black body to be interpreted. Bodily inscription, in anthropologist Paul Connerton's (1989) conceptualization, is defined by social practices through which memory is amassed in the body. A type of inscription is one's memorization of cultural postures and gestures. When different postures are introduced to the culture—to ceremonies or liturgies, for instance—then cultural stakeholders experience some awareness and appraisal of postural appropriateness. Connerton asserts that postures and gestures communicate something to the one who is familiar with the meanings of the idioms within that cultural context. In the case of Jungle Cat's performance, I evaluate the United States cultural context with regard to its racial and gender imagination about black men as distributed through literature and multimedia.

Literature on the construction of race in the United States' racial imagination has posited that the black male body is a locus for race and representation that is constantly interpreted. African American studies scholar Ronald L. Jackson argued that "the interpretations of mass-mediated inscriptions of the body reveal the hidden contours of psychic and institutional investitures that drive, indeed motivate, the producers of the inscriptions."[51] Jackson defines inscription as the ways the body is socially understood and treated as a discursive text that is read by interactants. He explores the extent to which the black male body is read in the American racial imagination of body politics.

Although theologically oriented scholars Dwight Hopkins (2006) and sociologist Michael Eric Dyson (1996) have considered the implications of these inscriptions in African American Christian religiosity, there has not been consideration about the ways these inscriptions have been interpreted in traditional gospel performance. Further, there have not been any linkages made between gospelized embodiment to broader African Diaspora understandings of black male corporeal politics in worship.

Spectators who characterize Jungle Cat's praise pole dance as blasphemous likely perceive a disruption of a heteropatriarchal social order when Jungle Cat's image and gesture challenges the negative images of black men to which they have been socialized. To behold and to listen to black men's spiritual intimacy with God contradicts the media's fixation on black male physical abilities over their spiritual disciplines. Citing feminist studies scholar Gina Dent, Ronald L. Jackson writes, "Because mass media and popular culture are predominantly littered with these negative images, it appears that they are unwilling to see black bodies positively, and this affects everyday looking relations."[52] These limited and negative images coupled with the notion that "the physical expression of masculinity in dance in the twentieth century has become associated with conveying queer potential. If the male dancing body is always already queer, this transgression against normative definitions of gendered and sexual behavior carries with it the penalty of punishment."[53] The mass media's *fantastic hegemonic imagination*[54]—adapting Emilie Townes's term—about black men's bodies reduces black men to their physical attributes inclusive of athleticism, physical strength, and sexual prowess. Thus when a heterosexual man views the black male dancer, for example, it may trigger a cognitive dissonance, if a white supremacist logic has been socialized to view black men dancing on "stage" as always peculiar, phallic, and not spiritual. Succinctly, black men's visible spirituality evokes a simultaneous navigation of male ideals, envy, surveillance, control, and humanization of black bodies. While the heteronormative beholder organizes their perception of and potential arousal from that body, men in particular negotiate the fine line between their internal suspicion of homosexuality and anxiety about interpreting one's own ensuing homoerotic haze.

The Complex Imagery of Men Physically Worshipping God

Jungle Cat's characterization of his movements is consistent with a form of Davidic worship that nurtures his relationship with God, in which the image of the divine encompasses a theology of incarnation and indwelling of the body by

an animating force. As mentioned before, a Davidic model of worship is an undignified approach to dance that permits the Spirit to moves upon the praiser's
permeable heart and body. The dancer is to use all that is within him (2 Samuel
6:14; Psalm 103:1), anytime and wherever, despite the disparaging gaze of other
humans, including those with whom he has been most intimate such as one's
spouse (2 Samuel 6:16). In some regard, spectators are expected to misunderstand, disapprove of, and find strange a man's dance. Davidic praise body language is communication solely intended for God's approval.

Furthermore, for Jungle Cat to dance before God within a Davidic model of
Christian worship is to deal with the dancer's and perhaps the observer's im-
agination of God's corporeality. Jungle Cat's "pole dancing for Jesus" suggests
movement to unite with God that is both erotic and mystic. Central to African
American Christian tradition is, for example, the belief that Jesus Christ
(Immanuel or "God is with us") has shared in the fullness of humanity's materiality and has made the body a sacred site for God's love toward humanity.
Theologian Dwight Hopkins argues in his exploration of African American
Christianity and the construction of the black male body that eroticism is
about sex and transcendence, working from the inside out to achieve pleasure
and the ultimate embodied sacredness. The possibilities for this embodiment
are understood in the ultimate demonstration of sacredness achieved through
life and death that for countless believers is proved and embodied in the person
of Jesus.

> For example, Jesus Christ, in Black Christianity, is body revelation of sacred life
> force. "Jesus Christ clearly signifies that God loves us in or bodies as uniquely
> embodied creatures." Simultaneously, the blues moan and groan out another
> revelation of sacred life force. In the blues, physicality and spirituality exist as
> a dynamic quilting of the life force among Black folk. The folk perceive a pow-
> erful, "spiritual function of the human body." The sacred and the secular, the di-
> vine and human coalesce. "For Black people the body is sacred, and they know
> how to use it in the expression of love."[55]

As a man uses the pole to signify Jesus Christ's body revelation and the cross, he
signifies more than the pleasure dimension of transcendence. He signifies Jesus
Christ's suffering on the cross—that in James Cones's black theology of liberation reading of the pole qua cross, resembles the nineteenth through twentieth-
century execution of African Americans on the lynching tree. And yet through
the work of Jesus the Christ on the cross Christians witness and await life after
death. Consequently, the struggle, on the part of orthodox African American
congregations, to discuss issues of gender and sexuality is ironic and a lost opportunity for liberation to scholars in black religious studies. Particularly since

Christianity is, as Michael Eric Dyson notes, "grounded in the Incarnation, the belief that God took on flesh to redeem human beings. That belief is constantly trumped by Christianity's quarrels with the body. Its needs. Its desires. Its sheer materiality. But especially its sexual identity."[56] Men's engagement with God's incarnation is even more complex, as they then explore their sense of God's metaphorically male materiality in worship. Citing Dyson, Victor Anderson advocates for a consideration of a black theology of homoeroticism that takes into account same-gender quarrels with the body in worship as well.[57] Though he engages in a solo practice and spiritual sustenance, Jungle Cat is jointly fitted with other believers. Moreover, the musical message warns that a schism occurs in the body of Christ when commentary comes from those within the body about his unconventional praise. Negative commentary is damaging to his sense of belonging.

A Black Theology of Homoeroticism

Taking a cue from Victor Anderson's proposition, I turn to evaluate men's Christian dance and movement through the lens of a pluralistic black theology of homoeroticism. Existential phenomenologist Lewis Gordon asserts that the metaphoric maleness of God, in a monotheistic religion, arguably gets in the way of men's worship in multitudinous charismatic black churches that adhere to hegemonic structures that socioculturally render black men's bodies invisible, closed, and hypersexual (Gordon 1995). In "Homoeroticism and the Black Heterosexual Male" (2007a), Stephen Finley considers Gordon's assertion about the metaphoric maleness of God and engages Jawanza Kunjufu (1997), Howard Eilberg-Schwartz (1991), and Jeffrey J. Kripal (2001) to expand on the implications of the metaphoric maleness of God, in the psychoanalysis of particularly black men's interwoven social, cultural, and theological conception of intimacy with God. Finley argues that in the monotheistic Christian religious tradition, the symbolically gendered attribution of God causes the language of men to break, entangling the meanings they generate in constructs of gender, sexuality, and desire. Thus the space to relate to God is confined. Religion scholar Howard Eilberg-Schwartz argues in his book *God's Phallus: And Other Problems For Men and Monotheism* (1991) that over time the male gendered language upon which Christian imagery is based, has evoked an uneasiness from the contradictions inherent in men's relationship with a God who is explicitly male.[58] The observer's uneasiness is cognitive dissonance that is induced while unraveling the meanings associated with religious symbols, along with God's phallus and maleness. The participants' uneasiness with the symbolism has necessitated a disembodied God, one that needed to be dismembered to erase the homoeroticism suggested in men's male relationship with God. The erasure of God's body over time has manifested, for example, by veiling the body of God in the sanctuary and the debates over the perceived feminization of men in church communities.

More to the point, the uneasiness evoked in Christian mystics' embodied symbolism is theologically and structurally followed along gendered and sexed lines. "God is imaged as a male with whom the male mystic erotically unites, the symbolism will by definition, be homoerotic for males."[59] A major dilemma is the homoeroticism evoked in Christian monotheism by the male demonstration of love for a male God. I pause to make a distinction between "homoeroticism" and "homosexuality." Homoerotic is symbolically same-gender relationships, in which there is desire to unite with the other and it is does not require a sexual enactment.[60] More specifically, in this context it is a man's love for a male God.[61] In his mysticism research, Jeffrey Kripal distinguishes between homoeroticism and homosexuality:

By this I do not mean to imply that most male mystics who employed erotic language to speak about their religious experience also engaged in homosexual acts, or even that most of these same mystics would have desired such acts within some culturally and historically specific register: an individual's use or appropriation of homoerotic symbolic structure does not necessarily reflect a subjectively felt set of same-sex desires or, more problematically still a "homosexuality" . . .

By "homoerotic," then I mean to imply the textual existence of a male-to-male symbolic structure in which mystical encounters are framed along same-sex lines.[62]

The metaphoric language that permeates the characterization of the human's relationship with God in biblical tradition is corporeal, erotic, and sexual, where—in heteronormative terms—God is male or a Bridegroom and humanity is imagined as female or a bride.[63] By imagining men as brides of God, believers were "partially able to preserve the heterosexual complementary that helped define the culture."[64] Likening God to man reifies patriarchy, polices women's bodies, and controls female spaces. Thus when men enter into "women's spaces" like men's gaze in the sanctuary during worship, their corporeality becomes inverted, swallowed up in the feminine role of the human's relationship with God that then reveals a disjuncture for men's conception of the self.

I found an additional clue to the erotic overtones generated when I weighed media coverage of Jungle Cat's performance in comparison to white women's similar devotional uses of the pole. When his praise gained momentum in 2011, there were also articles about free praise pole fitness classes soundtracked with Christian Rock songs that are held on second Sundays exclusively for (mainly white Christian) housewives at Best Shape of Your Life, in Old Town

Spring, Texas. In March 2011, KTRK-TV, a Houston ABC affiliate interviewed participants in a segment called "Spin Without Sin: Pole Dancing for Jesus." Crystal Dean, the instructor who is a former pole dancer, shared that the class is not about sex. They are taking care of themselves and pursuing closeness with the divine in an all female class.[65] Dean and the participants likened both the pole and their bodies to being a temple.

In a mystic manner, Tiffany Booth confessed: "I do feel a spiritual connection whenever you have the music on and it's singing about lifting you up and being closer to God. You do feel that." They even provided biblical support from Psalms 149:3 from mixing music, dance, and religion: "Let them praise His name with dancing; Let them sing praises to Him with timbrel and lyre." It is interesting that the gender-inclusive language within the verse they reference biblically supports Jungle Cat's praise pole dance. In addition to the biblical support, an ABC blogger who eventually posted the segment cited professor Thomas Tweed of University of Texas. "Some people of course would say that this is not the way; that it's too vulgar, it's too crass, it's inappropriate," Tweed said. "But I can imagine some Christians saying if it actually brings a husband and wife together as Christians to deepen the marriage bond, that actually it's okay." As one might imagine, there have been protestors, one of whom stood at the door and held up a Holy Bible in the window, as the women participated in class.

The Texas housewives are in many respects unmarked within a heteronormative construct. They overcome the symbolic barriers of using the pole for closeness to God through female homosocial bonding that further reinscribes heteronormativity. Ironically, even though students say the class is not about sex, part of the way that the housewives are able to conquer the public's resistance is through observers' interpretation of such practices as beneficial to both the Bridegroom *qua* God and their husband. Implied in such a gendered perception of the performance is the correlation made between a God conventionally constructed as male/bridegroom and the meaning of the pole as a phallic symbol. In this construction, women are arguably allowed to be sexually suggestive toward God. Moreover both the symbolic temples of the women's bodies and the pole are used for homosocial bonding in an erotic practice to worship a male God.[66]

On the other hand, due in large part to the imagined maleness of God, Jungle Cat's performance reinscribes symbolic barriers of men using the pole for closeness to God in a heteronormative construct. I argue that it is precisely his performed combination of the hypersexualized black male body, the male gendered God, and phallic symbol of the pole that overwhelm observers' reception of his dancing. His worship registers to them as a symbolically homoerotic performance. The majority of male dancers, not just black ones, are presumed to be gay until they prove their heterosexuality in dominant culture. Men are not

permitted to allow their spirituality to inform their sexuality, let alone be sexually suggestive in their worship to God. Men are not permitted to dance and
choose the movements, as instances of what ethnomusicologist Henry Spiller
observes to be simply dancing among Java men—"moving their bodies in ways
that seem free, in a context that seems self-evident, and engaging with aesthetic
values that seem natural."[67]

One disruption to Judeo-Christian heteronormative and patriarchal
constructions resisting feminization is the research on the polytheist strands
of Hebrew tradition that embrace God's feminine features. Of note is the
worship of the Hebrew goddess *Asherah* that Israelites worshipped publicly following their entrance into Canaan for about six centuries. *Asherah*
was represented as a carved, cylindrical figurine (made of wood or clay)—
a type of pole, totem, or tree—with an implanted or flared base. A number
of Egyptian figurines that have been found from the nineteenth century B.C.
show a female holding at one breast a circular object that researchers infer
is a "frame drum" (tambourine) or a molded bread cake (Dever 2005). "The
Lady *Asherah* of the Sea" was the chief Canaanite goddess in the pantheon,
the wife of *El* the chief God and the progenitress of the gods. In her husband *El*'s presence, *Asherah* would prostrate and he would inquire about her
requests. She is also described as a wet nurse to the gods (Patai 1990). With the
Asherah tradition, the phallic/penetration symbolism of the modern pole can
be interchanged with ancient nursing/endowment symbolism. According to
historian Matthew Kuefler, eunuchs who worshipped *Asherah* would publicly
castrate themselves before her pole,[68] and Christians considered this practice
of physical alteration unmanly. On the other hand, for men to cultivate their
interioriority on a pole toward a nurturing God is another means by which
God does the act of improving a person's interior disposition or inward attitude. In other words, it is manly to privately worship a nurturing God on the
pole, away from public consumption.

For men addressing their identity as they negotiate their intimacy with God,
the challenge is to unpack, organize, and reimagine God. For some, it is difficult to feel comfortable while publicly demonstrating their relationship with
a male-imaged God. It is this complexity in facilitating male closeness with
God in heteronormative constructs that compels me to ask afresh the question posed by Lewis Gordon, "Can men worship God?" Can men find ways to
publicly open up to God? As I consider Gordon's questions, there remains the
Pentecostal belief in the physical manifestation of the Spirit, a Holy Spirit that
enters in and indwells the believer. The believer is to welcome the indwelling of
the Spirit, whose entrance is a symbolic act of spiritual penetration. The imagery
of indwelling clashes with heteronormative masculinity, in which the male body
is to be impenetrable. One would have to consider the sociocultural signification

of embodied masculinity as impenetrable, and thus, incompatible with a God who indwells.

According to philosopher Lewis Gordon, within a heteronormative society, men's bodies are constructed and disciplined to assume a "closed identity," blocking entry into the body. Male bodies are perceived to protrude and to be without holes. They are not permitted to physically lose themselves, be overcome by or entered by any entity. Contrary to the gesturally open masculinity of Davidic undignified praise, this closed identity social construct also limits the body language of men, as their affect of admiration is stirred in worship. Impenetrable masculinity suggests that to be entered lessens a man's masculinity in the required, embodied surrender to God. To assume a closed masculine posture is in essence to lose one's capacity for worship, the space for God to indwell a man, and an opportunity for the Holy Spirit to "enter in" him.[69] Therefore in a Western heteronormative context, worshipping God becomes a moment in which a man's masculinity gets in the way of intimacy with God, prohibiting him from a deeper consciousness of and unity with God.

In this chapter I have explored Jungle Cat's progressive approach to music and movement as a means of conveying his pluralistic Pentecostal identity, in a body language that he recognizes as worship. Jungle Cat appropriates and deploys symbols that speak to him and his audiences in multivalent ways. Jungle Cat stands as an example of alternative expressions of masculinity. He destabilizes hegemonic notions of what gospelized masculine worship is imagined to look like and what those images reveal about men's identity. As Jungle Cat moves, he taps into a wider body vocabulary and broadens the symbolic possibilities of joining flesh and spirit in the act of worship in both public and private spaces. Whether or not the church's public square is willing to provide room, men of various sexual orientations are finding ways to cultivate their openness physically and spiritually. Moving beyond the public square and religious sanctuary, their practice is fashioned within the privacy of their homes, where they are free to allow the issues and emotions of their heart to flow. As spectators observe private performances via the Internet, it is certain that the intentions of the movements will get lost in translation and audiences' descriptions require a constellation of interpretations. Moreover, the rigid notion of masculinity constructed as a bodily enclosure is too confining for men. Perhaps Jungle Cat's devotional practice of praise pole dancing for Jesus will inspire other men to claim symbols and postures they can wield for God's glory.

While praise pole dancing defies hegemonic notions of masculine worship, men also engage in other forms of expressive culture that reinforce conventional masculinities. Gospel go-go is a male-centered music scene that illustrates an in-betweenness of black male attitudes within worship practices that is a different interpretation of muscular Christianity. Black male bodies are both inscribed and read for their conformity to the respectability politics of being culturally civilized and sexually disciplined men. My research on gospel go-go exemplifies the ways in which gospel musicians perform against the "flamboyant" gospel musician image. Gospel go-go musicians code their performance with macho and sometimes "hypermasculine" musical techniques such as singing, speaking, and playing instruments in lower ranges, while posturing in a manner that suggests their potential to be socioculturally unruly or religiously nonconforming. For them, Christian worship is an opportunity to express one's agency in cultivating their relationship with God.

4

"Peculiar 'Til I D.I.E."

War Cries and Undignified Praise in Gospel Go-Go Music

In the early 2000s, the gospel go-go scene was at the geo-political margins of Washington, DC–area black religious life. This was also a pivotal period when gospel go-go bands started to be included in regular worship services in congregations just outside of DC such as Ebenezer A.M.E. (Fort Washington, MD) and Community of Hope A.M.E. (Temple Hills, MD), despite other church leaders' reservations about the music's close aesthetic resemblance to nonreligious go-go. Spawned from the nonreligious go-go percussive funk music in the late 1980s and early 1990s, gospel go-go music addressed one of the popular concerns facing black religiosity: remedying black male absenteeism in church attendance through providing a local music idiom to which young men are attracted.

Occupying a sacred space between the church and the street, fans traveled throughout the metropolitan area to catch their favorite bands and party while practicing their faith in nontraditional settings. Since that period, young black men's facilitation of and attendance at these nontraditional events exemplifies what insiders call an "aggressive" masculine incorporation of the fire and desire it takes to set the atmosphere: exhibiting undignified praise[1] to God and fashioning "on fire" (exuberant), *phallomusicocentric* and *phallosonocentric* worship experiences. The notion of undignified praise is taken from 2 Samuel 6:21–22a to characterize David's dance with all of his might: ". . . It was before the LORD who chose me rather than your father or anyone from his house when he appointed me ruler over the LORD's people Israel—I will celebrate before the LORD. I will become even more undignified than this . . ." Gospel go-go participants fill the void in the black male underrepresentation in Christian worship, the crisis that was broached in the introduction of this book, while challenging negative perceptions of the music scene as evinced by the lives that are changed at the events.

Focusing on Washington, DC's gospel go-go music scene in the early 2000s, this chapter highlights the role of an understudied popular music in performances of socioculturally preferred black male homosociality. Evoking a street credible sonic aesthetic, I argue that central to the gospel go-go musicians'

Flaming? Alisha Lola Jones, Oxford University Press (2020). © Oxford University Press.
DOI: 10.1093/oso/9780190065416.001.0001

contribution to African American worship is a performance against the stereotyp-ical "flamboyant" choir director/singer image that we have explored so far.[2] In es-sence, the go-go music band is a symbolic composite of perspectives associated with the unmarked male-dominant categories of the musicians' pit and absentee men, who are talking back, providing musical contestation of the duplicitous preacher and choir director stereotypes. I aim to shed light on the musical and performative properties of what I observe is the performance of male *homomusicoenrapture* and *homosonoenrapture*, the same-gender sonic textures and visual dynamics that stim-ulate intense enjoyment that envelopes and propels gospel go-go participants. By sonic textures, I am referring to the sound qualities that illustrate a heterogeneous sound ideal[3] along sociocultural lines of performed gender expression that is geared toward men: the primacy of male singers and lead talkers rapping in a lower vocal range; the dominance of percussion and bass lines; the emphasis on instrumenta-tion that intensifies the lower frequencies dissociated with queerness in African American Pentecostal Christian worship;[4] and the interpretation of a simultane-ously street credible and spiritual warrior posture of masculine undignified praise.

Socioculturally, gospel go-go performers merge go-go music marginality with Christian practices of being "peculiar people," distinguishing themselves through their interpretation of a muscular Christianity persona, men who evoke sounds of battle in Pentecostal worship. These are men poised for war, a performance for which some believers have longed, as exemplified in the Williamson excerpt of this book's introduction. However, this performance simultaneously relies on the confinement of women's participation with a few women as lead singers and rarely as instrumentalists.

I begin by establishing the sonic textures that are tethered to a tumultuous go-go past that has positioned gospel go-go at the margins of society. Engaging that go-go past, I turn briefly to sketch the development of the music scene that gave rise to gospel go-go. Within the narrative about the emergence of gospel go-go into worship settings, there are queries about the stylistic configurations that I address with an examination of the extent to which they create a soundscape of men ready for battle. I evaluate musicians' methods for preserving local culture, navigating the indiscernibility of the message, and being heard socially. While participants claim the message that musicians deliver "makes the difference" or changes lives, I observe that there are also a range of sonic, spiritual, and organ-izational strategies that gospel go-go musicians deploy to facilitate an accessible worship experience for (non-)religious go-go enthusiasts.

Gospel Go-Go Aesthetic Development

Throughout the 1980s and well into the early 2000s, prominent Washington, DC church leaders expressed anxiety about accepting gospel go-go performance within traditional worship services because it is known as dangerous. As a result, concert after concert was held in nontraditional locations unaffiliated with a church. Due to an intracultural, classist bias against the nonreligious go-go music from which this gospelized genre is drawn, church leaders have also been reluctant to name gospel go-go as a resource for reinvigorating youth involvement. However, I have uncovered the fact that preeminent churches have come to culturally mine gospel go-go music's production of a masculine coded sonic safe space[5] to draw youth to their events for retreat, and to process daily urban hassles among peers. In addition to the sonic qualities, participants maintain that it is the artist's gospel message that distinguishes gospel go-go from its similarly endangered, nonreligious counterpart go-go. However, the public script about the lyrics that make gospel go-go distinct conceals the complex musical engineering at work in drawing men to worship through masculine coded sonic registers: the strategy of church leaders in deploying *homomusicoenchantment* and *homosonoenchantment*.

Within the musical social life of urban centers, and Washington, DC soundscape in particular, there is an acute sociocultural preoccupation with engineering an intense musical bottom that is purported to be sonically attractive to men. The musical bottom is comprised of the aforementioned vocal and instrumental amalgamation of lower frequencies notated in the bass clef of Western European notation represented in speaking and singing and that percolate in live gospel go-go music performance. Often capitalizing on gospel go-go musicians' gifts of what I call male *homomusicoenchantment* and *homosonoenchantment,* church leaders who invite the bands to minister benefit from the low budget musical pleasure derived from getting lost in the intense "beat" or rhythmic patterns of men's *live* go-go music that caters to perceived male tastes. The nonreligious, live go-go music aesthetic foregrounds lower frequencies through percussive instrumentation, electronic string and keyboard bass, and vocality that enthusiasts claim socioculturally registers as masculine sound. The lower frequencies are a crucial element of the rhythmic intensity because they fill in a gendered gap within the soundscape, while drawing men to attend worship. The heavy, lower instrumentation emphasis in the go-go music soundscape provides participants with a sonic texture and musicians with an external instrumentalization (music-making with instruments outside the body).

In the contemporary gospel music industry, audiences fetishize the musical bottom in vocal performance, due in large part to the scarcity of competent baritone and bass soloists.[6] Composer and contralto vocalist Dr. Ysaye Barnwell once said of composition voicing in a 2006 address to the Yale Institute of Sacred Music, "In contemporary gospel music, we have lost the baritone and bass vocal line." As a result, gospel enthusiasts perceive a symbolic, black masculine absenteeism in vocal performance. Even though the baritone and bass vocal lines do occur in other black sacred music genres such as quartet, chorale, anthem, and line hymn singing, the low male soloist is a delicacy in the African American worship soundscape. Speaking and singing in the lower register has multifaceted sonic meaning, as I referenced in chapter 2, with the baritone's "low vocal designation . . . prized for its stimulating timbral qualities, suitable for setting the mood for worship in the sanctuary and sex in the bedchamber."[7] Those sonic attributes are readily translatable to the gospel go-go music that shares the popular and sacred music orality aesthetics. "Unlike the high tenor voice, [the] baritone sonic persona is less likely to signify his queer potential in predominantly black gospel music contexts, and in many ways the conventionally masculine aspects of his voice normalize and thus mark as unexceptional the erotic aspects of his performance."[8] The baritone lead talker juxtaposed with the occasion crooning lead singer is key especially in a music scene where male rappers are encouraged to emote, whilst expressing the finer details of their life and in some cases perspiring and disrobing due to the heated concert stage. The combination of all of those responses to the energy generated in those spaces make for intense emotional connection and blurred sensual lines between participants: musicians and audience alike.

And of course, the instrumental musical bottom as represented in melodic and harmonic line notation of the bass clef has remained a driving force throughout black popular music performance. This musical bottom idolization prompts the following question about the gendering of sonic registers: To what extent have gospel go-go musicians sought a retrieval or preservation of the musical bottom that configure both vocal *and* instrumental textures with the objective of attracting men to Washingtonian communal worship?

Often referred to as an expansive "musical party," go-go is a rhythmic funk-derived music that developed in the Washington, DC area during the late 1960s and early 1970s. The scene gained momentum on the heels of the 1968 uprisings that swept throughout Washington, DC, Baltimore, Chicago, and other major cities following the assassination of Rev. Dr. Martin Luther King, Jr. In the aftermath, curfews were placed in effect in Washington to manage the "people out of control," who were outraged about King's assassination.[9]

South Carolina migrant Chuck Brown (1936–2011) is considered the godfather of go-go music. As an ex-convict and musician, Chuck Brown tried to find a way to keep nightclub-goers on the dance floor between sets. He utilized Afro-Caribbean instrumentation and musical elements to perform rhythmic groove transitions that would keep the party "going and going." Hence, "go-go" was born. His most famous songs are "Go-Go Swing (1986)"[10] and "Bustin' Loose (1978)."[11] Brown also established a tradition of critiquing police surveillance. In Brown's 1986 version of Louis Jordan's "Run Joe" (1948),[12] he said, using his baritone voice, "The po-lice-man is on the premises . . . What is he doing in here?"[13] Brown eventually released a gospelized go-go recording in 2005,[14] covering Andrae Crouch's "Can't Nobody Do Me Like Jesus" (1975) featuring Washingtonians Pastor Luke Mitchell Jr. and The New Olive Baptist Church, in which Brown and Mitchell concluded that of all their so-called friends, "Jesus is my friend." He recorded Edwin Hawkins' crossover gospel hit "Oh, Happy Day" featuring Y'anna Crawley and the Howard Gospel Choir founded by legendary alumnus Richard Smallwood.

By the 1980s, national concert promoters would hire go-go bands to open up for hip-hop artists when they came to Washington.[15] Unfortunately, the image of go-go as a pathologized music scene circulated when television and print media produced exposés in the 1980s about the illicit and sexually explicit activity at these events.[16] The alleged illicit activities at go-gos have served as justification for political leaders and law enforcement to close go-go clubs. Folklorists Kip Lornell and Charles Stephenson observe that go-go music scenes received even more of a bad reputation because of inaccurate portrayal in movies, documentaries, and videos,[17] but I contend that the fault lies not only with the entertainment industry. Cities are sites of social convergence, where systematic tension tightens between power-holders and the disinherited.

In the history of black cultural production, various iterations of urban youth culture have been portrayed as symbolic magnets for danger. Hip-hop events of the late 1980s, for example, were also considered dangerous after a shooting at a Run DMC concert during their Raising Hell Tour. Ice T's "Cop Killer" (1992) rap album that was recorded by his hardcore punk band Body Count was thought to spur violence against police officers. This bias even extended to the movie industry, whereas Spike Lee's film *Do The Right Thing* (1989) was feared to have the potential to incite riots. Go-go music media coverage in Washington, DC provides a case study of what Alona Wartofsky detected in the following passage as another product on which the media blames youth victimization and drug-related crimes:

> The music also survived something far more debilitating than clueless record executives. The crack epidemic hit Washington hard in the late '80s, and go-go shows became a magnet for trouble, in part because they attracted rival neighborhood crews quick to settle disagreements with gunfire. In 1987 a gunman sprayed bullets into a crowd leaving a go-go at the Masonic Temple on U street NW, and 11 people were shot. After several other well-publicized shootings, some resulting in fatalities, many clubs closed their doors to go-go promoters. The media and city politicians found an easy scapegoat in go-go. Some went so far as to suggest that the music's tribal beats riled up young people, that it made them uncontrollable and violent.[18]

There were 449 homicides in the city in 1997—statistics that earned Washington the label of "the murder capital" during this period. The rise in murders were accredited to "tribal beats that riled up young people" at go-go events and the crack pandemic. Citizens began to place pressure on government officials to do something about youth victimization. DC and Prince George's County politicians subsequently revoked the alcohol licenses of clubs that featured live go-go and eventually closed them. Unfortunately, Washingtonian youthful go-go scene participants were left without safe places to party. Journalism scholar Natalie Hopkinson (2013) has documented in her research go-go youths' strategies to remember uncountable narratives about violence, domestic war, and loss. They memorialize the deceased by wearing customized t-shirts that display the deceased's likeness and offer musical shout outs during go-go events, as I will briefly discuss later in this chapter.

Having participated in the development of the scene since the early 1980s, some youth in the go-go scene cultivated an alternative musical response to their trauma. A combination of gospel, funk, pop, and Afro-Latin jazz musics, "gospel go-go" has served as an evangelistic tool for participants facing urban violence, disenfranchisement, and discrimination in the early 1990s.[19] The local "parties" go-go musicians offer are noticeably inexpensive in comparison to their nonreligious go-go counterpart. Admission may cost $5 to $10 for gospel go-go band concerts versus a $25 to $60 entry fee for nonreligious go-go. Go-go enthusiasts would regularly leave a go-go set to attend a gospel go-go set for a good beat, especially if their favorite go-go band's venue has a long line. Gospel go-go musicians transfer into worship the performance of parties that keep "going and going." Their combination of a party with a "holy ghost workout"[20] does not diminish the gospel go-go event's potential as religious observance.

This go-go tradition of remembrance and memorialization resembles gospel go-go musicians' performances about the gospel of Jesus who Christians believe was resurrected from the dead. Gospel go-go musicians adaptation of go-go memorialization fills a void left from the decline of various African American communal lament or mourning practices comparable to the Negro spirituals, blues, and the New Orleanian second-line funeral processions. Likewise this coding of a street credible black male spirituality is similar to charismatic Christian models of undignified worship like musical "war cries" of spiritual warfare, during celebrative and ecstatic moments of worship, or even war cries that are chanted athletic events.[21] During war cries, it is permissible to make a joyful noise that can be anywhere from a yell to a growl to a scream—sounds that when black men make them outside of this religious context usually signal chaos, danger, or distress. Here is an organizing principle, a rallying cry, a sign that spiritual warfare is being waged and victory is already symbolically won.

In contradistinction to nonreligious go-go, I have also noticed that gospel go-go musicians privilege the message about Christian living over the go-go practice of recounting urban hassles and indulgences. The manner with which the rappers and talkers deliver the messages in the music is a distinguishing feature that closely bears a resemblance to the African American preaching tradition. While gospel go-go musicians characterize gospel as being Christian message-focused, their focus is ironic because customarily the vocalists' proclamation of the lyrics are indecipherable, reifying their resemblance with go-go performance, as they distance themselves theologically and socially from its nonreligious attributes. Musicians metaphorically sound convergence as they attempt to forget their prior knowledge of pain and pleasure, while using the go-go manner and style that is a symbolic vehicle for communal remembrance.

Street credible black male spirituality engages the intersection of race, class, gender, age, and death that religious leaders have neglected to engage. Musicians claim that variations of the male coded elements (heavy, percussive instrumentation, and soloist's talking styles that are in the lower speaking and singing range) draw youth to gospel go-go events, during which both men and women are permitted to worship, make noise, and play in a masculine-centered space that contrasts sharply with common perceptions of feminized church congregations. Distinct from male dominance, masculine-centeredness is the musicians' use of codes in performance that persistently direct the audiences' focus via the gaze and the hearing toward street credible masculine subjectivity and posture, even when women perform. In gospel go-go music spaces, participants are empowered to explore the sonic dimensions of spiritual combat and sociocultural catharsis, an aggressive posturing that is a sought-after competency for imagined masculine worship.

The Sound of Men Ready for Battle

My sister and I pull into the packed parking lot at about 9:30 p.m. For a few years, The Complex has been the place to go for gospel go-go.[22] The venue is located in Temple Hills, Maryland, next door to one of a handful of roller skating rinks in the Washington, DC metropolitan area. A few streetlights are scattered about the lot, along with an abundance of potholes. We swerve around them to find that the lot is full. There is barely any room to park on the periphery of the lot but we fit the car into a makeshift spot anyway. In the distance, I can already hear a "bounce beat" go-go groove emanating from inside. It sounds as though lead talker Cero Dos is on the microphone exhorting the audience to live for God, over the percolating percussion. We hop out of the car, and zip up our jackets. With our hands in our pockets, quickly we tiptoe across the lot in our jeans and black leather boots, and wait in line to get in The Complex. After a few minutes, we murmur among ourselves that the line better go fast because it is too cold to stand outside.

As we get closer to the metal double doors, I recognize the melody but cannot make out the words of the traditional praise and worship song they are covering. I start to nod and sing lyrics to the "praise and worship" melody I have known since I was a child, in a call and response manner. "Ooooooooooh, mag-ni-fy the Looooord! (HEY! HEY!) For He is wor-thy toooo be praised (Come-on! Come-on!)." The shouted calls are returned with customary go-go exuberance. I can feel the resonant pops as the congas are hit. The chime of the cowbells escapes through the closed doors and pierces through all the chatter outside. It has been ten minutes and the beat continues. All at once I hear the keyboard, congas, bongos, cowbell, drum set, and guitars interlock in an overwhelming groove. On the upbeat, the lead talker shouts, "Hosanna!" And the crowd sings back, "Ho-san-na! Bles-sed be the rock! Bles-sed be the rock of my sal-va-tion!"

By the time we make it into the foyer at 10 p.m., we are rhythmically bending and flexing our legs, bounce-swaying to the beat without releasing our hands from our jacket pockets. We arrive at the ticket table and pay $5 each. A band-leader walks by us with a stylishly torn t-shirt, jeans, bandana, and Timberlands.[23] He wipes perspiration from his face with a hand towel, as he presses past the line to open the door and step outside to talk on his cell phone. We are relieved that he opened the door because a gush of wind rushed in. The atmosphere is so thick that in the air we see steam rising from people's bodies. We peel off our coats and realize we are carrying more stuff than anyone else in the line. Very few folks were wearing coats or carrying purses like us. We are overdressed. It is obvious that this is our first time at a gospel go-go. I glance at the turned-off metal detectors, as we pass them and step into the main room. Regular nonreligious go-gos generally require high security measures because some participants violently settle neighborhood disputes at the events. At gospel go-gos, it is less likely that there will be incidents of youth victimization and so security is relaxed.

On the dance floor, everyone is huddled together. My sister and I decide to stand in the back, against the wall with some other ladies who were taking a breather. From this vantage point, we can see the depth of the crowd. Clusters of men, with some women interspersed throughout, throw arms around each other's shoulders, as they bounce and sway in a line right in front of the stage. On the floor, the crowd compacts itself and takes two-thirds of the space closest to the stage. And then a wave of the bounce beat instrumentals hits us. All over the room people part the crowd to make pockets of space for dance solos, duos, and teams, as the dancing participants respond through their signature "beat ya' feet" choreographies.[24] The lead talker on the microphone says in a baritone voice, "We're gonna try something new." A male vocalist sings their original song in a high, vibratoless tone. He cups the microphone with his hands and presses his mouth against it. His rhythmic melody is muffled, but I continue swaying to fit in with the dancing crowd, as the groove continues.

Combining Pentecostal and charismatic Christian aesthetics with Africanisms, gospel go-go performance practice is consistent with a muscular Christian interpretation of the Davidic undignified praise model. Gospel go-go undignified praise centralizes male gendered, sounded "work" and contrasts the ambiguously gendered choir director/singer sound, movement, and domains that I discussed in chapters 1, 2, and 3.[25] The gospel go-go musicians' undignified worship approach stems from familiarity with the live go-go music process in which participants "get to work" or "get down" through the participatory performance of sonic-somatic labor that has been practiced in African-derived cultures. By invoking sonic-somatic labor, I describe the interconnectedness of musical and bodily experiences in the audible pain and pleasure of intense, body moving sound production.

The emotive qualities of the gospel go-go vocal production are more discernible than the lyrics, due in large part to the dominance of percussion and sound engineering of its intensity, during live performances. Like musics cultivated in the antebellum South, musicians' incorporate contested masculine coded elements including "peculiar" vocalized interjections, imitating instruments[26] and machines, embodied memory, sound engineering techniques, street life narratives, and the prosodic use of instrumentation into alternative worship experiences. And yet negotiating rhythmic intensity in worship is not new, dating back to the early twentieth century, when musicians transferred rhythmic intensity from nonreligious dance music into Pentecostal holiness church music.[27] The percussion instruments are so dominant that it is easier to hear the vocalists' sounded exertion and release than it is to hear the vocalists' gospel message. Consequently, attendees rely on enthusiasts' shared memory of song lyrics that the bands cover.

The go-go aesthetic of vocalized exertion and release has been practiced in African vocal techniques (growls, grunts, calls, cries, whispers, etc.) with which speech acts are interwoven such as onomatopoeia of speech, rapid delivery of texts, and explosive sounds.[28] For example, these vocal techniques are deployed to reimagine the Pentecostal and charismatic Christian performance "War Cry" melodic motifs and similarly "shouting unto God with a voice of triumph," as cued in the lyrics and adlibs during ecstatic moments of worship and spiritual warfare.

The gospel go-go feature of sounded exertion and release is shared with other African-derived styles of field hollers, work songs, dirges, and boat songs that creatively organized participants, stemming from colonialism in the United States.[29] To deal with the grind of hard labor, participants engaged their surroundings, the field, urban, industrial, and even carceral soundscapes, by plying resonant, atmospheric sounds into musical components of their grooves. In fact, the heavy percussion in go-go music amplifies the musical textures that were once maintained through body percussion (claps, stomps, patting hips, etc.) in quotidian music-making of work songs and dirges in the South.

These "aggressive" elements signify on contemporary race and class tensions in Washington, DC live music scenes—tensions that stem historically from US colonial prohibitions against playing "talking drums" (one of several talking instruments) that may call together or provide notice between enslaved Africans through instrumentalists' mimicking of speech. Talking drums were central to black cultural experiences, so much so that according to musicologist Samuel A. Floyd Jr., the entire musical content of African-derived dance cultural expression such as the sacred ring shout can be subsumed under drumming. Furthermore, musicologist Eileen Southern asserted that enslavers made every effort to eliminate secret communication via "talking instruments," and thereby instilled anxieties about use of the drum among colonized Africans and their descendants.[30] Gospel go-go music preserves the local cultural practices that are endangered in the embattled go-go nightlife scene, where political officials have closed the majority of the clubs in which the bands played, thereby continuing prohibitions on drumming.

Despite these established tensions, gospel go-go brings into Christian worship traces of a culturally relevant, peer-guided strategy through which urban youth mourn loved ones—both Christian believers and nonbelievers—who have died due to youth victimization and other issues, while orienting themselves to God. The overrepresentation of masculine coded sound evokes for me the following question: In what ways are hypermasculine coded sounds—that is, the symbolic abundance of sounded masculinity—deployed to construct an unquestionably masculine safe space for worship and recreation?

There are at least two contradictions in church leaders' condemnation of gospel go-go through the 2000s. First, church leadership's dismissal of gospel go-go music was ironic because of the leaderships' call to diligently resuscitate black male underrepresentation in churches and prevent youth victimization. The masculine-centered go-go scene was a musical source to tap into that draws men into safe environments. Their negative assessment of gospel go-go stems from a legacy of social, political, and religious surveillance that monitors young black men and women as they gather to lift their voices, through a music style that was characterized by its sonic, visual, ambient, and social intensity. The following are some examples of nineteenth-century Washington, DC Black Codes surveillance and control practices that were pertinent to the city's history of religious and musical night-life and recreation: prevention of Christian baptism as a means to obtaining freedom; proscription of idle, disorderly, or tumultuous assemblages of Negroes; and the prohibition of secret, private, and religious meetings of colored persons, beyond ten at night.[31] Since the Black Codes, surveillance of musical nightlife has been cultivated through the clandestine "Go-Go Report" that is distributed throughout the Prince George's County Maryland police department.

> Prepared by the MPD's hush-hush Intelligence Branch, the report details which bands are playing at which clubs, and when. Police officials have been compiling the reports for a while now, and they've claimed the work helps them tamp down violence by tipping off the cops about events that might attract feuding D.C. gangs. But MPD has never really discussed exactly what's in the report, or released one publicly.[32]

The internally distributed document lists: the band names, one-off shows, weekly concerts, the times the clubs will open, and what time the shows will end. The police use this information to go to venues and monitor the crowds. Also, DC requires bands and clubs to hire police to protect the crowds. "We have 12 officers when we play in DC," said TCB manager Ben Adda in a 2010 interview for the Washington *City Paper*. Adda claims that his bands are targeted, especially since a recent shooting broke out after one of their concerts. Roberto L. Hylton, the Prince George's County Maryland police chief at the time, remarked about the incident and the Metropolitan DC nightlife:

> Although nightclub violence has been significantly abated in 2009, events featuring TCB continue to harm our communities. The PGPD stands shoulder to shoulder with our community leaders against the proliferation of violence masqueraded as entertainment.[33]

Consistent with other majority black cities, Washington's black citizens are sensitive to the historical and contemporary gaze and eavesdropping of city officials who monitor the musical, ritual, and recreational practices of black men. Ethnomusicologist Allie Martin is researching the extent to which Indigenous Washingtonians are standing their ground through the #MuteDC movement against silencing and sonically gentrifying policies such as the Amplified Noise Act of 2018 that criminalizes black musicians who are preserving, transmitting, and enjoying the sound of the nation's capitol.[34] In many regards, the clamor of gospel go-go signified black youths' response to the constraints of religious and political monitoring and suspicion. These regulations are a continuation of the constraints and practices that formed the US colonial "invisible church" in the hush harbors of the rural south. As a cultural byproduct of those remnant *Black Code* law enforcement practices, gospel go-go musicians have developed a highly visible and highly sonic sacred music practice.

Second, church leaders were opposed to gospel go-go as a way for youth to safely play and worship when curfew laws were in effect. Although the curfew laws are urban annoyances for some, they were potentially beneficial to church leadership's agenda. Host churches were unwittingly poised for captive audiences to facilitate the transformative nature of gospel go-gos, but ironically they were concerned about drawing a "street" element into their churches. They were concerned neighborhood disputes would be settled in their venues. However, gospel go-gos also present an opportunity to attend to traumatized youth in a musical language they recognize. To what extent, I wonder, did the remnant of discriminatory governmental policies (e.g., Jim Crow, *Black Codes*) influence black communities'—especially black males—worship practices in Washington, DC? On the surface the police monitoring is a threat to black youth's ability to move freely. Yet a deeper investigation reveals the local churches' culpability in controlling youth's music-making, even if by their own passivity in protesting the laws.[35]

National gospel artists have recognized gospel go-go's worshipful and marketplace potential. They have co-opted what insiders label as dated go-go rhythms and styles from the 1980s. Largely drawing upon the 1980s sonic textures and dance introduced to the international scene through Experience Unlimited's (E.U.) recording and popular video "Da Butt" from Spike Lee's *School Daze* soundtrack (1988), national gospel artists use rototoms, horns, cowbell, congas, and bongos to allude to the go-go textures. The "Da Butt" call and response song form of shouting out to participants with a "big ole butt" combined with various vocable responses such as "oh-ee-oh! Oo-oh!" and corresponding hip gyration, which are merely a reduction of the go-go experience, are incorporated into the gospel music mixes. Some examples include Tye Tribbett's "Victory,"[36] Karen Clark Sheard's "Prayed Up,"[37] Ricky Dillard's "Higher,"[38] Myron Butler's "Covered,"[39] and Israel Houghton and New Breed's "No Turning Back" featuring Aaron Lindsey from *Jesus at the Center* (studio version 2012, live version in 2013).[40]

Even Kirk Franklin did an impromptu live performance in 2011 of a more current "bounce beat" go-go style with his song "Before I Die" from *Hello Fear* (2011), combined with the "chop" dance movements in collaboration with a local band at First Baptist Church of Glenarden in Glenarden, Maryland.[41] Consistent with this gravitation toward confronting death and reveling in peculiarity, they sang,

> Get up and live right now, right now, right now
> right now, right now, right now, right now
> Get up and live right now, right now, right now
> right now, right now, right now, right now
> right now, right now, right now, right now
> Right before I die I gotta change

change how I think
change how I speak
I'm not the same
so when I speak
you don't hear the pain
no longer weak
with no one to
right before I die I gotta
become more like you
take up my cross
to count the cost
cause I was lost
that's why I praise you
you're the only God
I don't know what they do
But I know I used to be afraid to die
I used to be afraid to try
cause I was too afraid of knowing

In co-opting go-go style, national artists have brought the sound into houses of worship and illustrated the experiential resemblance in the joining of flesh and spirit that is performed in both nonreligious go-go and go-go in worship. Through an evocation of E.U.'s musical and danced performances of "Da Butt," they tap into participants' familiarity with the instrumental grooves and textures transferring into worship nostalgia a popularized musical cue for a communally performed moment of letting go and getting loose and funky in parties. But in my interview on the Pot Radio with master go-go percussionist Buggy "The General," he critiqued these "gospel" interpretations by national gospel recording artists from outside the Washington, DC area as being devoid of the go-go swing. The swing feel is cultivated through a multisensory live music experience that is intended to move the body acoustically and socioculturally. "You can't play this music," he added, "unless you have experienced it like Y'anna Crawley—get into the go-go. There is no other way!"[42] He references Washingtonian and former member of the Lissen Band Y'anna Crawley, who was a 2009 winner of Sunday Best.

Crawley's career marked by a versatility between live and recorded music performance.[43] She represents the current go-go scene, as well as the unsung contributions of Washington, DC–area go-go women that include keyboardist Maiesha and the Hip Huggers; Michelle Bowman; Cherie "Sweet Cherie" Mitchell-Agurs of the all-female Be'la Dona band; the Pleasure band; and vocalist Halima Peru, who also leads go-go style worship at Community of Hope

A.M.E. in Hillcrest Heights, Maryland. Furthermore, the national recording artists often lack the iconic physical engagement and thick percussive texture in their
performance, which suggests the performative desire to be prompted by the musical feature yet not be overtaken by it. Nevertheless, go-go musicians maintain
that go-go styles are more authentically generated, understood, embodied, and
apprehended as primarily a live music process and memory of pain and pleasure.

Instrumentation and Sound Engineering
Techniques: Intensity, Griminess, and Buzz

Growing up in northeast Washington, DC, during the 1980s and 1990s, go-go
music was a musical expression of being an indigenous, street credible black
Washingtonian. When my family moved out to Warrenton, Virginia, during
my middle school years, I encountered black Virginians who were bigger go-go
music fans than I was when I arrived. They would sing to me the song hooks and
beat the rhythms on the lunch tables. We would tune into WKYS 93.9 FM every
evening at 9:30 p.m. to listen to and record via cassette tape the go-go music they
played every evening during that half-hour. Throughout my public high school
years in the 1990s, I recall my peers attending go-gos: they would talk about the
hottest bands, go-go inspired t-shirt brands, and the gear they wore to be ready
for anything should a confrontation arise at the clubs. It seemed like most of
my friends started their own bands. Finally, when I was about seventeen years
old, I mustered up the courage to ask my parents to go to the WKYS 93.9 FM–
sponsored "battle of the bands" featuring the popular bands such as the Huck-A-
Bucks, Rare Essence, and Backyard band. Cautioning me to be wise and safe, they
allowed me to go with their blessing. They dropped me off at the venue. I stood at
the door by myself, watching the radio personalities and concertgoers enter the
Washington stadium, but I never went in. I was overwhelmed because I felt like
I had no context. I was a "church girl" who did not feel that I knew what go-go
music culture or even nonreligious music culture was. It wasn't until I went away
to school at Oberlin College and told people that I was from Washington, DC that
I realized outsiders' perceptions about the go-go music sound. They described
the sonic qualities as acoustically offensive. Peers from Detroit, Chicago, and
New York compared their electronic musics—house musics and hip-hop—to
go-go's "pots and pans" instrumentation or the percussive, tinny qualities of
1980s go-go music style that was popularized by the Experience Unlimited Band
(E.U.). That tinny texture within the percussive funk music is much maligned
when outsiders assess the scene and I would even acknowledge that insiders misunderstand its value; however, I would like to emphasize that that tinny quality
continues an African-derived sonic tradition of religious sound.

Gospel go-go participants experience an audible convergence of church and street, an in-between space where male youths practice a gospelized resistance tradition of commemoration despite social, cultural, political, economic, and historical traumas. Musicians recalibrate their go-go style strategies in worship to manipulate the audible convergence of religious and nonreligious identities through configurations of the gospel message and sound quality referred to as intensity, griminess, and buzz/hum.[44] According to gospel go-go sound engineer Aaron Hope, musicians use techniques that cram into small venues the band instruments, sound equipment, and resulting acoustic power suitable for a large stadium. In the Washington, DC area, sound engineer Reo Edwards is known for customizing stacked speaker cabinets also called "stacks" that could handle the stadium-sized power. Hope explained, "Imagine having a conversation beside a marching band. That is the power you are essentially expecting a gospel go-go vocalist to perform to with this style of sound engineering. Go-go sound engineers try to make the vocalists intelligible with that sort of power around them." Hope describes the speaker stacks or systems as including homemade, "life sized," rectangular components with subwoofers on the bottom of each stack, and the mid-high range speakers are at the top of each stack. The stacks are side-by-side. As Hope stated, "Reo's monitoring speakers are laid out on the stage in two sections. The front is dubbed 'frontline wedges,' which are the monitors that line the front of the stage specifically for the vocalist."[45] The stacks are so big that people stand on them to look down at performers.

Go-go style sound mixing brings to the fore the lower frequencies within the instrumentation to capture the kick drum, the talker or rapper, and the crowd's response as the talker or rapper turns the mic to the crowd. This sonic cocktail provides a continuous ambient vibration that is audible (described onomatopoetically as a "hum" or "buzz") and experienced in the body. It is interesting to note that the soloists who sing at length often have higher voices, which is logical due to the fact that higher singers are heard above the heavy low-frequency instrumentation and the lead talkers use of their lower vocal range. Feedback is inevitable when the vocalists turn the mic to the crowd. "Feedback is usually the enemy to listeners accustomed to digital sound," Hope remarked.[46] But go-go enthusiasts, much like rap and dub music fans, consider feedback a desirable ingredient in the live music experience. Feedback and heavy percussion signifies an explosive, sounded convergence that is also metaphorically echoed throughout the participants' lives.

While enthusiasts maintain that the difference between go-go and gospel is the message, I noted the intermittence of the musicians' message intelligibility to the audience. The dominant musical feature in the go-go aesthetic is the percussion section and not the vocalized sound. The textures submerge the sung and spoken lyrics as the vocalists proclaim them. Lead talker André "Dré" Hinds (I will refer to him hereafter as Dré) of Peculiar People band observes that

> [hip-hop] rappers come into the city and rap off tracks and they don't get as much love. They don't have the live sound when they perform. People want the energy from the bands—they want to feel them. Because we are talking about what we are passionate about, not smashing girls and doing drugs but we talk about living a life for Christ . . . That is what frees them up.

The musicians privilege the shared memories of pain and pleasure, love and loss embedded in the beats to which they move. The original objective of the go-go music form was conceived to keep folks on the floor, as I mentioned earlier. The embodied beats are then the vehicle through which participants are positioned to engage what musicians believe to be a life-changing, spiritual message. Over the expansive musical experience the lyrics register for the participants. I call this process of calibration "sounded convergence." The process of sounded convergence is musicians' untidy negotiation of musical and sociotheological change as gospel and go-go cocreate gospel go-go. This merge produces significant implications for gospel go-go communities that resound the scene's impact throughout their social lives. I argue for a threefold interpretation of sounded convergence, the multifaceted expressions of these characteristics may or may not occur simultaneously:

1) Sounded convergence is a worship experience in which musicians probe the limits of sonic intensities through a metaphoric and tangible enactment of spiritual warfare and geo-political striving.
2) Sounded convergence is an aesthetic that asserts performed acoustic imperfection is holy and just.
3) Sounded convergence is a process of recollection, reshaping, and/or inversion of sociotheological identity constructs into new designations—a new life of peculiarity.

Sounded convergence is useful for unpacking the role of sonic intensity in live gospel go-go and other Christianized pop musics.

Before I go any further, I would like to address my deployment of sounded convergence to account for the musical and social energy in gospel go-go. With regard to musical calibration as gospel go-go musicians combine go-go and gospel, I note the wide range of sonic textures in the black live music soundscape: amplified-muffled speech and singing, thick percussion layers, clamorous qualities, and the inability to hear oneself or the lead vocalists as distinct from the ensemble. These are characteristics of what Olly Wilson has coined as the heterogeneous sound ideal. It is "a common approach to music making in which a kaleidoscopic range of dramatically contrasting qualities of sound (timbre) is sought after in both vocal and instrumental music. The desirable musical sound texture is one that contains a combination of diverse timbres."[47] While this kaleidoscopic range is sought after in black live music, the buzzy heavy percussion qualities are "balanced" when beats from black live music styles such as hip-hop, dub, reggae, or go-go are incorporated into pop musics produced for the global marketplace. By balanced I mean that the more tonal instruments—the vocalists, keyboard, guitars, and horns—are made more prominent in the mixing of recordings. When insider participants subsequently hear go-go beats performed in Christianized pop music, the product lacks the intoxicating or grimy qualities, to borrow from my interlocutor Dré. In other words, he perceives the music tracks as sounding dull, polished, sanitized, or mute due to the removal of the sonic intensity. Thus the erasure of buzz signifies the extent to which the groove has been manipulated for mass consumption.

In fact, Dré and Aaron mentioned that the texture of the grooves were essential in our interviews. I asked Dré to expound on the importance of the intense energy in the live music. As the interview progressed, I realized that he described the texture and quality of the beats in the following explanation:

> **Dré:** Back when Junk Yard Band started, there was a gospel go-go group called TLC, in the early 90s. They all had the PA sound—that live sound—that straight from the street sound. It wasn't polished like the music on the radio. It was the DC sound—we have loved that griminess so much. We have always been our own people. Actually, you would rarely see bands go into the studio. It was always a live recording. I love to hear the griminess on the track. It is the identifier of the DC sound . . . I personally like the imperfection. I like to hear some mess-ups on the track.

With regard to Dré's point about imperfection, buzziness is a long-standing culturally desirable quality in broader African ritual aesthetics. This African musical aesthetic informs my examination of the multisensory merge between the gospel and go-go dimensions of performance practice possibilities. Moreover, I argue that the buzziness combined with lyric indecipherability is held in tension with church leadership's modes of organizing sound to emphasize the primacy of the voice(s). Go-go sound engineers manage the audio feeds to balance the output, ensuring that the instrumentalists' levels are not too intense to cause human injury or blowout the sound system.

Ethnomusicological research explores the ways grooves and beats are deployed in order to create community through participation and collaboration.[48] Music scholars such as Charles Keil have struggled to assess the "groovy processes and mysterious textures" that are generated through black music in particular.[49] In response to Keil's quandary, Kyra Gaunt observed that such "black musics often are used in the service of 'healing' the ills of Western culture, or the separatism of black difference, but rarely is participation in these musics sought after to embrace black difference or to allow blacks themselves to freely express in predominantly white settings."[50] I propose to unlay the theoretical complexity of the multilayered nature of "groovy processes and mysterious textures" through the lens of black difference Gaunt evokes that is illustrated through freely expressed gospel go-go.

My research is also in conversation with noise discourses on the intersection of black popular musics, orality, and religiosity.[51] In addition, while there have been recent publications on nonreligious go-go with a nod to its gospel counterpart gospel go-go,[52] there has not been an in depth consideration of the tensions that emerge when African American Christian believers practice this gospel go-go music style. While groove theory literature considers the extent to which music induces transcendence, musical cooperation, and gestural synchrony, I go further by focusing on the extent to which musical intensity or sound techniques in live music are key ingredients of the grooves and a vehicle through which political and theological figures monitor youth consciousness.

The process of sounded convergence is enacted in both gospel and go-go social life, when they combine to make the gospel go-go subgenre. Though go-go is nonreligious and gospel is religious, their musical masculinities are not mutually exclusive when paired side by side. There is no tidy divide between the masculinities performed in the two scenes; however, there is an imagined manhood in both scenes toward which participants aspire. As gospel go-go musicians sociotheologically adjust, the gospel aesthetic undergoes, for example, a reshaping of the musical masculinities pervasive in gospel spheres through its merge with go-go. Gospel go-go participants characterize male gospel performers in church as effeminate, queer, soft, holy, believing, or boyish (church boy, choir boy, etc.). At the same time, the go-go aesthetic that musicians perform undergoes a sanctification of musical masculinities when it merges with gospel. Nonreligious go-go masculinities are described as salacious, hypersexual, hard, traumatized, criminal, doubting, and abusive. Thus the musical progeny—gospel go-go performers—are permitted to explore a spectrum of musical masculinities, including the more blurred constructs, that are straight, ex-gay, hypermasculine, delivered, aggressive, mannish, soft, and abstinent from substances and premarital sex. These religious and nonreligious musical masculinities are able to coexist within worship qua gospelized go-go. Musicians demonstrate in their presentations of identity the processes by which attendees proclaim, question, remember, fall from grace, and "get back up" or recover from the fall over the course of an event; however, participants are not limited to these processes. They are encouraged to resist conforming to either a churchy or streetwise identity.

Message: The Distinction Between Gospel Go-Go and Go-Go

To understand the gospel go-go sonority further, I will delve into the distinction between it and nonreligious go-go as conveyed by participants. When I asked advocate Rev. Tony Lee about the differentiation between go-go and gospel go-go, he explained, "It is the message," which is a rhetoric-centered emphasis that reinscribes the music scene as masculine like the preacher's pulpit.[53] The difference in gospel go-go is much like what Deborah Smith Pollard observes in holy hip-hop, "the difference is that the commitment comes packaged in cleverly worded lyrics and raps that not only reference the Holy Bible but that may also link them to a variety of historical, cultural, and popular images."[54] Rev. Tony Lee adds that through strategic musical evangelism youths are drawn in droves. Some gospel go-go band members attest that "the combination of gospel and go-go is an effective way to spread the Christian message to young teens . . . it is a way for kids to get the message of God and enjoy the music they love" (Gore 2005). The strategic attraction is connected to the musicians' ability to provide the gospel in an idiom that they can recognize—the heavy percussion.

Leaders and others apathetic to gospel go-go have argued that an aspect of being a believer is to be peculiar, set apart, consecrated, and markedly different from those who are outside the church. Christian youths are to exemplify transformation by shedding their cravings and tastes that are associated with nonreligious activities. Theologically their lack of interest in worldly activities signifies the change that God has made in their lives. Also, gospel go-go detractors argue that nonreligious go-go styles are characterized by the "beat" that musicians produce using heavy percussion. In this context, "beat" is used to describe the rhythmic patterns and layering that musicians perform during the live music events. Gospel go-go makes the good news palatable to those whose noise and fury have been silenced elsewhere. In fact, church leaders and go-go music figures have characterized gospel go-go as too similar to go-go. Go-go percussionist and Christian believer Buggy "The General" has even characterized the beats as harboring more than similar music styles. He describes them as sharing "familiar spirits." Familiar spirits is a biblical term that refers to supernatural sources of temptations, habits, associations, bondages, and vices with which people struggle. They avoid them to pursue a deeper relationship with God (Leviticus 19:31, 20:6, 20:27; Deuteronomy 18:11; 1 Samuel 28:3, 9; 2 Kings 21:6, 23:24; 2 Chronicles 33:6; Isaiah 8:19, 19:3). Familiar spirits are a threat to a believer's maintenance of a pleasing relationship with God. Buggy who is credited with a lot of the popular go-go beats while playing for legendary go-go band Backyard Band and touring with R&B artist Raheem DeVaughn. He added, "When I made up those beats, I was not thinking about God. There was a difference for me between work and worship. [laughs] Yeah, I was not thinking about God." Fellow Percussionist and music minister Larry "Stomp" Atwater translated Buggy's comment, "He was thinking about the girls shaking their booty."[55] In other words, Buggy associates the rhythmic configurations he composed with the ways in which he was able to provoke the female participants to exert themselves through their danced responses to percussion calls. Another professional go-go percussionist and music minister confessed to me that he cannot regularly attend worship where go-go is incorporated. He needed a break. The style stirred up for him too many memories, associations or familiar spirits (i.e., carefree sexual behavior, marijuana use) from which he had been delivered. He did not want to struggle with the sensory memory in his worship, where he believed his focus should be on getting a message from God.

If the message is what distinguishes gospel go-go from nonreligious go-go, there remains the ironic negotiation of the shared musical feature of heavy percussion that impedes clear hearing of the message that is supposed to make gospel go-go appropriate. I notice that gospel go-go is distinct from conventional gospel that privileges vocal music, a domain that is frequently queered and feminized. Gospel go-go prioritizes both heavy instrumentation and talking in lower ranges, which are both culturally masculine domains. The vocalists' message is enveloped in layers of "beats." It is hard to hear the talker or the vocalists' lyrics and melodies. The more resonant components, the percussion and the bass line, are dominant in the performance. Because the go-go music aesthetic is based on covering popular songs or go-go rhythm patterns, new and unusual participants are drawn into the gospel go-go venues because of the familiar beat and not the message.

Gospel go-go musicians apply a layering of shared musical memory, combining praise and worship with core go-go beats, that draws from existing material as well. More seasoned Christians are familiar with the songs musicians cover and are able to sing along from memory. Musicians share the burden of discipling new converts by creating an atmosphere where participants become engrafted into the community through music-centered information exchange. Within go-go culture, rappers and talkers (who perform a similar function as rappers) like Dré are responsible for teaching visitors Christian values over the course of or series of event(s). From their perch, they instruct attendees on what the rules are in the gathering. Much like go-go, familiarity with participants is cultivated as talkers like Dré "shout out" or verbally acknowledge fans or family. Engaged newcomers seek, ask, and listen to their neighbors for the message that the vocalists are performing. The regular attendees who know the repertoire convey the message through shouted speech and corresponding dancing over the loud (dynamically intense) music. This engrafting is also an easy way for participants to memorize and embody the texts. After events participants hang out, eat, and invite each other to their churches or youth events. Gospel go-go encounters are merely a gateway to other trendy youth activities.

The Message of Peculiarity

While gospel go-go is comprised of elements that might attract men to worship, gospel go-go musicians pride themselves in being independent and mobile outside of church walls. They are disinterested in assimilating into conventional church culture. In 2009, Christian go-go music band Peculiar People (P dot P)[56] signed with the former management team of national go-go music sensation Mambo Sauce, best known for their single "Welcome to DC." I observed Peculiar People when they performed at churches and on college campuses in the Washington, DC area. I asked Dré to describe who was drawn to Peculiar People's performances. As he said:

> Young urban, hood men and youth go to the go-go. It is a male-dominated space. Man, for real. Not all men like praise teams and choirs . . . For real! It really is the energy, man. I believe that is what attracts the young men, and really urban, hood youth. It is the men who they see on stage. It is usually the men that they grew up with performing up there . . . They see themselves on that stage. It is the energy, the live sound that attracts men. That is what makes it so intimate because we come from where they come from. That is why they come, to hear their friends. Then they learn about Christ, as they see how passionate we are about the message.

Acknowledging the male dominance of the musical space, Dré claims that male attendees prefer to see their reflection on stage, supporting their friends as the actual performers. He maintains that the live sound energy attracts men. According to Dré, the percussion registers as masculine and "aggressive" to participants. This percussive accompaniment complements an intense vocal stylistic approach. The men sing and speak in various vocal ranges—from high to low. The lead talker is, generally a speaker using their lower range or bass timbre and the singer, tends to sing in a higher range or treble timbre. Go-go style performers use vocal "attack" techniques such as growls, screams, and yells that span the entire continuum of the conventionally male gendered vocal range and affect.

Peculiar People's message of being peculiar is a gestural and rhetorical articulation of social and theological convergence and an embrace of nonconformity.

High Hat	X	X		X	X	X		X	X	X		X	X	X		X
Snare		X				X				X				X		
Bass Drum	X		X		X		X		X		X		X		X	

Figure 4.1 Go-go "pocket beat" rhythm dictation by Alisha Lola Jones.

They perform peculiarity as a distancing of oneself from worldly influence and practicing critical thought about traditional Christianity. They start the song using a go-go "pocket beat" in 4/4 time that is represented in the Time Unit Box System (TUBS) with X indicating the pulse to be played (see Figure 4.1). As with all go-go rhythms, improvisation is performed, subject to various doubled and syncopated rhythm combinations within this structure:

I have attended several gospel go-gos, where they performed their popular song "Peculiar 'Til I D.I.E." It is so popular that as soon as the beat to the song "drops" or the groove starts, the crowd chants "D-I-E." Then the talker Dré calls out, "Peculiar 'til I . . . " The crowd continues, "D-I-E." Musically eclectic, Peculiar People incorporates praise and worship, hip-hop, and rock, among other styles. From the beginning of the song, the percussive accompaniment is "locked in the pocket" (the moment when participants achieve and stay in a "good" groove), as it simmers with Dré or Warchild's (rapper) vocal call and response. It is secured with the signature percussion roux of rototoms, timbale, drum set, bongo, conga, and cymbal instrumentation. I find that their expression of peculiarity is coded as a performance of streetwise African American Christian masculinity that is courageous, rambunctious, independent, and consecrated. The lyrics are as follows:

> Ay!
> Peculiar 'Til I D.I.E.
> Peculiar 'Til I D.I.E.
> Peculiar 'Til I D.I.E.
> Peculiar 'Til I D.I.E. (repeat)
>
> Peculiar 'Til I D.I.E., yeah no lie,
> Forever will I cry. (repeat 4x)
>
> They say we unusual
> That we plan to die before the funeral
> Atypical, we go against the norm
> We go against your form.
> We will not conform to the rules and regulations

That you got from your moms
And that she got from her moms,
Her grandma, who got it from her grandma
—the list just goes on.

They sayin' that we wrong,
Just notice that we do a lot of things
Because we heard it in a song.
(Where the truth at?)

What the text say
Are we following God?
Or are we walking just because we heard the pastor say,
"Follow me, we gotta do it this way."
That ain't peculiar at all,
Please practice your faith.

The next time that they step up in your face,
Just rock how you wanna rock
Praise how you wanna praise.[57]

At a glance, Peculiar People's "Peculiar 'Til I D.I.E." is the typical signature song of a go-go band, describing the characteristics of this particular band. It also serves as their creed; in the same manner traditional black churches list their confession of faith in their bulletin. "Peculiar 'Til I D.I.E." advocates for a peculiarity that may be interpreted in several ways: a biblical narrative, a critique of "church boys," and a Christianized street credibility. They consciously herald an interpretation of biblical Christian radicalism that stands as a corrective to the mainstream, salacious messages of go-go. This radicalism binds youthful, social, and religious peculiarity with the practice of holiness, consistency, and commitment until they die. It hearkens to the biblical vision of a *peculiar* people who are obedient to the voice of God. Peculiar people are treasured and chosen by God because of their courage in privileging God's voice above humans' voice (Exodus 19:5; Deuteronomy 14:2; 26:18; Titus 2:14; 1 Peter 2: 19). Peculiar People encourages listeners to witness and model their public demonstration of questioning church leaders and proclaiming God. D-I-E is an allusion to believers' aspiration toward discipline, to die daily to their flesh or carnal urges (1 Corinthians 15:31).

Peculiar People's creed acknowledges they identify in various ways. They are Washington, DC metropolitan youths dealing with urban hassles and microaggressions,[58] while grasping for a Christian hope. According to Dré, fans deal with hassles such as the requirement of permission slips for under age participants during curfew periods and the off-duty police presence required for the events in churches. This social and religious intersectionality is dealt with musically in the performance. Peculiar People fashions a place where enthusiasts envision their unique place in the world. Peculiar People promotes hope, resistance, marginality, and the "getting ignorant" posturing that it shares with traditional Washington, DC go-go music tropes, but there are gender and geo-class stakes within their peculiarity.

In this worship context, Peculiar People and their fans do not succumb to the institutional pressure to conform to what preachers say. Traditional gospel music is filled with hierarchical imagery and language: patriarchal (presumably male preachers) and maternal (natural mothers and leaders referred to as "church mothers"). Peculiar People's critical assessment of pastors (presumably chief male/father figure) and mothers within the "Peculiar 'Til I D-I-E" gospel go-go song narrative is noteworthy. Their message of autonomy in practicing one's faith, apart from the influence of even "the mothers of the church" is not typically endorsed in charismatic Christianity.[59] Mothers are perceived as organic Christian educators (lay ministers, Sunday school teachers, intercessors, bible study leaders, and priestesses of the single-parent home) and iconic moral models (Jones 2014). In removing theological intermediaries, they disrupt a social order that is organized by age, gender, household leadership, and church office rank. In addition, P dot P's irreverence disrupts broader sociocultural understandings of respectability politics. Peculiar People's message fosters critical thought about passively accepting church leadership's dogma. Gospel go-go participants truth-tell and confess sins that would be impermissible in a church service.

Like non-religious go-go bands, Peculiar People resides somewhere in-between church and street credibility, not wholly situated in either camp. On the one hand, plenty of gospel go-go musicians still have worldly habits like smoking, drinking, and premarital sex. They also launch their critique toward the "churchy" men who are fixated on church tradition, appropriate speech (see chapter 1), gesture (see chapter 2), attire, and attendance. Gospel participants in general convey gendered notions about men as they observe participants' "churchiness." For example, a "churchy" young man is referred to as "church boy" and never as a "church man." Referring to a male as a "church boy" suggests the perception that intense church participation diminishes one's manhood. As I set forth in chapter 2, for a boy or man to go to church and vocally perform is perceived to be feminine, submissive, and an repulsion to God and mankind. Popular gospel musician and producer Kirk Franklin, who as I mentioned has incorporated go-go styles in his music, reflected on this term in his autobiography:

> I think that another reason I got into so much trouble with sexual temptations during those years was that I was trying to fight my "image." I didn't talk about

my church activities very much at school, but some of the kids found about them and started teasing me. They called me "Church Boy."

I didn't mind so much when they called me "Church Boy." But they also called me "Mama's Boy" and started making jokes that I was gay, and that was painful. In the church, especially the African-American church during the seventies and eighties, homosexuality was a big problem. It still is in some places.[60]

Through Franklin's account, we learn that "church boy," "mama's boy," and I would add "*choir* boy"[61] are terms meant to call into question the sexuality and manhood of male participants. "Choir boy" is a term that has conventionally connoted one's sheltered life. I have observed that "choir boy" has been appropriated to characterize male musical (often obligatory) participation in music ministry. Its use in black church settings describes the gender rich metaphoric perception of musical participation. All the aforementioned terms (mama's boy, church boy, and choir boy) have been generated from narratives about how black single mothers or female head of households make church participation obligatory for black youths, especially males. Several gospel go-go musicians have described a feminine masculine choir director who has stuck out in their memories of church attendance. In addition, they expressed that they distanced themselves from churches where they are required to wear a suit and tie. When performing "nonchurchy" masculinity in gospel go-go, men are permitted to wear t-shirts and jeans. They can be demonstrative in a way that furthers a conventional muscular Christianity image.

The Posture of War and Getting Ignorant

Practicing a masculine undignified praise in a gospel go-go context is a performance similar to Reginald Williamson's defeminized church vision to gather men who are poised for battle, shared in this text's introduction. It is characterized by uniqueness, aggressiveness, accessibility, and openness to modes of entrancement induced by the groove. Somehow gospel go-go band Peculiar People has carved a space, fashioned a sound, proclaimed a robust message, and received invitations from faith communities and open-mics up and down the east coast to perform at their youth, college, and church events. Dré asserted that a large part of their appeal to audiences outside of Washington, DC is the "aggressive" and "masculine" nature of the music style that they perform. We find in Peculiar People's Christian go-go music an engagement with the street life that is absent from mainstream gospel music topics.

In the interviews I conducted with Dré, he also revealed that fans appreciated the spectrum of emotions that are performed in this male space.[62] A range of emotions that were not associated with black urban hypermasculinity in the popular US imagination. Gospel go-go bands weaved together the go-go beats (rhythmic patterns) and popular song covers as their rappers, talkers, and vocalists divulged deeply personal details of their developing faith, while navigating issues like urban hassles, loss, suspicion, and fatherlessness. They shared in an affirming community that is also focused on getting closer to God. Dré explained,

> To be honest with you we have a lot of our songs that we used to play kind of catch people off guard. Because as Peculiar People, we try to be more real to life. Not just real to life but transparent, man, in how we are, when it comes to the spirit. That just is being real and transparent. So, it kind of catches people off guard at churches.

Musicians deploy creative go-go grooves and beats to engage accounts of urban hassles, pain, and pleasure. "Real to life" meant staying connected to and clear about the contentious roots of go-go culture. It is truth telling. In fact, participants also describe the gospel go-go topic options as more "true to life." According to gospel go-go attendees that I chatted with at Peculiar People's performance at Ebenezer A.M.E. in Fort Washington, MD, the topics that are addressed within the worship are more relatable than the issues discussed within the worship services they attend at church. The gospel presented in go-go grooves signifies a musical forum for theological seekers to question, sense, believe, transition into, and urge Christian discipleship. It is also a space for new converts to develop a personalized theological meaning at their own paces. After their participation in an accessible gospel on Saturday night, gospel go-go enthusiasts forego church worship services on Sunday morning. They pursue this sense of authenticity in worship with an undisturbed groove.

Gospel go-go manager Preston Cobbs once said in an interview, "Because go-go is a music that was born in the streets, it's the streets that call for the go-go."[63] Gospel go-go participants combat the lure of the streets by turning their sights to how "unchurched" people who are familiar with church culture or newly converted Christians practice their faith.

> **Dré:** For the most part its been like a college day or a young people day or open mics, we've done that huh—crazy right? Our particular brand of music is kind of different. So, people are more receptive to the way we do it in terms of worship—not worship but more intimate songs.

In this comment, Dré suggests that they demonstrate a unique performance of intimacy with God. If we follow attendees' popular perceptions, it is peculiar to witness street credible men passionately perform closeness to God in a manner that is socially acceptable. Peculiar People's appearance and performance resembles young men that one might pass in so-called working-class, dangerous Southeast Washington, but they worship with a transparency that breaks down numerous stereotypes about African American men's capacity to unabashedly worship.

Alisha Jones (AJ): What is the experience like to go into these different cities with this type of music?

Dré: The experience? To be honest with you, we've played in churches and we've played in schools, colleges and stuff like that, out of town. And for the most part we are so . . . just excited about the energy of the music.

Huh, and that [fans] are like, "Wow what is this?" So, it really has been a good experience. A welcoming experience, to put it like that. And then just, the energy that comes with it and the passion that is behind it.

One should note the transferred go-go practice of covering Christianized pop songs. The practice of covering popular songs is a source of tension within the conventions of the genre and is one of the reasons go-go music is unable to traverse the local music scene. I asked Dré if Peculiar People covered top 10 hits to draw crowds that like go-go music. He assured me that while they do covers paying homage to go-go, pop, and Christian musics, they strive to create original music that is true to the musical intensity of the gospel go-go style.

Undignified praise also recalls the streetwise notion of "getting ignorant," as Elijah Anderson has observed, in order for young men to demonstrate courage, agency, and brawn in public space. In this case, it is middle-class black men's code-switching among other blacks, along the lines of geo-class identification. Their social versatility is indicative of a shared anxiety about adequately belonging to go-go street culture. "Getting ignorant" contrasts "respectability politics" that we briefly considered in chapter 2. Elijah Anderson explains street credibility as a way of being streetwise, through his interview with his informant Thomas Waters:

> The "street" repertoire of such individuals includes the strategy of "getting ignorant," which they invoke in conversations with others and enact in public to deal with supposed adversaries. "Getting ignorant" is taken to mean getting down to the level of a street-oriented person and capably adopting the supposed behavior of underclass blacks who would engage in loud talk and profanity and if necessary violence to deal with a public dispute . . . In the words of middle-class blacks, the posture and behavior Thomas Waters assumed is "getting ignorant," and because of caste behavior, such individuals can sometimes act out the script

rather convincingly. It is just this ability to switch codes situationally, going back and forth between middle-class propriety and an assumed "street" orientation, that allows many middle-class blacks to feel less nervous and constructed in public than their white counterparts.[64]

Originally, go-go musicians were from Southeast Washington, DC's black working class. The patrons were from all the quadrants in Washington, DC, including middle to upper middle blacks from Prince George's County. As participants of a subgenre of go-go music, gospel go-go musicians still feel the pressure to get ignorant or prove one's authentic go-go posture, "mean mug"[65] facial expressions, and credibility that is rooted in go-go musicians' working-class Washington, for example. When gospel go-go bands perform for festivals such as the National Council of Negro Women, Inc.'s annual Black Family Reunion, some fans have sneered until they heard the bands play.[66] In their performances, gospel go-go participants do not use profanity or are violent but they demonstrate the potential to be aggressive through their performance style. In order to reach the street oriented person, gospel go-go musicians get ignorant in gesture and posture to convey their identification with other underclass black people, who are perceived as thugs.[67]

Musicians do so, for example, by paying homage to various crews and neighborhoods through the lead talker's shout outs in their music to continue the go-go tradition. Dré stated, "The reason we put on hoods and we put on different sets in Washington, DC and Maryland and all that stuff—that's to show 'em love. That's like a unity type thing there, '152, 25, Uptown, Southside'—all that." When go-go rappers and talkers quote numbers in that manner, they are referring to go-go participants' date of death to pay homage.[68] "Uptown" and "Southside" are references to the neighborhoods of the participants who attend the go-go event. Dré is careful to acknowledge the shared memory of the death that looms in the air within the go-go music tradition. The musicians' facilitation of parties has broader implications for black youth's use of music to cope with loss by remembering those who have passed away. They pay homage to go-go participants who have died. The noisemaking in gospel/go-go music culture is a medium through which participants lament, wail, and mourn loss.

In many ways, as contemporary youths participate in gospel go-go music and movement, they undo the real and imagined fetters of remnant *Black Code* legislation that impacts their Christian religio-cultural life. When churches and community organizations refuse to host gospel go-gos, they remain outside of a culturally relevant ritual domain for recovery from trauma. The gospel go-go musicians create a party atmosphere where attendees are provided with space to exhibit potential for "getting ignorant" in social interactions.[69] Gospel go-go is concurrently preparation for spiritual and street warfare. To love go-go is to engage dialog about the uncertainty of one's mortality. No longer being afraid to die, but deciding to live right now. To love gospel go-go is to explore the certainty of life after death.

At the concerts, gospel go-go musicians are able to facilitate a complex negotiation of identities, a mixture of both African American Christian denominations and black socioeconomic statuses that might not otherwise occur in a nonreligious go-go event.[70] I have found that this particular convergence of multiple black identities within worship settings is an untapped field of inquiry. While there are some church leaders willing to have bands perform for alternative services, musician struggled with leaders to strategize about their collective ministry goals for the events and offer insight on retaining visitors. According to one of the musicians, some youth pastors hire the bands to "babysit their youth" and do not adequately pay bands. It is not so much that the band members are good at childcare but I presume that church leaders tap into the group's performed potentiality for "getting ignorant" or demonstrating street credibility to discipline and placate their youth.

Similar to the events Glenn Hinson observed of North Carolina sanctified music events in *Fire In My Bones* (2000), gospel go-go events function as services, even though the organizers do not always label them as such. The gospel go-go "altar calls" or moments during the events where participants are receptive to and publicly acknowledge conversion into Christianity bring in so many new converts that the local Christian community has noticed gospel go-go musicians' effectiveness.[71]After the altar calls, sometimes there are ministers or chaperones who speak with the new converts and give them information about finding a "church home," typically recommending that they visit the host church or ministry of the gospel go-go. It is interesting to note that several gospel go-go bands are formed by new Christian converts and amateur musicians, who want to continue the same sort of high-energy parties that they attended in nonreligious nightclubs. Seasoned go-go musician Buggy is concerned that musicians who put "gospel" in front of go-go styles are not doing the work to "crank" (do good go-go music) and get taught Christian principles. For the lead talker Dré, gospel go-go events became his alternative youth service where he could perform conflict resolution.

There are moments when some gospel go-go musicians claim the groove must be disturbed. Church leaders have expressed concern regarding the meanings attached to the beats and the traditional embodied responses to that music. Go-go music is associated with sensuous, suggestive, and arousing body-to-body movement such as grinding between two or more dance partners. Such movement and close contact is considered unbefitting believers in a worship service. Although physical intimacy is not encouraged at gospel go-go concerts, occasionally there are uninformed new attendees that move as though they are in a nightclub.[72]

For example, later in that evening sketched earlier in this chapter, on the stage of The Complex, the lead talker takes off his damp white v-neck t-shirt, wipes his face with it and reveals his singlet t-shirt underneath. He climbs onto the speakers and starts to proclaim. He stands with his feet shoulder width apart, hands clenched at his side, hips swaying, head bobbing, and surveys the crowd. And with his right hand he sweeps the mic close to his mouth. The music breaks and he yells, "Let's rock!" People start jumping right away and some can beat their feet to the go-go "bounce beat." I see the lead talker looks over at someone on the side and then quickly glance at the back of the crowd. Just like that two middle-aged women and a large man in his thirties rush into the crowd. A couple had started to grind together. One of the middle-aged women put her arm around the young lady, while the man took the young guy aside. The woman chaperone says to the young lady, "This is a gospel go-go. We don't dance like that here." The young lady and man said that they didn't know and that they heard the music next door. They must've heard the bounce beats at the rink and decided to join the party. The woman chaperone then hugs the young lady, pulls her and her male friend aside to chat further. The beat continues. I looked at my cell phone and it was about 11:00 p.m. The talker, who observed the resolved exchange from his perch on the speaker, then shouts, "Praise Harder! Praise Harder!" A vocalist screams in response, "Hey! Hey!" They say together, "We've got two hours to go, Let's rock!" Through various methods, the gospel go-go musicians manage believers' fears that partaking in the performance of go-go beats will corrupt them. Some musicians have talked about the conflict between focusing on lyric intelligibility and the prominence of the groove. In the preceding scenario, the couple responded to the "bounce beat" rhythm that Northeast Groover go-go band drummer Larry "Stomp" Atwater characterizes as a newer imitation of traditional go-go rhythms. Go-go "bounce beat" emphasizes every pulse in 4/4 time (Figure 4.2). In the TUBS graph of four beats shown, X represents a beat or pulse, "H" represents a higher pitch, and "L" represents a lower pitch in a percussion set. There are variations of these combinations over the duration of songs.

All the beats are played with various toned percussions. Some gospel go-go musicians want their fans to feel the groove more. They want the beat to be

High Hat	X	X	X	X	X	X	X	X	X	X	X	X	X	X	X	X
Rototoms	H	L	H	L	H	L	H	L	H	L	H	L	H	L	H	L
Cowbells	L	H	L	H	L	H	L	H	L	H	L	H	L	H	L	H
Bongos	H	L	H	L	H	L	H	L	H	L	H	L	H	L	H	L
Congas	L	H	L	H	L	H	L	H	L	H	L	H	L	H	L	H
Bass	X	X	X	X	X	X	X	X	X	X	X	X	X	X	X	X
Bass Drum	X	X	X	X	X	X	X	X	X	X	X	X	X	X	X	X

Figure 4.2 Go-go "bounce beat" rhythm dictation by Alisha Lola Jones.

embodied and reverberate. On the other hand, according to sound engineer Aaron Hope, gospel go-go bands such as Submission Band and Peculiar People have focused on lyrical intelligibility using repetitive anthems and chants, encouraging keyboardists and guitarists to suspend their parts temporarily, and having vocalists highlight words through their microphone techniques.

Gospel go-go musicians who use these musical strategies achieve intelligibility and change the traditional, "dirty" go-go sound. I asked Dré about how Peculiar People navigates the allure of the beats to attract new and unusual participants at the gospel go-go events. He was pastoral as he described how he doesn't want the listeners to just get caught up in the groove or entranced. Dré's colleague Stomp attested that one of the techniques he appreciated most about Peculiar People is that they stop the music or do a music break removing layers of heavy percussion and make the participants absorb to what they proclaim, in an effort to help them focus on worshipping and not just partying. Dré's response also exemplified his management of the musical intensity through musical breaks.

Dré: I know, I know being the leader of the band, I'm intentional about stopping the music and letting people hear what we are saying, bringing it back, especially at churches.
AJ: Why do you do that?
Dré: Why do I do that? 'Cause I know that the music in and of itself, that people can get lost in the music, in go-go music. They can just get lost in it like, like in the beat, in the congas, in everything that's going on. Because there's so many instruments that's going on, at the same time, I look out at that crowd and I can see people getting lost in it. Huh, and I think that because we're not just a regular go-go band, we're a Christian go-go band, its important that you catch what we're saying. I literally like to stop the music, repeat what we're saying, or anything that I think people are not getting or just try to bring out the song a little bit more. And then when I bring it back and they catch the words, then they're like "oh, yes!" And so now they see everything that's going on, on top of the words . . . Yes, I think its something that they have never heard before.

When Dré said, "they can just get lost in it," he was referring to the tendency to get entranced or to have transcendent experiences, when they explore their emotions and get physically locked in the expanded ritual of repeated music accompaniment and sonic stimulation over time. Citing Gilbert Rouget's work on music and trance,[73] ethnomusicologist Judith Becker writes,

Trance is practiced within a communal framework, is usually accompanied by music and often involves strenuous activity on the part of the trancer.

Institutionalized, religious trancing takes places with a context of sensual over-stimulation; the trancer is bombarded with arresting sights and sounds.[74]

Gospel go-go events are expansive, lasting for hours with songs that last over twenty minutes. They are strenuous in that most participants dance the entire time. Audiences are bombarded with sound techniques (i.e., distortion and feedback), instrumentation (heavy percussion), and vocal styles (i.e., low vocal register, growls, and ululation) in close quarters and close contact with other participants. Even though there is a sensuality at the events that distract participants, Peculiar People aspired to make sure their audiences walk away from the event with a clear message. This aspiration is consistent with local senior pastor and gospel go-go enthusiast, Rev. Tony Lee's sentiment that the most prized difference about gospel go-go is the message. The trendy beats draw the youth, but musicians must cut through the musical layers to get their attention during the performance.

Gospel Go-Go Griminess in the Sanctuary

Some Washington, DC–area pastors have made a space for gospel go-go musicians, but very few have managed to provide musicians with agency and mobility that is true to go-go culture. Rev. Tony Lee has what go-go musician insider's describe as the appropriate building facility for gospel go-go's musical intensity. This gospel go-go church holds services in the Iverson Mall of Hillcrest Heights, Maryland. Iverson Mall is located where the socioeconomic borders of the oft-disenfranchised Southeast Washington, DC black people and affluent Prince George's County black people ebb and tide. This African Methodist Episcopal church (A.M.E.), Community of Hope (COH) was started in the Legend Restaurant & Night Club (and strip club), with a sheet covering the bar. On Resurrection Sunday April 16, 2006, Rev. Tony Lee, who has been referred to as a John the Baptist and tradition outlier in ministry, started the first go-go church. Over the past decade, Peculiar People has been featured in worship services and recordings made at COH. Most churches do not have the instrumentation or sound equipment for proper gospel go-go performance. Bands that regularly play at COH utilize the sound engineers who are members and able to navigate the band backline and equipment requirements[75] and balance the sound. Rev. Lee has been esteemed as "the first gospel go-go and holy hip-hop pastor" by GospelGo-Go411.com. Since Community of Hope was established, Rev. Lee has worked with local leaders and the go-go Coalition to stop the violence[76] with the Behind the Beat go-go conference.[77] He has created a space, where go-go enthusiasts can promote love and enjoy safety, party, God-talk, and hope.

So, standing six feet two inches, with shoulder-length cornrows, and in his uniform of a t-shirt and jeans, Rev. Tony Lee and his Street Team meet the people where they are, descending upon Washington, DC nightlife, educating club-goers about HIV/AIDS, how to stop the violence, and teaching hope. Rev. Lee oversees a ministry of touring go-go musicians and vocalists who sojourn from as far away as New York and North Carolina to worship regularly on Sundays in their professional go-go music style service.

While faith leaders over the years have allowed gospel go-go musicians to use their space for infrequent weekend and nighttime youth events,[78] COH is the first church that has incorporated gospel go-go, along with other African American Christian music styles, into their regular Sunday liturgy in the main sanctuary. Informed by his experience as a youth minister of Ebenezer A.M.E. church (one of the pioneering churches to welcome gospel go-go into their sanctuary) and their excursions to The Complex (the aforementioned closed gospel go-go location of the early 2000s), Rev. Lee knows the potential impact of an edifice where go-go enthusiasts can praise in a manner that they understand. He claims that at these gospel go-go events, a large volume of young people would have conversion experiences that were unparalleled in regular morning worship. When The Complex became defunct in early 2006, there was no longer a venue where young people could "come as they were" to worship God. In the spring of 2006 COH was established as a timely response, promising no condemnation to hopeful go-go enthusiasts in their worship service welcome statement: "It doesn't matter when you did it, where you did it, how you did it, or if you woke up this morning doing it—this is a place where everybody has a chance."

COH has provided support for go-go and gospel go-go musicians to create a place where *everybody has a chance*. In 2009, they opened their doors to a four year-old band called Peculiar People, for their album release party. COH is a gospel go-go ally. A banner that read "The Year of the Turn Around . . . Community of Hope AME Church" hung behind them, on the stage, as they partied in the filled-to-capacity, storefront (mall-front) sanctuary of the church. In this sanctuary, they were able to play their grooves: Backyard Band's iconic "the unibomber beat," pocket beats, socket beats, and the newer bounce beats. They were permitted to dance, to soften the posture, to strengthen, and to worship. Like a regular go-go, the lights were turned down—basically off—or at least there was a dimmed lighting effect for the event.

Gospel go-go musicians practice their nonconforming faith in alternative locations, somewhere between church and the streets. In this chapter I have examined the extent to which gospel go-go musicians have carved a space, fashioned a sound, and proclaimed a robust message in a male-coded musical language that is attractive to DC-area black males youths. Gospel go-go musicians act as intermediaries between the street and the church, performing messages and enjoying the same beats that "worked out" their urban hassles, pain, and pleasure. Such discourses are tied to a legacy of controlling black youth's recreation and religious life, perceiving their participation through a lens of threat. Gospel go-go musicians deliberately tap into musical masculinities in a manner that shifts public perceptions of black male emotional capacity. That ability to attract young men and transform their lives is sought in communities where black male absenteeism is being evaluated. However, gospel go-go continues to be exploited and overlooked as a resource, because of the stigma associated with gathering young black men together. Their musical gifts are both attractive and despised. Participants epitomize the sacrality of the profane and the profanity of the sacred connecting similar people, style, and grooves, while the religious music is crafted to help young people find and practice their faith on their own terms. While there are fans and musicians who desire a separation between Friday or Saturday nightlife and Sunday morning worship, participants with whom I spoke seek ways of partying, being stylish, and having genuine expression about the sociocultural issues alienating them from God and deterring them from traditional church attendance.

In the next chapter, I consider what happens when gospel musicians embrace the queerness associated with the flamboyant choir director trope and actually disclose their queer identity. I delve into Tonex's controversial shaping of alternative, intangible spaces using a spectrum of encoded language that resists a hegemonic, muscular Christian image. Much like gospel go-go musicians, this preacher-musician embeds messages into his music and rhetorics in idiomatic SGL language and musical styles that black queer believers recognize. He diverges from his Pentecostal Christian organization's heteropatriarchal scripts and uses music to perform queerness in the public square in a manner that is unabashedly delivered from the opinions of other believers.

5

"Wired"

(De)Coding Tonéx's Unapologetic
Queer Body Theology

There was a lot of buzz among students at Howard University and in the media about Anthony C. Williams, also known as B.Slade or Tonéx, and his September 2013 performance at the Howard Theater's Gospel Brunch. Some students oppose his gospel brunch billing because his openly gay identity is contrary to their prohibitive biblical stance on homosexuality. The news of opposition to an openly gay gospel performer evokes prayerful support from his fans over social media throughout the week. Yet when I arrive to the venue on Sunday just before 11 a.m., I see no protesters. There is only a short line of people with a few DC gospel musician colleagues taking up the rear.

As usual, the seating is first-come, first-served, and recordings of the gospel greats the Clark Sisters, Fred Hammond, and Vanessa Bell Armstrong are playing in the theater house. Shortly after we sit, we are offered an all-you-can-eat brunch buffet. Just after 1 p.m. we hear, wafting from behind the veil of the stage curtain, Anthony C. Williams singing Richard Smallwood's "Total Praise." As the song progresses, the orchestral accompaniment is layered. Even though "Total Praise" was originally composed and recorded as a choir piece, numerous soloists such as Fantasia[1] have covered the song, tailoring it to their signature vocal approach.[2] At the end of the song, the curtains lift and Williams poses at the microphone stand as the crowd erupts in applause. He then sings, "He's Not Dead, He's Alive," from *Out the Box* (2004)[3] a selection that pays homage to the Jackson 5 by sampling the funky brass horn riff from the chorus of "Dancing Machine" (1973). He performs the reprise of the song and signifies on resurrection and mummies, as he does the Egyptian style or "King Tut" dance.[4] Three DC-based male background vocalists, Jeremy Lloyd, Clifton Ross III, and Jason Paul, accompany him: he calls this ensemble the "Vocal Ninjaz." The one-hour set includes hit gospel tracks from Williams's Tonéx catalogue: "Work on Me," "Make Me Over,"[5] "God Has Not 4got."[6] He also includes the classic hymn "I Need Thee Every Hour" by Annie Sherwood Hawks (1835–1918).

The manner with which Williams performs gives me the sense that we are located in a different arena, perhaps Jericho City of Praise in Landover, MD or the Verizon Center in Washington, DC, much larger venues in the area. As

Flaming? Alisha Lola Jones, Oxford University Press (2020). © Oxford University Press.
DOI: 10.1093/oso/9780190065416.001.0001

Williams sings, he makes large gestures, peering intently into the theater house, as though gazing into a football stadium sized crowd. He ends the set with a new song titled "Quench" and demonstrates his virtuosic Pentecostal tambourine playing skills. He beats it with his elbow, palm, and back of the hand. He rapidly sings at the vamp, "Stop quenching the Spirit! Stop quenching the Spirit!"[7] Williams exhorts that there needs to be a revival. All of a sudden he tosses the tambourine—in the manner of a "mic toss"—into the crowd. A female friend, who he later acknowledges in the show, catches the tambourine and continues the accompaniment that Williams is playing. Williams's song "Quench" gives the audience a foretaste of his new gospel album that he announces will be released in May 2014. This concert signifies that Anthony C. Williams is resurrected, "born again," as a gospel performer. He is making music on his own terms, as an openly gay Christian artist. Despite all of the protest beforehand, fans and latent detractors were more invested in witnessing what promised to be an entertaining return to the gospel music industry.

Preacher and musician Rev. Anthony C. Williams, III, popularly known as Tonéx, is an emerging icon in popular music because he embodies long-standing tensions and contradictions concerning queerness and African-American Christian identity in gospel music social networks. Throughout his Grammy nominated 2009 recording, *Unspoken,* the artist Tonéx explores the queer practices and intimacies that he contends are embedded in Pentecostal Christianity. Although these practices are not *openly* discussed—either in African-American Christian churches or on gospel recordings—his gospel performances as an openly gay man illustrate the self-disclosure toward which Tonéx believes all Christians should strive. At work in Tonéx's self-disclosure strategy are the performative transactions of his inhabiting, traversing, dismantling, and blurring the boundaries between the rhetorical domain of the pulpit, the vocal domain of the choir loft and platform, the instrumental domain of the musicians' pit and the participant-observers' domain of the audience or congregation.

Through the depiction of stories that have been classified as inappropriate, Tonéx advocates for a less sexually restrictive performance of faith, while challenging the "don't ask, don't tell" social contract in Pentecostal communities. "Don't ask, don't tell" reinforces the stigmatization of queer believers as leading double lives because they are shamed into non-disclosure. Adopting a queer listening, viewing, and recalling attuned to same-gender meanings, Tonéx's performances are read as a polysemous interpretation of "authentic worship," one that reveals a queer critique without jarring the prevailing heteronormative worldview in Pentecostal settings. Moreover, the polysemous meanings go undetected by those who are ignorant of or indifferent to queer ways of being. By examining "Wired" from Williams's last album under the Tonéx stage name,

I argue that men who desire men or discreetly have sex with other men have been conveying who they are in multivalent gospel performance, while Christian participants who subscribe to heteronormative constructs may be unaware of or even willfully oblivious to their modes of self-identification. The queer perspective presented in "Wired" and other tracks on the *Unspoken* album complicate the aural-visual trope of the flamboyant choir director who functions as a consumable cultural product of gospel music performance. The flamboyant choir director is traditionally derided for emoting and losing control, permitting spectators to observe the legibility of his bodily experiences and spiritual interiority, despite the fact that the stereotypical figure is disallowed from publically articulating queer experiences of worship and in everyday life. Tonéx resists that "don't ask, don't tell" social contract by divulging the unspoken. Specifically, he models standing in his truth, which includes the concerns and joys brought about through queer intimacy. In this chapter, I investigate the queer Pentecostal performative strategies behind the creative process of worshipping in Spirit and in truth, as Tonéx grounds his performances in bodily experiences recorded on the *Unspoken* album. By vocalizing unspoken bodily experiences for gospel music audiences, Tonéx guides his fans through an exploration of what it means to be wired—that is, the occurrence of the embedded, transferred, bestowed, gifted, ridiculed, and surveilled aspects of being a queer man in Pentecostal Christian community.

To probe Tonéx's creative process as an African-American Pentecostal gay man in this chapter, I consider how his public narrative as an ex-communicated preacher-musician informs his performance of identity, all the while queering the pulpit ministry domain reserved for hetero-presenting men. We look closely at his preacher-musician worship leader role to understand how his functional and spatial domains shape the nature of his contribution. Then I examine the ways preacher-musician Tonéx deploys rhetorical and musical devices to identify himself and issues pertinent to an intersectional understanding he shares with other same-gender loving men while utilizing this tradition. Using a queer listening of the rhetorical and musical devices in "Wired," I evaluate his performances of queer body theologies. This analysis reveals the sociotheological implications of being transparent about one's queer identity in gospel music scenes—implications about which discreetly gay men express anxiety.

De-Coding Preacher-Musician Performance

Possessing an arsenal of culturally relevant versatility in musical and rhetorical devices is central to preacher-musicians' craftsmanship as worship leaders and performers who move their audiences toward revelation and transformation.

Tonéx's ability to move effortlessly between singing, playing multiple instruments, and preaching is the performance of dominance within worship leadership facility and spiritual transformation. As a preacher-musician, Tonéx is a member of a tradition of ministers who are able to move seamlessly between performing music and delivering "sermonettes" or short, impromptu sermons. Preacher-musicians are a unification of two gendered worship roles in which men participate. The combination of these roles in one spiritual facilitator blurs the imagined gendered nature of the individual roles. Preacher-musicians are able to facilitate a ritual construction as mediators whose attributes resemble the gender ambiguity of God, the ultimate signifier of the creative power that is harnessed through worship. Analysis of the preacher-musician tradition must take into account the function of the gendered body, gendered spaces, and attire in participants' imagination.

From 1997 to 2009, Tonéx was both a musician in the gospel industry, and also pastor of Truth Apostolic Community Church in San Diego, CA, which is affiliated with the Pentecostal Assemblies of the World, Inc. (PAW). My first encounter with Tonéx's style was at the Gospel Music Workshop of America (GMWA) in New Orleans in the early 2000s. My father Alvin Augustus Jones, a journalist and music video producer for The Dream Network contracted to videorecord the conference, told me that I should attend his concert that was scheduled around 1 a.m. just after the midnight musical.[8] My father said to me, "You have got to see him perform." Tonéx was best known as a vocalist with a wide range, from a baritone to tenor, in addition to being a multi-instrumentalist.

Williams's preacher-musician skill set is an interesting case for African-American gospel rhetoric and orality analysis. As was discussed in the introduction, there are three intersecting "spatial genitalia" domains for preacher-musician formation—the pulpit, the musicians' pit, and the choir loft.[9] These spaces have been gendered: pulpit ministry as masculine, mannish, or virile; vocal music ministry as feminine, childish/boyish, or queer; and instrumental music ministry as masculine, mannish, or virile. Preacher-musicians who combine these skill sets in performance negotiate and possibly dismantle the gendered dynamics that bifurcate those domains. According to rhetorician Roxanne Mountford (2003), manuscript-based preaching in mainline Christian denominations has been traditionally conceived as a space where one demonstrates bodily control as a sign of masculinity. Mountford observes that manuscript preaching traditions consider speech pitch fluctuation, voice modulation, and embodiment as feminine. In contrast to mainline denominations, African-American Christian preaching traditions weave together manuscript, memorized, and extemporaneous preaching for men and women. It is an embodied and demonstrative tradition that prizes what homiletician Henry H. Mitchell (2008) calls the "celebration moment" in preaching. To achieve

the celebration moment preachers engage the congregant's emotions and deploy inflection and modulation in their speaking range during the sermon. "It
is universally true that people recall far better what they have celebrated well.
And they are more apt to grow in Christian behavior-areas about which they
have authentically rejoiced."[10] Citing Deuteronomy 12:12, Mitchell sets forth
that emotional or expressive celebration is biblical and acknowledges that most
mainline denominations are inhibited with regard to emotional celebration.
Tonéx connects African-American Christian preaching with gospel music performance techniques in a manner that allows for a wider range of speech-pitch
fluctuation, voice modulation, attire, and embodiment.

For years, Tonéx and his former wife Yvette Williams (née Graham) were
known for their visually vivid imagery, wearing coordinated provocative garb
during appearances and performances. They used highly provocative attire to visually signify a peculiar identity and draw attention to their message.
A performer's attire is an extramusical form of communication about their appropriateness in any given performance frame. The audience's interpretation
of a performer's attire is shaped by the context in which musicians perform. As
with speech, the meaning of any costume depends on the circumstances.[11] Tonéx
stylistically mixed conventionally female-gendered materials, including boas,
wigs, braids, faux locs, high ponytails, and hairpieces with conventionally male-
gendered attire such as fatigues, Timberland boots, and A-shirts.[12] His wife, on
the other hand, was not "butch," and did not adorn herself in an adrogynous
fashion. Thus early in Tonéx's career, he presented an androgyny that was un-
precedented for a married gospel artist and controversial with his gospel music
fans. In a 2008 interview, he explained this approach by claiming:

> I see myself as kind of an anomaly because there is some element of ambiguity
> to my style because I will be this [referring to what could best be described as
> his "West coast, thugged-out" garb], or I'll be radical with a Mohawk or you'll
> see me in a business suit . . . From a cultural standpoint, we are very intimidated
> by anything that is outside of the urbane approach.[13]

Tonéx's ambiguous style enables him to theologize his body, adorn or disrobe
it, and permits his body and attire to be decoded in performance. Expressing
a progressive African-American Pentecostal sexuality and body theology
through music, Tonéx intentionally pushes the boundaries of gender identity
while carving out new social and spiritual "homes" in gospel, through the performance of a robust body theology. Theologian James B. Nelson wrote, "Body
theology is not primarily a theological description of the body. Nor is it princi-
pally an ethical prescription for how we ought to express ourselves physically.
Rather, and most simply put, it is doing theology in such a way that we take our

body experiences seriously as occasions of revelation."[14] In so doing, Tonéx also gives voice to unspoken forms of gospel praise, using his musical performances to share his story, as well as uncover and celebrate scandalous topics concerning sexuality and bodily experiences in African-American Christianity. Performing these portrayals allows him to engage in the politics of race, sexuality, and stigma as an act of intervention.[15]

Over the years, for example, Tonéx has progressively exposed his body by baring his back or chest, while appearing shirtless or wearing low-rise jeans in his photos. Analysis of the preacher-musician tradition must take into account the use of the gendered body, gendered spaces, attire, and transformation and their function in participants' imagination. In our April 2010 interview, he discussed his concern about the fact that gospel music is filled with images of people who are not healthy, obese artists. In effect, Tonéx displays his body to model a muscular Christianity in which musicians take care of themselves in anticipation of a high performance life. English scholar Deborah Smith Pollard observes that he subverted gospel music's strict dress code to relate to the "unchurched" people to whom he ministered.[16]

> [Tonéx,] who often changes during the course of an evening from rocker to hip hopper to fiery Pentecostal preacher, explained later to the press that his goal that night was to convince audiences who are often caught off guard by his chameleonlike transformations to judge him and his colleagues, not by what they wear, but by the messages they present.[17]

Therein lies the challenge for gospel musicians and the ways they convey their message through the extramusical elements of their performance. Musicians cannot control the audience's interpretation and assessment of their entire presentation. Messages are communicated not only through what is sung, but also through how, when, and where performers present their bodies. The context of the musicians' attire is essential to how the audience perceives their competence. Traditional gospel music fans believed that Tonéx's "fashion-forward" image was a distraction that overshadowed the worship experience.

Musical and Rhetorical Devices for Coded Performance

To enhance his articulating body and spread the gospel message, Tonéx's *Unspoken* (2009) album incorporates, in a dense manner, various musical, gestural, and rhetorical devices of homage, bricolage, euphemism, provocation, and other codes of communication that openly queer and "straight" ally gospel enthusiasts recognize.[18] He and other queer believers perform—what I argue in the remainder of the book—forms of unspokenness to socially and theologically navigate the gospel music industry and worship settings: decoding (in this chapter), unspokenness (chapter 6), musical kinship through a queer past (chapter 1), and musical dominance (chapter 7). Pentecostal homosexual men's practice of (de)coding body theology is a part of gay socialization in heteronormative African-American Christian contexts. As gender studies scholar David Halperin observes, "The process of learning to be gay continues to include, now as in the days before Stonewall, a process of learning how to re-code heterosexual codes so as to make them serve the purposes of gay self-representation."[19] Tonéx's use of word play in multiple rhetorical devices is also consistent with what Samuel A. Floyd Jr. (1995), citing African American Studies scholar Henry Louis Gates Jr. (1988), has described as musical signifyin(g). Floyd also posits signifyin(g) as a traditional African artistic mode of psychological self-defense and self-empowerment that historically developed and intensified, while blacks coped with both white oppression and hostilities within African-American communities. English scholar Geneva Smitherman goes further and elucidates the ways in which signification (also called "siggin") is done among African Americans as a verbal art of insult to make a point or just for fun. Those signified are not supposed to take it to heart. It is a culturally approved way of talking about people indirectly.[20] Signifyin(g) is, in essence, a mode of resistance, coping, commentary, and creative processing to neutralize various inter- and intracultural hostilities. Floyd writes,

> In the black vernacular, Signifyin(g) is figurative, implicative speech . . . Signifyin(g) is a way of saying one thing and meaning another; it is a reinterpretation, a metaphor for the revision of previous texts and figures; it is tropological thought, repetition with difference, the obscuring of meaning (Gates 1988, 53)—all to achieve or reverse power, to improve situations, and to achieve pleasing results for the signifier.[21]

Similar to signifyin(g), Tonéx also performs the rhetorical device Thomas Turino refers to as "semantic snowballing." Drawing from Charles Peirce's semiotic theory, Turino describes this phenomenon as "the potential collecting of multiple layers of indexical meanings around the same sign vehicle due to co-occurrences of the same sign vehicle and different objects in varied contexts over time, but with potential traces of, combinations with, past associations."[22] Unlike semantic tools such as double entendre, semantic snowballing accounts for the simultaneous, staggered, and interwoven deployment of multiple meanings in modes of communication. Indeed, a given sign vehicle registers as both traditional and transgressive. By examining Tonéx's signifyin(g) on body imagery, we gain insight into the ways multi-layered coded testimony, with regard to sexual and gender identities, situates Christian believers within multiple debates. In addition, his performances cultivate an understanding of social problems within the overlapping social groups that comprise black Pentecostal Christian worship of God in spirit and in truth. Tonéx opens up creative possibilities for conveying authenticity in what constitutes the praise embedded in the testifying body during worship.

The Naked Truth: A Gospel Account of Coming Out

In 2004, Tonéx began making his bodily experience legible through a process of truth telling and affirming those whose queer identities have been hidden in sanctuary worship despite their significant contributions to the gospel music industry. After releasing the album *Out the Box* (2004), Tonéx's last recording with his culturally diverse group called The Peculiar People, he divorced his wife. Tonéx shifted into representing himself as an openly gay man and expanded the types of topics that he tackled in his music, while continuing to perform under the Tonéx stage name. He announced his retirement from gospel music in 2006.

In 2008, Tonéx released his controversial album *The Naked Truth* mixtape[23] in which he reveals that he was molested at six years old. One of my research goals is to uphold the complexity of pervasive molestation narratives that often frame talk about same-gender desire. In so doing, I hope to counter the stereotype that sexual violation is the only catalyst for same-gender desire. There are countless same-gender loving people who have never been sexually violated maintained that they have always desired people of the same sex.

The *Naked Truth* album cover art exhibits a figure, presumably Tonéx, with his bare, wet, and muscular back turned and with hands lifted.[24] It was the first album released by a gospel artist that carried a parental advisory label. Among the gospel music fan base, the imagery was sexually suggestive and (homo) erotic. Lyrical content on the track titled "Shock Therapy" registered as rebellious and exposing the scandalous and unspoken problems within African-American Christianity. On the track titled "Searching," Tonéx acknowledged that believers were raising questions about his sexual orientation saying, "Am I Post? Am I Trade?" Tonéx evokes black and Latino gay Ballroom culture with his use of the queer and situational sexuality terms "Post (gay)" and "Trade (gay)." "Post" gay popularly refers to men who do not label themselves by their sexuality, even though they may view themselves as gay. Within the gay Ballroom culture gender system, as written by gender studies scholar Marlon Bailey, "trade" gays are cisgender or biological males who live as men, are very masculine, and identify as nongay. In addition, "trade" also refers to a "straight-identified man who is paid either to have sex with a man as a trick or who dibbles and dabbles in homosexuality but does not consider himself to be or bisexual."[25]

In Yoruba Richen's documentary *The New Black* (2013), Tonéx claims that his music has changed. He released a lesser-known EP titled *Rainbow* (2008)[26] that displayed clues about his identity without explicitly making known his sexual orientation to the uninitiated. While reflecting on the *Rainbow* album, Tonéx maintained he told the truth the entire time so that his critics could not create a scandal. For biblically informed listeners, the rainbow illustrated in the cover art registers as a symbol of God's promise never to destroy the earth again through a flood (Genesis 9); however, the rainbow pattern is also readily associated with queer pride. The symbolism was a way of engaging the speculations he acknowledged in *The Naked Truth* album. The *Rainbow* album featured the following tracks: 1) "Rainbow," 2) "Sweet Tea," 3) "Eye Call," 4) "Gotta Love Me" (from the series *Friends and Lovers*), 5) "Standing In Truth" (from the documentary *Standing in Truth*), and 6) "Gone (Dedicated to Corey Hampton)." "Sweet Tea" is a curious song on *Rainbow* in which he sings,

> Brothers in Hotlanta, they be sipping on that sweet tea. Sisters in Hotlanta, they be sipping on that sweet tea. Catch me in the club, in the corner, sipping sweet tea. Catch me on the dance floor, sipping on that sweet tea.

"Hotlanta" is a portmanteau referring to hot Atlanta, which is known for its large, upwardly mobile, black gay population. With regard to the significance of "sweet tea," performance, studies scholar E. Patrick Johnson explains in his book *Sweet Tea: Black Gay Men of the South* that in black gay vernacular, "sweet tea" is a euphemism for gossip, "as in, 'Chile,[27] spill the tea' or 'Pour the tea!' or 'Chile, I have some sweet tea to pour!' Sometimes the word is not spelled out, but merely represented by the letter 'T.'"[28] According to Johnson, the letter "T" also indicates "truth," "as when The Lady Chablis says in her autobiography, 'I was successful hiding my candy! Y'know, my T, my Truth.' Here The Lady Chablis adds a nuanced version to 'tea' by translating 'T' as 'truth' that suggests that in the south gossip is a form of truth."[29] The song "Standing In Truth" that is featured on this album and that I will discuss later expounds on "T" as truth.[30]

"Eye Call" is another thought-provoking track title that Tonéx coined as "gospop" that implements word play based on body language. The phrase "I call" is its homophone. He sings a line derived from the biblical text Psalm 37:25. The lyrics are: "Never seen the righteous forsaken, nor his seed begging for bread. If you call him, he will answer. He'll do just what he said." Tonéx continues, "Eye call. He'll answer me when Eye Call. What should I do? (Wait on him)." My homosexual conversation partners interpret "eye[31] call" as a euphemism for black gay men's nonverbal communication with those to whom they are attracted, particularly their use of a lingering gaze. "Eye call" is also the act of telephoning someone for discreet sex. This song was reissued on the subsequent *Unspoken* album and renamed as "When I Call," suggesting what gospel listeners may interpret as a composite of the aforementioned Psalm 37:25, adding the idea of waiting patiently on the Lord (Psalm 27:14).

After rolling out mixtapes and albums for a few years that suggested his queer potential, Tonéx self-disclosed as a gay man and released *Unspoken* in 2009. Even though the album was Grammy nominated in the broad "urban/alternative," it went largely unnoticed in the gospel music industry.[32] In my interview with him in April 2010, Tonéx shared that he was intentional about the *Unspoken* cover art. It illustrates one of the many personal transformations that fans would remember upon seeing the cover, when he controversially wore yarn braids in his early 2000s performances. The likeness of a younger Tonéx is shown bound and gagged, with blue-lit eyes,[33] and his image is filtered through a blue tinged night vision lens. There is also a brick wall behind Tonéx, suggesting a scene for a prisoner-of-war facing interrogation. The image appears as though he is being punished or detained for something he did or knows.

In a 2010 *Lexi Show* interview on The Word Network, Tonéx asserted that he had had sex with men and that he did not need to be delivered from being attracted to men. He said homosexuality is not a struggle for him, which was a huge departure from the traditional Pentecostal script of compulsory deliverance. By 2011, he changed his brand from Tonéx (associated with gospel performance) to B. Slade, a reference to Brian Slade, the lead bisexual and androgynous glam rock character in the movie *Velvet Goldmine* (1998). His name change signifies a theological, social, and industry transformation. B.Slade[34] represents a gay or bisexual, dandy,[35] and international persona. In fact, most of the glam rock artists were British, white, and androgynous. Examples of glam rock personae are David Bowie, T. Rex, and arguably at different points Bryan Ferry.

Tonéx's musical perspective is notable because at the height of his gospel career, from 1998 to 2000, he was one of the most sought-after performers. Other well-known male preacher-musicians with whom he has performed dealt with sensitive issues around their sexuality during the same time. Tonéx's self-disclosure occurred in an era of coming clean and restoration into the fold. For gospel artists, the confessing of faults mentioned in the introduction became a public relations strategy to maintain their fan base. Some examples include: choir director, producer, and pianist Kirk Franklin discussing his porn addiction; gospel singer, guitarist and composer Fred Hammond lamenting his divorce; gospel vocalist, pianist and composer Donnie McClurkin freely discussing his "deliverance" from homosexuality; choir director and organist Tye Tribbett admitting to cheating on his wife with a member of his group; gospel rapper and producer D.A.Truth admitting to cheating with his best friend Tye Tribbett's wife; choir director James Fortune seeking restoration following indictment on domestic violence charges; and producer and vocalist J. Moss litigating a child support case after conceiving a child outside of his marriage. Most recently, composer and vocalist Deitrick Haddon has talked about his wife's adultery and he shared on the show *Preachers of L.A.* about his child conceived out of wedlock.[36]

Even though they miss the mark within a Christian ethic, their self-disclosures, nevertheless, realign them with a heteronormative vision of relationships. Consequently, these individuals, along with others who trespass in this fashion, ask for forgiveness. As a part of the measure to discipline them, usually these figures have been "sat down" by their spiritual leader. Being "sat down" requires that a minister take a break from service ideally to start the process of repentance, receive counsel from their spiritual advisors, and eventually be restored back into the fold of the faithful. They are then usually given disciplinary options that provide measures for reconciliation without the threat of dismissal from the church fold. Williams is, in contrast, *not* asking for forgiveness and thus was excommunicated from his ecclesial affiliation.

On gospel music recordings, musicians have avoided issues pertaining to same-gender desire, sexuality and relationships. Participants who explore queer sexualities may do so in alternative performance and ritual spaces that are welcoming and affirming to LGBTQ expression such as house music and electronic dance music (EDM) clubs. The late "godfather of house music" Frankie Knuckles claimed that the house music dance floor is a space of thanksgiving for African American and Latino participants. He once said in an interview with the *Chicago Tribune*:

> God has a place on the dance floor . . . We wouldn't have all the things we have if it wasn't for God. We wouldn't have the one thing that keeps us sane—music. It's the one thing that calms people down.
>
> Even when they're hopping up and down in a frenzy on the dance floor, it still has their spirits calm because they're concentrating on having a good time, loving the music, as opposed to thinking about something negative. I think dancing is one of the best things anyone can do for themselves. And it doesn't cost anything.[37]

For example, one can find gospel performances about gay sexuality in LGBTQ nightclub scenes. In "Feeling the Spirit in the Dark" (1998), E. Patrick Johnson observes that nightclub participants enjoy house music mixes of traditional gospel.[38] The snowballing of musical components within house music thickens the ritual and liminal dimensions of the party. In nontraditional performances, participants adorn themselves in attire to convey their identity, discuss gay sexuality, and feel the spirit. Outside of these alternative spaces, Pentecostal participants perceive conversation about gay sexuality as out-of-place or obscene material that is wholly inappropriate for gospel performances and recordings. Tonéx uses a wide range of tools to incorporate these matters into gospelized styles. He uses signifyin(g) in "Wired" to create a shared sacred safe space for participants to express various identities that cannot be conventionally communicated in mixed sociotheological settings. Even though Tonéx divorced his wife and self-disclosed his homosexual identity, gospel enthusiasts have speculated about whether he had been wired with queerness, hetero-presenting through his marital status while on the down low and playing with gender expression for all of those years. I observe that he had been telling fans who he is for a long time, but the heteronormative gospel music culture was not equipped with the tools to decipher the queer communication embedded in his work.

"Wired": The Significance of Metaphor

In "Wired" from the 2009 *UnSpoken* album, Tonéx pays musical homage to both the New Jack swing era of the late 1980s and early 1990s and electronic dance music (EDM) styles more broadly. Popular New Jack swing artists include Teddy Riley, Guy, and Bell Biv Devoe. It combines hip-hop and contemporary R&B styles, and employs drum machines, clap tracks, and hardware samplers as core instrumentation. On the track, Tonéx demonstrates mastery of Michael Jackson and Prince's iconic vocal styles and showmanship. Interweaving their musical styles together, he imitates, for example, Michael Jackson's pitched screams and classic adlibs, quick fire, nasal sung-spoken lyrics, audible inhalations, and staccato "uh"[39] as an affixed syllable and phrase punctuation. Tonéx also uses Prince's instrumental style of cyclical, layering components of the rhythmic section over the course of a song. Tonéx is creatively molded into a composite of their iconicity, showcasing their musical facility and, in the process, contributing to and distributing their international artistic legacy through gospelized tributes.

The title "Wired" is fraught with meanings describing a person who has been implanted, embedded, gifted, contaminated, infused with, or surveilled by something. With this assortment of stylistic features, listeners have questioned whether this track should be labeled as a gospel music recording or something else, but a tidy stylistic classification of this track is unnecessary within the tradition of African-American signifyin(g). Perhaps the signifyin(g) practices of some African-American performers lend themselves quite well to performances that are intentionally ambiguous in their construction of both gender and genre. As Floyd explains, these signifyin(g) practices work "by commenting on other musical figures, on themselves, on performances of other music, on other performances of the same music, and on completely new works of music. Moreover genres signify on other genres."[40]

To include this song in gospel repertoire, listeners have also stated that gospel music is defined by whether or not the lyrics convey the "good news" message of the Holy Bible, much like gospel go-go and holy hip-hop enthusiasts. The lyrical messages of "Wired" are quite remarkable in this regard, prompting the question: For whom might this song be good news? The first verse starts with references to lines from traditional gospel lyrics. The rhyming couplets would begin with the phrase "When I think of," followed by a typical series of issues for which participants are thankful. As the singer delineates the issues, he or she conveys heartfelt gratitude by personalizing the lyrics.[41]

The second verse continues this lyrical pattern but deviates from common-place topics. Tonéx revises the usual topics and adds rhetorical possibilities, disrupting the expected reference. After the first chorus, he sheds musical layers of the accompaniment with a musical break, allowing the reverberation of the muffled, distant, and pulsing bass from what sounds like a Roland TR-808 drum machine to remain in the background of an EDM club-like sonic backdrop. As the pulse continues, Tonéx exclaims,

> When I think of
> All the STDs that should be up in my body.
> When I think of
> All you've done for me,
> It really makes me wanna rock your Body.
> Colossians is the fullness of God in bodily form.

The exposed heartbeat-like pulse accompanying the verse sonically indicates contemplation and the suspension of time, a liminality that is similar to what one might experience as they await and reflect on the results from an STD test, or as presently referred to, STI test.

Tonéx proposes a different way of understanding life-and-death through a contested gospelized performance of his reflection on sexually "risky behavior" for marginalized believers. His performance of this taboo topic give spectators access into the homosexual domain of concerns that are managed through modes of discretion/deception. Borrowing from Mary Strine, Beverly Long, and Mary Frances Hopkins, performance studies scholar Dwight Conquergood contends, "Performance is an essentially contested concept . . . Thinking about performance as 'an essentially contested concept' locates disagreement and difference as generative points of departure and coalition for its unfolding meanings and affiliations."[42] Performance breaks boundaries, remakes worlds, and has the capacity to cultivate understanding of contentious social issues such as same-gender love-sex positivity.[43] In addition, Tonéx expands the religio-cultural performance possibilities of performing openly queer testimonies, in what performance studies scholar David Román posits as an act of intervention into the conversations about race, sexuality, and AIDS that pathologize black gay men as prone to STD/STI infection,[44] especially since there have been advances in HIV/AIDS preventative treatments such as TRUVADA aka PrEP (Pre-exposure prophylaxis).[45] Tonéx intervenes using a variation on gospel texts, rhyming schema, and musical styles.

With regard to the narrative contour of the song, this "celebration moment" about seronegative status seems to come out of nowhere—that is, until one goes back and listens to the very beginning of the track that starts with an eerie dream sequence, amid mechanized sound effects that register like clicks from a film reel or factory equipment. Tonéx narrates the following:

> When I was 6 years old,
> I grabbed a bobby pin and I stuck it in a light socket.
> I should have died, but I think something happened.
> I think something got in.
> I think something took over.
> I think that was the moment I got wired.

Although these lyrics can be interpreted more than one way, my gay conversation partners provided queer listening of and feedback about the song that sheds light on queer bodily experience.[46] The introduction features the illustration of a queer-coded, and diminutively phallic symbol of bobby pin being inserted into a "light socket," an euphemism referring to sexual intercourse, specifically "barebacking." Typically associated with white gay men, barebacking refers to what Tim Dean calls "unfettered intimacy" or casual sex without condoms (2009).

It is taboo for artists to mention in gospel music performance the crises queer believers face, let alone to express praise for escaping the consequences of sex outside of a monogamous, heterosexual marriage. Homosexual musicians' avoidance of these topics in gospel impedes another terrain of spiritual healing—that is deliverance from ignorance about believers exploring their sexual preferences. There are three aspects of queer signifyin' at work in the case study of "Wired." First, Tonéx's signifyin' on barebacking (condomless sex) among homosexual/gay men is a form of what performance theorist Richard Schechner calls "dark play" in that only some knew that he was discreetly communicating with other homosexual men. In play theory, dark play is a form of play in which some of the actors participate and are unaware of their engagement in the game. It may seem innocuous to some, dark to others, and it is a subversion of the meta-communication[47] because in a heteronormative context only gay men and their allies would gather the connotations of his music. Unfortunately, barebacking reinscribes the assumption that there is an end to HIV/AIDS, a message that is pervasive throughout white communities that have access to trans-/queer-specific sex education, testing, health care, and medication such as antiretrovirals (ARVS), according to journalist Steven Thrasher.[48] He emphasizes that black men aren't having more sex; however, they do have sex across age ranges. Without access to the aforementioned products and services, the condomless sex movement has wildly different implications along racial, socio-economic, and intergenerational lines for black men who have sex with men. Second, while the tainting of blood is the imagery underscored in gospel settings with regard to HIV/AIDS transmission, the contextualization of his exposure to STDs/STIs with the opening soliloquy suggests semenic transmission. Third, homosexual "barebacking" scenarios are a depiction of "deep play" in queer relationships. As anthropologist Clifford Geertz explains it, deep play is a game where the stakes are so high that players are drawn to risk, deception, life-and-death, and sheer thrill.[49] Gay men's sexuality has been constructed, for example, as always unsafe and in need of protection through condom use, even in monogamous relationships. This recording reinterprets barebacking as a high-risk game through an intervention of good news that men are protected with more than condoms. God knows their sexual desires and clandestine experiences. God will protect them.

A barebacking interpretation came as a surprise to young and majority self-identified heterosexual black Christian listeners with whom I have spoken. When I asked gospel musicians in Washington, DC about their first impressions of "Wired," bareback sexual practices were not among the interpretations they put forth. They expressed that Tonéx was merely performing an incoherent fantasy that stemmed from his traumatic experience. One should note that their interpretation that Tonéx was incoherent is shaped by the Pentecostal community's belief that he is "of a reprobate mind" (corrupted beyond hope of redemption) due to his unapologetic queer identity. They also said that they were not paying attention when the monologue portion played on the track. The audience's mixed levels of attention represent the varied (dis)engagement that occurs for the audience, when performers layer multiple symbols and metaphors. Overwhelmed participants unfamiliar with the performed code disengage from what they perceive as incoherence, and thus reinstalls the open secret.

I observed a similar instance of varied audience (dis)engagement, while attending an evening open mic at a storefront church in December 2013. One of the newest male members of the church performed a track from his mixtape titled "Broken Kids," which is a cover of the song "Pumped Up Kicks" (2011) by Foster the People. I looked around to see if anyone else sensed the queer idiom the performer evoked with the term "kids." "Kids" or "children" are synonyms for men who are a part of the queer community. After he performed,

I stepped outside to ask attendees whether they interpreted a queer connotation. I asked my friends if they knew about what he was singing. Why was he singing about kids at an ostensibly adult event? One female attendee remarked on the male performer's t-shirt design, with a "bedazzled cross." She suggested his gay identity by inserting voguing[50] arm gestures, as she sang "Broken Kids." Another male musician mentioned that he knew the original track. Later, an elder of the church reflected on his performance at dinner and noted that when the performer recently joined the church, he shared his testimony of deliverance from being gay. The elder expressed interest in interpreting what the song revealed about healing broken identity and the journey to deliverance from same-gender love.

I contend that it is precisely when the code or manner with which the performer communicates symbolically thickens or when the content indexically thickens that researchers should pay closer attention. At the time of the *Unspoken* album's release, for example, Tonéx had recently divulged that he was molested as a child. Tonéx's personal testimony was expressed in coded fashion on "Wired." His testimony underscores a theme of youth sexual violation that is common in African-American church and gospel circles. Tonéx implicates participants in their passive action toward handling this type of abuse. For him to suggest that his early sexual experience with the man of the cloth "wired," embedded, or stimulated his queer sexual appetite implicates that minister and the church, and is particularly striking and unusual for a gospel recording. Such praise and "celebration moments" are also relevant for women survivors who have escaped the consequences of nonconsensual or violent sex. This musical performance of a testimony in which he postulates that God allowed him to find a way of escape, while maintaining his queer identity, foreshadowed what Tonéx would reveal six months later about identity as an African-American Pentecostal homosexual man on the taped television interview that was yet to be released.

Bad Blood Discourse, Barebacking, and Alternative Bonds

The stigmatization of STD/STI transmission can be traced to the history of black men's health in the United States. Within a US context, STDs/STIs hearken to a multilayered "bad blood" discourse with which black men have contended, most notably since the Tuskegee Syphilis experiment (1932–1972). Blacks cooperated with the Public Health teams to get free medical care for "bad blood" but were instead unwittingly infected with syphilis. In a reflection on James H. Jones's *Bad Blood: The Tuskegee Syphilis Experiment* (1981), Martin Levine considered the connections between the efforts of the Division of Venereal Disease and the Center for Disease Control. He wrote,

They say we have bad blood. Nearly forty years ago, they told some Black men they had bad blood ...

The team used this term because they felt it meant syphilis in rural black jargon. It was their understanding that the exact medical word, syphilis, would be incomprehensible to illiterate blacks. But bad blood meant far from syphilis. Blacks used it as a catchall expression for a bevy of ailments. Bad blood denoted headaches, indigestion, pellagra, sores, fatigue, general aches and pains, and numerous maladies.[51]

Black men's folklore and shared memory of that injustice contributes to the gendered and racial anxieties that linger about health care, prevention, and treatment that has contributed to the overrepresentation of black people in the AIDS pandemic narrative.

In a lecture delivered at Indiana University, journalism scholar Steven Thrasher uncovered the criminalization of HIV exposure the perception of the "blackness of AIDS." The notion stems from several systemic issues: black communities' lack of ARVs and President Bill Clinton's Crime, Housing, and Welfare bills that led to black homelessness, joblessness, and poverty.[52] President Bill Clinton's signed bills include: Glass Steegal Repeal in 1999; Defense of Marriage Act in 1996; Violent Crime Control and Law Enforcement Act in 1994; "Don't Ask, Don't Tell" in 1993; and Personal Responsibility and Work Opportunity ("Welfare Reform") Act in 1994. These meanings and legacies are negotiated when homosexual men decode their STD/STI status as a social metaphor, through which they interpret the body, embodied experience, and bodily disease. Unfortunately, one of the ways in which stigmatization is reinforced is through the legal and social consequences one anticipates occurring should they disclose that they are infected with a contagious virus, especially a contagion that disproportionately linked with what are considered abominable sex acts. To withhold seropositive status is illegal in 19 US states, and it is illegal to expose others to HIV in 28 states, according to the Center for Disease Control and Prevention.[53]

As mentioned earlier, it was not until recently that forthright performance about navigating gay sexuality was found in mainstream gospel. As I evaluate the ways in which these socially stigmatized diseases or health conditions threaten one's sense of a relationship with God, it is conspicuous to me that there is a lack of popular musical theology around bodily experiences that cause shame. In consideration of the unusual nature of Tonéx's performances, the following questions emerge: For what audience does he perform? In what ways does Tonéx's gospelized praise about STD/STI avoidance and prevention register as transgressively connecting to queer modes of signifyin(g) about their sexuality?

Let's return to "Wired" as a Christian educational tool that becomes effective through a revelation about homosexual unfettered intimacy texts. Tonéx can perform this song in a manner that caters to the sensibilities of a gospel clientele largely unfamiliar with the networks built around incurable disease, death, and dying, while reaching even farther to those who are familiar with the deeper networks cultivated within the bareback sexuality movement. In a manner that is not perceived as overtly sexual, he gestures toward the bareback movement and to Pentecostal homosexual men. The bareback discourse encompasses a debate about disease prevention versus unfettered intimacy. It is important to emphasize that black gay men are disproportionately impacted by HIV/AIDS infection due to issues surrounding cost barriers, miseducation, and lack of access to healthcare.[54] Therefore, anxiety about prevention is at the fore of African-American male bareback discourse. Philosopher Tim Dean elucidates that white gay men participate in a sexual freedom movement that resists the threat of contamination with the virus as a deterrent for unprotected sex. Condomless sex activists de-center STD/STI infection in the debate on what it means to be a sexually active gay man. In fact, contamination is an opportunity to construct an alternative notion of bonding that does not privilege procreation as the indicator of family ties:

> The AIDS epidemic has given gay men new opportunities for kinship, because sharing viruses has come to be understood as a mechanism of alliance, a way of forming consanguinity with strangers or friends, Through HIV, gay men have discovered that they can "breed" without women. *Unlimited Intimacy* does not take for granted what might seem obvious, namely, that bareback subculture is all about death. For some participants, bareback sex concerns different forms of life reproduction and kinship.

Bareback sexuality is an expression of kinship within white gay networks that transgresses prevention warnings to which homosexual men adhere. On gay social networks, there are men who actively seek partners who have fully disclosed that they are infected with the virus and desire condomless sex. Thus homosexual men destigmatize a seropositive status and disclosure. They do not allow a man's seropositive status to be a deterrent from casual sex. Deliberate transmission of the virus is against the law, and thus condomless sexual practices are kept underground in gay networks. However, white gay men are more likely to have access to healthcare and treatment to manage infection should they contract HIV/AIDS.

In the Huffington Post, activist Charles Stephens added to the predominantly white perspectives on barebacking and wrote about the extent to which loneliness is a driver among homosexual men in condomless sex. He offers that risky sex is not just about homosexual men dancing with death:

> Risk is a sensibility, an awareness, a desire, I think, to feel deeply, to feel something, because so many of us feel a kind of numbness, which is how we cope with being marginalized. There is pleasure, certainly; we are not merely the bleakness we endure. But there is suffering, which is the absolute core of oppression, another realm that neither HIV prevention nor LGBT politics has ventured into in a meaningful way.
>
> Barebacking is not a drive toward death or an inclination toward reckless behavior, as some alarmists would suggest. It's about people wanting to live life at its deepest. Sexuality, in whatever manifestation, is life-affirming. Sex between us, in our various roles and explorations of pleasures and fetishes, is rich in symbolism, which may be one of the few outlets for expression for those of us who are denied other means.[55]

African-American Pentecostal gay and "ex-gay" men have broached issues of "risky sexual behavior" via social media, using spiritual language to convey their explanatory models for STD/STI infection. For example, Tonéx introduced me to the work of Carless Hardin, who has discussed STDs/STIs as *spiritually* transmitted diseases" resulting from "risky" sexual behavior with same-gender loving partners.[56] Hardin reveals his casual sex experiences with prominent, itinerant gospel musicians as a means of publicly exposing their "freakiness." Hardin asserts the following about homosexual music ministers and preachers, "We have been out of the closet. It is no longer a hiding place." His interpretation of STDs/STIs is also informed by a belief (common among Pentecostals) that sex outside of committed relationships creates soul ties or spiritual connections with one's partners because of the exchange of blood. The sexually transmitted disease is held as a somatic symptom of a spiritually compromised life. Succinctly put, one takes on the spiritual baggage of the people with whom they have sex. The baggage manifests as hardships that can only be brought about through sexual intercourse. With the use of bareback imagery, Tonéx crafts a web of meaning that is lost on people outside of gay networks. It is specifically through gospel performance networks of gay men that interventions around STD/STI and HIV/AIDS transmission occur, where they can discuss the multiple risks of unprotected sex.

Hardin's spiritually transmitted disease concept has been articulated by commentators before him. Indeed, within Hardin's explanation lies equal concern for addressing quarrels with the body and spirit. African-American Christian homosexual men with whom I have spoken resist barebacking culture's virus-centered approach to gay men's health because it separates

spiritual implications from corporeal ones. For Hardin, sexual healing is inextricable from spiritual healing. He is committed to a more liberating STD/STI
data about African-American Christian homosexual men and the people who
love them. Hardin teaches about their sexuality by focusing on resurrection from
the death-dealing silence. African-American Christian homosexual men's commemoration of the power of the blood that was shed by Jesus Christ is a tradition
that focuses on overcoming suffering.

Gay and "ex-gay"[57] gospel musicians understood the nuance of Tonéx's new
message. For example, during a 2010 address to the Church of God in Christ
convocation in Memphis, Pentecostal pastor and gospel recording artist Donnie
McClurkin responded to buzz surrounding Tonéx's assertion that homosexuality
is not a "struggle." As I mentioned in chapter 1, Pastor McClurkin had already
become the first prominent African-American gospel artist to claim deliverance
from homosexuality. Along with his openly lesbian theological opponent Bishop
Yvette Flunder,[58] McClurkin laments that church leaders in the body of Christ
banish individuals who have been sexually violated by other believers. It is perhaps ironic that Flunder, Tonéx, and McClurkin concur on certain points. They
are, for example, on one accord with their urgent appeals to church leaders to
address the issue of sexual identity and the tragic suicide attempts of youths who
question their sexual orientation. They diverge in their messages of deliverance
from (McClurkin) versus affirmation of (Tonéx and Flunder) queer identities. In
fact, Flunder and Tonéx interpret McClurkin's admonishment as a manifestation
of McClurkin's self-loathing, as a closeted gay man seemingly in denial of the
ways in which he is "wired" in their estimation. Pastor McClurkin's commentary
is yet another instantiation of quarrels within African-American Christian and
gospel conversations that are being undertaken, utilizing various rhetorical and
performative devices. We will return to this genre of commentary in chapter 6.

Within body theology, one of the dominant ritual symbols is the blood that signifies purity and purification through the shared suffering of Jesus Christ. During
the last few years of Tonéx's tenure as pastor, Horace E. Smith, M.D. was the presiding bishop of PAW, the organization in which Tonéx was ordained. Bishop
Smith is senior pastor at Apostolic Faith Church and a physician specializing in
pediatric hematology and oncology at Children's Hospital in Chicago. His medical insight on the blood provides a theological lens through which Tonéx's PAW
fans may understand the significance of blood. Dr. Smith eventually set forth
in *Blood Works* (2011) that there is power in understanding the properties and
functions of blood as a spiritual metaphor for internal spiritual attacks on the
body of Christ. Among the expertise provided in his book, Smith argues that in
the spiritual world the most significant internal pathogens are sinful desires. His
examination of blood as a life force element and spiritual metaphor resembles
the dynamics of traditional Pentecostal social and theological assessment of

quarrels with the body, but he goes further in exploring the intersection between spirituality, sexuality, and gender expression. Smith has presented on changing perceptions regarding the LGBT participation in Apostolic churches, during the "Can LGBT People Be Active in My Church?" workshop at the P.A.W., Inc. 2013 Pastors & Ministry Leaders Summit.[59]

In homosexual Pentecostal men's multiple consciousness, Christian signification intersects with racial significations that are preoccupied with tainted blood. For those living with STDs/STIs, in what other ways might performances of gospel music cultivate a theology of healing or wholeness? Furthermore, how do African-American Christian men identify and acquire musical repertoire relevant to the unique theological, sexual, and epidemical issues they confront? In what ways is this message coded and decoded on and off the stages of gospel performance?

Songs about Incurable Illness and Faith

"Wired" resides in a repertoire of songs in which artists have attested that God protects, heals, and delivers believers from terminal and protracted diseases like HIV/AIDS. While there are innumerable songs that address healing, I would like to highlight a gospel song that addresses incurable or stigmatized disease. I trace the roots of such a gospelized response repertoire to the height of the HIV/AIDS epidemic. Musicologist Paul Attinello provides a framework for constructing gospelized repertoires of HIV/AIDS reflection. Attinello sets forth that while artists in other performing art forms such as theater responded to the AIDS epidemic, there was a deficit in musical responses.[60] Those who did respond resorted to avoiding specifics in the language deployed that cultivated an uncontroversial empathy in the public soundscape. Musicians at the time used tropes and idioms that were common to their genres, weaving together dense codes within their works. The songs operate "completely by implication rather than direct, unmistakable reference ... It would be easy for (a song) to pass without comment in the normal stream of hits on any radio station."[61] The uninitiated listener misses the meaning of the words that were incorporated.

"Where is Your Faith in God" (1985) by Rev. James Cleveland[62] is an example of a song about a backslider dealing with a disease that could not be cured. A Christian says to him, "You say you've been sick, tell me about it. You said you are sick and you don't think you can get well. Where is your faith?" Rev. Cleveland died shortly after recording it due to alleged complications from AIDS.[63] While it is not a song about being protected from the disease, it theologically engaged concerns about the HIV/AIDS pandemic in a discreet manner. Moreover, the reflection portrayed in the song was supported by the gospel artist's experience.

Another gospel artist, DeWayne Woods, catapulted into prominence with a song about his healing from HIV/AIDS. His song "God Still Heals" (2006) declares that "I once was sick and now I am healed. And I know that it was nothing but the grace of God... I'm alive today to testify that God still heals." For both artists, embodied wholeness is achieved through one's faith.[64]

Another example in classic gospel is "Thank You" by COGIC-raised Bishop Walter Hawkins from the *Love Alive IV* (1990) album.[65] Alto soloist then referred to as Rev. Yvette Flunder performed, "Tragedies are common place, all kinds of diseases, people are slipping away." The term "disease" is a metaphor that includes all ailments and avoids the sense of obscenity that the term "STD/STI" or "HIV/AIDS" would evoke. Hawkins's lyrics can minister to the cancer patient and the person with the common cold or pneumonia. The song also ministered to the emerging marginalized community of gay and straight HIV/AIDS patients, to whom Hawkins preached what he called a radical theology of inclusive love at his church, the Love Center Church in Oakland, California. HIV/AIDS was then and remains the most stigmatized STD/STI in black Pentecostal churches.[66]

One of Hawkins's most notable congregants was the late gay disco performer Sylvester James, who succumbed to the virus a few years prior to the recording release. Later, when Tonéx changed to the B.Slade brand, he paid homage to Sylvester James by recording the cover "You Make Me Feel (Mighty Real)" in 2011, singing falsetto while dressed in androgynous styles. Anne-Lise François expounds on his vocal and performance style: "Falsetto is Sylvester's truth... Sylvester's example is central then to my argument for falsetto as artifice, as a vamping and performance of otherness, and, by extension, as a metaphor for alternative, fictive spaces, which uncover the untruth of the real. But this example also helps to re-emphasize the forced nature of falsetto singing and to remind us of its being the only voice available, unwanted, unchosen, used by default."[67] TV One's documentary series *Unsung* (2011) covered the fact that Hawkins received a lot of criticism for his ministry to members like Sylvester James who were affected by and infected with the virus. For Hawkins to advocate for protection from and treatment of HIV/AIDS would have been more distracting than his mere acknowledgment that people are "slipping away" from diseases in general. Yet HIV/AIDS was held in gospel music spheres as an invisible threat and curse for the promiscuous and the queer. Hawkins's truth telling about the mass loss had to be judicious, along with other preacher-musicians who navigated its impact on the gospel community. With the emergence of the HIV/AIDS pandemic, there manifested a growing need to construct mature African-American Christian notions of sexual healing. Like Hawkins, Tonéx demonstrated in the *Unspoken* recording ingenuity around conveying what is impermissible to communicate in gospel performance. This ingenuity stems from the perception that those whose identities are on the margins of Pentecostal embodied theology are unable to find a safe space to come as they are, without injury being enacted upon them.

In this chapter I have examined preacher-musician Tonéx's negotiation of queerness and worship in spirit and in truth by addressing stigmatized bodily experiences. Tonéx's use of rhetorical devices such signifyin(g) opens up possibilities within the African-American Christian theological imagination, performance, and discussion. As we learned in chapter 1, members of the broader Pentecostal community view queer sexuality as a malady with which one struggles and from which one should be set free. Tonéx demonstrates strategies for homosexual men to creatively perform a progressive black sexuality that stretches beyond traditional Christian beliefs regarding what is appropriate to celebrate and praise God about corporately among other believers. Queer participants' discussion and performance of their sexual experiences has been considered inappropriate in gospel music; however, Tonéx's performances provide a counter-narrative to the notion that African-American Christian same-gender loving men are always down low, low down, or hiding "in the closet." As a homosexual man, Tonéx allows his expression about bodily experiences to do work on its own, while performing his identity through musical styles homosexual men may recognize.

In the next chapter I consider shared memory, bodily expression, and silence as forms of nonverbalized art that gospel musicians use to communicate something, when verbalization is censored, inadequate, or inappropriate for the social context. I continue analyzing Tonéx's *Unspoken* album as not only a crafting of alternative space but also a facilitation of a ministry of presence for those who are personally processing unspoken queer experiences. As I mentioned here, Tonéx released *Unspoken* after his *The Naked Truth* album, which was the first parental advisory by a gospel artist. The *Unspoken* album that followed symbolizes a ministry of presence for queer men dealing with unspeakable matters and challenges the heterosexist assumptions in black male absence literature. For whom is black male presence in church safe and restorative? What are the ways in which a man's presence in church is socially and theologically sacrificial?

6

Ritualizing the Unspoken

Memory, Separation, and the Rhetorical Art of Silence

Gospel musicians have made and discussed several quotes that encapsulate the circulating homoantagonistic statements queer believers hear as traumatic disincentives for self-disclosing or even attending churches regularly. When queer believers like Tonéx decide to "come out" to their loved ones, thereby rejecting deliverance, they typically experience one of the severest punishments in Christianity—their loved ones socially separate from them. In numerous performances, Tye Tribbett asserted that homosexual men and lesbian women ought to abandon queer identity—as though their sexual orientation was symptomatic of a spiritual infestation of the community—and ought to undertake an ideal heterosexual lifestyle. "Come out of lesbianism. Come out of homosexuality," was Tribbett's exhortation on his freshman, recordbreaking album *Victory Live!* (2006). One gay A.M.E. musician in Chicago told me that he used to be a Tribbett fan and liked his sound, but Tribbett's call to come out was so off-putting that his music became inaudible and intolerable, triggering severe feelings of rejection. And thus Tribbett's music became a sonic impediment to setting the atmosphere for that musician.

The expression "come out" can be interpreted in several ways. First, to "come out to" refers to the instance when lesbian and gay people reveal their sexual identity to their community and loved ones. Second, Tribbett derived his terminology "come out of" homosexuality from the biblical phrase "to come out from" found in 2 Corinthians 6:17 (KJV): "Wherefore come out from among them, and be ye separate, saith the Lord, and touch not the unclean thing; and I will receive you." In the text, "them" refers to unbelievers, unrighteous, "pagans," or "idolaters." Believers are to separate from unclean things and unbelievers, which are habitually understood to include queer people in gospel settings, so that God will receive or accept the righteous. Queer believers like neo-soul recording artist Donnie Johnson experience this separation from other believers both as God's abhorrence of him and human's disagreement with his way of life. "Somebody told me one day that God does not like me," Donnie testified at the 2014 "Are All the God's Afraid of Black Sexuality?" symposium mentioned in chapter 1. If same-gender loving believers do not "come out from homosexuality," other Pentecostal believers designate them or one's association with them as what

Flaming? Alisha Lola Jones, Oxford University Press (2020). © Oxford University Press.
DOI: 10.1093/oso/9780190065416.001.0001

Franklin calls a "big problem"[1] or a spiritual threat, epitomizing the group of people God dislikes, as we will discuss later in this chapter. To contest the notion that God does not like gay people, my interlocutors have focused on the ways in which God's presence is experienced in their work. As with most music ministers, transformation through their worship leadership and creative production is the ultimate evidence. Tye Tribbett's and Kirk Franklin's statements illustrate the heteropatriarchal[2] metanarratives in popular gospel music and publications that construct homosexuality as a condition from which believers who self-identify as gay or lesbian must "come out" or be delivered, as was discussed in chapter 1.

"There is no way you can listen to his music and not feel the presence of God," my openly gay research conversation partner asserted as we listened to a recording of an iconic gospel artist in November 2011. "His anointing is unmistakable," he said further, "and it is beyond me why his homosexuality matters to anyone. Without question, his gifts have brought millions of people to God. He is gay. Telling people would mean undoing his life's work. All you have to do is experience his music. Nothing else matters." My informant's compelling remarks illustrate the dissonance found in gospel music scenes as artists who skillfully set the atmosphere for worship, while counting the cost for disclosing their queer sexuality, especially when not self-identifying allows them to maintain a measure of comfort.

In this chapter I continue exploration of Tonéx's *Unspoken* album to consider unspokenness as a means of decentering the primacy of and dismantling the violence enacted through rhetoric in African American worship leadership, while bringing to center the power of presence in ministry when the posture of standing in one's truth is assumed. The multifold notion of standing in one's truth is a theopolitical principle that symbolizes a queer ministry of presence. It is characterized by multisensory conformations of unapologetic public and private worship, aesthetic appeal, social discretion, affirmation, contestation, intercession, and demoralization, while fostering spiritual efficacy—experiencing one's ability to usher in God's unmistakable presence, thereby disputing negative aural-visual connotations of the instrumentalized queer body as a deterrent. Standing in one's truth is also submitting oneself to that contested instrumentality, a musical self-giving trait, functioning as a barometer for setting the atmosphere, despite participants' prejudiced behavior toward the worship leader being used by God.

In the face of a queer shaming public, Tonéx ritualizes discretionary devices within gospel contexts where homosexuality is abhorred, considered a "big problem," and made more problematic than heterosexual men's sexual indiscretions. Throughout gospel folklore, discourse about the unspeakable encompasses various performative aspects of gospel that include "speaking in tongues"[3] and the accompanying process of interpreting them, being "slain in the

Spirit"[4] and the arduous task of spiritual leaders or attuned believers recounting dreams and delivering prophecies to other believers.

In what is to follow, I turn my attention to unspokenness as a worship posture in the face of censorship. I start by briefly exploring churchgoers' portrayals of hypocrisy about heterosexual and hetero-presenting men who are able to promote homophobia, while they recover from their own sex scandals without being ex-communicated or shunned like homosexual men. Through the lens of ritual theory and Cheryl Glenn's notion of "unspoken" as a rhetorical art of silence, I examine gay gospel participants' communication devices even when they are silent, juxtaposing that rhetorical art with pervasive narratives of queer musicians who assume a liturgically and socially submissive stance to sing their own death knell after homophobic sermons. In church spaces, what are the ways in which queer musicians who assume a socially submissive stance perform a negation of their self? I then consider Tonéx's move from the ritual of unspokenness to the performance of "standing in truth" as a means to engage the perception that homosexuality or queerness is a problem. Close attention to Tonéx's songs unveils erotic, traumatic, and unutterable narratives of same-gender spiritual and physical intimacy in Christian rituals.

Preachers Get a Pass

In African American Christian and gospel settings, preachers and musicians regularly deliver sermons regarding ideal manhood as evinced by the traditional role men play in households. Men who do not perform or define their masculinity or manhood by their participation in traditional households as provider, progenitor, and protector are denied "real men" status. Sociologist Richard Pitt · observes that when men do not fit into those household leadership categories, "the performance of Black masculinity becomes predicated on a particular performance of Black sexuality and avoidance of weakness and femininity."[5] Examining Jawanza Kunfuju's accounts that I mentioned in chapter 3, Reggie Williamson in the introduction and other remarks presented at the beginning of this chapter, the congregation is imagined as a feminine domain. Thus, men's performance of heterosexuality and avoidance of weakness and femininity manifests in rhetorically equating committed male congregants' participation with inadequacy. Furthermore, Pitt suggests that to be confirmed as gay in the historically black "church family" is to potentially suffer or to socially diminish a man's manhood. For a man to be gay, it is interpreted as being less than a real man. It constitutes failed manhood. A man's diminished manhood is suggested with people's use of terms that were used to ridicule Kirk Franklin such as "church boy," "mama's boy," and "choir boy." Such stigmatization is unfortunate because his adoptive mother

Gertrude Franklin was his earliest supporter, taking him in when he was abandoned by his biological mother. Born Kirk Smith, Mother Gertrude Franklin was Franklin's biological great aunt and a widow whose surname he assumed upon adoption. She resold aluminum cans to raise money and invested in his private and church music education. He said of Mother Franklin in an *LA Times* interview, "She taught me everything. She taught me how to respect people and respect myself, and that's something I'll never forget."

More to the point, embedded in believers' deployment of these terms is the metanarrative that men are at risk of being verbally and socially infantilized, castigated, and/or castrated when they demonstrate commitment to their church, their mothers, vocal music or even dance ministry participation. All of which are viewed as emotive approaches to worship in which one's inner life is displayed. In essence, men who are actually present in historically African American Pentecostal churches risk being belittled for their gravitation to those congregations where women are empowered to lead.

Perhaps those derisive terms have influenced Franklin's signature vocal style that is more of a talking lead soloist (rapid, staccato, raspy, and situated in the lower speaking range), which registers to gospel listeners as a masculine vocality. His vocal style resembles what we observed in gospel go-go and in many ways this is why he was an ideal, impromptu collaborator with local DC musicians. These infantilizing and feminizing terms, among others, are uttered in the pews, in the pulpit, and in the public square as code phrases for men and boys who are homosexual or gay.

> The word "homosexuality" may rarely be used in a Black pulpit. Instead, it is replaced by code words—punk or sissy—that reflect not only a distaste for how a man might behave in the bedroom, but how he might exhibit effeminate behaviors, the rhetoric spoken from Black pulpits indicts their romantic-sexual performance by accusing them of flawed gender performance. By conflating sexuality with gender, the performance of Black masculinity becomes predicated on a particular performance of Black sexuality.[6]

The pulpit, arguably the most powerful space in African American Christian worship, is a symbolically phallogocentric platform from which heterosexist rhetoric is delivered in the worship. Among gendered spaces in black churches, the pulpit is constructed in opposition to the symbolically "unmanly" or boyish gospel choir loft that is a platform for the art of musical and gestural rhetorics. In chapter 2, I recounted a contradistinct instance in which Bishop Walter Thomas redefined the pulpit as an opportunity for alliance by expressing kinship and alumni affinity to promote acceptance of Patrick Dailey's gift. Such a gesture of education about and goodwill towards androgynous, queer, transgender, or gender-fluid musicians is not enacted normally in African American gospel contexts.

To distance themselves from the perception of being socially feminized or castrated on the account of their vocal participation, Franklin and Tribbett have performed similar heteropatriarchal rhetoric within gospel music and sermonettes throughout their career. As I mentioned in chapter 5, both men also faced reprimand due to their sexual indiscretion within their heterosexual marriages. Franklin revealed in his book *Church Boy* (1998) that he had a pornography addiction. In Tribbett's "Lift Every Voice" (2010) interview, he confessed to an extramarital affair with a woman in his singing group. Yet Franklin and Tribbett were still received by believers after they confessed their faults and repented for their sexual sin. They were also both friends with Tonéx. One might presume that Franklin and Tribbett would stand alongside Tonéx when he disclosed his unapologetic queerness, but Franklin and Tribbett distanced themselves from Tonéx.[7] In addition, Tonéx experienced financial loss as performance engagements were cancelled and he was "blacklisted," as he puts it, in the gospel music community. His livelihood was jeopardized after he plainly spoke the truth about his identity.

Instead of performing heterosexuality or avoiding the appearance of "feminine weakness," Tonéx confessed to being homosexual to his fans but did not repent for it. He does not consider being gay a sin; instead, it is the way that God created him. It is his identity. Tonéx claimed in *The New Black* (2014) that his decision to change to the B.Slade brand was like being born again. Even though he lost a lot of friends, he gained a new community that he did not anticipate, many of whom were unfamiliar with his previous Tonéx brand. The aftermath of the risk Tonéx took confirmed discreet queer believers' fears that to self-identify as homosexual or to confirm being in a same-sex partnership means that they just may face the humiliation of a church family who suddenly knows them not. Such anxiety about separation prompts me to ask afresh the question W.E.B. du Bois posed in *The Souls of Black Folk* (1903): "How does it feel to be a problem?" Tonéx's case, like so many others, illustrates a constellatory consciousness in which vocation, sexuality, gender expression, and religious belief map onto his experience of being perceived as a menace. As I compare Franklin, Tribbett, Donnie Johnson, and Tonéx's narratives, I observe that the problem homosexual men pose is a perceived threat to fraternal bonds and men's economic advantages maintained in heteropatriarchal communities. The collective manages anxiety about the potential of men "womanning up," queering, or any type of embodied gender unification of men with women in worship. For a man to appear like a woman before God is the unspeakable.

At the core of Pentecostal black preaching is reproving and ostracizing sin, with the most evocative messages focusing on sexual sin, while queer sin is described as the most repulsive. While preachers divulge their testimonies about heterosexual premarital and/or extramarital relationships, they are less likely to share about their queer and/or "questioning" sexual past. To distance themselves publicly from any woman-likeness, queer potential, or androgyny, some black male preachers or preacher-musicians perform contradictory public and private scripts about morality, regardless of their sexual preferences. And stereotypically, black male preachers are described as hypocrites, who rail against sexual sins while they succumb to their own moral failings. Sociologist and preacher Michael Eric Dyson (1996) related a service during which a preacher delivered a sermon about the transformational power of God. The preacher warned, for example, about the pitfalls of sex outside of marriage and proclaimed that God can turn lust into love, thereby giving the saints a better relationship with God. By the end of the sermon, the congregation responded to his sermon by erupting in shouting and handclapping. The other preachers on the dais thanked him for the sermon. Dyson reflected on the contradictions displayed in that moment

> Sex, after all, is a difficult subject to treat in the black church, or, for that matter, in any church. This is indeed ironic. After all, the Christian faith is grounded in the Incarnation, the belief that God took on flesh to redeem human beings. That belief is constantly trumped by Christianity's quarrels with the body. Its needs. Its desires. Its sheer materiality. But especially its sexual identity.[8]

After the service, the congregants let the preacher know how moved they were by the sermon. When the worshippers left, all of the men retreated to the pastor's study. There were no women present. Then the visiting preacher asked the pastor of the church, "Who is that woman with those big breasts who was sitting on the third aisle to my left?" The preacher said further, "Damn, she kept shouting and jiggling so much I almost lost my concentration." And by the end of the exchange the pastor assured the visiting preacher that he would look into fixing him up with the woman. As the result of the events of that day, Dyson "learned, too, how dishonest we're sometimes made by the unresolved disputes between our bodies and our beliefs."[9] With regard to the spatial genitalia designations of the church, the pulpit was that pastor's perch from which he surveyed the pews for his next potential sexual conquest. The visiting preacher performed the public script that the believers expected to facilitate their "high time" in the Lord, and the private script displaying his lust before his colleagues permitted, irrespective of his teachings, while protecting his pursuit of clandestine romantic and sexual rendezvouses. Some of the homosexual men with whom I have spoken have observed that sort of scenario play out and have expressed a resentment toward the philandering heterosexual men who are insensitive and condemning of gay ministers' and musicians' sexual needs.

Numerous homosexual men choose to remain in conservative and "fundamentalist" (biblical literalist) black churches, while navigating contradictory heterosexist teachings that are contrary to their "out" identity that is lived in other contexts. In the artist now known as B.Slade's "Black Sheep" from *The Children* (2012) mixtape, I find a response to the perception that being homosexual is a problem. He reinterprets marginalization as an intracultural black Christian role of being set apart. "We are a sheep from another fold, then we must reach out to all souls. Our wool is black but not our souls. Jesus will never let you go." B.Slade advocates for sheep of another fold Jesus referred to in John 10:16 (NLT): "I have other sheep, too, that are not in this sheepfold. I must bring them also. They will listen to my voice, and there will be one flock with one shepherd." The pretext is that Jesus The Good Shepherd knows his sheep and they know him (v. 14). Jesus lays down his life for his sheep (v. 15). Instead of avoiding the perception of being problematic, B.Slade advocates for focusing on the incarnated God's steadfastness that is exemplified in Jesus who will never let God's sheep go. Sheep represent animal sacrifice on the behalf of mankind and is a signifier of human martyrdom. B.Slade challenges the notion of where the problem lays, and interprets sheep as same-gender loving people who also love The Lord and cruel saints in the dominant culture, despite the believers' ridicule of queer sexual orientation and gender expression.

Countless patrons have come to revere gospel music as a remedy for spiritual maladies, and queer musicians tend to administer that remedy through performance and recordings, contributing to the vitality of the Christian worship in creative ways. I contend that the musician's peculiarity is a "secret ingredient" in the production of the music. The largely heteropatriarchal patrons' consumption of the music—despite their perception of gay musicians' sexuality as unethical and reprobate—is bewildering. The musicians are expected to be demonstrative, passionate, queer, sensuous, and/or carnal. In essence, "problematic people" perform gospel music. Tonéx recalled, for example, when his father Anthony Williams Sr., who was a bishop in the Pentecostal Assemblies of the World, would prescribe that Tonéx listen to gospel records "to get back on the right track." "I think what he meant was that he wanted me to go back to my roots or I guess what he thought was my foundation. But the people that he wanted me to listen to were gay too" (The New Black 2014). Donnie McClurkin (who I broached in chapter 1 and will discuss further in chapter 7) also has written in his book *Eternal Victim/Eternal Victor* (2001) that attending church and participating in music ministry were a means to get in the presence of God and escape the social conflict surrounding his identity.

I pause here to focus on a problematic, latent feature of McClurkin and Tonéx's listening practices and the composition of their soundscape: using gospel music as a coping mechanism without critical analysis and selection of the repertoire.

Both listened to gospel music with awareness of discrete queer identity performance and of those identities being associated with predatory behavior amounts to gradations of soul murder. Intense music-making and listening—both live and recorded—become the gateway drug and tool for grooming prey. I cringe as I think about how many queer believers, some of whom were victims of child abuse, are made to return to musical abusers, listen to the music and message of their perpetrators and then, forced to create a logic that discredits their discomfort and disconsolation for the "greater good of the community." This is a form of church-facilitated, sonically-induced Stockholm syndrome. The sense of these tensions re-emerge in chapter 7, as we consider why some musicians stop the music. The cultivation of these "logics" are not only a form of sonically-induced trauma bonding, but it persistently causes a disconnect in perceiving solidarity with women who boycott predator's music as a means of survival and punishment.

Ritualizing the Unspoken

Ritualizing the unspoken is a performance of one's interiority in a manner that is socially read as either a strong or a weak trait based upon one's culture. English scholar Cheryl Glenn conceptualizes the "unspoken as a rhetoric of silence." The meaning and interpretation of a person's silence is contingent upon their social-rhetorical-context.[10] Within African American Christian contexts, ritualizing the unspoken is contingent upon a combination of the biblical African and postcolonial United States' social-rhetorical context. Glenn acknowledges that the unspoken is rooted in a metaphorically gendered biblical account in which it was desirable for women to be silent (1 Timothy 2:11–12). "And, besides, silence itself is not silent: it is the origination of sound, the sound or creative flow of being."[11] Within a Christian context, silence has been socially constructed as representing passive, empty, stupid, or disobedient behavior. Speech was a divine gift and metaphorically gendered male. I, too, resist the notion that silence is always a mark of passivity or concealment. Silence also functions as a mode of active communication.

Music ministry provides a safe space for black men to emote and to explore deep desire, in spite of a hegemonic US culture that discourages men from showing their feelings publicly. As I mentioned in chapter 5, *Unspoken* is Tonéx's proposal for new and improved forms of authentic worship placing eroticism and gender nonconformity at the forefront of performances, at the risk of being separated from unaccepting faith communities. Tonéx reflects on personal matters that gospel music fans mark as taboo conversations about sexual and gender identity. His argument is that ultimately God is the judge of his worship competence. The title *Unspoken* is a play on the biblical notion of God's intimately communicated insights to a set-apart individual, while they are elevated in the heavenlies. Refer to 2 Corinthians 12: 4 (KJV)—"How that he was caught up into paradise, and heard unspeakable words, which it is not lawful for a man to utter." To worship God "in spirit and in truth" (John 4:24) is thus seen as a radical assertion of identity that has particular saliency within a Christian context. What does it mean for Tonéx to perform the unutterable with regard to discreet sexual identity? What kinds of counter-narratives do his performances embody, and what might his performances tell us about the closeting or silencing of African American Christian same-gender loving (SGL) men? As gay believers are coded and recoded through performance, "unspoken" stories become emblematic of a confidentiality and security that may only be sufficiently bestowed by God.

Tonéx explores his understanding of authentic worship on *Unspoken* tracks by diving into musical signifyin(g) strategies that I broached in chapter 5. He combines references to musical and written literature to inquire about the practice of unspokenness in authentic worship. Tonéx suggests in his lyrics that believers perform both independence (create unique meaning) and conformity (enact familiar behavior), while being present or silent in worship. I conceptualize the ritual of unspokenness as a form of ministry of presence, which is conventionally one's ability to stand alongside another person with care and love. Ministry of presence through unspokenness is to be present and in solidarity with the disinherited in contested spaces, while using gesture and rhetoric to diffuse the death-dealing blow of homophobic sermons and everyday speculative conversations about a believer's queer potential and/or victimization. I would also add that unspokenness as a ministry of presence is a form of self-sacrifice; a ministry to silently be in contested communities that even cause a person to subject him or herself to socially intimate violence and aggression. The following excerpt from the title track depicts a musical scenario, where a participant explores unspokenness in worship:

> The organ plays,
> The service begins,
> It's time to pray
> But before we begin,
> "Does anyone have a prayer request?
> For a loved one?
> The Lord, He knows what's best for you."
>
> It's me, it's me, it's me, oh Lord,
> Standing in the need of prayer.
> I need thee,

Oh, I need thee.
Hands up in the air
Because this prayer is unspoken.
I can't say a word
because this prayer is unspoken.
Those who know the prayer of faith
Please hear my devotion.
I'm in need of intercession.
This one's Unspoken.

This one's private,
I can't tell nobody.
What I did last summer,
I can't tell nobody.
Let me see you signify by raising
Your right hand.
I know I'm not the only one
With this circumstance.

The narrator illustrates the participants' observant and reflexive role in prayer. During the first verse, he observes a worship scene with an organ playing in the background. In a harmonized call, an announcement is made for those present to submit petitions on behalf of themselves or a loved one. Then the narrator, presumably playing the role of intercessor, concludes: "The Lord, He knows what's best for you." Praying for others is a transformative ritual of spiritual support for those in need and also comfort for the person petitioning on their behalf. They integrate individuals into community through the praying ritual. In the chorus, he musically signifies on, "It's me, it's me, it's me, Oh Lord, standing the need of prayer."[12] This passage is derived from a traditional Negro spiritual that has become illustrative of the sensual and ecstatic tarrying tradition[13] in worship throughout African American church folklore.[14] Tonéx uses *sotto voce*[15] lead and background vocals over a moderate New Jack Swing-era groove. The rhythm section, particularly the drum set, is foregrounded in the accompaniment, which features little harmonic variation. Although Tonéx sings a small melodic range at first—reiterating one pitch—he gradually shifts his vocal registers, strengthens his timbre, employs ad lib virtuosity, and exchanges his whispery timbre for a fuller and brassy vocal quality.

The musical protagonist escapes self-deception by "coming out" in the presence of God ("It's me, it's me, oh Lord It's me, it's me, oh Lord "), by adopting a stance of confession ("standing in the need of prayer"), and with a gesture of total submission ("hands up in the air"). The details of the petition remain unspoken, presumably concealed from other humans, while it is gesturally submitted in public worship. Tonéx suppresses the confidentiality of the matter on his heart by silently lifting his hands because he realizes the Creator knows his matters anyway.

Tonéx's *sotto voce* vocal quality conveys that even though this prayer is unspoken, his internal devotion is not restrained completely. He persists. This performance of sung unspokenness illustrates an impression that silence is a rhetorical art, a space from which speech is created. "Praying gay Christian men" is a common image evoked throughout my interviews with gay informants and within queer theological discussions. For example, most of the homosexual men with whom I spoke claim they have prayed and sought God for deliverance from what Paul mentions in the Holy Bible as "a thorn in his flesh," which is a way to construe "problematic" sexual inclinations. For homosexual men, "this prayer, like the struggle they were having, was personal and private" (Pitt 2010, 44). This personal and private presentation of the prayer is illustrated as Tonéx sings "This one's private—I can't tell nobody. What I did last summer, I can't tell nobody." While signifying on the popular horror film *I Know What You Did Last Summer* (1997), he describes secretive, censored speech about presumably damnable gender expression and queered sexual tastes. In many ways, the ritualization of the unspoken would not exist without the belief that to claim a problematic identity means risking estrangement from other believers. Silence is a strategy for remedying being perceived as a threat to the fraternal bonds within church leadership and the lucrative economy of gospel music production.

Homosexual men's silence is not without purpose. Silence is musical and operative in worship spaces that privilege rhetoric. In the silence, intimate bonds are formed that are discreet, and intentionally maintained by men within sanctified communities for their safety, comfort, and management of scrutiny. A silent worshipper praying or meditating is engaged in modes of knowing, composing, and generation, according to poet George Kalamaras in *Reclaiming the Tacit* (1994), in various religious practices. Performance studies scholar Jason King explains that intimate bonds are formed in silence as a mode of communication:

> These bonds may themselves be outside of formal speech, outside of the potential for coherence and articulation—in the same way that sound carries a formal power that lies outside the valence of text. In this case, silence does not necessarily denote a lack of communication. Silence is a realm of possibility unto itself. In the supposed gap between official discourses which work to silence invisible public displays of queerness, and thus underground discourses circulated by marginalized audiences, silence becomes reconstructed not only as knowledge, but also as sentimental kinship ("one of the children").[16]

This deafening silence, while fostering kinship, may unfortunately incite an observer's perception of discreet sexuality and identity as a deceptive practice. In addition, believers' condemnation of same-gender desire has reinscribed a silencing, a "don't ask, don't tell" arrangement so that gay people can function without judgment from their church family.

Openly queer, Pentecostal-raised clergy Bishop Yvette Flunder and Tonéx have mentioned to me that it was their prayerful practice of questioning the divine about their identity that conditioned them for what they call a shamanic role within music ministry.[17] They believe that they have creative traits emblematic of their queer identity, endowing them with access to the supernatural and the ability to wield their creativity to navigate good and evil. Comparable with the North American and Asian notions of the shaman, in African traditions there is a large body of literature with trickster characters, which are silent in the natural world and important communicators to God and humans. According to anthropologist Philip Peek in "Re-sounding Silence," unspokenness in African folktales represents respect, sagacity, esoteric knowledge, and serenity. Deep silence can also be the manifestation of social power and the presence of a deity.[18] Silence is a sign of wisdom and it is incorporated into initiation rituals: "The loss and then relearning of speech and language effectively stand for death and rebirth."[19] There are also tales about silence regenerating the initiate and cultivating the silent one's inner state. The following Yoruba tale illustrates the merits of a well-developed inner state:

> The king invited the animals to a great feast, and offered a prize to the best dancer. The animals danced energetically before him, each showing off its own most striking qualities—the elephant its grave dignity, the leopard its beautiful coat and sinuous agility, the gazelle its spectacular leaps and so forth. When, at the end of the dance, they gathered around the king to hear his judgment, to their surprise and displeasure he awarded the prize to the tortoise ... "And so it is that I awarded the prize to the tortoise," said the king, "for it is only I who can see the dance is entirely inside him!"[20]

A moral of the story is that those in power interpret silence as they wish. Another interpretation is that only the sovereign are able to discern one's interiority. African traditions of silence are an empowering interpretation of interiority development. Thus, silent individuals' well-developed inner state is discerned by the most powerful through their consistent facilitation of efficacious encounters with God in worship.

In *Unspoken*, Tonéx illustrates unspokenness through portraying gestural responses to God. He riffs off of the pop performer or hype man call phrase to "throw your hands up" in live concert settings. He sings, "Hands up in the air because this prayer's unspoken." This line may be interpreted in four ways: 1) the unspoken is musically performed; 2) the unspoken is communicated through body language; 3) there are certain matters that one might keep discreet in worship; and 4) other participants may observe lifted hands as an emotional representation of a resolved personal conflict in the presence of God. His illustration of hands up in the air is also a variation of Karen Clark Sheard, "If I Can't Say A Word, I'll Just Wave My Hands," from her *2nd Chance* (2002) album that describes indescribable goodness of God. I discussed in chapters 2 through 5 the extent to which the black male body is read, often sexualized, and subjected to surveillance and control. Contrary to popular notions of coming out of the closet, black gay men's bodies are read in what English scholar Maurice O. Wallace calls a sociovisibility (2002). Citing Wallace, gender studies scholar Marlon Bailey argues, "Sociovisiblity is the corporeally arresting consequence of a kind of picture-taking racial gaze that fixes or frames black subjects within a rigid and limited grid of representational possibilities."[21] The sociovisibility of the black gay man can be used as an advantage, when they are able to wield the spectator's perception. Sociovisibility is also a means by which heterosexist spectators identify targets in order to enact microaggressions upon them. As E. Patrick Johnson asserts, "The Black homosexual becomes the site of displaced anger for the Black heterosexual, the scapegoat used to thwart his own feelings of inadequate manhood."[22]

The ritualizing of the unspoken is empowering for homosexual men, while worshipping in their community; however, gay men are disempowered in worship when they are inclined to request prayerful support, but instead leave matters unspoken while in crisis to avoid confusion. Tonéx asserted, in my interview with him, that participants appear to be transparent in their church families but do not divulge the most controversial aspects of their life. They remain silent in their deepest moments of crisis. He resolves that this silencing is counterintuitive to the believers who are otherwise instructed to worship God in spirit and truth. To what extent does the worship context restrict believers ability to sing their truth? An examination of Pentecostal music performance would suggest that queer musicians are expected to "shut up and sing."[23]

Singing a Death Knell

Through impromptu music, testimonies, and prayer, believers attest to spiritual transformation as the result of musicians' tailored response to a move of God in the preached moment during altar call. Music performance at altar call is intended to seal the sermon that was preached. Worship in the midst of challenges is a stimulating event in which participants explore embodiment, sensuality, and sexuality, but African American Christian homosexual men are frequently discreet about the challenges that are related to their "problematic" sexual identity. For example, the anxieties one experiences while awaiting results from an STD test after a bareback rendezvous are off-limit topics for prayerful support. In what ways might their management of social and theological tensions queer prayer requests through public worship and intercession?

Dyson attests to homophobic preaching moments that are met by SGL men's singing—a type of unspokenness by diffusing spoken words with musical communication.

> One of the most painful scenarios of black church life is repeated Sunday after Sunday with little notice or collective outrage. A black minister will preach a sermon railing against sexual ills, especially homosexuality. At the close of the sermon, a soloist, who everybody knows is gay, will rise to perform a moving number, as the preacher extends an invitation to visitors to join the church. The soloist is, in effect, being asked to sing, and to sign, his theological death sentence. His presence at the end of such a sermon symbolizes a silent endorsement of the preacher's message. Ironically, the presence of his gay Christian body at the highest moment of worship also negates the preacher's attempt to censure his presence, to erase his body, to deny his legitimacy as a child of God. Too often, the homosexual dimension of eroticism remains cloaked in taboo or blanketed in theological attack. As a result, the black church, an institution that has been at the heart of black emancipation, refuses to unlock the oppressive closet for gays and lesbians.[24]

While I am unsure how everyone "knows" the musician is gay, Dyson's observation conveys the irony of that moment between homophobic proclamation and queer affirmation. Homosexual men's navigation of the preacher's performance of sermonic denial is an intentional ritual in which the queer singer re-presents the significance of his presence, by sonically and creatively diffusing the contentious rhetoric that was preached. Queer musical re-presentation also has implications for community building and affirmation. I call this ritualizing of the unspoken a process, which is rooted in the theatrical nature of ritual. Social scientist Emile Durkheim (1912) established that ritual is set and repeated action that expresses a community's values and cultivates "social solidarity." Durkheim urges that even though rituals convey religious ideas, rituals are not themselves ideas or abstractions, but performances staging patterns of behaviors or texts. A ritual distinguishes between the sacred and the profane in that the sacred is what the community values most. Durkheim posited that ritual not only incorporates individuals into community, but intensifies in times of crisis. In essence, rituals are thoughts in action or thoughts as action with those characteristics that resemble theatre.

Homosexual men's disciplined and repeated socially silent posture in the face of reoccurring anti-gay sermons and teachings is a ritual that discreetly cultivates solidarity with other SGL participants present, absent, and ex-communicated. To avoid postures and presentation that may be construed as weak or effeminate, feminine-presenting men resort to social practices that are interpreted as closeted, evasive, low down, vague, or deceptive. They do so, I argue, to assuage believers' social and theological apprehensions about queer people coming out or letting slip[25] any effeminate characteristics in gospel settings. They also remain in community as unconfirmed gay people by performing familiar patterns of sacred behavior (i.e., hands raised or waving hands) and texts (i.e., vernacular speech, scripture, songs) that flow throughout gospel communication. Further, ritual unspokenness, whether a sung response or conventional silence, is "a strategic way of acting" and thus a form of ritualization as set forth by ritual theorist Catherine Bell. "When analyzed as ritualization, acting ritually emerges as a particular cultural strategy of differentiation linked to particular social effects and rooted in a distinctive interplay of a socialized body and the environment it structures."[26] Within unspokenness, gay participants value discretion and perform ritual unspokenness as a cultural strategy to diffuse the rhetorical omission by using similar devices. They are socialized to do what Richard Pitt labels as compartmentalization of their strong religious identity from their committed homosexual sexual identity.[27] SGL men's compartmentalization is not a healthy approach to fully engrafting into networks of support, but this approach to sharing their religious identity is a way of avoiding separation by selecting in what ways and with whom they will belong.

Standing in the Truth and Dealing with Bad Faith

Worshipping "in spirit and in truth" is a key motivation for public worship that resembles *standing in the truth*. Tonéx posits that musicians and ministers performing in gospel should reveal personal truths, in order to be competent as spiritual leaders and relevant artists. His performance of this inspirational song was a dress rehearsal for the reception that he would experience when he officially identified himself as gay two years after its release. It was also his way to cure himself of bad faith. Two years prior to releasing *Unspoken* and his "coming out" on the Lexi Television show (2010) that airs on The Word Network, Tonéx recorded the title song[28] for the unreleased *Standing-N-Truth* (2008) documentary on African American HIV/AIDS awareness and prevention.[29] In a musical style that resembles classic R&B, he portrays a same-gender loving man who defines the characteristics of truth. Truth is imagined as standing,[30] conveying one's entire story (including those events that happen behind the scenes), facing one's fears of finding out their HIV status, and exploring deep knowledge of real love. He sings, in the manner of an altar call remarks, "Obtaining knowledge gives you (or gave me) power. So, don't you waste another hour." This phrase is a biblical composite of Proverbs 4:5 (In all thy getting, get understanding) and Hosea 4:6 (my people are destroyed for the lack of knowledge).

The "Unspoken" album concept suggests that there is silence to be broken and speech to be uttered, but it is somehow withheld. The biblical reference to worship the Lord "in Spirit and in truth" (John 4:24) is an example of some of the attributes for authentic interior disposition that I raised in chapter 2. Tonéx explained to me that one's environment should not influence one's expression of their spirit or interior authenticity nor their lived reality. In fact, in response to the question, "What does worship in spirit and in truth mean to you?" He stated:

> I always thought worshipping in spirit and in truth meant with the Holy Ghost or the Holy Spirit and then also in whatever state the flesh or carnal side can be honest about that versus in deception . . . Not deception of others but more so self-deception. That you think that you are fooling yourself by not acknowledging these things and you are trying to mask it over—sometimes with emotions of that environment and a lot of people are not finding the healing or self-examination or introspection because it is more of a culture, a cliché, then it is an actual reflection. If you are going to worship in spirit and in truth then it means that God knows anyway who we are, what we are, where we go, what we do . . . So, not just in church but in every aspect you should worship in spirit and in truth.[31]

In his response, Tonéx observes that other worshippers benefit from manifestations of the spirit that are prized in musical performance. There is less of a focus on musicians' personal pursuit of the truth. Tonéx believes that to worship God in spirit and truth requires eschewing self-deception. He also recommends that participants should strive to be unmasked in every social and religious context. Moreover, Tonéx suggests that gospel musicians and ministers ought to welcome multivocality in worship. Diverse perspectives inevitably include those who have been marginalized or those ostracized for sins committed against them by other believers. For him, nondisclosure renders one's worship impotent because the worship is not transparent. In other words, truth-telling is coming clean and confessing faults. It is essential for another level of worship and in a biblical sense, participants overcome by the word of their testimony (Revelation 12:11b).

Tonéx describes standing in the truth or self-disclosure as one's avoidance of self-deception. His focus on self-deception calls to mind philosopher Jean-Paul Sartre's (1956) notion of "bad faith," which is

[a] lie to oneself within the unity of a single consciousness. Through bad faith a person seeks to escape the responsible freedom of Being-for-itself. Bad faith rests on vacillation between transcendence and facticity [sic] which refuses to recognize either one for what it really is or to synthesize them.[32]

Sartre also distinguishes practicing "bad faith" from being a liar. A liar actually tells her/himself the truth but denies it to others in words and with negating actions. Bad faith includes the additional step of lying to self. With regard to the racial imagination, philosopher Lewis Gordon (1995) expounds on Sartre's bad faith concept to include the anti-black racist implications of "bad faith," known colloquially as self-hatred, by interpreting it also as a particularly racial "negative mode of being" in which one denies certain identities within both the self and the world. Bad faith occurs in those instances when a person actively convinces himself in a Sartre sense that "I am not who I am" or in a Gordon sense that "I am a black man who is not a black," or in Tonéx's critique "I am a SGL who is not same-gender loving." The opposite of bad faith is "good faith," which is one's sincerity and candor to oneself and to the world. Ultimately, Sartre argues that bad faith affects one's experience of transcendence and reality. In place of Sartre's notion of transcendence, Tonéx uses the concept of "anointing" or the divine approval that is manifested through one's work, which includes instances of participants' personal transformation. Tonéx proposes that self-deception threatens the manifestation of the anointing in a person's ministry and life. For him, anointed queer believers exhibit the most extraordinary creative and shamanic abilities.[33] Queer individuals who live their peculiarity out loud are gifts to the supposedly homogeneous communities in which they fellowship.[34] Queer self-selection or omission of testimony is antithetical to his interpretation of worshipping God in spirit and in truth. Tonéx followed his inclination to close the chasm between gospel participants by using Unspoken to minister to LGBT enthusiasts in a language and style that he knew they would recognize, while suggesting his queerness to a broader gospel audience.

In what ways may a homosexual man stand in the truth of censored queer texts? Tonéx's use of signifyin' in "Sneeze," GLOR3X," "Bl3ND," and "F@ce Down" unmasks contested submissive and feminized male body theologies precisely because he musically treats terms and debates that are not commonly discussed in gospel. "Unspoken" symbolically provokes listeners to bear witness to peculiar, plausible, and real scenarios, and to judge the unutterable aspects of Christian customs that are recounted in problematic biblical texts and transmitted through contemporary worship without close inspection.

Recording the Unspoken Biblical Tradition

In my 2018 article "'You Are My Dwelling Place': Experiencing Black Male Worship as Aural Eroticism and Autoeroticism in Gospel Performance,"[35] I tackle the imperceptible techniques in which vocal worship leaders explore sexuality and sensuality by deploying a virgin, celibate, queer, sensual, and romantic listening of gospel performance.

> Within the twenty-first-century, historically African American Pentecostal settings in which gospel music is performed, there is a long-standing tradition of ministers presenting songs and delivering sermons that promote sexual abstinence among unmarried individuals, encouraging listeners to wait until they get married to have sex. Essential prescriptions for maintaining chastity in the Worth the Wait movement include prohibitive teachings that Christian believers should guard their hearts, minds, and "gates" (i.e., ears and eyes) from sexually suggestive or erotic contemplation, pornographic entertainment, and self-pleasure through masturbation. Yet the songs and sermons through which such messages reach the "gates" of the congregation are themselves a physical and embodied discourse that—for many listeners and performers—can be understood as erotic and pleasurable . . . Furthermore, there is no consideration of the pleasure vocalists themselves may derive, concurrently maintaining Christian piety while providing forms of musical sexual healing[36] for others.[37]

To establish a Christian genealogy of queer believers' texts, I extend that research by considering the extent to which Tonéx recounts the queer, homoerotic, concealed, and questionable nature of prophetic healing traditions through a queer interpretation of "Sneeze," a song that illustrates a resurrection experience. The mechanized musical elements on this track pay homage to the 1981 synthpop hit "Tainted Love" by the British duo Soft Cell.[38] While utilizing a reoccurring synthpop boom-chi-chick rhythmic pattern, "Sneeze" has a thicker accompaniment texture. The synthesized instruments and highly auto-tuned solo voice range are studio technological advances that are incorporated into the texture.

The song is loosely based upon a composite of two similar Hebrew Bible resurrection accounts involving the prophet Elijah (1 Kings 17:17–24) and the prophet Elisha (2 Kings 4). In 1 Kings 17:17–24, the widow with whom Elijah had stayed, requested that the prophet resurrect her son from the dead. He took the boy to his chamber. He then stretched himself over the boy three times, while asking

God to let the boy live. The boy sneezed three times and was resurrected. Then Elijah carried the boy to his mother to tell her that the boy was alive. According to a similar 2 Kings account, Elijah's successor Elisha went into a room with a child who was already laying on the bed, closed the door, and the parents left them alone for Elisha to pray to the Lord. To heal the young boy, Elisha lays on the child in a peculiar manner, using a body-to-body approach. The parents did not question his approach to healing their son. Also, the story never gives the child's account of the events.

Tonéx adapts the Hebrew Bible story to depict the boy's modern first-person perspective, illuminating the omission of his perspective in both accounts. In first person voice, the boys says,

> Guess it wasn't supposed to happen from jump.
> Nine months later I appeared as a lump.
> Persecuted from the day I was born,
> I didn't know I had some lessons to learn, to learn, to learn.
> Start popping, start sneezing . . .
> You don't have to cry no more.
> I've gotta go tell somebody what the Lord has done for me.
> Stop sneezing (Achoo!),
> Stop sneezing (Achoo!),
> Stop sneezing, Can't stop sneezing (Achoo!)
> You see the prophet laid on top of me
> He said that I should live and not die
> That's why I sneeze.
> Had an aneurysm when I was twelve, I grabbed my head and fell.
> Then the prophet drove in from out of town
> and told my mama he knew how to get down.

Instead of testifying that he was resurrected from the dead, the boy tells his mom that she "doesn't have to cry no more." The boy is more concerned about his mother than himself. His solo voice then enacts a musical call and response where the background vocals tell him to stop sneezing. The boy replies, "Achoo!" Tonéx's sung, auto-tuned, prepubescent-like sneezes continue to soar higher and higher, as he is asked to stop sneezing. The background vocal response "bless you" progressively spirals out of control, in an ascending stepwise melodic pattern.

In ancient times, sneezing symbolized a near death experience or acted as a gift from the gods. The gods would bless an individual and the sneeze was the result. Since the nineteenth century, medical researchers have found the nasal passage and genitals are connected through the parasympathetic nervous system.[39]

As a result, they have linked fits of sneezing to inducement by sexual ideation, arousal, ejaculation, and orgasm.[40] In this case, the sneeze is the remnant of the boy's resurrection and functions as a euphemism for a peculiar administration of a "gift from God," a resurrection from death that is thinly separated from the parameters of sexual arousal.[41] In the call and response of the recording, the background vocals represent the community who placates the boy's symptoms. The boy can't stop sneezing after his healing. His involuntary sneezing suggests that the sneeze is both a blessing and curse. He sings, "I'm feeling good from my head to my shoes," alluding to the conflation of pleasures and pains that come with resurrection and childhood sexual violation. He will carry the markings of a queer healing for the rest of his life. It is also interesting that the mother is implicated in the song as a passive and silent gatekeeper, who believed what the prophet told her. "He told my mama he knew how to get down."[42] Clearly the widow would do anything to resurrect her son, her charge and anticipated contributor to the household. Does that mean that she would exchange his death for another affliction, such as the challenge of deciphering the prophet's questionable physical behavior for the rest of his life? Or place upon the child the affliction of sneezing? Until the end of the song, he repeats the chorus and concludes with the final stanza, "You see, the prophet laid on top of me. He said that I shall live and not die that's why I sneeze." This imagery of the prophet lying on top of the boy is more akin to what happened in the 2 Kings account.

Through reiteration of this phrase, Tonéx illuminates the absurdity of the adults' lack of critical thought about the prophet's sexually suggestive, intimate, and concealed interactions with their son. He voices the boy's story. Tonéx's depiction of this imagery echoes renderings of queer encounters in the homosocial bonds of churches, where surviving young men often attribute their queerness and even feminine masculinity ("effeminacy") to a man of God touching them inappropriately or coercing them into sex. Frequently, these boys or young men are from households headed by single or widowed women.[43] Like sneezing, the young men's social queerness is linked to a perceived physical signification or social residue of those encounters. Consistent with the research, men later return to the church for deliverance from a struggle with the desires that members in churches introduced to them, as McClurkin, Pearson, Flunder, and other have said.

This musical account of body-to-body rituals is fascinating commentary to compare with the August 2012 bishop consecration footage of Bishop Wayne T. Jackson's controversial administering of a body-on-body prostration ritual with two male candidates, a ritual Jackson said he has done since 1998. He claims that the ritual represents a transition from a death of self to a resurrection, attaining a spiritual promotion to bishop. The Detroit Pentecostal organization Impact Ministries International's ceremony revealed a peculiar and—because of the same-gender, intimate nature of it—homoerotic tradition, when the bishop laid on top of the two candidates. After the video was released, Bishop Jackson and other ministers defended the ritual.

One female bishop in the fellowship characterized it as true consecration pageantry, the ritual "pomp and circumstance" with which other believers should become more familiar; however, during her consecration, she declined participation in the body-on-body prostration. Her abstinence from the ritual reveals her concern with the intimate nature of the prostration. It would have been perceived as obviously inappropriate imagery if a woman were incorporated into the ritual. This evokes the following question: What about the same-gender nature of this body-on-body ritual was less queer than a coed ritual?

While a comparative inter- and intradenominational liturgical analysis of prostration would be fascinating, it is outside the scope of this book. From a musical standpoint, I found it curious that the popular song "I Give Myself Away" (2009) by William McDowell was performed as the consecration ritual music. It is a song of self-sacrifice and surrender to God's will. The musical refrain was the call and cue for Bishop Jackson's ritual response of literally leaping into laying on top of the men. The congregation and music ministry were positioned, by virtue of their musical call, as complicit in setting the atmosphere and framing of the ritual. Through the collective reiteration of the chorus, it was unclear about whom and in what manner the candidates would "give (themselves) away." Since I reviewed that consecration footage, I have witnessed other Pentecostal prostration rituals at consecrations at Sweet Holy Spirit Church in Chicago but not in a body-on-body manner.

Tonéx's track "BL3ND" encompasses the entire recording's ethos, encouraging listeners to shed self-deception. Similar to Prince's acoustic "How Come You Don't Call Me" (b side of 1999, released in 1982), the tribute continues with exposed vocals and features the rhythm section of his band. It starts with an *ostinato* of just lead vocals, congas, and electric bass guitar. One may perceive the acoustic depth of the space where the percussion was recorded. Advocating for a Christian peculiarity, he immediately interrogates the listener,

> Do you really wanna be like them? Do you really wanna act like them? Do you really wanna sound like them? Why do you try so hard to blend?

With a layering of slight melodic variation, vocal harmony, and rhythm section variation, he then describes why blending with others does not work.

> You wonder why they hate you. You wonder why they tolerate you. You wonder why you have to be you, yeah. Because you try too hard to blend. You wonder

why they spite you no matter how hard you try. Because you never blend in with them you are unique in God's eyes.

In the next stanza the chordal keyboard accompaniment begins. The drum set enters, double-timing the rhythmic pattern. He argues that blending goes against the unique way that God created us. God's thoughts toward us are the only one that matters. In other words, God has called us to be peculiar.

"GLOR3X" examines the euphoria achieved in a believer's embodied and indwelled worship. It pays homage to Prince's falsetto gospel vocal style found in "Come," "Pheremone," and "Orgasm" from his *Come* (1994) album, while utilizing a popular exclamatory Pentecostal colloquial response "glo-ray" that expresses joy and affirmation of a message. With my multiple-consciousness as a listener of religious and nonreligious genres, the title *Come* centered the vocalization of euphoric experiences: beckoning, close proximity; an offertory for a conversion experience induced by transcendence; sexual climax; and its homonym "cum," the material biological evidence of climax. Both Prince and Tonéx tapped into the black radio quiet storm format of mood music (inspired by Smokey Robinson's 1975 *A Quiet Storm* album) to simulate the historically black Pentecostal and gospel music practice of "setting the atmosphere," a progenitor to the nascent, related genre of gospel mood music.[44]

Although Prince did not subscribe to Pentecostal belief, he did subscribe to faith traditions with similar sexually conservative religious beliefs and drew from the Pentecostal and gospel music traditions to take people there, that is, to happiness, joy, love-making, to heaven. His vocal musicality in particular is interesting to me because of his extended vocal range from baritone to falsetto at any given moment, vocal ranges and styles that we know sonically simulate anywhere from pillow talk and climax.

Prince's "Pheremone" points toward this same interconnectivity that emphasizes the chemical reactions the body generates not just for love-making but also in the intimate space of music making and consumption. Like in the erogenous zones used for singing, one has to stimulate the hedonic hot spots of the body to generate and secrete pheromones. And this activation is required in both the religious and nonreligious domains of music performance, regardless of one's aspirations of being sexually muted. Exploring these connections may relieve the stigma surrounding related forms of euphoria in musicians' pursuit of maintaining that euphoria. It helps us to decipher the subsequent addictions that iconic artists such as Prince, Whitney Houston, and Michael Jackson have succumbed to as the result of an occupational hazard, the alluring nature of the embodied music making enterprise.

In "GLOR3X" Tonéx depicts an orgasmic experience of being in the presence of God. His vocal style incorporates panting, growls, and squalling rooted in African American preaching. Tonéx likens experiencing God's presence to being "kited" or high on drugs. In the second verse, he describes the thick atmosphere, "Don't mind the smoke, its *Shekinah*,[45] there's nothing finer." "Shekinah" is a grammatically feminine Hebrew term that expresses the dwelling or settling of the presence of God in the earth.[46] According to anthropologist Raphael Patai in *The Hebrew Goddess* (1990), there are several accounts from Talmudic sages, for example, who saw or heard Shekinah in her earthly manifestations. In the mystic Kabbalistic literature, Shekinah communicated mysteries in her appearances. Thus, Tonéx's performance suggests that when the feminine Shekinah entity envelops a man, it is a sounded queer process that occurs here on earth.[47]

Enjoying God's atmospherically thick presence, Tonéx then shrills, in a D'Angelo style falsetto, "I'm gonna stay here," while sonically alluding to its similarity to basking in a kited state, chemically-induced high state, or a sexual afterglow. "I love the way I feel. The Holy Ghost is real.[48] I can feel it in my bones." Then he launches into the chorus, panting a sung repetition of "glo-ray" on an ascending scale melodic sequence and layering in the harmonic texture as it is repeated. He squalls, "Chills up and down my spine. Its real," articulating the sensuous nature of the Holy Ghost as it indwells. He adds, "Raise your hands and say glo-ray. Some of y'all know what I am talking about this evening. There is nothing like the presence of the Lord." He ad-libs that in the presence of God "there is fullness of joy." Tonéx demonstrates that worship informs one's transcendence, sensuality, and satisfaction.[49]

The recording concludes with "F@ce Down"—a title that I call a semantic *boulder* due to the loaded nature of its potential symbolism. Depending on the listener, F@ce Down has either sacred or obscene implications. He uses his lower, "manly" coded baritone register with rock style accompaniment that features a lead guitar solo in the introduction. A Pentecostal interpretation of "face down" refers to the practice of prostration, where one kneels or lays face down in humility and awe before God to crucify one's flesh.[50] In the chorus we hear, "Get down, down on, face down." He encourages that true confession is good for the soul. He advises that one should pursue the life of a servant, where God increases and humans decrease their will. An explicit or even obscene interpretation of "face down" is also a modern expression that is suggestive of a sexual position in which the male or female receiving partner is crouched on all fours (i.e., doggy-style or sexual "bottom"). The sexual suggestiveness also implies that submission to God informs the more intimate dimensions of a believer's life.[51] In some ways the face down posture of prayer, like pole dancing as a form of liturgical dance, is a practice that serves a dual function of cultivating piety and sensuality. Attention to the dualisms and multiplicities in these metaphors and practices reconcile believers' Dysonian "quarrels" with the spirit and flesh are marked as taboo, despite the fact there is proven experiential and scientific evidence of these linkages.

Performing the Gospelized Unspoken

Like gospel go-go musicians, Tonéx has taken his devotion outside of the church and conveys the issues of his heart in more appropriate welcoming and affirming settings. Even though Tonéx's "own received him not" in "compulsory hetero-normative" black Christian circles, he reclaimed his space, asserted that he is still here and a member of the gospel community in yet another milestone moment. In February 2011 B.Slade, who is the artist formerly known as Tonéx, returned to the gospel industry by debuting under his new brand at a Bonnerfide radio pre-event concert of the gospel music industry's beloved Stellar awards. The event was held at a local club in Memphis, outside of the sacramental confines of a church sanctuary. B.Slade is a brand that records and performs music that "reads" (popular black gay vernacular for finding a flaw in someone/thing) the church's silence about the misuse of power and sexuality. He performs gospel style tunes and music utilizing same-gender loving sexual imagery. According to Tonéx, the organizers felt that this neutral space, outside of a church setting, would allow for liberality in music and body language.

B.Slade took to stage wearing a grey blazer adorned with a glitter-encrusted mask on his shoulder. The removed mask signified his realness in that space. When I asked him if there was a story that he wanted to tell in that performance, he was very clear that he wanted to speak for himself:

> The first story was that regardless of what's happening, I am still here. We want people to sing it. We cannot go by what we see and talk about faith, without a tangible challenge. So just showing that I had to walk by faith and not by sight to even show up at that event . . . Of course, in the performance I was paying homage to Michael Jackson. Though Michael Jackson has gone on, I believe that I caught the glove, continuing that performance excellence. They may have thought that I fell off the planet . . . I am not dead. I am still alive—which of course pays homage to the death burial and resurrection of our Lord and Savior Jesus Christ. It served several purposes all in one song. It had many meanings.

Like the narrator in the song "Unspoken," the most important thing for B.Slade was to be present with and heard by other believers, despite the ways he was rejected from gospel networks. In the statement, he describes a glove being passed to him from Michael Jackson to him. This passing of a glove is an allusion to the biblical tradition of Elijah's mantle being passed to Elisha. The mantle signified by the glove is an inheritance in which the recipient is doubly blessed with their predecessor's anointing upon receipt.

B.Slade is paying homage to Jesus Christ, while performing in first-person pronouns, is another sort of reverential and compacted semantic snowballing that could be perceived as blasphemous. One could interpret the song lyric as B.Slade is not stating that he is like Christ, but rather that he embodies and personifies Christ. Such a move is an aggressive metaphoric rebuttal against the assertion that he is of reprobate mind. As he performs Christ through the song "Work on Me," he gathers and depicts the associated symbols of Jesus's blood, the anointing as represented in Christ, incarnation, setting the captives free, persecution, martyrdom, and resurrection that demolish the constraints of death.

> And then "Work on me" that was just a favorite. I was tryna make sure that I did songs that did very well on the charts ...
>
> And then "Believer" to let them know that I have not lost sight of who I am in Christ, what I do for Christ and that I believe in God. And I believe in the gospel of Jesus Christ. Um and even more specifically, I said that I would not do "Make Me Over" because I knew that was what the public would be expecting and secondly the Lord has already made me over. So, I did not need to sing a request about him making me over again and again and again and again. And if people need that song to minister to that area of their life, it is recorded and they can play it as many times as they want. But I am not just gonna sing a song like that because it is something that the public wants to hear and I am not singing it from a place where I really don't need Him to make me over.

B.Slade's decision to perform "Work On Me," instead of "Make Me Over" was resistance against the notion that God did not intentionally create him queer. He is resistant to reinscribing the pervasive pathologization of queer people. He also did not want to enact self-loathing that could be harmful for those in attendance questioning their identity. Setting aside his new, more-secular B.Slade song catalogue for the evening, he maintains that he gave them the nostalgia they wanted. He sang his Tonéx catalogue and not his newer B.Slade repertoire. And they sang with him, as he sang. While performing "tipping"—dance movement that alluded to gay Ballroom, nightclub, and voguing scenes, B.Slade brought in what theologian emilie townes calls the "warrior chants and unquiet spirits" of his exiled gay and lesbian Christian family in a never before witnessed gesture toward reconciliation. The attendees knew the tipping movements, they danced in synchrony, as they sang nostalgia. He sang so that they would perhaps reconsider that he was of a reprobate mind and perhaps believe again that he belonged with them. He told a compelling story: "I'm not dead. I'm alive ... and I believe."

African American preachers' heteropatriarchal sermons are a pervasive performance of provocation among African American Christian believers and gospel participants. Preachers deliver homophobic messages and sermons to distance themselves from resembling feminine-presenting men or gay people. Homosexual musicians manage these tensions by engaging in performances of unspokenness. In a Westernized Christian context, silence may register one as passive, effeminate, and/or a powerless participant. In an African context, the unspoken persona, in many ways, is perceived as one who is knowledgeable, possesses a well-developed inner state, and is empowered to discern the efficacy of those who speak against them with anti-gay rhetoric. Tonéx's *Unspoken* minds the gap between anti-gay and unspoken rhetorical arts by voicing contested chronicles. Performance of the unutterable chronicles provides a means through which believers observe a fuller account of biblical heritage. This chapter examined multiple perspectives as conveyed through silence, gesture, and speech is perhaps a glimpse of believers being able to truth-tell together. In chapter 7, I consider the performance of Donnie McClurkin's contested sexual identities that deploy discreet social navigations. I look at examples of an ex-gay or delivered homosexual man's performance of heteropatriarchal, Pentecostal Christian scripts regarding sexuality.

7

Church Realness

The Performance of Discretionary Devices and Heteropresentation in the House of God

In both black church folklore and comedy the flamboyant choir director is a trope, highlighting the ways in which gospel music is an aural-visual performance art, a site for scrutinizing performer's sexuality and gender expression. When I ask male music ministers who is the paradigmatic flamboyant gospel choir director that evokes that stereotype, they mention James Hall (Chapter 3) and Ricky Dillard overwhelmingly. Dillard exemplifies an over-the-top presentation of masculinity that encapsulates gospel performance of identity. A Chicago native and former house music DJ, Dillard is a Stellar award winner and Grammy nominee. He is a highly visible and demonstrative figure who cues the choir and instrumentalists, using singing, speaking, and bodily movement. According to gay spectators, Dillard is described as dancing in a provocative manner, to say the very least. By provocative, I am denoting his style of sonic and visual gender expression against which my self-identified heterosexual conversation partners say that they intentionally perform as in the case of gospel go-go musicians. In short, the heterosexual and heteropresenting musicians characterized Dillard's style as having an indistinguishable queer aura, due in part to his lack of public commentary about the style of directing and dance he performs.

A facet of the gospel public's commentary is Dillard's deployment of iconic sonic textures and gestures that resemble queer performance cultures such as the house music associated with the black and Latino gay Ballroom culture on the international music scene. One of his notable televised performances was on the 2008 Stellar awards with his group "New G" (also known as New Generation), during which they performed the song "Worked it Out."[1] Continuing the house music practice of covering existing repertoire (as with go-go music in DC), the song is signifying on "Jesus Can Work It Out," recorded in 1980 by Dr. Charles Hayes and the Cosmopolitan Church of Prayer Choir in Chicago. Starting the performance at the drop of the drumbeat on the kick drum and snare, Dillard says in the higher register of a strained baritone range reminiscent of a 1990s R&B ad lib, "Aw, yeah!" He represents the baritone contingent of vocalists who are often displaced in contemporary gospel music voicing. Lower voices are usually forced into singing treble timbres because artists are no longer composing

Flaming? Alisha Lola Jones, Oxford University Press (2020). © Oxford University Press.
DOI: 10.1093/oso/9780190065416.001.0001

for baritone and bass choral participation. He stands front and center with the choir behind him on the stage, claps, and calls three times, "Said he worked it out." The choir replies enthusiastically each time, "Worked it out!" Then as they sing the chorus, while simultaneously beginning "choirography" (a vernacular term referring to choreography for choirs) by doing the Bart Simpson dance in synchrony. Ricky Dillard & New G incorporated various dance moves into the performance; however, it was the musical reprise and dance he led at the end of the song that caused a buzz among gospel insiders. He said, "Well, the Bible says that David danced before the Lord with all his might [places his hand on his chest]. The spirit of David is coming upon me. Can I dance? Can I dance?" Tonéx and several artists associated with the gospel industry described Ricky Dillard & New G's danced exit as evoking specifically black and Latino gay Ballroom culture such as voguing and duckwalking.[2] According to gender studies and performance theorist Marlon Bailey, Ballroom culture is centered on "inner-city LGBT individuals' dress, dance, and vogue to compete for prizes and trophies."[3] Voguing is a performance culture that was made popular in the mainstream when it was featured in the documentary *Paris is Burning* (1990). Later Madonna appropriated vogue performance in the video for her song "Vogue" from her 1990 album *I'm Breathless: Music from and Inspired by the film Dick Tracy*. Though there were several noticeably popular or secular dance forms woven into Dillard's performance, it was the dance that closely resembled voguing and duckwalking from gay Ball culture that stirred controversy. Moreover, the house music scene in which Dillard got his start "is the signature sound of Ballroom culture,"[4] serving as the sonic texture for the gospel song. House music and Ballroom culture cultivate performance traditions that explore authenticity, mimicry, power, and play.

While his performance bore strong resemblance to gay Ballroom culture, he has neither publicly disputed nor confirmed a connection to queer identity—a neutrality that is quite common in "don't ask, don't tell" heteronormative social arrangements. In fact, I argue that given the tension and politics of outing, Dillard's disclosure of a queer sexual orientation is less useful to speculate than examining the aural-visual iconicity LGBTQ spectators noticed in his performance. By iconicity, I am referring to the theoretical concept within semiotics that theorist Charles S. Peirce mined to analyze resemblance between symbols.[5] The ways in which one symbol may bring to mind another symbol: moving one's arms to form a picture frame and freeze a pose resembles taking a picture. Dancing that same choreography while walking resembles voguing and squatting while doing similar arm gestures is iconicizing duckwalking. In other words, in assuming a queer viewing and listening of Dillard's performance as a form of play on a televised gospel platform, what work might a performed queer resemblance (un)do in homoantagonistic religious settings?

Queer spectators viewed this performance as comingling the two domains—church and Ballroom culture—in a manner that provides entertainment for spectators who overlap with both spheres. Through Dillard's presumed evocation of Ballroom culture in public gospel performance, his performance style registered to queer observers as an inverse of an emerging competition category within the Detroit Ballroom scene in the late 2000s that participants refer to as "church realness" or "church cunt realness."[6] Educing from the church realness category's designation of the performed protocols and ostentatious attire associated with Pentecostal culture, *church (cunt) realness* indicates performers' shared sociocultural memory, transference, resemblance, tailoring, and deconstruction of gendered roles such as the church Mother, usher, or deacon. In performance theorist Marlon Bailey's assessment, there are two primary functions of realness in black gay Ballroom culture:

> As a Ballroom-created standard, this criterion requires adherence to certain performances, self-representations, and embodiments that are believed to capture the authenticity of particular gender and sexual identities. These criteria for performative gender and sexual identities are established and function within a schema of race and class. Racialized, classed, gendered, and sexualized performances, self-presentations, and embodiments give realness its discursive power in both the Ballroom scene and in larger society . . .
>
> First, it is a guide that members use to construct, rehearse, and hone, their performances and the presentations of their bodies to compete, be judged, and snatch trophies at Balls for enacting the most "real" gender performance for a given realness category. Second, realness is based on individual and communal recognition of what I will suggest is the way in which members enact their realness performances to create the illusions of gender and sexual normativity and to blend into the larger heteronormative society to avoid homophobic discrimination, exclusion, violence and death.[7]

Based on a visual epistemology, creating the illusions of gender and sexual normativity to blend into larger heteronormative society is a means by which queer-inflected men are able to maintain their livelihood in the gospel music industry and status in churches. Frequently, church realness contenders reenact the ecstatic moment within worship of shouting, during which the Spirit of the Lord moves upon them. Simultaneously, the minoritized group of queer believers is elevated by playing with the dominant heteropatriarchal culture's willful obliviousness that prohibits gay believers from disclosing who they are without reprisal. Thus, Dillard's performance evokes the questions that form the basis of this chapter: To what extent have gospel artists identified, implicitly or unwittingly, with gay culture in their live national performances?

Since homosexuality is considered a sin in historically black Pentecostal traditions, gospel enthusiasts find out about artists' queer sexual history re-currently through their self-disclosure of deliverance from homosexuality as established in chapter 1.[8] Yet both homosexual men and men delivered from ho-mosexuality share a knowledge, memory, and/or imagination of same-gender attraction. Having established the sociocultural policing of the aural-visual features within gospel music scenes, I am interested in the ways in which kinship remains unavoidable among musicians with shared knowledge of same-gender attraction regardless of their self-identification. Moreover, in many ways, hetero-presenting men and gender-conforming men prop up what French philosopher Jacques Derrida coined as the *phallogocentric* features, that is, the privileging of men's speech in Pentecostal worship as a strategy for performing conformity in church realness as well. Their performances of identity inadvertently bol-ster bolster what French feminist Luce Irigaray calls the "the phallic economy" of Pentecostal settings which maintains a web of sociocultural activity aimed at managing perceptions of black manhood: create a male-centered worship ex-perience, fixate on black masculinity, and dislike exploration of same-gender affinities.

I return to Pentecostal Pastor Donnie McClurkin from chapter 1, who is the most popular musician that has disclosed his identity as delivered from homo-sexuality. Prompted by McClurkin's deliverance testimony that he preached at the 2010 Church of God in Christ (COGIC) convocation, this chapter engages gender studies and performance theory to examine music-centered Pentecostal worship and the ways in which he performs a church-oriented masculine iden-tity that I denote as church realness. I argue that men's performance of church realness in historically black Pentecostal churches is the deployment of sung and spoken heteropresentation and gender conformity. The objective of the perfor-mance is to blend in and assert dominance in gospel music heteropatriarchal forums in a manner that has been socioculturally imposed upon them. While church realness relies on identity performance, I am not advocating for an an-alytical lens to verify an individual's self-identification. Heteropresentation is characterized by what one displays about oneself and not by what one identifies or believes about oneself. Instead, I examine the extent to which church realness is a sustained performance of spiritual vitality that relies on socially undetected queerness. In this ethnography of McClurkin's demonstration of spiritual vitality, he engages public imagination and spiritual experience to defuse rumor[9] that he is queer and thereby maintains his sense of belonging in his religious com-munity. Through an analysis of McClurkin's self-presentation, I consider the fol-lowing questions: To what extent do men perform a heteronormative manhood in Pentecostal worship? What techniques do they use to perform a distance from designated queer features that are perceived as religio-culturally off-putting?

Heteropresentation requires modes of competent communication and interaction with other men in mixed company that sets the atmosphere within a performance. I call this performance of heteropresentation modes discretionary devices in which men present themselves in a manner that distances them from queer characteristics and resembles a more heterosexual identity. Men's performance of discretionary devices affords them the ability to engage with their extended networks, while escaping scorn and estrangement in their church homes. On axes of power, play, and performance, I find same-gender loving men have the potential to perform church realness with various combinations of the following strategies: 1) using musical performance to prove worship leader competency; 2) employing multiple rhetorical and performative devices to convey heterosexuality; 3) assessing the context climate or local theology[10] in which they perform; and 4) identifying and engaging diverse theological conversation partners to create kinship. For different reasons, men deploy the discretionary device of church realness to construct a sustained heterosexual identity that blends into the compulsory heterosexuality of conservative African American church and gospel music settings. While deploying a queer listening and viewing of gospel music scenes, let us now draw from previous chapters and turn to McClurkin's self-disclosure before a gathering of COGIC to observe his subtle intertwining of worship and performance that aligns with a church-oriented black manhood.

Stop the Music

The COGIC is the largest historically black Pentecostal organization in the United States. The annual COGIC convocation includes worships services, concerts, and workshops. As I mentioned in chapter 1, when we look at the religious traditions cultivating marketable musical talent, innumerable acclaimed gospel vocal musicians, songwriters, and keyboardists were raised and/or trained in the COGIC tradition: Dr. Mattie Moss Clark, The Clark Sisters, The Winans family, Pastor Kim Burrell, Bishop Yvette Flunder, Edwin Hawkins, Bishop Walter Hawkins, Pastor Daryl Coley, and Pastor Donnie McClurkin.

You may recollect that I mentioned McClurkin is a COGIC preacher-musician; the senior pastor of Perfecting Faith Church in Freeport, New York; an award-winning recording artist, and a producer on the TV show *Sunday Best*. McClurkin is the most popular black gospel artist to identify as "ex-gay" or delivered from homosexuality. He asserts that he was not "born this way."[11] In response to his message, McClurkin was disinvited in 2013 from the Rev. Dr. Martin Luther King Jr. Memorial concert in Washington, DC due to the organizers' concerns about his preaching against homosexuality.[12] COGIC is notable for engendering famous gospel musicians who have successfully attracted nonbelievers as their patrons. COGIC is also well-known for homoantagonistic and anti-feminization sermons and remarks that emphasize a disdain for men who demonstrate womanlike qualities in their gender expression.[13]

A believer's pursuit of deliverance from homosexuality in public self-identification and private practice functions in several ways. Chief among those functions in the public square is presenting oneself as abjuring duplicitous behavior such as being "down low" or bisexual. In McClurkin's *Eternal Victim/Eternal Victor* (2001) he describes relationships with men as perverse, specifically male leaders who were socially duplicitous and sexually inappropriate in their behavior.

And as I mentioned in chapter 6, McClurkin (2001) asserts that gospel music performance became a means through which he experienced spiritual deliverance that helped him to escape anxiety and trauma. The benefits he detects in music participation resemble the properties one might observe in musically induced flow, escapism, and/or trancing, during which musicians and listeners may lose themselves through and in the pleasure derived from sonic and somatic qualities of vocal and keyboard music production. Relatedly, I contend that his interactions as a youth with women or Mothers of the church would have been characterized as queering, diminishing his manhood with perceptions conveyed in the terms "mama's boy" or "choir boy" due to his affinity for Mothers of the church and vocal music-making. It is McClurkin's embodiment of these affinities as a formerly gay man that iconizes the music-centered expression of identity along gender lines.

At the one hundred and second COGIC convocation in Memphis, Tennessee, in 2009, Evangelist Joyce Rodgers exhorted and prayed for the attendees while speaking in tongues during the youth altar call. Following her intercessory prayer, McClurkin stepped forward to speak. Right before he began to preach, McClurkin raised his open hand– a stereotypically feminine, open position described in chapter 3 – gesturing to the instrumentalists to stop playing the music as he delivered the sermonette so that they would not be distracted from his message. "Hear me out," he instructed the believers present, cuing that what he was about to say is serious. This is a key performance move for McClurkin as he attempts to balance the gendered and sexualized liturgical domains that he engages as a preacher-musician: the masculine-coded and presumed heterosexual domain of the pulpit and the feminine-coded and presumed queer domain of vocal music participation.[14] As I mentioned in chapter 1, McClurkin said "They are covered by gifts and they are covered by music." With that phrase, McClurkin described the gift of music-making, one who possesses beguiling properties which compose a realm of concealment for believers who are presumably negotiating spiritual struggles with queerness. Unlike Flunder and Tonéx's embrace of queerness as a shamanistic trait, empowering them to handle good and evil in the spiritual realm, McClurkin cautions that music-making is a deflection which prevents believers' deliverance from perverse identities.

Allow me to draw your attention to two contentious reasons that McClurkin offered for stopping the music. The first reason McClurkin stops the music is to warn the young adults about the ways in which music-centered activities are used to lure them into sexual exploration. Here I would emphasize that the *telos* of the Pentecostal worship services is the altar call when people experience transcendence—tapping into a spectrum of experiences that range from ecstatic to trance-like—souls are won, new converts are identified, and people are healed. During the altar call, music is usually played to support the flow of the spirit but at this moment he breaks tradition. The second reason for stopping the music is that Pastor McClurkin claims that there was an overrepresentation of discreetly gay and feminine masculine musicians. Therefore, their participation as music ministers precludes them from responding to the altar call and receiving the deliverance from the queer sexuality that he claims to have experienced. And thus his instruction to stop the music signals his insider perspective that queer believers use their musical gifts to deflect attention from their spiritual needs.

You may recall from chapter 4 that the lead talker for Peculiar People enacts the same move of stopping the music with a raised, closed first to keep the audience's attention, especially when people seemed to be lost in the musical rhythms and not attuned to the message they were proclaiming. In both performance styles, a hypermasculine go-go lead talker and a "nonhomosexual" preacher-musician emphasized the importance of utterance, participant's singing and speaking using their mouths. Reminiscent of trancing, the practice of getting lost in the music more precisely intersects with McClurkin's and Dré's theological perspective in which they hold music as a potential distraction to the ritual work of deliverance and salvation. Indeed, music performance can be a means through which participants escape trauma and disengage from actively participating in the spiritual work of achieving transcendence through worship leadership. Conversely, some Pentecostal believers have asserted that musically induced deliverance is essential to completing the spiritual work. Gospel vocalist Tonéx's father instructed him to listen to gospel music to navigate spiritual ailments.[15] However, in the 2013 documentary *The New Black,* Tonéx points out that irony lays within the remedy that his father prescribed.

> I remember my father's prescription for getting back on track was to go listen to some gospel records. I think what he meant was go back to my roots—I guess what he thought was my foundation, but the people I was listening to, they were gay too.

Perhaps Tonéx's account supports McClurkin's concerns about music preventing deliverance, and if that is the case Flunder would argue that believers would have to throw out most of the beloved repertoire. "Gospel music is gay music. Our most popular songs were written and recorded by gay musicians," she asserted in our October 2015 personal conversation. COGIC-raised minister Bishop Carlton Pearson expounds on the grounds for the irony in using gospel music as a remedy because the music itself is believed to be composed by scores of discreetly gay musicians:

> Most of the prominent music of the church, at least for the last 50 or 60 years has come through many men who had homosexual tendencies. And who were very creative, very spiritual, almost mystical and they wrote our music. So, we sang their songs and cursed [identity] theirs at the same time.[16]

These deliverance listening practices have three implications. First, like culturally competent musicians, McClurkin and Tonéx are able to flow, generating music that is Spirit-inspired, each knitting together the community he serves.[17] In fact their narratives suggest that they used music as a means to create private and portable sanctuary within the conventional public sanctuaries they frequented.

Second, the anxiety and irony to which Donnie McClurkin and Tonéx refer unwittingly reveals another layer of meaning cultivated in vocalist's musical participation that positions one's deliverance as a sexual orientation in and of itself—neither homosexual or heterosexual—but rather as a music-centered expression of pleasure through the use of their bodies in service to God, church, and the community. Their vocal music and ministry participation creates a kinship that remains regardless of their self-identification, positioning gradations of queerness as the quality of a musician's facility. Participation is the fabric of their kinship, wherein the musical soundscape provides a sphere in which they are bonded sonic-somatically fluid, malleable, relative, and promiscuous. Vocal music making is a love language unlike any other. In the heteropatriarchal contexts of Pentecostalism, the activity is embodied, symbolically fashioning intimacy through same-gender discovery and revelation of musical semiotics as vocalists negotiate: sensations and objects of desire within the texts; sonic-somatic intimacy through collaboration with other musicians; sonic iconicity and indexing of pleasure; and adoration of a God conventionally constructed as male thereby depicting a love and preference for the highest, attractive attributes of "real" manhood.[18] Customarily fostered through various apprentice and collaborative relationships, musicians' sociocultural knowledge of ministry, intimacy, and discretion is transmitted through the ministry of music. Performing in music worlds of worship, "delivered" men have shared experiences of the unspoken aspects of pleasure, sexuality, and sensuality while drawing close to the divine.

Third, I hear McClurkin's concerns as more than wariness about spiritual contamination, liturgical focus, or musico-enchantment. Simultaneously, worship participation readily touches their minds, bodies, and spirits, during one of the most opening activities one can engage: skillful worship. On a psychological level, the potential compounded meanings of that worship soundscape to which sexual predators are likely to be drawn and contribute musically adds to a sense of spiritual obstruction. As I mentioned in chapter 6, intense, music-making and listening—both live and recorded—are fashioned as the gateway drug and instrument for priming sexual conquests. Like McClurkin and B.Slade, victims of sexual abuse are made to return to musical abusers. They are made to listen to and ascribe sacredness to their music and message. And then, they are forced to create a logic that discredits the discomfort and disconsolation they feel, for the "greater good of the community." Again, this is a form of church facilitated, sonically-induced Stockholm syndrome.

Orality

While McClurkin is the most popular formerly homosexual preacher to deliver those 2009 altar call remarks at the convocation, the message against feminine-presenting and/or homosexual men was not new. Instead of using music to deliver the believers, McClurkin relies on the traditional COGIC script of deliverance by using harsh language to coerce the queer believers to come forward in large numbers. His use of the rhetorical template registers to me as an internalization of homoantagonistic and transphobic rhetoric. Since McClurkin's testimony about deliverance from homosexuality in the early 2000s, he has been outspoken about young men and women being disproportionately "turned out" or introduced to homosexuality in the church. McClurkin's statements are in line with a conventional COGIC convocation heteropatriarchal script of incendiary language that has been sustained by preachers and speakers such as Evangelist Frances Kelly[19] and Pastor Kim Burrell.[20] Their sermons chasten queer and gender-nonconforming people. For example, "sissy" is a problematic term that has been a fixture of the annual COGIC convention as a way of describing men exhibiting feminine gender expression and flamboyance, often while participating in musical performance. Unlike other preachers who deliver the anti-homosexual sermons from a third-person perspective, McClurkin preached the sermon in first-person, the embodiment of a living epistle to be read for sin. Such as designation symbolically makes for an even more compelling sermon about the potential for gay believers to experience spiritual transformation. An important admission that McClurkin made was that he was entrenched in contemporary gay gospel music networks as a "(fore)father". McClurkin stated that youths are drawn to "perverted" sexual exploration at music-centered events such as late-night gospel musicals.

As McClurkin reconciles his past sexual identity and gender expression with his aspiration toward efficacy in ministry, he is able to tap into discreet modes of communication with, social assessment by, and deliverance ministry to believers with queer knowledge. In the sermonette to the COGIC convocation, McClurkin asserts that the youth's gay sexual orientation or unconventional gender expression is a perversion that stems from fatherlessness and inappropriate intimacy with adult male predators that include church leaders. McClurkin admonished:

> They have been failed on many, many points . . . They have been raised without fathers. They have been left empty and hurt. And, the very one's of us that have been their forefathers have failed. Hear me please. Hear me please. The very ones of us that were over the generations failed; myself included . . .They are being tainted and they are being turned by people in their generation.

While facilitating the altar call, McClurkin assumed culpability and chastised those who have not accepted the deliverance he claims to have experienced. To be sure, my point here is neither to dispute nor affirm McClurkin's self-identification as delivered from homosexuality. I argue, however, that McClurkin's rhetoric deflects observers' perception that he maintains gay social knowledge, maneuvers, and performance that are undetectable to heteropatriarchal gospel music patrons.

> I went to Mason Temple and sat at the musicals. No. NO. NO. NO. No. NO. NO. NO. Where are the fathers? We have many instructors but we don't have many fathers. Where are the fathers that will embrace the boys and say, "No. No. No. He can't have you. He can't have you. He won't have you." Where are the fathers that say, "I will not kill you. I will not condemn you but I will nurture you."
>
> And today I am overwhelmed in this holy convocation because I see feminine men. And listen, do not applaud like it is a bash. It is because we failed. It is not their fault. It is not the children's fault. It is because we failed.
>
> We didn't father our children. We didn't cover our children. We didn't discern the seed and we didn't uproot it. We failed our boys. We failed our girls.[21]

I have repeated portions of his remarks from chapter 1 to return to McClurkin's focus on fatherlessness. The message aligns with various teachings that address black male absenteeism in the home as being linked to absenteeism in the church. His sermonette challenges the notion that a mere black male presence is enough. He is advocating for a greater quality in their ethics of care and ministry of presence. McClurkin was a victim of incest and credits his former gay sexuality to molestation by male family members. "The men who do not father" refers to the lack of appropriate love languages and interactions with men in the home and church. His use of "instructors" refers to trustworthy adults, presumably men in this context, who introduce young people to sexual activity in an inappropriate manner. McClurkin's reflection on absent fathers is ironic, especially in light of his public repentance for being absent in his son's life.[22] Also, he offers that fatherly men should not provoke or condemn but nurture the young men who they observe questioning their gender expression and sexual identity.

And yet, it was McClurkin's condemning remarks about gospel vocalist and producer Tonéx's self-disclosure as unapologetically gay, during the altar call that was widely circulated among COGIC Christian and gospel fans. The succeeding excerpt is from his remarks that he proclaimed with tears, illustrating that he knows firsthand what God can do.

> We talk about the Tonéx situation and it is only turning their hearts further away from God and making them believe that such conversation is real when it is not real. It is not real. It is not real. It is not real. It is not real. God did not call us to such perversion. God didn't call this generation to such perversion. God did not call you, young people, to such perversion. Your generations have lied to you. Society has failed you. The only way you can find real hope is in Jesus Christ. That is the only way that you can find deliverance. I tell you of the truth. [speaks glossolalia] If it hadn't been for this Jesus, I would be homosexual to this day but he is a deliverer.

McClurkin is one of several Pentecostal ministers, including officials in Tonéx's former Pentecostal Assemblies of the World organization, that have deemed Tonéx as being of a "reprobate mind" (cf Romans 1:28), thus discrediting as heretical his message of welcoming and affirming LGBTQ believers. In response to Tonéx's stance as an unapologetically gay Pentecostal, the PAW community provided him with two choices: seek deliverance to be reconciled back into the fold or be unrepentant and released from affiliation with the fold. As I mentioned in chapter 5 Tonéx proclaimed unashamedly that he did not need deliverance from homosexuality and consequently, he became disaffiliated from various Pentecostal organizations. Using Tonéx's rejection as a fall from grace scenario, McClurkin admonished the youths at the convocation not to follow Tonéx's example and revealed four points of contention about gay discourse: 1) naming musical events as a site for gay youths; 2) opposing Tonéx's narrative that being openly gay is a real identity; 3) accrediting fatherlessness with the prevalence of gay youth; and 4) asserting deliverance from homosexuality is possible.

However, as I reviewed the footage with my openly gay music ministry colleagues, they repeatedly expressed their skepticism about the anti-gay nature of his remarks saying statements such as, "His slip is showing"; "That queen" (with an eye roll); or "He needs to just come on out of the closet." When I asked for clarification about how they knew he was queer beyond rumors that they heard, they said just listen to what he is saying and how he is saying it. In other words, they were suggesting that in his mode of communication he was unwittingly revealing his familiarity with and perhaps comfort within gay culture through socio-cultural multilingualism.

Ball Commentator as Preacher

By assessing the extent to which the COGIC convocation attendees presented themselves authentically, McClurkin's remarks iconicized a privileging and internalization of the paradigmatic commentator in a black and Latino Ballroom competition about which Marlon Bailey writes, demonstrating the primacy of orality in black Pentecostalism and its overlapping characteristics with LGBTQ performance culture. Like the commentator on the platform of competitions one might hear on the show *Pose* (2019) or the documentary *Paris is Burning* (1990), McClurkin speaking as the preacher on the platform observes the performance of identity and helps discursively produce the gender and sexual formations, while asking the metaphoric judges or congregants in this case to assess the performer's successful unmarking of queerness.[23] The human objects of our collective gaze are assessed for both their presentation of authenticity and illusion.[24] And in his assessment, they are found to be wanting spiritually and performatively within a realm of church-centered realness that privileges heteropresentation at all times. Both Ballroom culture and Pentecostal hierarchy are male-dominated and assesses the maintenance of heterosexual, cisgender performance. What distinguishes Pentecostalism from Ballroom culture is that men are expected to avoid feminine masculinity, traits that are read as evincing sexual queerness. There is no acceptance of varied expressions of masculinity. In fact, I contend that the qualification valued most is men's performance of identity, rather than their precise naming of their identity, experience, and truth.

Still, traditionally, Pentecostal black churches do not reward homosexual men who are honest about who they are.

Like a commentator in Ballroom culture, McClurkin used the mic in his role as a preacher and pastor in that moment to describe the scene, helping to discursively produce the gender and sexual formations. Instead of being performed on a runway, the convocation was the frame for analyzing the performance of stable, church-oriented masculinity. Similar to how the commentator would prompt the judges, McClurkin asks the gathered believers to scrutinize the performance of gender nonconformity in their midst. However, his self-identification as delivered from homosexuality in itself undermines his assertion. McClurkin's movement from one sexual orientation to another (homosexual to nonhomosexual) through intangible, spiritual means illustrates the symbolic fluidity of identity in the very act of undergoing deliverance. Thus, that fluidity becomes the basis for the persistent suspicion that he and other believers face when they share their testimony, an anxiety-inducing task for all involved.

Shedding light on the aims of the Ballroom systems, Bailey stresses that the realness criteria are hinged on the desire to blend into heteronormative society. A successful performance of realness minimizes any sign of deviation from heteronormativity. As a result, when church realness is exhibited in Pentecostal spheres men must present a persona that encompasses some configuration of interiority, chastity or monogamy, heterosexuality, and nonfeminine masculinity. To adhere to heteropresentation of black Pentecostal manhood, they distance themselves from any appearance that they are promoting homosexuality or men's exploration of feminine domains.

As I reviewed McClurkin's personal narrative in *Eternal Victim/Eternal Victor* (2001), he confirmed his development of versatile communication skills as my conversation partners suspected. McClurkin avoids social dissonance by deploying what I previously discussed in chapter 6 as discretionary devices that distance him from perceived queerness.[25] Discretionary devices are techniques employed by presumed or confirmed queer men to distance them from perceived queerness; examples include evasion, silence, unrequited heterosexual love, suggestion of interest, forms of play, and ex-gay self-identification. For instance, McClurkin explained that when he was homosexual he developed a social bilingualism that permitted him to communicate with other gay men in mixed social company. Resembling the "down low"or bisexual narrative, the concept of social bilingualism is not new, connoting ingenuity and social anxiety about one's personal presentation, but the implications of using such modes of communication in music ministry have not been explored. According to linguist Donald Winford, social bilingualism or multilingualism are instances of code-switching, when a speaker alternates between two or more languages.[26] McClurkin divulges that he would "converse one way with people in general, and a completely different way with members of [his] secret inner circle, yet in the same lifestyle. It was something like radar. No matter where you were, you could detect others with the same lifestyle; as well as be detected."[27] His ability to converse in various ways with diverse people is essential for what performance theorist Richard Schechner calls "dark play" in that only some knew that he was discreetly communicating with other homosexual men. While it may seem innocuous to some, dark to others, it is certainly a subversion of the meta-communication[28] of heteronormativity in gospel settings that I previously discussed.[29]

On the one hand, discretionary devices are empowering for men in that they are tools for discretely engaging one another in public. On the other hand, discretionary devices are disempowering for those who are left out in performances of "dark play." Performance theorist Richard Schechner wrote further, "Playing in the dark means that some of the players don't know they are playing . . . Dark fantasy involves fantasy, risk, luck, daring, invention, and deception. Dark play may be entirely private, known to the player alone . . . Dark play rewards its players by means of deceit, disruption, and excess."[30] In fact, McClurkin's "ex-gay" label deflects from observers' sense that he maintains the homosexual social knowledge and maneuvers that heteropatriarchal gospel music patrons do not detect. As a result of researching this multilingual discretionary device in his narrative, I elected to do a queer listening and viewing of the footage—that is, to observe his remarks with attention to potential black gay signifyin(g).

In the aforementioned sermonette, McClurkin he addresses the role of musical social life in queer gender expression and sexual identity. Allow me to reassert that my point here is neither to dispute nor affirm McClurkin's self-identification as "delivered" from homosexuality; however, I argue that he is able to communicate with homosexual believers in a more precise manner due to his social knowledge from his queer past. As a worship leader, he assesses others' queer potential, which may expose him to temptations by "familiar spirits" (see also chapter 4) of sexual queerness. In mixed company, in plain site he engages queer believers "under the sound of his voice" and traverses social networks that are otherwise too inconspicuous for gay allies to cross.

Within his exhortation, McClurkin "reads" the gay and lesbian believers in the event. "Read" is a popular black gay vernacular for finding a flaw in someone or thing, in a performative manner, as mentioned earlier. Also, McClurkin used several signifiers that evoke black gay Ballroom and homosexual cultural terms[31] such as "house," "(fore)father," "turned (out)," and "children" or "kids"—all of which are colloquial terms used to construct metaphoric belonging and kinship among participants in black and Latino Ballroom culture.[32] On the one hand, he implicates the churches in the tainting, embedding, sowing, or wiring of the young people with a queer identity. On the other hand, McClurkin preaches a message similar to gospel artist Tye Tribbett's position that homosexuality is not God's ideal or natural, and thus being gay is not a legitimate identity.[33] His assertion of those claims was a manifestation of his internalization of the COGIC convocation script that has been delivered by several preachers such as Bishop Earl Carter and Evangelist Frances Kelly, who will be discussed shortly. At once, McClurkin adapted what registered as gay vernacular and posture while chastising them with what they already know about themselves.

Reviewing McClurkin's sermon further, I am struck by the manner with which he challenges the notion that a person's self-identification as gay is "real." He trembled and wailed:

> I stand here looking at young people that are not even comfortable. They talk about being real. They are not comfortable being real.

In the sermonette, McClurkin conveyed two meanings of "real": the conventional meaning referring to youth's display of authenticity and the queer meaning of identity performance. In gospel contexts, I call this deployment of multivalent terminology a "church realness." Bailey explains, "realness as a theory of quotidian performance offers a way to understand, primarily, how in society beyond the Ballroom scene, all gender and sexual identities are performed."[34] McClurkin refers to authenticity by saying, "making them believe that such conversation is real when it is not real" or authentic. He code-switches: "Talk about being real" or performing identity. "They are not comfortable with being real" or being who they are. His evocation of "real" is a missile of critique, loaded with transgressive queer meaning. McClurkin deploys the queer term of "realness" that is used in black gay Ballroom culture performance practice as pointing out a flaw in how the young people were carrying themselves.

In actuality, like McClurkin suggested and his colleagues have acknowledged, conservative denomination conventions and gospel music conferences are where "the saints" purchase pornography in their hotel rooms and participate in what same-gender loving gospel vocalist and activist Bishop Yvette Flunder calls "anonymous clandestine encounters."[35] According to one of my openly homosexual interactants, a healthy contingent of participants who attend the COGIC convocation and music conferences like Gospel Music Workshop of America and the National Convention of Gospel Choirs and Choruses use established networks and technology such as popular gay male websites and gay apps to meet up with other men. On those sites, it is common and expected for men to state the rules of engagement: "I am a down low man looking for . . ." or "I am an HIV positive man seeking an HIV positive man." When I evaluated the apps, I learned that like Facebook or Twitter, the sites have a GPS feature. It is a little bit more sophisticated in that the user can see other men's proximity to them. For men who would like casual sex, they can use this feature to get a sense of the distance of prospective partners. In fact, some of my gay conversation partners attested that close proximity is a primary criterion for casual sex. One should note that the GPS tracking remains on even if the user is offline. For cellular phone users, the GPS feature can be turned off when they take the battery out of their phones. This means that while in worship homosexual men can get a sense of who in their proximity is homosexual without speaking to each other in public; this includes any homosexual artist who subscribes to the social media website or application and has their phone on their person. Thus, the subscriber emits a signal without uttering a word or disclosing their identity to those who are not on the social media websites, which is a multi-media form of dark play. In the following section, I consider the extent to which delivered as a form of church realness is a discretionary device that provides men with the tools to assume religious, social, and cultural dominance in Pentecostal settings regardless of their sexual orientation. By doing so, men's public presentation and not their self-identification permits men to maintain their social networks, livelihood, and kinship to men with shared experiences.

Delivered as a Form of Church Realness

If one were to rely on popular discourse, being a musician delivered from homosexuality—that is, being nonhomosexual—is a sexual orientation that is a music-related sensorimotor stimulation of the entire body and that is triggered by musical inducement.[36] However, I observe that being delivered from homosexuality provides a vantage point into sociocultural interactions, identity fluidity, and spirituality informed by transformation that is imagined as always in flux, as processual. This rhetorical maneuver of declaring one's deliverance status is one of several tools black male gospel artists use to deal with the theopolitics of self-identification in gospelized contexts in which black masculine anxiety is pervasive. Black men's sexuality, interiority, spiritual animation, and stability of transformation are always monitored. As a result, men go through drastic measures to demonstrate compliance even if doing so is inconsistent with their quotidian life. At stake is the protection and security of black church fragility.

I have observed McClurkin perform distance from queerness as forgetting, disgust with, and social separation from queer men who remain "in the life." Such distancing is articulated in spiritual language of deliverance. As I wrote in chapter 1, Pastor McClurkin concludes the chapter titled "A Seed is Planted" in his book with an emphatic (suggested by its capitalization in the original text), multireferent statement "I AM DELIVERED"[37] that is variously interpreted as an apologetic or polemic proclamation. "I AM DELIVERED" in many ways cues his fan base that he is certain and spiritually fit, with the help of the Holy Spirit, to continue to lead them competently in worship. "I AM DELIVERED" suggests that he has repented and turned from what some believers consider to be destructive sexual practices. Succinctly, Pastor McClurkin navigates public perception and asserts, in a Pentecostal idiomatic language, that he is not of a reprobate mind, like Tonéx has been designated. And McClurkin is still fit to readily set the atmosphere.

The proclamation is consistent with common Pentecostal language of healing and spiritual transformation, where believers are imbued with the power to turn away from the deepest temptation. As an apologetic, McClurkin argues against skeptics who claim deliverance from homosexuality is impossible or unsustainable. His theological stance is that the seed of homosexuality can be plucked up with the word of God. The phrase "I AM DELIVERED" is a polemic engaging those familiar with what McClurkin calls the "underworld" of homosexuality in black churches and the community to whom he publicly denies the rumor that he is a down low or discreetly gay man.

McClurkin's ex-gay self-identification evokes strong critique from some openly gay believers, most notably Bishop Yvette Flunder, who asserts that his negating characterization of "ex-gay" is a symptom of self-loathing and rejection of his true or natural sexual identity. Sociologist Richard Pitt described this negating self-identification as characteristic of an "identity confusion" stage.[38] He connotes openly gay critics' suspicion of ex-gays stems from their own personal experiences of unsuccessfully attempting to avoid same-gender attraction. Pitt recalls:

> In discussing their own failed attempts to reject the homosexual identity, a number of the men ridicule so-called "ex-gays," arguing that they do not believe that God has truly taken away the person's homosexual orientation. They suggest that the men have only changed their behavior, but that there has been no actual change in their feelings or orientation toward men.[39]

It is hard for McClurkin to refute Pitt's critique and intimation that he is a homosexual man in denial about or performing distance from who he is. Pitt maintains that African American conservative churches both cultivate and despise sexual subcultures of same-gender loving and homoerotic believers. "The sexual subcultures keep people," Flunder contends, "on a treadmill of getting delivered and getting bound, getting delivered and getting bound, getting delivered and getting bound."[40] Flunder's accusation of McClurkin's self-loathing also suggests that he is less than forthcoming or that he is on the down low in his current sexual activity. As I examine McClurkin's narrative, I find the term *homolatent*, as coined by black queer feminist scholar Moya Bailey, useful in assessing the sociocultural tensions he faces. Bailey sets forth

> "homo" to foreground the same gender orientation of the behavior and "latent" to foreshadow the "pathological" potential of queer desire's rupture into the real. For those who are unable to transition successfully, their "latent" powers manifest as a penchant for violence and nihilistic destruction waged on those closest to them. The violent nature of homolatent interactions sets it apart from traditional nomenclature used to describe same-sex attraction. Unlike "queer," "homosexual," or "same gender loving," *homolatent* attempts to address the abjection of desire.

One's penchant for violence can also be self-inflicted through self-negating, self-denying, or homo-antagonism toward people who remind a person of their past. The spread of these rumors has been fueled by the fact that he is over fifty and has never married. Even when he was reportedly engaged to Nicole C. Mullen, he was derided in the media for being disingenuous about his intentions to marry the woman he was dating.[41]

In several respects, the "naturalness" of who this is, though displayed in performance and public personae, is found in his private and portable sanctuary of gospel music. I witnessed McClurkin's construction of sanctuary on March 10–11, 2014 at the St. Sabina revival, and I am drawn toward McClurkin's and other itinerant preacher-musicians' construction of various extended sacred communities into church families. He constructs extended church homes like St. Sabina where he did the revival that may be more fitting than the Perfecting Church where he is senior pastor or the COGIC denomination where he was ordained, allowing for a spectrum of heuristic identity performances without the risk of separation and public humiliation should he be unsuccessful in his performance of normative gender role competence. As an ex-gay man, McClurkin retains traces of social discretion devices that permit him to maintain connection to men with whom he shares a queer knowledge and memory. These devices are similar in style and gesture to African American modes of communication referred to as signifyin', the cultural practice of ingenuity in word play that are combined with queer-oriented adaptation and identity performance.

Altar Call: Musical Dominance and Anti-Homophobic Kinship

Black Pentecostal preachers who sing frequently shift gears, using their musical gifts or skills to engage the worship service attendees. In essence, some ministers who are like Pastor McClurkin draw on their more culturally prized ability to sing to seal the celebration moment in the service. Music ministry is his comfort zone. However, moving along the spectrum of oralities—that is, from preaching to singing—is also a way of tempering the gendered meanings associated with the pulpit and music ministry domains.

McClurkin's narrative provides a broader understanding of discretion, especially when one's sexual history has been stigmatized. I am struck by the extent to which discretion provides space for recovery and reconciliation from the stigma placed upon male victims of imbalanced, sexualized same-gender power. Sociologist Erving Goffman's (1963) examination of stigma is useful to understand common modes of managing what Goffman calls "spoiled identity." Stigma then refers to the shame a person may feel when their identity is spoiled in some way. Within black Christian communities, for example, there is a taboo against addressing the homoerotic dimensions of arousal, intimacy, incest, and pleasure among men, especially if those encounters occurred in music-making spaces. Finding spaces of worship that function as a socially clean slate, where one is not constantly read through their past, is important for any person who is trying to thrive in their quality of life.

As I participant-observed the revival featuring Pastor Donnie McClurkin on March 10–11, 2014 in a Catholic parish called the Faith Community of St. Sabina, I realized the distinction between inhabiting a "church home" versus belonging to the metaphoric Body of Christ. When believers reside in the Body of Christ, they experience freedom of being and expression that permits them to explore kinship and like-mindedness in various ways. In the United States' popular religious imagination Catholicism is considered theologically conservative, much like McClurkin's COGIC denomination.[42] However, the senior pastor, Polish American Father Pfleger is known for his theologically inclusive and social justice driven sermons. He is affiliated with majority-black progressive organizations such as the Samuel Dewitt Proctor Conference and Trinity United Church of Christ. The church Father Pfleger pastors is inclusive in its community engagement but its theological leanings are not readily apparent on the church website "About Us" section:

> The Faith Community of St. Sabina is a Word-based, Bible teaching church that believes in the power of praise and worship. We are a spiritual hospital where all are welcome and invited to "taste and see the goodness of the Lord." Our purpose is to nurture and develop spiritually mature Christians who are trained leaders and who are not confined by the walls of the sanctuary, but can penetrate the world in order to present God's way of living as a divine option.[43]

McClurkin's "appearance" at St. Sabina is a means through which he attempted to diffuse the damage he made that caused him to be disinvited to the MLK memorial celebration.[44] By ministering to a more progressive congregation, perhaps he sought to diffuse tensions cultivated from his previous "heterosexist" or deliverance focused messages.

As the revival comes to a close, Chicago gospel legend Dr. Walt Whitman moves from the left arm (stage right) of the "cross-shaped" sanctuary to the front. He sings a verse and chorus of "God Is" (1979) by the late Rev. James Cleveland,[45] as an "altar call" song. Then the ensemble sings the verse and chorus. McClurkin starts to sing the verse an octave higher than Whitman sang it, approaching the edges of his vocal range. Beside him, knelt a dapper white record executive who passes him a glass of water in between each phrase he sung. When McClurkin concludes the song, he moves from his chair behind the pulpit over to the piano on the right of the sanctuary and begins to play, while Dr. Whitman holds the mic for him. He plays and sings traditional hymns and Christian contemporary songs but the Catholic parishioners do not seem to know the repertoire he chooses. McClurkin then points out that this repertoire is falling out of practice, one of the big concerns that he and fellow producer

Daniel Moore of BET's *Sunday Best* have encountered throughout the auditions and show run.

I was impressed by the homosocial, intimate, and playful nature of the impromptu worship that they led that night. All of the soloists after the sermon were men. I believe that Donnie McClurkin's performance of the melody in an octave higher than Whitman represents more than McClurkin singing in his *tessitura* or comfortable range. I could hear that McClurkin kept ascending, vocally pushing the limits. On the surface, his musical gesture was one-upmanship. McClurkin ascended musically, singing the melody higher than Whitman, toward the extremes of his range. By doing so, he asserted a sung signification on being a musical or metaphorically sexual "top," which is a vernacular term used to describe a person's personality, sexual position preference, or social dominance.[46] At St. Sabina, he was permitted to assert dominance outside of the rhetorical or masculine domains of the Pentecostal worship, which is his secondary talent. Instead, he enacted a form of gospelized treble timbre transcendence that was a self-identification of social dominance among his musician and preacher peers.

Preachers deliver sermons during altar call to invite attendees to accept their spiritual deliverance. Much of the language they use to illustrate the nature of sin is offensive but it prompts people to distance themselves from sinful behavior. As an ex-gay preacher and musician, McClurkin embodies insights into the spiritual struggle with queerness. Using shared language, preachers can communicate in a precise manner with queer believers to prompt their deliverance from spiritual strongholds. For McClurkin, deliverance is imagined as a process to separate himself from essentialized homosexual communication, history, and practice; however, discretionary devices of church realness permit ex-gay and homosexual men to be conciliatory about the dynamics of how they identify each other.

In this chapter, I interpreted queer(ed) men's use of a "church realness" in gestural and rhetorical performance as a vital tool to construct homes. Men who perform church realness attempt to allow their religious and queer identities to coexist while they fellowship in their primary communities of faith. They do so both to belong with their church family and transcend surveillance of their values and practices. To avoid dissonance with church home social values, black queer and ex-gay musicians may elect to use discretionary devices to connect with extended church families and other networks. For those outside the world of gay social circles to interpret discretionary devices, they must be nimble in how they decipher complex arrangements of understanding in which musicians engage in dark play in the formation of gender identity, imagination, and rumor. Heterosexist performances, both on the part of preachers and musicians, put same-gender loving musicians in the difficult position of choosing livelihood or truth.

8

"Preaching to the Choir and Being Played"

An Altar Call

Traditionally, "preaching to the choir" is a metaphoric saying that characterizes a speaker communicating with an audience who presumably share the speaker's perspective. However, my research demonstrates that the preacher's perspectives and choir's perspectives are more precisely described as adjacent on the perch of the sanctuary stage. And yet, for many of the people who come from historically Black Pentecostal traditions, the premise of this research, following discourses surrounding the flamboyant choir director stereotype, is metaphorically preaching to the choir. I agree that this book preaches to the choir through both metaphoric shared experience, while always contesting the power structures that assert dominance over subordinate singing domains in the phallomusicocentric and phallosonocentric networks of the historically Black Pentecostal tradition. Exposing these narratives points toward embedded toxicity that threaten the bonds believers say they seek to solidify and protect.

"Never trust women. Women are the enemy." Several homosexual men have divulged to me that their mentors cautioned them with this advice not to trust women, as they began to explore the social implications of accepting their sexual orientation. In disclosing that they have received that advice, my research conversation partners signaled to me that they never thought they would be able to share such intimate details about their piety, desires, and relationships with a cisgender heterosexual woman from the Word of Faith movement. To speak freely with me in interviews was for innumerous conversation partners the beginning of an undoing of distrust based on the notion that we are in competition, vying for attention among the scarce supply of "(un)available" men and the resources associated with the "(un)available" men's status. Unfortunately, the men's confession that they were notified to be conciliatory to women did not indicate an instant embrace of me or other women, nor should it. Developing trust is a process. I have observed a few of these relationships flourish, and then there are some relationships where I sense through less than forthcoming communication and their subsequent lack of advocacy for women on issues such as equitable compensation of ministry leadership hierarchy that our boundaries are still in tact. I have heard expressions of envy and experienced sabotage of

Flaming? Alisha Lola Jones, Oxford University Press (2020). © Oxford University Press.
DOI: 10.1093/oso/9780190065416.001.0001

developing heterosexual relationships in which attractive men's sexual duality is intimated. Many of my brothers in music ministry perceive themselves to be disempowered to enact any substantive, sociocultural change for themselves, let alone the women whose misogynistic experiences are so similar to their own. They, too, are waiting, campaigning to be chosen. And when I follow where the money flows, I detect the true substance of where alliances lay. Musicians are beholden to preachers whose heteropresentation is safe-guarded and reinforced in a heteropatriarchal power structure, the merits of which have been glorified and internalized by the people most oppressed by it. The heteropatriarchal power structure is engineered to dominate symbollically feminine domains. Those invested in the structure's flourishing—presumably men, but ironically women can be its most vehement proponents—seeking to become dominant, and even queer men internalize these aims. All the while, openly gay men are kept in place and out of the running for primacy in the decision-making ranks due to the constant looming fear that their identities will be used against them. In short, we are being played against each other like crabs climbing to the top of a barrel with a sealed lid on top of it.

Conversely, I have heard similar, negative perceptions about gay men that warn women of the deceptive down low man. "They are backstabbers," I've heard a Mother of the church say. Several women have echoed a question posed to me by a female caller when I was interviewed about my research on radio: "How am I supposed to relate to gay men? What use do I have for them?" My response to them was what would it look like if we understood closeness and intimacy as inclusive of and more than sexual possibility in relationships. Homosexual men have always been a fixture in our lives as godfathers, uncles, cousins, fathers, brothers, (un)available love interests, benefactors, and ministers.

Both of these perspectives challenge the assumptions that just because men and women share the same domains, their shared occupancy does not denote shared understanding or affinity. Although in many ways women and homosexual or gender-nonconforming men may be socioculturally compatible, it does not mean they are talking among themselves. Not every woman has a "gay husband" or best friend, and many gay men are without cisgender heterosexual companions. In fact, these social variations suggest that there are times that men and women music ministers do not seem to hear each other over the music. And their anxieties and apprehension evinced the need to discover the ways in which we are much more than our erotic potential. We are human beings with social and cultural formations. Obviously, men and women can love each other deeply without having to consume each other, and that is sacred territory. At the very basic level, believers gain much by pursuing a profound understanding of sisterhood and brotherhood that fosters transparency, care, trust, hospitality, and mutual critical affirmation without having to consummate that love through sexual intercourse. And perhaps it is the very domain of collective music-making, the cocreation that it fosters, where an unspoken consummation materializes.

More than the coupling of women with gay men in vocal music participation is the impenetrable work spouse relationships that occur between the preacher and the chief musician. Protected by compensation arrangements and confidentiality expectations that favor the pastor as boss, that coupling is the dominant working relationship in African American Christian religiosity. With this in mind, I wonder what are the ways in which men's collective participation in vocal music ministry has come to function as a form of eunuchoidism to handle women in churches, while granting access to men who are phallogocentrically oriented, at the very least via their servile affinity for phallomusicentrism or multivalent male-centered music-making. Undoubtedly, there is a pervasive investment in men's cocreation after their own kind, a creative enterprise that reasserts dominance and pre-eminence. The unspoken connections and privileges afforded through this system are beguiling to the very best of men. And yet I am committed to spark a change, however slow it may be.

With these tightly knitted dynamics interwoven into the fabric of historically African American Christian religious music life, I am compelled to do the work of prizing the advancement of women. This advancement must be done through the invaluable opportunity for women to speak for themselves. Our project does not absolve men from the imperative to stand in solidarity with women as they seek equity in church and denomination leadership structures.

Through my transcongregational research, I have found numerous performances of black male presence on which scholars have not focused: various alliances, private worship, male homosociality, ministry of presence, and itinerancy. Each performance of black male presence portrayed something unique about who they are and the means by which they realize their relationship with God. On the one hand, there are ways that preachers may provide space and demonstrate alliance with performers who exhibit queer potential. On the other hand, ex-gay Donnie McClurkin's performances of both distance from and familiarity with queerness permits him to communicate a precise message in conservative African American denominations and organizations hearing and viewing. Musicians' itinerancy may allow them to create broader communities that welcome and affirm their sexual identity, as performers find supplements for what their church home may be unable to provide. Jungle Cat's performance was a case study on the dissemination through the Internet of a private praise pole dance footage that challenged notions about the interpretations generated when his black male body moves and is inscribed with social meanings, while he engaged a symbol that carries gendered erotic meanings in the popular imagination of US viewership. In addition to movement, I found with Tonéx that presence may also be performed through other rhetorics such as coding, polysemous vernacular, and unspokenness as a ministry of presence. Gospel go-go is an example of a masculine-centered approach that is organized around performing against feminine masculine gospel performances that are imagined to be pervasive in church musical spaces.

I embarked upon this research on performers' rituals and social interactions in gendered gospel music to consider the extent to which ethnomusicology may elucidate discourses on black male absenteeism in African American worship. I was particularly attuned to the demonization and invisibilization of black male bodies in worship and the public. In response to this observation, I wanted to offer research that addressed those issues. The media inscribes black men's bodies with various meanings that have generated narrow imaginings of their bodily experiences, presenting them in hypermasculine athleticisms, closed postures, hypersexual intimacies, and carnal masculinities. Black men are rarely presented as deeply spiritual and divinely connected beings. Andrew Caldwell's case study teaches us that as we seek to deliver people, we must be careful about our own misconceptions that reinscribe or replace one perceived "affliction" with another. With Jungle Cat's performance of praise pole dance, I challenged a popular perception of black masculine athleticism and proposed a broader understanding of black male spiritual body language through praise pole dancing. With Patrick Dailey's performance of high-singing, he exhibits performers' anxieties around posture and stance when they sing in uncanny countertenor vocal ranges and repertoire. For researchers to analyze black male presence, there must first be an exposure to the diversity of black male images and sounds so that they may be comprehended even in their most peculiar presentations.

There are also various hegemonic African American Christian gendered spaces, words, and attire that black men are expected to use to worship, and when they diverge from those expectations participants may be distracted by their performance of stylistic independence. Preachers and instrumentalists are constructed as masculine, vocalists are imagined as feminine or queer, and preacher-musicians inhabit an androgynous performance realm. The pulpit, musicians' pit, and even the pastor's office that is out of the performance frame proper are imagined as the masculine spaces. The congregation, the platform, and the choir loft are envisaged as feminine spaces. I remain curious about the perceived peculiarity in their gendered performances function—those moments and participants who observers discussed long after the music stopped. The exploration of black men's performance of gender and sexuality in gospel music and black Christianity, with a focus on Pentecostal men, is crucial for understanding the performative mechanisms that draw or put off gospel audiences.

The performances covered in this book revealed additional themes that are outside of the scope of this project, but I hope to unpack these observations in my research moving forward. Black Christian male performers and their observers are socialized in male-centered theologies and ideologies such as muscular Christianity, compulsory heterosexuality, and heteropatriarchy constructs that influence assessment of the extent to which musicians attain "ideal manhood." These constructs offer rigid ideas of what men sound and look like when they worship. While believers adhering to those constructs aim to restore men as the head of households and as participants in churches, I have found that there are limits others place upon men's levels of commitment. Men are perceived as too committed to their families, especially mothers, and overly involved in certain church activities, especially feminized musical domains such as singing and dancing. Men also absorb compulsory heterosexual values and exhibit misogynist behavior to dissociate from any hint of feminization or queerness.

Male performers of various sexual orientations prize peculiarity, realness, truth, memorialization, discretion, and authenticity in performance discourse, which is in opposition to the dominant perceptions distributed in the media that focus solely on men's deceptiveness and lack of social conscience. The men's use of these terms prompts me to ask different questions about the ways they understand and practice them: In what ways do they play with notions of realness, truth, and authenticity? To what extent are their understandings and enactments of these terms a reclamation of self-identification, despite social and theological constraints? While there is merit to suspicion about men's deceptive behavior, I am interested in meeting that suspicion with broader analysis of men's techniques of self-disclosure. Men lifting their voice, moving, coding, demonstrating potentialities, and being represented are some means through which they reveal who they are and in ways they deem appropriate or useful. The hegemony interprets these means to be peculiar. Nevertheless, these peculiar strategies are laden with participants' meaning and familiarity.

As I have dug into the Judeo-Christian roots of gospel and African American Christian practices, I am anxious to continue taking a deeper look into the divine feminine in language and imagery. Asherah- and Shekinah-based traditions have offered to me questions about the omission and suppression of God's nurturing characteristics in worship. These findings bring me full circle to the work that I began at the beginning of my research and published on "mother iconicity" and play in gospel music (Jones 2014). I am confident that my work on men's worship and gospel performance will stand in critical dialogue with my future research on the "open secret" of feminine-inspired worship.

I must admit that I have left some things unspoken in this book. Perhaps these omissions are a symptom of my ambivalence about dealing with the burden to be forthcoming. Since I am a theologian, Pentecostal insiders expect for me to have a theological agenda driving my research. When I speak of the burden to be forthcoming, I am acknowledging 1) a trend in the frequently asked questions that I have received as I have conducted my research, and 2) a transformation in my perspective and practice.

In a conversation with a seminary colleague, she asked the following question about my research topic: "Where is the theological critique?" I tried to convey to her that I have conducted my research as an ethnomusicologist and part of that role is to lay bare the choices the musicians make and the theology that informs those choices. While I do have biases informed by experiences, beliefs, and identity, it is not my role to craft an apologetics of any sort, at least that is not my intention. Her response was that proper gospel research must include a theological stance. She said, "I get the sense that your agenda is to be more welcoming and affirming. Is that your agenda? I don't know, but I think that is what you are doing."

"Welcoming and affirming" is a term used in Christian churches to identify themselves as safe places for LGBT people. I have always been struck by the stance it symbolizes. The phrase evokes such passionate responses from conservative black Christians. In myriad ways, "welcoming and affirming" is perceived as a theological deviation from biblical literalist ideas about being set apart from those who do not believe and are not righteous. Unfortunately, some Christians do not accept unrepentant queer people into their community as they are. For some believers, saying they are "welcoming and affirming" is interpreted as condoning behavior that is not biblical.

I have even thought long and hard about the passion the phrase "welcoming and affirming" initially evoked in me. As I have reflected over the years about the reoccurring notion of hospitality, I have heard and attended performances that have inspired my present research agenda. There are three performances that have resonated with me in this regard. The first is Jungle Cat's performance to Bishop Hezekiah Walker's 2004 recording of "I Need You to Survive" (2004). I would like to point out that the musical and gestural rhetoric in the performance stood out to me: "I won't harm you with words from my mouth, I love you. I need you to survive." After reviewing Jungle Cat's footage over and over, I was both provoked by his performance to make commentary about his worship and humbled by the caution suggested in his performance to reflect on the ways my commentary about his private praise might be harmful to him.

The second performance is the recording by B.Slade (the artist formerly known as Tonéx) titled "Bi Our Love" from *The Children* (2012) album, based upon John 13:35: "By this shall all men know that ye are my disciples, if ye have love one to another" (KJB). I appreciated that B.Slade signified on more than one aspect of love with the use of "Bi" in the title. "Bi" is a homophone for "by" that is used in the original song. "Bi" also suggests bisexuality and eros. He covered Peter Scholte's "We Are One in the Spirit" (1966), which suggests agape:

> We are One in The Spirit,
> We are One in The Lord.
> We are One in The Spirit,
> We are One in The Lord.
>
> And we pray that all unity may one day be restored.
> And they'll know we are Christians by our love,
> By our Love,
> Yes they'll know we are Christians by our love.

B.Slade's interpretation of this song challenges an inclination to distance oneself from other believers who are different from the majority, while being one in the Spirit and one in the Lord.

Lastly, P. J. Morton performed the *Cheers* (1982–1993) television show theme song to close his show at the Double Door club in Chicago on a Sunday night. The performance illuminated for me the perennial philosophy that faith addresses people's longing to belong and to be known by name. The Grammy award-winning New Orleans-raised Morton is gospel recording artist Bishop Paul Morton's son and a member of Maroon 5. His ability to turn the function of the nostalgic theme song into a benediction at the end of his show was remarkable. Morton and his band invited the audience to participate by singing three-part gospel harmony, facilitating a transcendent experience in the club. After he left the stage, people's hands remained raised as they continued to sing repeatedly: "You wanna go where everybody knows your name." The longing acknowledged and hospitality stimulated in Morton's performance contrasted the reoccurring personal narratives I encountered throughout my research, where men conveyed rejection from and harm in their church homes. In essence, people are searching for homes that are not musically offensive.

These three "gospelized" music performances and recordings are instructive to me about what Christian hospitality might sound like. I interpret the commonality in these performances as remarking on the lack of hospitality, love for, and knowledge about the Others within Christian communities. And the lack of hospitality, love, and knowledge concerns me. Consequently, I suppose that I accept a characterization of my own efforts as welcoming and affirming to all of God's children. Let me make it clear that I do not intend to describe Christian believers as loveless or without compassion. I am just not sure that their love is perceived by all of God's children. My agenda is to prompt a reflection on the strategies by which believers may better excel in love.

The last frequently asked question is: In what ways does this research influence the work you do in the academy, ministry, and in public facing programming? I envision three main purposes for it. First, I envision that my research will be a tool to continue critical inquiry into the formation of identity in contemporary gospel and black Christian music as social life research. Second, I have already started to facilitate workshops and training for church leaders seeking strategies for addressing black male representation in churches, gender, sexuality, and HIV/AIDS awareness and prevention as a consultant. All of these topics are closely linked to the musical lives of believers. Lastly, I convene art-based events that are geared toward empowering young black men in low-income and high minority neighborhoods through Genius for Men and Move and Shake Women public programming. I have found empowering young black men is inextricably linked to uplifting young black women. My team at InSight Initiative and I provide a range of public arts education such as training and concerts that incorporate the resources that I have found, during this research. My aim is to present musical uplift in a language that everyday people will recognize.

The best way to deal with the taboos that bind is to make sure that scholars and practitioners not only research to find the answers to the questions surrounding identity formation, but that we also remain in relationship and conversation with the communities we seek to inform and for whom we seek to advocate. My hope is that this research is a bold conversation starter to get everyday people talking about how to best facilitate encounters with God that allow ministers, believers, and seekers to come as they are without wrath or doubting. At the core of such a welcome and affirmation will be the development of practices, resources, and training with both head and heart to ensure transformation spreads like wildfire to all in need of change.

Appendices

APPENDIX A

Gospel Go-Go Music Lineage

Beginnings

The following lineage was assembled and accessed on GospelGoGo411.com and has been edited for clarity:

Originators: Joshua Generation, Gideon Band
Pioneers: Submission Band (SMB), Xodus Band (XB), Proclaimers of Christ (POC), Ten Commandments Band
New Creation Band (Original)

Gospel Go-Go Movement

Trilogy Band, Krazy Praise (KP), Jammin' Jeff's Band (formally of Northeast Groovers), Young Prophets (YP), Turning Point, In His Image (currently The Unseen Movement), God's Blend Band, Young Disciples, Incorruptible Band (ICB), Living Sacrifice (an all female band), Psalms 100, Psalms 150 Band (currently Rezurrection Band), Posse 4 Christ, Redemption Band

Da Next Generation

Peculiar People (P dot P), Critical Revelation (CRB),
Mission Band, The Unseen Movement, Agape Band,
Vertical Band, Future City, Heaven Sent Band (made up of current go-go veterans including Lil Benny, Yanni, Kal'El and Others), New Creation Band (also known as Gospel Church Band), Fully Committed Band, Remixx Ensemble, Blynd Faith Movement, Maximum Sacrifice, Unleashed, Vessels 4 Christ (V4C), Chosen Generation

Peculiar People: Sound Requirements List

Electrical Power Source Requirement

- 2 /20amp circuit of AC power

General Band Setup Information

Vocalists: 4 Vocalists: lead, rapper, and 2 singers.
Keyboards: 4 keyboards (2 Musicians)
Lead Guitar: 1 acoustic and 2 electric, has own amp, requires 2 DI Input Boxes
Bass Guitar: 1 bass guitar, has amp/bass rig, XLR output on back of amp
Standard 5-pc Drum Set
Percussion: 4 congas and 4 timbales, various rack percussion and world accessories
Stage Size Required: 24' x 18'

Required Equipment List

Mics/Inputs

- (4) Shure SM58s
- (8) Shure SM57s
- Shure BETA 52
- (4) Audix f-10s & (2) Audix f-15s (Drums)
- (6) DI –Boxes or
- Beringer Ultra-DI PRO DI800

FOH

- Allen and Heath GL2400-24
- (4) dbx 1066 Compressor/Limiter/Gate
- (2) Presonus ACP-88 8-Channel Compressor/Gate
- dbx DriveRack PA Processor
- dbx 120A Subharmonic Synth
- (2) Yamaha SPX2000
- DeltaLab Effectron II ADM 1024
- (4) Dual 18" Subwoofer Cabs
- (4) 15" 2-way Mains
- (2) Crown Micro-Tech 5002VZ Amplifiers
- (2) QSC PLX3602 Amplifiers
- TASCAM CD-RW800SL

Stage Monitoring: (4 Mix Monitoring System Required)

- Peavey RQ 1606 Monitor Mixer

- (2) Rane RPM 22 EQs
- dbx AFS-224 Processor
- (4) QSC PLX2502 Amplifiers
- (4) Wedge monitors (vocals)
  - Mix: All vocalists, keyboards and guitar
- (2) Dual 15" 2-way Cabs (keyboards)
  - Mix: keyboards and Lead vocalist
- (1) Dual 15" 2-way Cab (Drums)
  - Mix: bass drum, snare, toms, congas, keyboards and Lead vocalist
- (1) Dual 15" 2-way Cabs (Percussion)
  - Mix: congas, snare, Lead vocalist

For questions, comments, and concerns please contact Jessie Julien at thepeculiarpeople@gmail.com.

APPENDIX C

JULY 2010

Below is a list of GO-GO Bands playing in and around the DC area from July 8-22, 2010

Friday, July 9, 2010
Club: LePearl
Location: 7929 Central Avenue
    Capitol Heights, MD
Doors Open: 7pm – 12am
Featuring: TCB, XIB, ABM

Friday, July 9, 2010
Club: Legend
Location: 3225 Naylor Road
    Temple Hills, MD
Doors Open:
Featuring: Backyad Band

Friday, July 9, 2010
Club: Glendale Firehouse
Location: 11900 Glenndale Blvd
    Glenndale, MD
Doors Open: 7:30pm – 1am
Featuring: TOB, ABM, UEB,
Renegade, MTM

Saturday, July 10, 2010
Club: The Skyboxxx
Location: 3435 Leonardtown
    Waldorf, MD
Doors Open: 10pm – 2am
Featuring: ReAction, ABM, XIB,
UEB

Friday, July 9, 2010
Club: Capitol Heights Ballroom
Location: 5400 Norfield Rd,
Capitol
    Heights, MD
Doors Open: 5pm – 11pm
Featuring: ReAction, Allstars,
UEB, AAO, New Action

Saturday, July 10, 2010
Venue: Tucker Road Pool
Location: 1770 Tucker Road
    Fort Washington, MD
Doors Open: 7pm – 12am
Featuring: ReAction, XIB, ABM,
Renegade, Allstars, UEB

Saturday, July 10, 2010*
Club: Onyx
Location: 817 Southern Avenue
    Oxon Hill, MD
Doors Open:
Featuring: ABM, UEB, GameOva
*Indicated in PG Band Schedule

Friday, July 9, 2010
Club: CFE
Location: 7758 Marlboro Pike,
    Forestville, MD
Doors Open: 12am – 4am
Featuring: Backyard Band

Bestselling author and lecturer has spoken at almost every college and has been a featured guest on Oprah, BET, MSNBC and the Al Sharpton Show.

Dr.Jawanza Kunjufu IS COMING TO "YOUR CHURCH"

What is your church doing to empower Black boys?

What is your church doing to engage Black male teens?

What is your church doing to attract and keep adult Black males?

What is your church doing to stop the Schoolhouse to Jailhouse Pipeline? What are you doing to reduce the suspension and dropout rate?

Do gangs & negative rappers have a greater influence on our youth than your church?

How can your church reduce crime?

What is your church doing to empower former inmates never to return?

To schedule a date contact

African American Images
P.O. Box 1799
Chicago Heights, IL 60412
Phone 708-672-4909 X737
Fax 708-672-0466
Web
www.AfricanAmericanImages.com
E-mail
customersvc@africanamericanimages.com

Invite Dr. Jawanza Kunjufu to speak at your church. Simply check the boxes below for your topic selections & return the flier to Ms. Smith's attn. at the email address above.

"SATURDAY"

☐Male Youth Workshop,☐Parent Workshop,☐Raising Black Boys,☐How to Increase Males in Your Church,☐How to Increase Male Volunteers,☐Male Retreat,☐What is Your Church Doing to Stop the Schoolhouse to Jailhouse Pipeline?,☐How to Attract and Keep Millennials,☐How to Put Black Men Back to Work,☐Stop the Violence

"SUNDAY SERMON"

☐ Saving Black Men, ☐What Happens When a Man Meets Jesus, ☐ Black Lives Matter, ☐ The Black Church Matters, ☐ Men's Day, Father's Day, ☐ Legacy of Martin Luther King, ☐ Black History Month Celebration, ☐How to Put Black Men Back to Work, ☐ Stop the Violence

Adam! Where Are You? Why Most Black Men Don't Go To Church, Developing Strong Black Male Ministries, Countering the Conspiracy to Destroy Black Boys, Raising Black Boys and many more!

P.A.W., INC. 2013 PASTORS & MINISTRY LEADERS SUMMIT
Bonaventure Resort and Spa Weston, Fla
THURSDAY, DECEMBER 12, 2013
Plenary Session 3 ● 4:10pm – 5:40pm
Can 'LGBT" People Be Active In My Church?
Bis Horace E. Smith M.D. Presenter

PASTORS, LEADERS AND SEXUAL EXPRESSION IN TODAY'S CHURCH
- There Are LGBT persons in your Church!!
- Do you know them?......Do you want to?
- How are they identified?
- What do you do when they 'come out' to you?
- Can they be active in your ministry?

ENGAGING THE PRIMARY ISSUE: HUMAN SEXUALITY
- WHAT DO WE UNDERSTAND ABOUT HUMAN SEXUALITY?
- IS SEXUALITY OR SEXUAL IDENTITY A CHOICE?
- HOW ARE WE HANDLING SEXUALITY AND SEXUAL EXPRESSION IN THE PRESENT CHURCH?
- HOW BROAD IS OUR UNDERSTANDING OF REDEMPTION AND RESTORATION?

WHAT IS HUMAN SEXUALITY?
Sexuality is in fact a Divine gift. Human beings are created as sexual creatures by a holy and righteous God. We all therefore have been wonderfully and fearfully made, and we need to have a total vision of life and our existence in which love and salvation permeate every area of our lives---including our sexuality.

LEVELS AND DYNAMICS OF SEXUALITY Chromosomal Sex: Hormonal sexuality: Gonadal Sexuality: Internal and External Accessory organs and their behavior: Neurological/Brain development: Gender identity: The psychology of sexuality: Spiritual and Biblical dimensions of sexuality

L.G.B.T.: LESBIAN, GAY, BISEXUAL, TRANSGENDER: Defining the Community
The LGBT community, sometimes known as the gay community, is a loosely defined grouping of lesbian, gay, bisexual, and transgender and LGBT-supportive people, organizations, and subcultures, united by a common culture and the civil rights movement.

LGBT STATISTICS: The Williams Institute: University of California School of Law
- An estimated 3.5% of adults in the United States identify as lesbian, gay, or bisexual and an estimated 0.3% of adults are transgender.
- This implies that there are approximately 9 million LGBT Americans, a figure roughly equivalent to the population of New Jersey.

- Estimates of those who report any lifetime same-sex sexual behavior and any same-sex sexual attraction are substantially higher than estimates of those who identify as LGB. An estimated 19 million Americans (8.2%) report that they have engaged in same-sex sexual behavior and nearly 25.6 million Americans (11%) acknowledge at least some same-sex sexual attraction.

TERMINOLOGY AND DEFINITIONS
Sexual orientation
"Sexual orientation" is the preferred term used when referring to an individual's physical and/or emotional attraction to the same and/or opposite gender. "Heterosexual," "bisexual" and "homosexual" are all sexual orientations. A person's sexual orientation is distinct from a person's gender identity and expression.
Gender identity
The term "gender identity," distinct from the term "sexual orientation," refers to a person's innate, deeply felt psychological identification as male or female, which may or may not correspond to the person's body or designated sex at birth (meaning what sex was originally listed on a person's birth certificate).
Gender expression
Gender expression refers to all of the external characteristics and behaviors that are socially defined as either masculine or feminine, such as dress, grooming, mannerisms, speech patterns and social interactions. Social or cultural norms can vary widely and some characteristics that may be accepted as masculine, feminine or neutral in one culture may not be assessed similarly in another.
Transgender
A broad range of people who experience and/or express their gender differently from what most people expect — either in terms of expressing a gender that does not match the sex listed on their original birth certificate (i.e., designated sex at birth), or physically changing their sex. It is an umbrella term that includes people who are transsexual, cross-dressers or otherwise gender non-conforming. Not all people who consider themselves (or who may be considered by others as) transgender will undergo a gender transition.
Transsexual
A transsexual person has changed, or is in the process of changing, his or her physical and/or legal sex to conform to his or her internal sense of gender identity. The term can also be used to describe people who, without undergoing medical treatment, identify and live their lives full-time as a member of the gender opposite their birth sex. Transsexuals transitioning from male to female are often referred to as "MTFs." Similarly, female-to-male transsexuals are frequently called "FTMs."

GENDER IDENTIFICATION: SEXUAL ORIENTATION AND THE CHURCH
The Abrahamic religions of Judaism, Christianity and Islam, have traditionally forbidden non-heterosexual and non-vaginal sexual intercourse (both of which have been variously labeled as sodomy), believing and teaching that such behavior is sinful and derived from the behavior of the residents of Sodom and Gomorrah.

Today, several denominations within Christianity and Judaism accept gay, lesbian and transgender members and permit the ordination of openly LGBT candidates for ministry.

Global Alliance of Affirming Apostolic Pentecostals: GAAAP
Copyright 2013 Bis Horace E Smith M.D. Presenter

(GAAAP) is an LGBT affirming, Oneness Pentecostal denomination, headquartered in Thonotosassa, Florida.

GAAAP was organized in 2007 by Rev. Robert Morgan of Tampa, Florida. GAAAP originally began as a ministerial fellowship, with 17 ministers by early 2008.

In April 2010, GAAAP merged with Apostolic Restoration Mission (ARM), formerly known as the National Gay Pentecostal Alliance (NGPA). NGPA had been the first LGBT-affirming Apostolic denomination, having formed in 1980 in Schenectady, New York.

By late summer 2010, the organization claimed 50 ministers in 19 States and 5 nations. It was in 2010 that GAAAP amended its constitution to become a denomination and began to affiliate churches. Another significant development in the administrative structure of the organization was the official consecration of Robert Morgan and Robert Stamper as Presiding and Assistant Bishops respectively in August, 2011. The organization hosts an annual leadership retreat in February, in Tampa, FL and an annual ONE Conference that rotates between cities.

The church is non-trinitarian in theology, holding to the belief that all the fullness of God resides bodily in Jesus, and teaches that repentance, water baptism by immersion in the name of Jesus Christ, and the Baptism of the Holy Ghost are essential elements of the Apostolic era church that must be retained in the church of God today. They also believe that speaking in tongues is the initial physical evidence of the baptism of the Holy Ghost. The church is affirming of gay people but doesn't not promote itself as a gay organization.

THE BIBLE AND SAME SEX ISSUES: AUTHORITY OF SCRIPTURE

Among Christians, the Bible is the highest authority in theological and ethical matters.

The question is, what does authority mean?

Does authoritative mean perfection, or inerrancy or complete consistency?

TWO BASIC VIEWS OF BIBLICAL AUTHORITY

- o The a priori view says that the Bible is authoritative in all of its parts and is so prior to interpretation. This affirmation is made not on one's own experience, but the teaching of another such as a parent, teacher or pastor.
- o The experiential or existential view says that the Bible is authoritative only in those parts that are existentially engaging and compelling—that give grounding and meaning to existence. This avowal can be made ponly after and in the light of one's own interpretation.

HERMENEUTICS: THE PROBLEM WITH INTERPRETATION

Determining What Matters In Scripture

The interpretation of a text is always strongly governed by its context, and this context is two-fold:

1. The literary and historical/cultural context of the text
2. The religious, intellectual, and cultural context constituted by the interpreter's pre-understanding, presuppositions, or social location.

There is no completely objective interpretation. We never have the Bible as it is in itself. We always have it from some—limited—point of view.

CHANGING ATTITUTUDES

What are the spectrum of possibilities regarding these issues among contemporary Christians?

1. Homosexuals as degenerates: prior to 1960 almost all Christians saw homosexuality as sin.
2. Homosexuals as diseased: Mainline Protestants in the 1960's began to make a distinction between homosexual orientation (disease) and homosexual practice (sin).
3. Homosexuals as disordered: in 1974 the American Psychiatric Association dropped homosexuality from its list of mental diseases. However the APA did recognize a category "sexual orientation disturbances," which did not include all homosexuals but designated those who were disturbed by, in conflict with, or wished to change their sexual orientation, and those who were subjectively distressed or socially impaired by their homosexuality.
4. Homosexuals as differently ordered: this view allows that if the condition is the result of complex causes—genetic and environmental, beyond the control of the individual, then a 'cure' cannot be expected and homosexuals should live out their orientation.

BIBLICAL PASSAGES REGARDING HOMOSEXUALITY
OLD TESTAMENT
Gen 19:1-29   Jud 19   Lev 18:22 20:13

NEW TESTAMENT
Rom 1:18-28   1 Cor 6:9-10
THE WITNESS OF JESUS AND PAUL: Teaching Love and Grace

"LGBT" ACTIVITY IN MINISTRY?

THE CONUMDRUM AND THE RESPONSIBILITY OF SOULS: IS THERE NO BALM IN GILEAD?

SUGGESTED READINGS:

THE HOLY BIBLE

HOMOSEXUALITY AND THE BIBLE: TWO VIEWS
Dan O. Via and Robert A. J. Gagnon

THE SAME SEX CONTROVERSERY
James R. White and Jeffrey D. Niell

ARTICLES ON SEXUAL ORIENTATION AND GENDER IDENTITY
Rev Chris Glaser M. Div
The Bible and Homosexuality: A Christian View
Gender Identity and the Bible: Jewish and Christian Perspectives

Issues of Sexual Orientation, Gender Identity, or Gender Expression:
What Should the Church Do?

HUMAN RIGHTS CAMPAIGN: (Official Website)
WORKING FOR LESBIAN, GAY, BISEXUAL AND TRANSGENDER EQUAL RIGHTS
Copyright 2013 Bis Horace E Smith M.D. Presenter

Notes

Introduction

1. The Stellar Awards were first awarded in 1984 by Don Jackson the founder of the Stellar Awards Gospel Music Academy (SAGMA) to recognize artists in the gospel music industry. It is the first of two major award shows to focus on the genre. The other is the Gospel Music Association's Dove Awards.
2. See Jones (2018).
3. "God chaser" and "God catcher" are allusions to a genre of charismatic Christian worship manuals such as Tommy Tenney's *The God Chaser: "My Soul Follows Hard After Thee"* (1998) and *The God Catcher: Experiencing the Manifest Presence God* (2000) that explore the posture of effective worship.
4. Here I acknowledge that "gospel music" is a term that I deploy to account for the music industry catchall designation consolidating myriad black sacred music traditions under its umbrella, that is, emphasizing the production of black charismatic worship for devotion, aesthetics, pleasure, and profit.
5. Ritual approaches to God in the Hebrew Bible were often done through smoke from sacrificial offerings (Exodus 29:14, 18).
6. For example, "And the angel of the Lord appeared unto him in a flame of fire out of the midst of a bush: and he looked, and, behold, the bush burned with fire, and the bush was not consumed" (Exodus 3:2).
7. In Exodus 24:17 (KJV), for example, it is written, "the sight of the glory of the Lord was like devouring fire on the top of the mount in the eyes of the children of Israel." Some other passages of fiery God encounters are: "a pillar of fire" (Exodus 13:21–22; 14:24); "the Lord descended by fire on Mt. Sinai" (Exodus 19:18); and "God is a consuming fire" (Hebrews 12:29).
8. Smoke is a frequent signifier of fiery God encounters: "And mount Sinai was altogether on a smoke, because the Lord descended upon it in fire: and the smoke thereof ascended as the smoke of a furnace, and the whole mount quaked greatly" (Exodus 19:18).
9. "The angel of the Lord appeared unto him in a flame of fire out of the midst of a bush" (Exodus 3:2).
10. Acts 2:1–4, New Living Translation.
11. The term "feminization" carries erotic connotations of the femme domination of butch submissives in bondage, discipline, submission, and masochism/sadomasochism (BDSM) practices (Ramet 1996).
12. I found two versions of Williamson's "Defeminizing the Church: Will This Encourage More Men to Attend?" presentation: the first presentation was created in 2011, and a second, longer presentation, created in April 2016, was designed by Paul Davis.

13. Misogynoir is a portmanteau coined by queer black feminist Moya Bailey, combining misogyny and noir to convey the disdain or dislike directed toward black women.

14. "These Hoes Ain't Loyal" (2013) signifies on the controversial song by popular R&B recording artist Chris Brown, who fell from grace in 2009 amidst accusations that he battered his then girlfriend, pop recording artist Rihanna.

15. Sunni Muslim ethnomusicologist Aliah Ajamoughli pointed out in a lecture on November 31, 2018 at McCormick Theological Seminary in Chicago, the imprecision in his deduction about the reasons for the overrepresentation of men attending mosques. In traditional Islamic belief, women's domain is domestic, that is, in the home and not in the mosque. What then emerges is an inverse problem in which women are absent in mosque participation.

16. "Pastor Jamal Bryant Sermons 2016—These Hoes Ain't Loyal," YouTube, posted by Jamal Bryant Sermons, April 23, 2016, https://www.youtube.com/watch?v= yPlX5gQNyk8.

17. It is not lost on me the compounding irony Bryant created through the assertion "these hoes ain't loyal" in the sermon, as a man who has admitted publicly to being a philanderer. As a minister, I believe that such an assertion in a sermon titled "I am My Enemies' Worst Nightmare" is pastoral malpractice and implies that anyone who does not keep his confidence, including women with whom he has had clandestine sexual affairs, is disloyal regardless of the fact that he trusted them enough to cheat with them. Further, he suggests that he has the propensity to make matters difficult for people who reveal his indiscretions.

18. For more religion scholarship that examines black men's worship, see also Finley (2010) and Boyd (2011).

19. African American women have researched black women's overrepresentation and contributions to black churches. See the research of Butler (2007) and Gilkes (2000).

20. This data was found in the 2014 Pew Research on "Attendance at Religious Services," https://www.pewforum.org/religious-landscape-study/attendance-at-religious-services/, last accessed November 29, 2019.

21. Maternal pedagogy refers to techniques that take into account the ways in which the intersection of gender, literal and symbolic familial relationships, motherhood, nurture, and learning matter for the transmission of information. Various scholars have written extensively about this concept: see Onuora (2015), O'Reilly (2013), and Zhang (2007).

22. Bishop Yvette Flunder has voiced this observation in several forums that I have attended. One instance is during a panel at the "Are the Gods Afraid of Black Sexuality?" symposium that was convened by African American religion professor Josef Sorrett who is the director of the Center for African-American Religion, Sexual Politics, and Social Justice (CARSS) at Columbia University in 2014.

23. During my research, I have encountered several accounts of gospel musicians tapping into the passions stirred in worship to God as the result of converting love songs to Gospel songs. For example, Richard Smallwood posted on Facebook on October 18, 2016 that his song "I Give You Praise" was written in his twenties, originally titled "You Are Love," and intended for a female love interest (Jones 2018, 11).

24. Jones (2016, 218).

25. Jones (2016, 217).

26. Jones (2016, 217–218).

27. I use the term "preacher" and not "pastor" to denote the male rhetorical role to which participants frequently refer in African American church folklores. "Preacher" emphasizes the main function of pulpit ministry, which is the delivery of homily and other rhetorical styles. While pastors engage in pulpit ministry, their role emphasizes shepherding responsibilities or congregation-care.

28. There are several memoirs about the "pimp preacher" figure in African American churches including Herbert Brown's *Pimps in the Pulpit* (2012), Gerald Gibb's *The Pimp and The Preacher* (2006), and Bruce Henderson's *Pimp to Preacher: Evangelism 911 With a Former L.A. Pimp* (2013), to name a few.

29. "But if I say I'll never mention the Lord or speak in his name, his word burns in my heart like a fire. It's like a fire in my bones! I am worn out trying to hold it in! I can't do it!" (Jeremiah 20:9, New Living Translation). Rev. Shirley Caesar is one of countless recording artists who have popularized the phrase "It's just like Fire" in her gospel recording "I Remember Mama" (Jones 2014). The phrase is also the basis of the Glenn Hinson's ethnographic research found in *Fire in My Bones: Transcendence and the Holy Spirit in African American Gospel* (1999).

30. "Chi chi man" originally referred to vermin in Jamaica but grew to encompass corrupt people. It is widely acknowledged, however, that "chi chi man' is slang on the island for "a gay." Grotesquely signifying on the Christmas carol refrain melody "Do you hear what I hear?" ("Little Drummer Boy"), T.O.K. sings in "Mr. Chi Chi Man": "From dem a par inna chi chi man car / Blaze di fire mek we bun dem! From dem a drink inna chi chi man bar / Blaze di fire mek we dun dem!" ("Those who gather in a fag's car / Blaze the fire, let's burn them! Those who drink in a fag bar / Blaze the fire, let's kill them!"). A similar Jamaican term that proposes aggression toward gay men is "batty man," "batiman," "batty boy," and "batty bwoy" that is heard in the song "Boom Bye Bye" in which Buju Banton sings lyrics that encourage the assault and execution of gay men: "Boom bye bye / inna batty bwoy head / Rude bwoy no promote no nasty man / dem haffi dead. ("Boom [the sound of a gunshot], bye-bye, in a faggot's head / the tough young guys don't accept fags; they have to die"). Jamaican dancehall is a global pop music that permeates the US soundscape—especially urban centers—and is a stylistic influence on various gospel music artists.

    David Usborne, "BBC Plays Burn Gays Reggae Hit." *Independent*. Sunday, August 19, 2001.

    Leah Nelson, "Harmonies of Hate Promote Violence Against Gays to Millions in the United States and Elsewhere," Southern Poverty Law Center (SPLC), February 27, 2011, https://www.splcenter.org/fighting-hate/intelligence-report/2015/jamaicas-anti-gay-murder-music-carries-violent-message.

31. Jones (2018, 6).

32. Walker (2005, 3).

33. "Signifyin(g)" is a way of simultaneously representing the vernacular and conventional pronunciation of the terms signifyin' and signifying.

34. "Sexual healing" references the euphemism for physical satisfaction through sex that was coined by soul music tenor Marvin Gaye in the 1982 song "Sexual Healing" from the Motown album *Midnight Love*.

35. Jones (2018, 4).

36. That phrase in context reads: "'[A] sexuality' might be a person's position vis-à-vis the means of expressing and/or enacting relationships of intimacy through physical pleasure shared, accepted, or given. For some of us, it might be that the most intense and important way we express or enact identity through circulation of physical pleasure is in musical activity, and that our 'sexual identity' might be musician more than it is 'lesbian,' 'gay,' or 'straight.' Be that the case or not, one might expect a significant amount of bleed through between a person's musicality and a person's sexuality as conventionally defined (that is, as genitally focused enactment of intimacy through the circulation of pleasure). If music isn't sexuality, for most of us it is psychically right next door. If our musicalities and our sexualities are psychically next-door neighbors, how might we experience a crossover between the two?" Cusick (2006, 71).

37. Johnson (2008, 184).

38. Louis Vuitton or LV is said to be a brand popular among homosexual men in gospel music networks. "Holy Ghost Enforcers Episode 6" (2014).

39. "Praise the Lord, everybody. Oh, Praise the Lord, everybody. Don't act like you don't know him because I do, hunh? Praise the Lord! Listen. Giving praises to God who is truly the head of my life. Giving honor to the pastor of this fine church—you know who he is 'cause I do, hunh?"

40. Rumor and other forms of speculative communication such as conjecture and accusation do a work all on their own without any verified evidence. This is due in large part to the biblical conviction that believers should abstain from the appearance of evil (1 Thessalonians 5:22).

41. Jones (2016, 217).

42. Ibid.

43. Jones (2016, 220).

44. My father, Rev. Dr. Alvin Augustus Jones, who served as a general manager for a gospel music radio station and copastor of Miracle Faith Centre at the Uline Arena with my mother Rev. Dr. Martha Butler Jones in Washington, DC, during the 1980s and 1990s, made me aware of this network of known queer concert organizers and decision-makers.

45. Mississippi Children's Choir (1992).

46. Levy (2002).

47. Boyd (2011, 100–101).

48. Anthony C. Williams has several stage names associated with his solo and instrumental artistry. "Tonéx" (used 1996–2008) and "Tonεx" (used 2008–2010) are his most popular brands associated with gospel music-making. In 2010, he changed his name to Brian Slade, also known as B.Slade, which is a reference to a glam rock character by the same name in the movie Velvet Goldmine (1998). Other names include but are not limited to the following: T.Bizzy, The Black Maverick, T'Boy, O'ryn, and Pastor N8ion. I use Tonéx throughout this book unless I am indicating a particular period or citation.

49. According to the openly gay young men with whom I toured as a musician, "Mt. Sinai Church" is known for the many discreetly gay men who lead its demonstrative worship. Since that time period, the pastors of "Mt. Sinai Church" have been called to task for anti-gay preaching by their openly gay congregants. In response to the criticism, "Mt. Sinai Church" has launched a ministry for gay people who seek deliverance.

50. Sylvester James biographer Joshua Gamson has written that James used his and her pronouns interchangeably. However, popular texts often refer to James as "he/his/him." Gamson (2005).

51. Bishop Eddie Long was previously characterized as hypermasculine in his attire and rhetoric. That style gained in popularity as a way of signifying healthiness in a sociocultural environment of HIV/AIDS anxiety. Long would preach while wearing "muscle shirts" and/or vests that emphasized his physique. Bishop Long protested vehemently against various LGBTQ legislation as well. Critics speculated for years about the ways in which his hypermasculine presentation may be overcompensation for his sense of inadequacy, self-loathing, or a means to deflect other's detection of visual and social signs of his queer potential. Heterosexual observers overlooked his stylistic approach that registered as a "trade" or queer athletic presentation to homosexual believers with whom I have conversed. Bishop Long's case furthers critics' claims that preachers who deliver homophobic messages are themselves queer or questioning their sexuality.

52. Among black homosexual believers, "spiritual son(s)" registers as a coded, multifaceted designation that likely connotes a queer love interest with biblical literalist black church culture resonances so as to escape close scrutiny. Similar terms range from familial to militaristic to monarchal: father, godfather, brother, godson, unc(le)/nephew, mentee, adjutant, armor bearer, king, and dad/son. Typically, these designations preserve a hierarchal imbalance of power and create the conditions for trade or situational sexuality. At the very least, these terms capture gradations of intimate homosociality.

53. Boyd (2011, 95).

54. Hairston (2010, 18–21).

55. 2 Samuel 11.

56. 1 Samuel 18:1.

57. When I shared with a distinguished homiletics professor about my research in April 2013, he confessed that he was taught in seminary that one has not preached well unless they have reached an orgasm while delivering their sermon. I was struck by the correlation made in his ministerial formation with the proclamation of the word and self-pleasure (eroticism). I have heard voice pedagogues make similar remarks to depict the sensations, memory, and imagination vocalists may tap into for strengthening their "breath support" to sing. I include the dimension of a minister's self-pleasure to figure in as an element of various schools of thought about preacher-musicians' technique, particularly with regard to vocality (Jones 2018, 14).

58. Jazz trombonist Wycliffe Gordon has interpreted the deacon's moan on his album *The Gospel Truth* (2000).

59. More succinctly, men sleeping with men and forming private alliances is a means of survival for men who are poor and a form of leverage for men who are interested in achieving status within the church hierarchy—a hierarchy that privileges compensating male ministerial staff.

60. Ruth Manuel-Logan, "Juanita Bynum Confesses to Affairs with Women," *NewsOne.com*, July 17, 2012, https://newsone.com/2025697/juanita-bynum-gay-lesbian/.

61. Aisha Jefferson, "A Gospel Singer Slims Down and Comes Out," *TheRoot.com*, April, 2, 2011, https://www.theroot.com/a-gospel-singer-slims-down-and-comes-out-1790863396.

62. Behavioral health strategist, documentarian, and founder of Black Men's Xchange National, Inc. (BMX), Cleo Manago coined the term "same-gender loving" (SGL) in the early 1990s. On the BMX website, the organization provides the history for the term SGL: "The term was created in 1990 as a [black] culturally affirming homosexual identity. SGL was adapted as an afrocentric, alternative to what are deemed Eurocentric homosexual identities (e.g., gay and lesbian) which do not culturally affirm or engage the history and cultures of people of African descent." Manago (2010).

63. For example, clinical psychologist Carlton W. Parks observes, "African-American disadvantaged youths are less likely than Euro-American youths to self-label as gay male, lesbian, or transgender youths" (Parks 2001, 41).

64. Walser (1993, 111).

65. I also draw from ethnomusicologist and black sacred music practitioner Mellonee Burnim, who confessed to the tensions of not fitting neatly into the demographic of her field site. She describes this as an "insider-outsider" position (Burnim 1985).

66. Awkward (1995, 4).

67. Brown (1999, 88).

68. Hill (1993, 345–346).

69. Bishop Vashti M. McKenzie notes that "neither the Bible nor history denies that women . . . have contributed much to their societies and the growth of the church" (McKenzie 1996, 2).

70. Ibid.

71. According to Alice Walker in *In Search of Our Mother's Gardens* (1983), womanism is defined as the following:

    1. From *womanish*. (Opp. of "girlish," i.e. frivolous, irresponsible, not serious.) A black feminist or feminist of color. From the black folk expression of mothers to female children, "you acting womanish," i.e., like a woman. Usually referring to outrageous, audacious, courageous or *willful* behavior. Wanting to know more and in greater depth than is considered "good" for one. Interested in grown up doings. Acting grown up. Being grown up. Interchangeable with another black folk expression: "You trying to be grown." Responsible. In charge. *Serious.*

    2. *Also*: A woman who loves other women, sexually and/or nonsexually. Appreciates and prefers women's culture, women's emotional flexibility (values tears as natural counterbalance of laughter), and women's strength. Sometimes loves individual men, sexually and/or nonsexually. Committed to survival and

wholeness of entire people, male *and* female. Not a separatist, except periodically, for health. Traditionally a universalist, as in: "Mama, why are we brown, pink, and yellow, and our cousins are white, beige and black?" Ans. "Well, you know the colored race is just like a flower garden, with every color flower represented." Traditionally capable, as in: "Mama, I'm walking to Canada and I'm taking you and a bunch of other slaves with me." Reply: "It wouldn't be the first time."

3. Loves music. Loves dance. Loves the moon. *Loves* the Spirit. Loves love and food and roundness. Loves struggle. *Loves* the Folk. Loves herself. *Regardless.*

4. Womanist is to feminist as purple is to lavender.

72. Lawless (1988, xi).

73. Crawley (2008, 313).

74. Crawley (2008, 315).

75. Brooks (2006, 6).

76. Ibid.

77. This is an excerpt from correspondence with the author on January 28, 2015.

78. See also Griffin (2006); Brett (1994); and Dyson (2001).

79. Marcus (1995, 97).

80. Marcus (1995, 110).

81. Madison (2012, 16).

82. According to the editors of The Crunk Feminist Collective in their 2012 anniversary post in which they examine birthday sex as self care, they interpret insight from a key feminist, "Patricia Hill Collins told us a long time ago that an ethic of care is an integral component of a Black feminist epistemology. She suggests that an ethic of care prioritizes individual expressiveness, together with a respect for emotions, and a capacity and commitment to empathy."

83. Boyd (2011, 1).

84. There has been much scholarship about African American Great Migration to Chicago narratives (1910–1930 and 1941–1970). Religion scholar Wallace Best has written that since the Great Migration Chicago resides in the African American imagination as a place to which people move, "as an integral part of the deliverance motif" (Best 2007, 1). Accounts about the exodus of blacks from the southern US to the northern US have privileged the stories of black men searching for better employment to provide for their families in Chicago. Grant Park in Chicago was the locale where Barack Obama announced his acceptance of the presidential nomination to bring change to the nation's capital. In comparison, Washington, DC has become a site for gathering black men to present themselves in solidarity for social justice (reproduction rights, same-sex marriage, violence, drugs epidemic, and HIV/AIDS, etc.), direct action (mentorship, apprenticeship, and presence) and mobilization. The momentous March on Washington for Jobs and Freedom, during which Rev. Dr. Martin Luther King Jr. delivered the "I Have a Dream" speech (1963), and the Million Man March that was convened by Minister Louis Farrakhan (1995), are two examples. In 2009, Washington, DC was the site where the first African American President Barack Obama stood with his family on the Mall that was once

ascended by King and Farrakhan, embodying the complexity of attaining "best Black manhood" (Boyd 2011, 2). Like Boyd, I acknowledge that there is "something slippery about contemporary masculinity that needs to be (solidified) in traditional spaces" (Boyd 2011, 2).

85. In Boyd's reading of Philip Brian Harper (1996), he defines black masculine *anxiety* as the call for black racial authenticity and its attendant racist discourse is the result of "a profound anxiety about the status specifically of African-American masculinity" (Boyd 2011, 4).

86. "Black on black violence" is a highly contested term that attributes an inequitable racial uniqueness to black people who enact violence within their community. White people commit the majority of their crimes, for example, in their community too and those crimes are not referred to as "white on white crime." The development of this term is extensively covered in David Wilson's *Inventing Black on Black Violence: Discourse, Space, and Representation* (2005).

87. Melissa Harris-Lacewell is presently referred to as Melissa Harris-Perry.

88. Taylor (2008, 92).

89. Walton (2009, 9).

90. Dyson (1996, 79).

91. (Jones 2016, 222).

92. Hawkeswood (1997, 39).

93. Hawkeswood (1996, 40).

94. Hopkins (2004, 186–187).

95. Hopkins (2004, 183).

96. Dyson (2001, 313).

97. Ibid.

98. West (2001, 306).

99. Harris-Lacewell (2006, 126).

100. Boyd (2011, 2).

101. Ross (2008).

Chapter 1

1. Kiki The First Lady, "Donnie McClurkin Is Getting Married . . . . . . To A Woman! Fellow Sanctified Singer Nicole Mullen!," on the 95.5 R&B for the Lou, https://955thelou.com/1973903/gospel-star-donnie-mcclurkin-is-getting-married-to-a-woman-fellow-sanctified-singer-nicole-mullen/.

2. I would like thank my colleagues Gregory Melchor-Barz, William Cheng, Henry Spiller, and Tes Slominski for their close review of early versions of this chapter. They are invaluable editors and conversation partners.

3. "Interview w/Tymel Thompson . . . but first . . . ," YouTube, posted by Larry Reid, August 5, 2019, https://www.facebook.com/LarryReidLive/videos/2284496634981336/?q=larry%20reid%20live&epa=SEARCH_BOX.

4. Hairston (2009, 26).

5. According to performance theorist Richard Schechner, there are at least four perspectives from which rituals and ritualizing can be comprehended: structures, functions, processes, and experiences. Structures are what rituals look and sound like, how they are performed, how they use space, and who performs them. Functions are what rituals accomplish for individuals, groups, and cultures. Processes are the underlying dynamic driving rituals; how rituals enact and bring about change. Experiences are what it's like to be "in" a ritual (Schechner 2006, 56).

6. Schechner listed seven functions of performance: to entertain; to make something that is beautiful; to mark or change identity; to make or foster community; to heal; to teach, persuade or convince; and to deal with the sacred and/or the demonic (Schechner 2006, 46).

7. Pentecostal ministry that focuses on deliverance from homosexuality is akin to the predominantly European American evangelical Christian "pray the gay away" ministries that seek to rehabilitate gay believers to be heterosexual. "Pray the gay away" is also the title of a 2011 episode in the television series *Our America with Lisa Ling* that aired on OWN TV that explores the lives of people who are trying to reconcile homosexuality with Christianity. Subsequently, sociologist and gender studies scholar Bernadette Barton released the book *Pray the Gay Away: The Extraordinary Lives of Bible Belt Gays* in 2012. See "The Naming Project" portion of the episode on the OWN TV YouTube channel at https://www.youtube.com/watch?v=AvAHCMRN86o.

8. Among the men I research, they self-identify queerness in ways that highlight their African American identity. Many of the men prefer the following terms to distinguish themselves from the dominant, racial, political, and socioeconomic experiences of European American gay men: homosexual and same-gender loving (SGL). In this chapter, I use the term "homosexual" because of its popularity in the gospel industry discourses and parlance.

9. Reference Revelation 12:11 KJV.

10. Diverging from Pentecostal sensibilities that cringe at the thought of ministry being viewed as performance or for spectacle, I do conceive of deliverance ministry ritual as performance to account for the planned and skilled qualities of what is presented to the public. I adopt Schechner's definition of ritual that cinches to the concept of performance: "Performances—whether in the performing arts, sports, popular music, or everyday life—consist of ritualized gestures and sounds. Even when we think we're being spontaneous and original, most of what we do and utter has been done before—by us even. Performing arts frame and mark their presentations, underlining the fact that artistic behavior is 'not for the first time' but enacted by trained persons who take time to prepare and rehearse . . . A performance may be improvised—but as in jazz or contact improvisation dance, most improvisations consist of arranging and moving through known materials" (Schechner 2006, 52). Following sociologist Emile Durkheim's concept of ritual as thought in/as action, Schechner writes about sacred rituals as "those associated with, expressing, or enacting religious beliefs. It assumed that religious beliefs involve communicating with, praying, or otherwise appealing to supernatural forces. These forces may reside in, or be symbolized by

gods, or superhuman beings. Or they may inhere in the natural world itself—rocks, rivers, trees, mountains—as in Native American and Native Australian religions." Schechner (2006, 53).

11. Twelve years after "He Delivered Me," Daryl Coley recorded the song "Deliverer" and released it on the 2005 *Just Daryl* album.

12. In his testimony about choosing to sing for Jesus, Coley recounted to Hairston that his life was changed during a Gospel Music Workshop of America (GMWA) when he spent time with recording artist Danniebelle Hall. "I was at the Gospel Music Workshop of American in Houston, TX and for the first two or three days Danniebelle and I just hung out and she really ministered to me. The Spirit of the Lord had her there for that purpose. She talked to me. She felt the pull. What the Lord essentially said to me was that he had preordained people who would be blessed by the ministry that he had deposited in me and if I'd have chosen a secular career—of course, he had an alternate plan. But I made a decision to be in the ministry—not just to entertain, but this really became a ministry to me once the Lord explained to me his purpose for my life" (Hairston 1995).

13. In the article, Coley explains that he was music director for Sheila E.'s (née Sheila Cecelia Escovedo) father Pete Escovedo. Escovedo is an Oakland, California-based Mexican-American jazz bandleader (Hairston 1995).

14. After his parents divorced when he was a child, Coley's mother raised him with his two siblings. They attended a Baptist church called Mt. Zion Baptist in Oakland, California where Rev. W. A. Holley was pastor. Coley spent most of his adult life in Pentecostal networks working as a music director for Church of God in Christ (COGIC) musicians such as Edwin Hawkins, Walter Hawkins, Tramaine Hawkins, and Sylvester James (Hairston 1995).

15. Coley deployed a similar musical move on the word "through" of the first song of the album "The Comforter Has Come."

16. Research on phonology and the use of articulators in laryngeal activity while speaking is found in "Loose Lips and Silver Tongues, or Projecting Sexual Orientation Through Speech" by speech-language-hearing scientist Benjamin Munson and linguist Molly Babel. They provide a crash course on speech production in their research on the intersection between speaking and sexual orientation, "A finer-grained look at speech reveals a situation that is many orders of magnitude more complex than this simple conjecture would suggest. The first level of complexity comes when considering sounds that are not produced with an open vocal tract. Acoustic models of these sounds, including fricatives sounds such as /s/ and /ʃ/, and the stop sounds like /p/, /t/, and /k/, are much more complex than those of vowels. The complexity of modeling the articulation to acoustics process leads to a reduced ability to determine the inverse, that is, to determine articulation when given acoustic output. The second level of complexity comes when considering that many, if not all, of the anatomic and physiologic factors that influence speech production can be countered by active articulatory movements" (Munson and Babel 2007, 421–422).

17. Jones (2014).

18. Over his career, Coley said he was influenced by Helen Stephens, Nancy Wilson, Sarah Vaughn, Gloria Lynn, Caravans, Thomas Whitfield, Rev James Cleveland, Benny Cummings (Hairston 1995).

19. Bailey (2013).

20. "Comforter" refers to the Holy Spirit, a term that rhetorically gestures toward the sensuous qualities of the Spirit's presence.

21. Coley and Vandross share many professional characteristics. Both of them were known for their behind-the-scenes musical production as composers, arrangers, and session vocalists who had an ability to blend with sopranos and altos and an extended vocal range that was not easily defined. Vandross's health was scrutinized as well due to his fluctuating weight, especially during that Wimbley tour. News outlets and fans speculated about Vandross's sexual orientation and whether he was healthy and intimated that he was living with the blood-related ailment HIV/AIDS. Vandross's discretion about his sexual orientation and health positions his aural-visual iconicity to be a well from which Coley drew to perform meaning in a multivalent way.

    "Exclusive: Luther Vandross Tells Tim Lampley 'Weight' Question Bothers Him," YouTube, posted by Timolampley, August 28, 2012, https://www.youtube.com/watch?v=-_kJWDBsbGw.

22. Vandross (1987).

23. Other male gospel figures known for a similar style of attire include Tennessean choir director and recording artist O'landa Draper and television personality Dr. Bobby Jones. For samples, please view Adilson Morais' "My Soul Doth Magnify the Lord" by O'landa Draper, YouTube, posted May 13, 2013, https://www.youtube.com/watch?v=EJ23-5PpT_0, last accessed March 25, 2018. Also, as seen at GMA Dove Awards' 3:05–3:06 mark of this footage "Dr. Bobby Jones GMA Honors Featurette," YouTube, posted on December 9, 2015, https://www.youtube.com/watch?v=fJIohxhH8fc.

24. During Pastor Daryl Coley's Live streamed memorial services his female colleagues Vanessa Bell-Armstrong and Yolanda Adams mentioned that he loved to collect Louis Vuitton items (April 2, 2016).

25. There are several biblical texts that refer to women's menstrual and men's semen discharge as a symbol of impurity. The impurity of men's semen discharge is referenced in Leviticus 15:16–18, 32 and Ezekiel 23:20. The majority of the scriptures on discharge focus on women's menstruation (Leviticus 15:19–30, 18:19, 20:18; Ezekiel 18:6, 22:10, 36:17; Luke 8:43–46).

26. "Speaking in tongues" is a Pentecostal Christian manifestation of being filled with the Holy Spirit. It is a practice of xenoglossia in which a person speaks a language that they do not know. Commonly, Pentecostals joke among themselves about other Christian's style of speaking in tongues, if a believer repeats syllables or articulates their tongues in a noticeably or likely unintelligible manner, suggesting that they may not actually be speaking another language.

27. BET Networks (2018).

28. This practice of harvesting audio and video clips for mixtape music production is a popular satiric style in social media. There are several cases in which voices from

Black eye-witnesses featured news footage commenting on ecstatic events have been used in mixtapes. Kimberly "Sweet Brown" Wilkins was made famous when her 2012 news footage audio was used of her saying, "Ain't nobody got time for that!" Antoine Dodson's 2010 news footage was also widely distributed when he said, "Hide your wives, hide your kids."

29. Jones (2018).
30. Jones (2016, 218).
31. Jones (2016, 218).
32. Pearson (2014).
33. One observer compared Andrew Caldwell's "womens" to the queer stereotypes performed in the reoccurring Men on Film sketch of *In Living Color* (1990–1994) on FOX, where two black gay and gender-nonconforming men talk about male actors, do signature gestures such as "two snaps up," and call male celebrities "mens." Their use of "mens" was not a vernacular expression attributed to Black gay men's every day speech styles but rather the sketch was a display of two hetero-presenting actors' hyperbolic portrayal of Black gay linguistic flourishes that emphasize an affixed, lingering "s" as a final consonant to already plural words in speech. For that observer, Caldwell's use of "womens" was read as a queer transposition of the cultural reference that betrayed his assertion that he is no longer gay.
34. Munson and Babel (2007).
35. Research on speaking and sounding gay abounds. See. Bowen (2002); Gaudio (1994); and Munson and Babel (2007).
36. Campbell (2008, 154).
37. Memes are humorous images, GIFs, texts, or footage that are often combined with popular sayings that are created for the purpose of being widely circulated on the Internet.
38. Blake furnished a videotaped apology to Caldwell in the following excerpt: "On Saturday evening, November 8, one of our more than fifteen speakers used terms and spoke in a way that was offensive and inappropriate. Though he alone was responsible for the nature and tone of his remarks, it was on my watch that this took place. Even though I was not present at the service on that night, as presiding bishop of the Church of God in Christ, I apologize for what seemed to be a harsh, uncompassionate, disrespectful spirit on the part of that speaker. I also apologize to Andrew Caldwell, a young seeker for the Lord, who came forth and made statements on that night regarding his change of heart and his purpose in life. His testimony literally went viral and has brought upon him criticism and sardonicism. We extend our love, our prayers, and our support to that young man as he seeks to know God and to serve God." COGICPR (2014).
39. American studies scholar Roderick Ferguson writes, "Queer of color analysis presumes that liberal ideology occludes the intersecting saliency of race, gender, sexuality, and class in forming social practices. Approaching ideologies of transparency as formations that have worked to conceal those intersections means that queer of color analysis has to debunk the idea of race, class, gender, and sexuality are discrete formations, apparently insulated from one another. As queer of color critique

challenges ideologies of discreteness, it attempts to disturb the idea that racial and national formations are obviously disconnected" (Ferguson 2004, 4).

40. "Struggle" is a catchall Pentecostal term to denote one's process of striving toward spiritual freedom from sin and demonic oppression. According to the *Official Manual with the Doctrines and Discipline of the Church of God in Christ* (1973), demons are evil spirits belonging to the unseen or spiritual realm; are embodied in human beings; and can be subdued and conquered (1973, 50–51). Same-sex sexuality is perceived as demonic due to the fact that it is a bodily experience that detaches sex from being exclusively for reproduction that is central to biblical literalist teachings about creation. In a biblical literalist sense, it is sinful for individuals to engage in sexual behavior outside of heterosexual marriage and for purposes other than reproduction.

The term "struggle" is also deployed as a gendered and sexualized vernacular term for men who seek accountability as they distance themselves from homosexual activity and desires. Even though Pentecostal holiness theology emphasizes the biblical teaching derived from texts such as Mark 9:29 that asserts "this kind can come out by nothing save by fasting and prayer" (1973, 51), preaching is juxtaposed with music-making as a preferred method for addressing individuals' homosexual inclinations. To facilitate deliverance rituals in worship, there are several restorative and contentious rhetorical strategies ministers deploy throughout the deliverance sermon repertoire that include the following: using biblical literalist interpretations of scripture regarding same-gender intimacy; associating queerness with musical participation; recounting personal narratives of deliverance; praying or "touching and agreeing" collectively with those who "struggle" with homosexuality; scorning people who struggle with same-sex desire and queer gender expression; and praising those who testify in a manner that publicly distances themselves from their lesbian, gay, bisexual, transgender, and queer (LGBTQ) genealogy.

41. Greene-Hayes (2017).

42. Included in sexual misconduct literature are a spectrum of violations such as molestation, rape, and age-based transgressions of pedophilia, hebephilia, and ephebophilia.

43. McClurkin (2001, 37).

44. McClurkin (2001, 39–40).

45. McClurkin (2001, 45).

46. McClurkin (2001, 39).

47. In 1906, W. E. B. DuBois argued in his seminal book *The Souls of Black Folk* that the great challenge of the twentieth century is the problem of the color line. The color line demarcates what DuBois observed to be "a peculiar sensation, this double-consciousness, this sense of always looking at one's self through the eyes of others, of measuring one's soul by the tape of a world that looks on in amused contempt and pity" (1944, 2) The double consciousness that he described was that sense of surveillance, the "unresolved strivings" in being both an American and African.

48. Even though McClurkin's description of being bilingual resembles the African American sociocultural practice of what W. E. B. Du Bois called double-consciousness, his narrative exposes the ways in which DuBois's double consciousness concept is heteropatriarchal and does not account for a prism of consciousness,

which includes sexuality, gender expression, class, and religious identities, to name a few facets that reflect a Fergusonian queer of color analysis. Moreover, DuBois's sense of the peculiar problem of the color line is gendered, presuming that the preservation of black manhood will uplift all Americans of African descent. Black women's rights are problematically colonized by black men's prerogative.

49. Snorton (2014).
50. King (2003).
51. Hairston (2009, 26).
52. In Pentecostal contexts, bisexuality does not seem to be a legitimized identity.
53. "Donnie McClurkin & Evangelist Joyce Rodgers Talks to the Youth COGIC," YouTube, posted by williamstempleCOGIC, January 8, 2011, https://www.youtube.com/watch?v=gJEonFztD0w&t=144s .
54. Muñoz (1999, 4).
55. Greene-Hayes (2018).
56. "Mother of the church" is a vernacular term referring to female lay leaders and socio-cultural pillars in historically black Protestant congregations.
57. McClurkin (2001, 41).
58. McCune (2014, 9).
59. Rowan (2006, 43–44).
60. As a cisgender, heterosexual, African American woman who is a divinity school trained Word of Faith preacher, conservatory trained musician, and ethnomusicologist of religious music in the African diaspora, I know a lot about being regarded as a "differently-abled" believer as I inhabit the margins of several communities. For instance, some believers have viewed my womanhood as an inferior designation, barring me from the highest ranks in church leadership. My womanhood is imagined as an inherent disadvantage, a natural condition from which there is no deliverance. Due to my sex, subordination is my plight, so heteropatriachally influenced leadership maintains.
61. Smallwood (2019, 44).
62. Young (2016).
63. McClurkin (2001, 43).
64. However, it is not lost on me the irony of McClurkin's bestowal of empathy while evoking derision about his own deliverance narrative.
65. Jones (2016, 218).
66. Boyd (2011, 94).
67. Although Burrell was raised COGIC, her congregation is not affiliated with the organization nor does COGIC recognize female pastors.
68. Treble timbre is a term coined by musicologist Naomi André in her 2006 book *Voicing Gender: Castrati, Travesti, and the Second Woman in Early-Nineteenth-Century Italian Opera,* which describes voices that are notated on the treble clef.
69. The doctrinal constellation that is central to the cultivation of a religio-cultural rejection of homosexuality among Pentecostal holiness believers is the doctrines of demonology (demons), anthropology (man), hamartiology (sin), and soteriology (salvation). A Pentecostal holiness doctrinal framework for deliverance practice is

found in the Church of God in Christ's (COGIC) *Official Manual with the Doctrines and Discipline of the Church of God in Christ*. The COGIC theological framework is concerned with believers' attainment of holiness and successful resistance of demon influence. Demons manifest through human's bodily experiences described as demonic possession, and demons are entities that combat goodness in humankind (50). Within the doctrine of anthropology, COGIC sets forth that "the body is the means whereby moral values in the soul may hare [*sic*] expression" (53). And thus, bodily experiences and expressions are perceived as indicating either the sinful or transformed nature of a person's moral fiber. Sin is "the volitional transgression against God and a lack of conformity to the will of God" (56). Citing II Timothy 2:14 as the scriptural basis, COGIC teaches that sin is transmitted to all humans through "the blood of the human race through disobedience and deception motivated by unbelief" (55). For humankind to be restored to the intended state of holiness from which it has fallen, humankind must be born again. "Born again" is a vernacular term for salvation (the doctrine of soteriology). "[Soteriology] deals with the application of the work of redemption to the sinner and his restoration to divine favor and communion with God. This redemptive operation of the Holy Spirit upon sinners is brought about by repentance toward God, which brings about Conversion, Faith, Justification, Regeneration, Sanctification, and Baptism of the Holy Ghost. Further in the manual, sanctification is a core theological concept from which the pursuit of deliverance stems. "Sanctification—That gracious and continuous operation of the Holy Ghost by which He delivers the justified sinner from the pollution of sin, renews his whole nature in the image of God and enables him to perform good works (Rom. 6:4; 5:6, 11, 12; Col 2:12; 3:1, 2; Gal. 2:19; I Thess. 5:23; II Cor. 5:17; I Cor. 6:15, 20; Jer. 31:34; St. John 6:45; Ezek. 36:25–27; Phil 2:13; Gal 5:24; Titus 1:15; Heb.9:14) (p. 56–57)."

70. Marcus Jones. "'We're Followers and We're not Following God': Pharrell Williams Warns Against Looking at Internet for Answers," Premier, posted October 15, 2019, https://www.premier.org.uk/News/World/We-re-followers-and-we-re-not-following-God-Pharrell-Williams-warns-against-looking-at-internet-for-answers.

71. Caldwell divulged this information on December 31, 2016 and January 23, 2017 through Facebook live stream. On December 31, 2016, he posted a live stream with this caption: "I don't have anything else to say about #KimBurrell except sweater dresses are not her friend; and she should give refunds to all the gay men that sowed into her ministry and helped her when nobody else was checking for her. Other than that, carry on." And then on January 23, 2017, it appears a third party posted his video: "He's spilling all the tea on 'Celebrity Big Kim Burrell.'"

72. Perry (2017).

73. Jones (2016, 216–217).

74. Jones (2016, 227–233).

75. Pearson (2014).

76. McClurkin (2001, 39).

77. Woodard (2014).

78. Pearson (2014).
79. Woodard (2014, 37).
80. Fredrickson (1971, 114).
81. Woodard (2014, 31).
82. Frequently, in an analysis of white dominance over enslaved people equate animal slavery with human chattel slavery conditions in the colonial United States. In *Habeas Viscus: Racializing Assemblages, Biopolitics, and Black Feminist Theories of the Human*, African American Studies and English scholar Alexander G. Weheliye contends that it is dangerous to link human slavery with animal slavery: "Moreover, post humanism and animal studies isomorphically yoke humanity to the limited possessive individualism of Man, because these discourse also presume that we have now entered a stage in human development where all subjects have been granted equal access to western humanity and that this is, indeed, what we all want to overcome. It is remarkable, for instance, how the (not so) dread comparison between human and animal slavery is brandished about in the field of animal studies and how black liberation struggles serve as both the positive and negative foil for making a case for the sentience and therefore emancipation of nonhuman beings" (Weheliye 2014, 10).
83. Joy DeGruy (2017).
84. A social contract is a term coined by Jean-Jacques Rousseau in *The Social Contract* (1762) connoting an agreement among members of a group in society. Rousseau (1968).
85. Pearson (2014).
86. Cane (2016).
87. See also Kelefa Sanneh's "Revelations: A Gospel Singer Comes Out," *The New Yorker*, January 31, 2010.

Chapter 2

1. A version of this chapter was previously published in *The Oxford Handbook of Voice Studies,* ed. Nina Sun Eidsheim and Katherine Meizel, 35–51 (New York: Oxford University Press, 2019).

   There are several, annual gospel music conferences that facilitate networking, training, performance, and recording of the repertoire. Examples of other comparable gatherings are the National Convention of Gospel Choirs and Choruses founded by gospel music pioneer, Professor Thomas A. Dorsey and Edwin and Walter Hawkins Music and Arts Love Fellowship Conference that was convened by brothers Edwin and Walter Hawkins.

2. The Dream Network was the first black-owned Christian television network in 1990s, co-founded by Alvin Augustus Jones and Martha Butler Jones. It was aired on DishTv, DirecTV, and SkyAngel.

3. The Word Network is a Jewish American-owned television network based in Southfield, Michigan geared toward African American viewership. " 'Some Day' The New Psalmist Baptist Church Mass Choir with Soloist: Patrick Dailey," YouTube,

posted by New Psalmist Baptist Church, September 15, 2011, https://www.youtube.com/watch?v=GKjX7uBJktA&t=385s.

4. SSAATTBB is an acronym within choral arrangement that refers to the first and second soprano, first and second alto, first and second tenor, and first and second bass choral voicing.

5. Jones (2016, 217).

6. Carter conducted the renowned Morgan State University Choir for thirty-four years, from 1970 until his passing in 2004.

7. Interview with the author and Patrick Dailey on November 11, 2011.

8. According to musicologist Naomi André, "In their own time, the castrati voices were altered voices and would not occur without a type of surgery called orchiectomy" (André 2006, 18). Castration, orchiectomy, or gonadectomy are surgical, chemical, or any other procedure in which men lose their testicles and thus become sterile and greatly reduce the production of testosterone hormone.

9. André (2006, 18).

10. André (2006, 20).

11. Kemble (1863, 106).

12. As I consider the expression of "singing high," I draw a division between the countertenor vocal designation and the term "falsetto." Both countertenor and falsetto are Western classical singing notions, but falsetto is a stylistic device used in other musical genres as well. Among many vocal pedagogues, falsetto pertains to men's vocal style or affect that is perceived as beyond their normative vocal range. According to vocal pedagogue Richard Miller, "In the international language of singing, falsetto describes that imitative female sound that the male singer is capable of making on pitches that lie above normal male speaking range" (Miller 1996, 121). In African American music performance, Anne-Lise François's research on falsetto use in gospel-influenced disco, she counters that the popular assessment of falsetto as a gimmick is a hegemonic perspective. She argues that the foundation for analysis of falsetto style is built upon "1) the falsetto voice's homelessness with respect to either gender, and 2) its legitimacy within what is itself a Diaspora-formed or exilic tradition" (François 1995, 443). The intangibility in the gender homelessness imagery captures the cost for men who sound castrated or androgynous without a physical condition to blame for their musical distinctiveness.

13. Southern (1997, 236).

14. Southern (1997, 477).

15. Jones (2018, 3–21).

16. Jones (2016, 217).

17. Smith (1995); Cheatham (1997).

18. Southern (1997, 249). See also Story (1993); and Eidsheim (2008).

19. Shirley (2012, 262).

20. François argues that one of the "nonconformist" ways in which black men have lifted their voice to higher heights, independent of and despite limited performance platforms, is through falsetto style in pop music such as disco and soul. François examines, for example, falsettist Curtis Mayfield's contribution that "In the same way,

it might be said that he can't help but sing in falsetto; the haunting otherworldliness of his voice is forced and urgent. In a world where 'the price of meat is higher than the dope on the street,' there is no choice but to sing in the register of the other (world). Falsetto is the only way to make oneself heard in a world which is already a lie—the white-owned world which is also that of one's suffering community. To go 'back to the world' then is to be made to sing—to assume the voice of otherness—so as to express precisely that in one's self and one's vision which is denied fulfillment in this world. But to reclaim the world is also to urge the present with reiterative emphasis in the knowledge that one's inner ghosts have no other place to go" (François 1995, 444–445). African American men's falsetto singing signifies a means through which men sound transcendence to cope with social injustices. They also vocally sound a wide range of topics that demonstrate their ability to feel and skillfully perform for listeners who are embedded in various cultural matrices (Jackson 2000,13). Black male high voice soloists/falsettists have musically transcended in popular, gospel, and Western art music that merits in depth research and cannot be exhausted in this chapter. In Western art music, African American countertenors include Derek Lee Ragin, Ken Alston Jr., Victor Trent Cook, Tai Oney, Matthew Truss, Cortez Mitchell, and Patrick Dailey. In popular music, black male high-singing vocalists include Smokey Robinson, Philip Bailey, Thomas Allen, Jr., Claude Jeter (Swan Silverstones), Bryan McKnight, Maxwell, Prince, Curtis Mayfield, the Stylistics, Al Green, Ron Isley of the Isley Brothers, Little Richard, and El DeBarge. In gospel music black male high-singing vocalists include Richard Smallwood, John P. Kee, Rance Allen, Anthony C. Williams (formerly known as Tonéx), and many gospel quartet singers. This is by no means an exhaustive list of black men who sing high.

21. André (2006, 3).
22. Leonardi and Pope (1996, 28).
23. Koestenbaum (1993).
24. Leonardi and Pope (1996).
25. André (2006, 18).
26. André (2006, 12).
27. Leonardi and Pope (1996, 25).
28. François (1995, 445).
29. Composer and conductor Scholz further defines androgyny as "the union of the physical characteristics of male and female in our being and the notion of asexuality, a characteristic of spiritual beings, especially angels" (2000, 7).
30. Halperin (2002, 29).
31. I would like to fully disclose that I worked for Richard Miller as a laboratory assistant (2000–2004) at the Otto B. Schoeplfe Vocal Arts Center (OBSVAC), Oberlin Conservatory in Oberlin, Ohio.
32. Miller (1993, 13).
33. Vocal pedagogue Richard Miller maintained that countertenors are more likely to achieve agile movement in rapid passages and embellishments. He writes further that such an approach allows for easy control of dynamics. Miller also clarifies that

countertenors who sing in falsetto should not be confused with those who sing *voce piena in testa* (full head voice) (Miller 1993, 13).

34. Miller (1996,123).

35. The Word Network's demographics and programming format is described on its website as follows:

> The network has gained recognition as the network of choice for African American programming by featuring ministries, an informative Christian focused television lineup and gospel music . . . The Word network recognizes that music is a large part of the Christian experience, and offers line up of gospel artist, interviews, videos and musical specials featuring artists such as Marvin Sapp, Kirk Franklin, Mary Mary, Donnie McClurkin, Hezekiah Walker, J. Moss, Deitrick Haddon, Cece Winans, Byron Cage and newcomers such as Wess Morgan and VaShawn Mitchell, to name just a few. (The Word Network n.d.)

36. Interview with Patrick Dailey and the author on November 11, 2011.

37. Melisma is a group of notes sung on one syllable or vocable.

38. Feldman (2007, 26).

39. Interview with Patrick Dailey and the author on November 11, 2011.

40. Halperin (2002, 27).

41. Voice Studies Now Conference at UCLA, January 29–31, 2015.

42. The meme was distributed by @ChurchOfFunny, which is a Facebook, Twitter, and Instagram social media handle known for featuring Black church humor. The image of the woman's nonverbal facial expression upon seeing her Boaz or her love interest in the choir illustrates the popular ridicule of men who sing soprano or sing high.

43. "Chile" is a vernacular form of "child," which is a term of endearment.

44. Interview with Patrick Dailey and the author on November 11, 2011.

45. I deploy "minister" as a signifier of social peculiarity, as one who is set apart, and who demonstrates social and theological discipline to God and humankind in presentation, posture, and attitude.

46. Interview with Patrick Dailey and the author on November 11, 2011

47. Shirley (2012, 274).

48. For more on respectability, consult White (2012).

49. Even though Pentecostal worship leaders do not perform *en travesti*, an instance in which en travesti occurs in gospel music performance is through the production of plays and movies. For instance, the basis of writer, producer, and movie studio owner Tyler Perry's fortune is performing en travesti as the reoccurring, black woman title role *Medea* in his gospel plays in the late 2000s to mid-2010s. Womanist and black feminist critical analysis of his portrayals of black of women can be found in the edited volume *Womanist and Black Feminist Response to Tyler Perry's Productions* (2014) by L. Manigault-Bryant and Tamura Lomax. Other black male comedians have made a fortune imitating and dressing as black women with gospel music in the soundscape of their portrayals: Eddie Murphy, Martin Lawrence, Jamie Foxx, and Keenan Thompson, to name a few (Braxton 2017).

Chapter 3

A version of this chapter was previously published in *Esotericism in African American Religious Experience*, ed. Stephen Finley, Margarita Guillory, and Hugh Page Jr., 314–330 (Boston: Brill Academic, 2014).

1. The biblical phrase "when the Spirit of the Lord moves" references II Samuel 6:14 and alludes to musical repertoire depicting David as a praise dancer and psalmist in Contemporary Christian Music repertoire. One of the most popular performances of musical masculinity in the gospel music singer-songwriter Fred Hammond's "When the Spirit of The Lord" from his 1998 *Pages of Life* album (Butler 2014).

2. Psychologists Antoon Geels and Jacob A. Belzen propose five dimensions within mysticism discourse: experiential, ideological, ritual, intellectual, and consequential (Geels and Belzen 2003, 9).

3. Within the "ritual dimension," they list isolation, meditation, contemplation, prayer, mystical weeping, and visualization as examples ritual types (Geels and Belzen 2003, 9).

4. Jungle Cat (2009).

5. Hezekiah Walker & The Love Fellowship Choir (2002).

6. Camacho (2006).

7. Jones (2018).

8. Burleigh (1994).

9. In Mircea Eliade's work, *The Sacred and the Profane: The Nature of Religion* (1987) he traces the early development of the sacred and the profane concepts. Eliade defines the sacred as something that manifests and shows itself within religious experiences as wholly different from the profane.

10. Souhern (1997, 130–131).

11. Ibid.

12. Hedgeman (2007, 18).

13. Curry (2004, 11).

14. Turner (forthcoming, 169).

15. Fred Hammond and Radical for Christ, *The Spirit of David,* Benson Music Group, released March 30, 1997.

16. Butler (2014, 17).

17. Kirk-Duggan (2004, 217–233).

18. "Full Monty" is British slang of uncertain origin that means everything that is wanted or needed; the whole thing.

19. Crawley (2008, 309).

20. McGinn (1992, xvi).

21. Ibid.

22. Belzen and Geels (2003, 8–9).

23. Elsbeth Meuth interprets tantric celibacy as "sexual energy channeling and transmuting for other purposes than the bedroom." She also referred me to Stuart Sovatsky's writing on tantric celibacy as "a sex-positive, body- affirming attitude, for it is a path of

sublimation, not repression" (Sovatsky 1999, 5). In Sovatsky's estimation, tantric sublimation is the negotiation of a paradox—eros literally becomes sublime.

24. Mallakhamb is derived from two Marathi words: *malla* and *khamba*. *Malla* means
wrestler and *khamba* means a pole. For a sense of the mallakhamb fetes, see the following footage: Sangnam Institute of Indian Martial Arts, "The Topmost Mallakhamb
Players Vol. 1," YouTube, https://www.youtube.com/watch?v=6FTBrtifKYQ, last
accessed February 24, 2015.

25. Other forms of US male pole use include acrobats in the circus, firewomen and
men's use of the pole in firehouses, and the grease pole tradition among Italian
Americans at the Italian Market festival: "Grease Pole Climbimg Competition,"
http://www.italianmarketfestival.com/grease-pole.html. Also, grease pole climbing
is popular among Philadelphians during numerous festivities such as the 2018
Eagles parade: Tricia L. Nadolny and Holly Otterbein, "The Wildest Things Heard on
Philadelphia's Police Scanner during the Eagles Parade," The Philadelphia Inquirer,
February 8, 2018, http://www.philly.com/philly/super-bowl-lii/eagles-parade-
police-scanner-philadelphia-20180208.html.

26. Cage (2005).

27. Georgia Mass Choir, "He's All Over Me," 1996.

28. Richard Pitt and George Sanders sets forth in "Revisiting Hypermasculinity: Shorthand
for Marginalized Masculinities?" (2010) that hypermasculinity is a construct that
upholds a minority identity.

29. See Appendix C for a full list Jawanza Kunjufu's workshops.

30. Kunjufu (1997, 67).

31. E. Patrick Johnson explores the stories of gay men in gospel performance in the
chapter "Church Sissies" in his book *Sweet Tea* (2011).

32. Jones (2016, 217).

33. Leonard Greene, "Jilted Bishop Launched Scandal Campaign Against Gospel Artist
After Romance Was Spurned: Lawsuit," the *New York Daily News*, June 15, 2017, http://
www.nydailynews.com/new-york/jilted-bishop-launched-smear-campaign-gospel-
artist-suit-article-1.3251360.

34. Snorton (2014, 98).

35. In his essay on Bill T. Jones, Gay Morris examines how male dancers were viewed
as suspicious because of their choice to dance. He argues that this suspicion is in
Victorian codes. In other words, the very desire to move as only ladies were to do was
held as effeminate. Morris (2001, 246).

36. Watson (2007, 91).

37. Snorton (2014, 106).

38. Boyd (2011, 61).

39. Male femininity refers to men's display of attributes and symbols that are conventionally associated with women.

40. Johnson (1998, 403).

41. I have witnessed an exploration of the sensual, sexual, and spiritual, while a semi-
narian at Yale Divinity School. During an ecumenical chapel service, for instance, a

New Testament professor preached a homily based on a Song of Solomon Chapter Four, while a staff member bellydanced to illustrate the eroticism of the biblical text.

42. Communication, media and religious studies scholars Curtis D. Coates and Stewart M. Hoover found that "Evangelical and mainline Protestant men are both reflexive about their own media practices and conversant with dominant public scripts about the media" (Coates and Hoover 2013, 146–147).

43. "Bro. Franklin (Offering Time)," footage of Bro. Franklin "dancing like David as usual" at Redeemed Christian Church of God—Pavilion of Redemption, posted by "iamsotc," June 23, 2009, YouTube, https://www.youtube.com/watch?v=8pUAnrVWUkk.

44. "Bro. Franklin's Testimony Part 1," interview with Jugo TV about Bro. Franklin's Testimony, posted by SayoJugo Awofodu, December 6, 2009, YouTube, http://www.youtube.com/watch?v=Oei72F2ZEmM.

45. Caleb Brundidge, "About," accessed July 13, 2014, http://www.calebbrundidge.com/About.html.

46. "Twirl" is also a euphemism for the demonstrative associated with whirling, "flamboyant" gay man.

47. Morris (2001).

48. Burt (2001, 221).

49. Burt (2007)

50. hooks (1992, 116).

51. Jackson (2006, 1).

52. Jackson (2006, 2).

53. Burt (2007, 233).

54. *Fantastic hegemonic imagination* is neologism conceptualized by womanist ethicist emilie townes: "Combining Michel Foucault's understanding of the imagination and Antonio Gramsci's use of hegemony, I develop how the imagination—the fantastic hegemonic imagination—'plays' with history and memory to spawn caricatures and stereotypes" (Townes 2006, 7).

55. Hopkins (2006, 189).

56. Dyson (1996, 306).

57. Anderson (2004, 310).

58. Eilberg-Schwartz (1994, 1).

59. Kripal (2001, 19).

60. Finley (2007a, 311).

61. Eilberg-Schwartz (1994, 2).

62. Kripal (2001, 18).

63. Howard Eilberg-Schwartz explained, "Marriage and sexuality are frequent biblical metaphors for describing God's relationship with Israel. God is imagined as the husband to Israel the wife; espousal and even sexual intercourse are metaphors for the covenant. Thus when Israel follows other gods, 'she' is seen to be whoring. Israel's relationship with God is thus conceptualized as a monogamous sexual relation and idolatry as adultery. But the heterosexual metaphors in the ancient texts belie the nature of the relationship in question: it is human males, not females, who are imagined to have the primary intimate relations with the deity" (Eilberg-Schwartz 1994, 3).

64. Eilberg-Schwartz (1994, 37).

65. "Woman Offers Christian Pole Dancing Class in Houston" (2014).

66. In international coverage, Anna Nobili headlined as "a lap dancer turned nun angers Pope." She describes herself as "La ballerina del Signore (the ballerina for God)" in Rome, Italy. Before male cardinals and bishops, Nobili twirled around a wooden crucifix that was laid on the ground. Even though the cross was not erected, it signified a shared memory of the crucified body of Christ. The media's framed the combination of Nobili's past as a lap dancer, the cross, and the bishops and cardinals gaze to eroticize the interpretations of her praise. Within a tradition where leadership is organized in homosocial groups, she facilitated a coed ritual, in order for God's presence to enter their midst corporately.

    In their Catholic homosocial leadership structure is that all the participants have taken a vow of celibacy. Nuns like Anna Nobili are to be a bride of Christ. In this example, we find that in coed settings, she is to be self-contained in her mystic practice. Men may not observe her embodied closeness with God.

    Subsequent to her performance, Alicia Trujillo reported that the Pope eventually reprimanded Nobili. Her monastery was shut down for "suspicious activity," not befitting their holy designation. These contrasting media receptions of women dancing at the foot of the figurative and proverbial cross reveal distinct social sensibilities about eroticism that are demarcated along gender, color, and denominational lines. Alicia Tujillo, "Lap Dancing Nun Performs for Church," *BBC News*, July 13, 2014, http://news.bbc.co.uk/2/hi/7988322.stm.

67. Spiller (2010, 119).

68. Kuefler (2001, 257–258).

69. Stephen Finley concludes that "The impervious, fully armored, black male body is an impediment to finding meaning in the black Church in that worship of God is a homoerotic entry into the body" Finley (2007b, 18).

Chapter 4

1. Washingtonian music minister Stephen Hurd is one of several artists who have recorded renditions of "Undignified" (2004) written by Matthew Redman. The song illustrates the sort of actions one might take while worshipping God with the exuberance of David.

2. The performed flamboyant choir director stereotype has been blamed as a deterrent to men who do not identify with that model of masculine vocal music leadership in historically Pentecostal Black church worship. In contrast, the presumed predominantly heterosexual, virile, and cisgender male leadership is situated in the pulpit and the "musician pit" in churches (Jones 2016, 225–226).

3. Wilson (1983, 1–22).

4. Jones (2018).

5. Here I adapt the term "safe space" as applied by Beverly Daniel Tatum (2003, 77).

6. Jones (2018).

7. Ibid.

8. Ibid.

9. Denise Kersten Wills, "People Out of Control: Remembering the 1968 Riots," *Washington Post*, April 1, 2008.

10. Chuck Brown & The Soul Searchers (1986).

11. Chuck Brown & The Soul Searchers (1979).

12. Jordan (1948).

13. Chuck Brown & The Soul Searchers (1986).

14. Chuck Brown (2005).

15. Lornell and Stephenson (2009, 31).

16. One marker of disenfranchisement is that Washingtonians have adopted the slogan "Taxation Without Representation" on their license plates in protest for having to pay federal taxes without the right to vote in Congress. This tax designation is due to the fact that Washington, DC is a federal district and not a state.

17. Lornell and Stephenson (2009, 206–227); Jones (2018)

18. Wartofsky (2001).

19. Gospel go-go has been sustained over four gospel go-go music historical phases: originators, pioneers, gospel go-go movement, and da next generation (see Appendix A, "Gospel Go-Go Music Lineage."

20. Hopkinson (2002a, T21).

21. The Pentecostal "War Cry" motif was made popular by the late Bishop Kenneth H. Moales Sr. (1945–2010). At the time of his passing, Moales was presiding prelate of the Pentecostal Church of Jesus Christ, pastor of Cathedral of the Holy Spirit in Bridgeport, CT, and former president of the National Convention of Gospel Choirs and Choruses (NCGCC) founded by forefather of gospel music Thomas A. Dorsey. "War Cry" has been performed in congregational celebration moments for decades. It is traditionally sung on the "o" vocable and alternates with musical moments of shouting, clapping, and/or stomping. The following video clip includes footage of Moales singing the motif during a worship service: "Bishop Moales Leads the War Cry," YouTube, posted by havinastroke, July 18, 2010, https://www.youtube.com/watch?v=Me3CWI6iR6U.

22. Natalie Hopkinson (2002, 2013) and Sheri Dennis (2002) have written about the significance of The Complex as a Christian go-go alternative venue.

23. In high school, I was told that in addition to the practicality and style of wearing Timberland boots, people wear them as weapons to go-gos to be able to stomp on others should a fight break out.

24. "Beat ya' feet" is a Washington, DC dance style that resembles combination of break dancing and miming (Hopkinson, 2002c).

25. Researchers have observed in other Christian movements an exploration of musical performances that depict a muscular Christianity aesthetic. For instance, sociologist Amy D. McDowell explores performances of muscular Christianity in Christian hardcore punk in her article "Aggressive and Loving Men: Gender Hegemony in Christian Hardcore Punk," in which she argues that such performances have gained popularity among White Evangelical youth since the 2016 presidential election. https://gendersociety.wordpress.com/2017/04/20/

aggressive-and-loving-men-gender-hegemony-in-christian-hardcore-punk/?utm_
content=buffer9216e&utm_medium=social&utm_source=facebook.com&utm_
campaign=buffer.

26. Floyd (1995, 57).
27. Southern (1997, 456).
28. Nketia (1974, 189).
29. Southern (1997, 151–204).
30. Southern (1997, 172).
31. Snethen (1848).
32. Rend Smith, "Exclusive: A Look at MPD's 'Go-Go Report,'" *Washington City Paper*, http://www.washingtoncitypaper.com/news/city-desk/blog/13062005/exclusive-a-look-at-mpds-go-go-report.
33. Liz Skalski and Alison E. Walker, "Man Shot, Killed in Capitol Heights After Go-Go Concert," Gazette.Net, http://www.gazette.net/stories/12292009/prinnew141120_32574.php.
34. Martin (2019).
35. Curfew laws dwell in a heritage of race, gender, and youth based policing such as those regulations enforced during Jim and Jane Crow and Black Codes eras. Forms of these laws have continued under the auspice of youth victimization prevention but it is debatable their effectiveness in influencing a decline of youth casualties. The Juvenile Curfew Act of 1995 distributes the responsibility of and security expense for surveillance of youth from the police to churches and the schools at which gospel go-gos are held. Because of this Act, go-go music patrons under 17 years old are prohibited from freely moving about Washington, DC from 11 p.m. and 6 a.m. on Sunday–Thursday and 12:01–6 a.m. on Friday and Saturday, often in effect between July and August. Like most urban centers, those are the months during which there is an increase in youth victimization. Such laws are crucial to the Washington, DC social life because the curfew is in effect during hours when nocturnal go-go events are traditionally held. Persons under seventeen years old are exempt from curfew enforcement if they are with their parent or are at an official school, religious, or other recreational activity sponsored by the District of Columbia, a civic organization, or a similar group that will take responsibility for the juvenile. If they violate the law, they are subject up to a $500 fine and up to 25 hours of community service. See Appendix C.
36. Tribbett (2006).
37. Clark-Sheard (2010).
38. Dillard (2014).
39. Butler (2010).
40. Israel Houghton & New Breed (2013).
41. Kirk Franklin's impromptu live performance was captured in "DC Teaches Kirk Franklin How to Chop {Gospel GoGo}" (2011).
42. Interview at The Pot radio on April 10, 2015.
43. Jones (2014, 679–680).
44. Personal interview conducted in May 2014.
45. This is an excerpt from follow-up email in June 2014.

46. Due to advances in technology, there are various recording techniques and effects that engineers can use to edit imperfections. They may eliminate feedback, use compression for the vocalist, and provide clarity for the various musical lines. Sound engineer and go-go Aaron Hope explains that gospel go-go sound engineers understand that while those imperfections are offensive in popular music sounds, they are desirable in the go-go aesthetic. Gospel go-go musicians want the sound to remain "dirty."

47. Wilson (1992, 329).

48. Reagon (1985, 1992, 2000); Floyd (1995); Wilson (1992); Maultsby (1990); Kelley (1996); Rose (1994); Gilroy (1993, 1993); Hall (1982, 1992); Davis (1990, 1998); Griffin (2001); Mahon (2000); and Ramsey (2001).

49. Keil (1995, 5).

50. Gaunt (2006, 121).

51. See Rose (1994), Pinn (2008), and Rommen (2007).

52. Stephenson and Lornell (2009) and Hopkinson (2012).

53. Jones (2016, 223–224).

54. Pollard (2008, 153).

55. Radio interview at The Pot radio on April 10, 2015.

56. The Peculiar People band members are MayDay (vocalist), Warchild (vocalist), Deborah "Jlyrical" (vocalist), Brandon "Chiavo" (guitar), Ronald "Trae" Saunders (drums), Aaron Hope, Nate Rhodes, and Jay Julien.

57. "Peculiar People (Peculiar 'Til I Die)" (2008b).

58. "Microaggression is a term used to describe racial assaults that are 'subtle, stunning, often automatic and non verbal exchanges which are 'put downs' by [whites]" (Russell 1998, 138).

59. One should note the gendered gaze of the patrons with whom they musically reason about their faith. As with other gospelized styles, the patrons are overwhelmingly women, girls, and femme identified fans.

60. Franklin (1998, 39).

61. The "choir boy" stereotype was recently staged in a play with original gospel music and arranged spirituals called Choir Boy (2013) written by Tarell Alvin McCraney. It is the coming of age story of a gay African American youth, set at an all-boy preparatory school as he vies for lead soloist of the school's legendary gospel choir.

62. My initial interviews with Dré were conducted in March 2009.

63. Hopkinson (2002a).

64. Anderson (1990, 172–173).

65. "Mean muggin'" is a vernacular term for a hard, frowning facial expression.

66. Carpenter (1993).

67. Hopkinson (2002b).

68. Hopkinson (2012, 38).

69. See also Harris (1999a, 1999b, 1999c, 2002); Hopkinson (2002a).

70. In contrast, its nonreligious counterpart go-go is infamous for being the site in which geo-class and moral tensions collide.

71. Harris (1999), Hopkinson (2000d).

72. Hopkinson 2002a.
73. Rouget (1985, 6–12).
74. Becker (2004, 1).
75. See Appendix B, "Peculiar People Sound Requirement List."
76. The phrase "Stop the Violence" is attributed to KRS-One's 1989 response to the murder of Scott La Rock who was a founding member of Boogie Down Productions and a young man during a concert featuring Boogie Down Production and Public Enemy. KRS-One started the Stop the Violence Movement as a national hip-hop campaign to cease violence in African American and hip-hop communities.
77. Lornell and Stephenson (2009, 237).
78. Gowen (2001).

Chapter 5

1. Jones (2015).
2. Smallwood (1996).
3. Tonéx (2004).
4. Williams's dance is similar to the Egyptian style dance, where dancers move head and arms in different directions resembling Egyptian iconography. The Egyptian style dance is referenced in The Bangles' song "Walk Like an Egyptian" (1986). His dance moves may also be called the "King Tut" dance which was first performed in a novelty song by Steve Martin on Saturday Night Live in 1978. King Tut is a nickname for Egyptian Pharoah Tutankhamun, whose tomb artifacts were being exhibited at the time of his performance in New York at the Metropolitan Museum of Art 1976–1979. Martin later recorded the novelty song as commentary on the United State's fascination with ancient Egyptian artifacts.
5. Tonéx (2004).
6. Tonéx (2002).
7. The phrase "Stop quenching the Spirit!" is a warning against grieving or stifling the Holy Spirit (1 Thessalonians 5:19).
8. I was told that one of the advantages for convening music conferences in New Orleans is that they are flexible about the times when music concerts can be scheduled. When I attended GMWA in 1999 and 2000, I recall concerts that were scheduled well into the morning.
9. As I have mentioned in the introduction and chapter 1, in gospel performance, the "choir loft" is gendered as a female space. The choir loft is distinct from the musicians' pit, which is conventionally gendered as a male space.
10. Mitchell (1996, 30).
11. Lurie (1981, 12).
12. "A-shirt" is short for athletic undershirt. A-shirts may also be (problematically) referred to as "wife beaters."
13. "Lexi Show (Tonex) Part 3," YouTube, posted LexiTelevision, September 11, 2009, https://www.youtube.com/watch?v=Yg5EhnbZqkA.

14. Nelson (1992, 9).
15. Román (1998, 155).
16. Deborah Smith Pollard also writes, "When artists make garment selections that go beyond the traditional boundaries of the black Church or gospel music world, they generally do so for several reasons. What may appear to be a flagrant disregard for the rules of dress and decorum can be more appropriately understood as the existence and assertion of multiple identities with 'the body of Christ,' the name Christians use to refer to fellow believers and their institutions. Whereas earlier generations seem to have prioritized projecting a certain image through attire—'I am Christian and, therefore, not worldly'—a growing number of turn-of-the-century gospel artists are selecting ensembles and accessories that underscore the various identities they embrace and that allow them to declare through their selections, 'I am young *and* Christian *and* 'fashionably correct.' Such perceived proclamations are controversial in some circles because they highlight the existence of differing values and aesthetics, divergent interpretations of relevant Scriptures regarding adornment and the body, and challenges to denominational mores in the Black Church and gospel music worlds, where, for years, many viewed conformity as a sign of membership" (2008, 80–81).
17. Pollard (2008, 96).
18. Tonéx (2009).
19. Halperin (2002, 31).
20. Smitherman (1986, 118–119).
21. Floyd (1995, 95).
22. Turino (2008, 237).
23. Tonéx (2008).
24. In my interview with Tonéx, he said that he did that cover because too many people in the gospel music industry are fat. He wanted to challenge them to be healthy. He added that he believes gospel artist Kirk Franklin copied him and used a similar concept, displaying his muscular body in the cover art for *The Fight of My Life* album (2007). On the cover, Franklin was featured standing in a boxing ring with his chest bare and standing over what appears to be his former self, while being held back by a referee. Franklin's bare chested portrayal registered for many fans as erotic and egocentric.
25. Marlon Bailey elucidates the various gender system categories within gay Ballroom culture in his book *Butch Queens Up in Pumps: Gender, Performance, and Ballroom Culture* (2013). He explains that "Trade" and "Men" are similar categories. "In the gender system of Ballroom culture, Men participate in the community, either directly or indirectly, and are usually romantically involved or have sex with Butch Queens or Femme Queens. Men do not typically identify as gay, often identifying as straight or bisexual instead. Men are usually very masculine and, if they participate in balls, they compete in realness categories. Some Men participate in house activities but do not walk balls. The Man category is both a gender category and a sexual one because of the joined ideas of sexual practice embedded and ascribed to the identity. Men are similar to what is known as Trade in black LGBT culture at large . . . Men also have

romantic and sexual relationships with Femme Queens, which is consistent with their identifying as straight because Femme Queens live as women. Conversely, a few Men who are involved in relationships with Femme Queens do identify as bisexual even if they do not see themselves as gay; hence, they are not Butch Queens" (Bailey 2013, 42).

26. Tonéx (2008).
27. "Chile" is a variant of child.
28. Johnson (2008, 17).
29. Chablis (1996).
30. Sweet tea "is also an adjective used to modify spaces, places, events, sex acts, and types of dissident sexual agents" (Johnson 2011, 17).
31. "Eye" is also a euphemism to describe a man's phallus.
32. Sanneh (2010).
33. In my interview with him, Tonéx mentioned that his critics referred to the illustration of him with blue-lit eyes as representing a demonic possession. He countered that the critique is ironic because his eyes were blue in the same manner that Christ has been depicted as being a blue-eyed Messiah, even though he is historically of a darker hue.
34. B.Slade aurally resembles the imperative phrase "be slayed." "Slayed" is a black gay vernacular term that means that one killed or overwhelmed spectators with their performance. As in "He slayed in his performance in the opening of the Grammys!"
35. For more research on black dandyism, consult English scholar Monica Miller's book *Slaves to Fashion: Black Dandyism and the Styling of Black Diasporic Identity* (2009).
36. Jones (2017).
37. Kot (2014, 1.1).
38. "Hold My Mule" (1989) by gospel music icon Rev. Shirley Caesar was the remixed song that Johnson referenced in the article. The house remixes and other variations of the original recording re-emerged in 2016 and 2017 on social media. While Caesar was flattered by the renewed popularity of her song, she did not like that musicians started making new recordings, using her voice without consent and proper attribution for nonreligious purposes that contrasted with her holiness beliefs. Her dissent with the repurposing of her song is notable, especially because she is known for collaborating with and validating secular artists (Jones 2014).
39. The "uh" sound is represented by "ə" (schwa) in the International Phonetic Alphabet (IPA).
40. Floyd (1995, 94).
41. The following lyrics exemplify this practice: "When I think of His goodness and what He's done for me. When I think of His goodness and how He set me free . . . I can dance, dance, dance, all night."
42. Conquergood (1995, 137).
43. Conquergood (1995, 138).
44. Román (1998, 155).
45. Presently, in 2019, the United States has one of the highest retail prices for PrEP of around $2,000 per month, even though the US government was an early investor in the scientific advances that produced it.

46. This queer listening was prompted by remarks from queer musicologist and dance scholar Daniel Callahan's during my Ethnoise! graduate student workshop at the University of Chicago in 2012.
47. Schechner (1993, 38).
48. Amanpour and Company (2019).
49. Geertz (1973, 432–433).
50. Voguing is a mode of gesturing and dancing that was made popular by the documentary on black and Latino gay ball culture in New York. Madonna then appropriated voguing in her interpretative hit "Vogue" (1990). She was subsequently critiqued for her use of the art form.
51. Levine (1998, 127, 130).
52. Thrasher (2019).
53. "Disclosure of HIV Status", Center for Disease Control and Prevention, https://www.cdc.gov/hiv/policies/law/states/exposure.html.
54. Arnold and Bailey (2009).
55. Stephens (2014).
56. "Carless Hardin—The Pulpit Uncensored," 9:13, YouTube, posted by "OeauxHaHa," November 4, 2011, http://www.youtube.com/watch?v=kxDxwS4SmxQ.
57. "Ex-gay" is a controversial term that describes a person who refrains from engaging in same-sex relationships, and presumably works to replace homosexual desires with heterosexual desires and behavior, perhaps in order to pursue heterosexual relationships. People who subscribe to ex-gay movements have formerly self-identified as LGBTQ. In common Pentecostal parlance, this ex-gay status is described as being delivered from homosexuality.
58. Bishop Yvette Flunder, Shirley Miller, and Dejuaii Pace are rare examples of female gospel artists who have openly self-identified as lesbian. Instead, discourses about women's sexuality focus on the "problem" of single motherhood.
59. Bishop Horace Smith, M.D. provided resources on the discourse regarding LGBT participation in a workshop handout for P.A.W., Inc. 2013 Pastors & Ministry Leaders Summit attendees (see Appendix D, "P.A.W., Inc. 2013 Pastors & Ministry Leaders Summit Handout").
60. Attinello (2006, 222).
61. Attinello (2006, 225).
62. Cleveland (1985).
63. Graham (1994).
64. Additionally in the discourse about deliverance from sexually transmitted disease, "Let Go, Let God" (2006) is a hit single Dewayne Wood that was marketed through his interviews debuting the single as a testimony about his healing from HIV/AIDS. Woods (2006).
65. Hawkins (1990).
66. For many years, there have been rumors surrounding whether Walter Hawkins's queer sexuality was the impetus for his divorce from Tramaine Hawkins. During Columbia University's "Are the Gods Afraid?" conference at First Corinthian Baptist

Church in Harlem, NY on October 24, 2014, his close friend Bishop Yvette Flunder shared that Hawkins was never permitted to be fully who he was in the public's eye.

67. François (1995, 447).

Chapter 6

1. Recording artist Kirk Franklin writes, "I think that another reason I got into so much trouble with sexual temptations during those years was that I was trying to fight my 'image.' I didn't talk about my church activities very much at school, but some of the kids found about them and started teasing me. They called me 'Church Boy.'

   I didn't mind so much when they called me 'Church Boy.' But they also called me 'Mama's Boy' and started making jokes that I was gay, and that was painful. In the church, especially the African-American church during the seventies and eighties, homosexuality was a big problem. It still is in some places" (Franklin 1998, 39).

2. I use the term "heteropatriarchal" to connote systems in which heterosexual presenting men subordinate and assume access to women or feminized groups. I use this term instead of "homophobia" because I do not interpret the primary function of these comments as conveying disdain for homosexuals (though that is an effect). I interpret the remarks to demonstrate a type of social dominance consistent with a muscular Christianity theology that pursues re-establishing male leadership in conventional family roles.

3. I conceive of "speaking in tongues" as a ritualizing of a believer's indecipherability while privately or publicly using divinely inspired vocables to communicate through prayer with God in what is called one's "heavenly language," xenoglossia, or glossolalia. If this practice is enacted publicly, it is believed to be incomplete or invalid if it is done without another believer interpreting, with the help of the Holy Spirit, special prayerful communication that is otherwise indiscernible to others gathered.

4. "Slained in the Spirit" is a nonecstatic mode of trancing in which a believer or seeker (presumably) involuntarily lays on the floor as a result of a leveling move of the Spirit.

5. Pitt (2010, 40).

6. Pitt (2010, 40).

7. Tye Tribbett reunited with Tonéx in performing during a worship service in Washington, DC at Ebenezer AME in fall 2013. Tribbett stated a revised position about homosexuality in the April 2014 issue of *Sister 2 Sister* magazine. He claims that while homosexuality may come naturally, it is not God's best.

8. Dyson (1996, 80).

9. Ibid.

10. Glenn (2004, 9).

11. Cheryl Glenn writes further, "Thus it is even when we imagine that we are experiencing environmental silence, something makes a sound. If the washing machine is not running, then the furnace or water softener is. Traffic moves along the streets, cushioning the sounds of walkers and talkers. Birds signal one another as they fly overhead or roost in trees. When we experience the locational silences of funeral homes,

libraries, or courtrooms, environmental sounds—even speech—leak into silence. When we share silence communally with others, when two or more solitudes come together, at religious or musical events, someone always coughs, sneezes, or clears the throat. And when we practice silence on a personal level, our own breathing and beating accompanies use wherever we are, no how silent we try to be. Yet according to our Western culture, in each of these settings, we say we are experiencing silence when we are conscience of these silences" (Glenn 2004, 9–10).

12. This phrase in the song derives from a traditional spiritual in which the singer confesses that the prayer is for them.

> *It's me, it's me, oh Lord*
> *Standing in the need of prayer;*
> *It's me, it's me, oh Lord*
> *Standing in the need of prayer.* Not my mother, not my father
> But it's me, oh Lord
> Standing in the need of prayer. Not my brother, not my sister
> But it's me, oh Lord
> Standing in the need of prayer. Not my elder, not my leader
> But it's me, oh Lord
> Standing in the need of prayer. Not the preacher, not the sinner
> But it's me, oh Lord
> Standing in the need of prayer.

13. The practice of "tarrying" for the Holy Spirit stems, in large part, from the 1906 Azusa Street Revival in Los Angeles, CA, during which participants reported that the Spirit was poured out among them. They began to demonstrate divine gifts such as speaking in other tongues "as the Spirits gives utterance" (Acts 2). This manifestation of spiritual gifts was seen as a modern-day fulfillment of biblical prophecy and a continuation of early Church practices in which Jesus's disciples waited or "tarried" for the Holy Spirit to descend during Pentecost. David Daniels III argues that tarrying for the Spirit is one of several practices that "reflected more of the religious ethos of the 19th century than the 20th." He describes tarrying as "a Pentecostal counterpart to the Baptist mourner's bench" that serves as "a form of contemplative prayer," though which Pentecostal believers "experienced conversion, sanctification, and Spirit baptism by the sovereignty of God" (Daniels 2001, 280).

14. As I mentioned in chapter 3, in James Baldwin's first novel *Go Tell It on The Mountain* (1952), he depicts the tensions around participants' contemplation and self-disclosure during a prayer service in which he references the song "It's me, it's me, oh Lord."

15. *Sotto voce* means below the voice, in an undertone or barely audible voice (as in an aside).

16. King (2000, 430).

17. Bishop Yvette Flunder described herself as a shaman at the Are the Gods Afraid of Black Sexuality?" two-day, interfaith conference at Columbia University's Center on African American Religion, Sexual Politics & Social Justice (CARSS) in New York City on October 24, 2014. Tonéx used the term in the 2010 interview with the author.

18. Peek (2007, 23).
19. Peek (2007, 24).
20. Leinhardt (1985).
21. Bailey (2013, 56).
22. Johnson (2003, 37).
23. "Shut up and sing" is a term that was popularized by the European American country music group Dixie Chicks and is the shortened title of their 2006 documentary *Dixie Chicks: Shut Up and Sing*. The phrase was derived from various country music detractors' quotes in which they expressed dissent with the group's political stance. Variations of that phrase have been applied to other entertainers and athletes such as the African American football player Colin Kaepernick amid his protests against police brutality by taking the knee or kneeling on one knee during the singing of the US national anthem.
24. Dyson (1996, 104–105).
25. "Letting slip" alludes to several vernacular expressions derived from historic anxieties around women allowing their unmentionable undergarments show. Since then the phrase, refers to being vulnerable or an incompetent performance of gender identity in gay vernacular. For example, Patrick Dailey mentions men *letting their slip show*, that is, displaying feminine masculine gender expression, while audition for heterosexual, cisgender roles (see chapter 2).
26. Bell (2009, 7).
27. Pitt (2010, 41).
28. The song was also released on the *Rainbow* EP (2008) mentioned in chapter 5.
29. With regard to the documentary, I received the following description from a documentary producer and University of Chicago PhD candidate Tadhi Coulter: "A first of its kind documentary, Standing-n-Truth: Breaking the Silence weaves the personal narrative of African American men, women and children in the face of the HIV/AIDS pandemic, transcending differences of sexuality, class, and gender. The voice of one man (Tim Daniels) allows others, who have been silenced, ostracized, and discouraged, to reflect on their own personal stories, while emphatically and empathetically constructing and integrating strategies for reducing individual and collective stigma. An array of the following popular-opinion leaders share intimate experiences of stigma, shame, and silence: David Malebranche, MD, MPH, Beny J. Primm, MD, Gail E. Wyatt, PhD, Vickie M. Mays, PhD, MSPH, Kevin Fenton, MD, PhD, Michael Eric Dyson, PhD, Congresswoman Maxine Waters, Bishop Yvette E. Flunder, Kym Whitley, Mari Marrow, Pamela Williams, and Sheryl Lee Ralph. Directed by: Tim Daniels Produced by: Tim Daniels, Rorie Burton, Tadhi Coulter."
30. Standing imagery is pervasive throughout gospel music repertoire. It represents courage, stable faith, solitude, and certainty in God. For example, Pastor Donnie McClurkin's most well known song is titled "Stand" (1996).
31. Interview with B.Slade and the author on March 27, 2011.
32. Sartre (1956, 628).
33. Though it is outside the scope of this chapter, it is worth noting there are ways in which Tonéx and Sartre differ in their conceptualization of self-deception or "bad

faith." For example, Tonéx would disagree with Sartre's conflation of homosexuality with pedophilia.

34. While many black Christian communities may be discursively constructed as homogeneous in terms of sexual orientation, I contend that closeted queer individuals are "hidden" in the sanctuaries of black worship. I read Tonéx's call for an audible (and visible) peculiarity as a plea for recognition of the radical heterogeneity of black gospel spheres.

35. Inspiration for the approach taken in this paper comes from the music and religion section panel entitled *Gendering Gospel Music* at the 2015 American Academy of Religion (AAR) conference in Atlanta, Georgia, which featured the religious music scholars Charisse Barron, Cory Hunter, Cheryl Townsend Gilkes, and myself. A conversation arose about the gospel music industry's ambivalent reception of artists' recording love song albums. As we discussed the intended audience for these works, a participant argued that there is no eroticism cultivated through gospel music performance. They contended that the objective of gospel music is to worship God, implying that worship is to the exclusion of sexual arousal and desire. Several attendees, including myself, disagreed with this assertion. This exchange prompted me to probe how music scholarship on the performance of gender and sexuality could be a lens through which I analyze the indecisive reception of the album, and led to this larger discussion of erotic listening and performance.

36. "Sexual healing" references the euphemism for physical satisfaction through sex that was coined by soul music tenor Marvin Gaye in the 1982 song "Sexual Healing" from the Motown album *Midnight Love*.

37. Jones (2018, 3–4).

38. Soft Cell (1981).

39. Bhutta (2008).

40. Sneezing following intercourse is also referred to as "honeymoon rhinitis." Monteseirin et al. (2002, 353–354).

41. Fantham (2006).

42. There was only a widow who dealt with the prophet in the 1 Kings account. Though the father is mentioned in the second Kings resurrection account, he is not mentioned at all in the song.

43. Pastor Travis Greene—who was mentioned in chapter 1—is one of many believers whose story complicates the queer resurrection narratives. His modern story legitimizes the belief in being raised from the dead. The first time he was resurrected as a "still born." In an interview with Tamara Young of Jet magazine, he said, "A couple of radical things happened in my life. When I was born—on the spot, my mother said that I wasn't breathing. My skin color was purple, and doctors immediately said that I was stillborn. My mother and father just started praying and believing God, and He performed a miracle." The second time he was brought back to life as a four year old pronounced dead after falling four floors out of a house his mother lived in at the time in Germany. "Then, when I was four-years-old, I fell out of a window and I was pronounced dead. They covered me with a white sheet. But, then my mother came, she picked up my lifeless body, and prayed to God to give me my life. He did it. The

crazy thing about it is they kept me in the hospital for a couple days, then as we were leaving, I told my mom, "I remember falling from the window, but I never hit the ground. Right before I hit the ground, a man with a big hand caught me. I couldn't see his face because it was so bright, but I heard a voice that said, 'Do you want to go home with your mom or come with me?' I looked up and said, 'I want my Mom.' He said, 'This time you're going home with your mom. Next time, you're coming with me.' I said, 'Excuse me Sir, what's your name?' He said, 'Son, my name is Jesus'" (Young 2016).

44. Jones (2018).

45. The Hebrew term *Shekinah* is translated in English as "the dwelling" in which the presence of God descended to dwell upon humanity (Deuteronomy 11:14, 23:16 6, 11: 27. 2; Nehemiah 1:9).

46. *Shekinah* is not a term that is found in the Holy Bible but has gained popularity in Pentecostal circles. *Shekinah* is often conflated with the term *shakhan* found in Exodus: "Moses could not enter the Tent of Meeting, for the cloud rested upon it, and the glory of the Lord filled the Tabernacle (Exodus 40: 35)."

47. In 2018, I wrote about Charles Anthony Bryant's performance of ascending to a celestial dwelling and one's musical embodiment of a dwelling place in the article "'You Are My Dwelling Place': Experiencing Black Men's Aural Eroticism and Autoeroticism in Gospel Performance." This interpretation of dwelling in Richard Smallwood's composition "I Give You Praise" (1989) is in contradistinction to Pentecostal Second Testament or New Testament notions of the Holy Spirit as a divine entity that indwells the believer (Jones 2018, 9).

48. R&B/Funk artists The Bar Kays' "Holy Ghost" from the *Money Talks* (1978) album compared love qua eros or sexual desire to feeling like the Holy Ghost.

49. Gospel artist Israel Houghton recorded a reggaeton style gospel song about satisfaction titled "With Long Life (He Will Satisfy Me)" (2007).

50. There are several gospel songs that describe being prostrate before the Lord such as recorded in "Beyond the Veil" by Daryl Coley on *Daryl Coley Live: Live at the Bobby Jones Gospel Explosion VII* (1996).

51. F@CE Down has broader connotations similar to the yoga poses of "downward facing dog."

Chapter 7

1. "Ricky Dillard & New G Worked It Out" (2017).

2. Sanneh (2010).

3. Marlon Bailey writes further, "Three inextricable dimensions constitute the social world of Ballroom culture: the gender system, the kinship structure (houses), and the ball events (where ritualized performances are enacted). What members refer to as the "gender system" is a collection of gender and sexual subjectivities that extend beyond the binary/ternary categories in dominant society such as male/female, man/woman, gay/lesbian/bisexual, and straight. Ballroom members conceive of sex,

gender, and sexuality as separate but inextricably linked categories. Ballroom gender and sexual identities serve as the basis of all familial roles and the competitive presentation and performance categories at ball events" (Bailey 2013, 5).

4. Bailey (2013, 2).

5. Turino (2008, 237).

6. Some videotaped examples are "Mercedez Ellis Loreal Giving the Children Church Realness At Oz!!," YouTube, posted by House of Hung Realness, October 31, 2013, https://www.youtube.com/watch?v=pewU7e9whrk; "The Red Realness 10s," YouTube, posted by Kiki Vidz, December 4, 2016, https://www.youtube.com/watch?v=AlseoiE5oWA; "Church Cunts," YouTube, https://www.youtube.com/watch?v=m6OEePySPl4—Mother Leviticus.

7. Bailey (2013, 55–56).

8. Jones (2018).

9. Once conceived and uttered, rumors have a life of their own. In *The Psychology of Rumor* (1965), Gordon W. Allport and Leo Postman address fans' fascination with and distribution of unsubstantiated claims about celebrities, black male gospel musicians in this case. Allport and Postman argue rumors are circulated in relationship to the importance of the issue to the speaker and the listener. At a rumor's most basic level, it represents that the speaker knows something the receiver/listener does not know.

10. In her book *Preaching as Local Theology and Folk Art* (1997), homiletics scholar Lenora Tubbs Tisdale argues, good preaching (and music ministry) "not only requires its practitioners to become skilled biblical exegetes. Also, it requires them to become adept to 'exegeting' local congregations and their contexts, so that they can proclaim the gospel in relevant and transformative ways for particular communities of faith" (xi).

11. Former Motown recording artist Archbishop Carl Bean contests McClurkin's assertion in his controversial 2010 book titled after his #1 hit, *I Was Born This Way: A Gay Preacher's Journey Through Gospel Music Disco Stardom and a Ministry in Christ*.

12. Harris (2013).

13. Jones (2018).

14. Jones (2016, 223).

15. Sanneh (2010).

16. "Independent Lens | The New Black | Faith Gave Tonéx the Courage to Come Out to His Fans | PBS," YouTube, posted by PBS, June 10, 2014, https://www.youtube.com/watch?v=rFK38cDKLnI.

17. Musically induced deliverance may bring about what Mihály Csikszentmihalyi theorized as optimal experience or flow. For Csikszentmihalyi, flow is "a state of concentration so focused that it amounts to absolute absorption in an activity. Everyone experiences flow from time to time and will recognize its characteristics: people typically feel strong, alert, in effortless control, unselfconscious, and at the peak of their abilities. Both a sense of time and emotional problems seem to disappear, and there is an exhilarating feeling of transcendence" (Csikszentmihalyi 1990, 1).

18. Finley (2007b, 16–19).

19. In 1982, for example, Evangelist Frances Kelly preached a sermon on women's night during the COGIC convocation admonishing women and men present against the desire to be popular by changing words of "worldly" songs to make the gospel message "contemporary." She said further that one must be careful not to look like the world by coloring and cutting hair into trendy styles. "Once we start looking like the world, don't nobody say nothing to us, you see. Because they are scared you won't sing no more." She described how those believers with musical gifts are not being disciplined because leaders do not want to offend the church entertainers. Among the many issues she outlined was her concern that young people are being misled by the idea that sex is a lifestyle. Evangelist Kelly retorted that sexuality is the magnificent handiwork of God for men and women to enjoy together. "He made man, and male and then he female. No in between . . . I get so sick of sissies I don't know what to do," she exclaimed. Evangelist Kelly's sermon is one of many that conflate sexual orientation with gender identity. More than anti-gay, her pronouncement that there is "no in-between" with regard to gender identity is an alienating message for gender nonconforming, intersex, and transgender people who seek to reconcile their spiritual and bodily experiences with their gender expression. Moreover, one's gender identity may or may not correspond with their sexual orientation. "COGIC Convocation" (1982).

20. As I have written in chapter 1, COGIC-raised Pastor Kim Burrell has come under fire for preaching a similar homoantagonistic message in which she asserted observed a feminine masculine believer with what she calls a "homosexual spirit" that she associated with "perverted behavior." What is key in her remarks is that she views his homosexuality as a form of demonic oppression from which he needed deliverance or the spiritual change that would manifest as heterosexuality. However, many spectators of the Burrell footage concluded that she revealed an antiquated view of the relationship between gender expression and sexuality. Further, her remarks caused injury to the men that she referenced in their absence as being sinners.

21. "Donnie McClurkin & Evangelist Joyce Rodgers" (2011).

22. Hairston (2009, 26).

23. Bailey (2014).

24. Bailey (2014, 67).

25. See chapter 4.

26. Winford (2003, 15).

27. McClurkin (200, 39–40).

28. Schechner (1993, 38).

29. Marlon Bailey examines a similar practice in black Ballroom culture and how LGBTQ male youth "construct homes." Bailey finds that this practice challenges "assumptions of homogeneity of sexual behavior in African American men, as well as a lack of appreciation for the dynamic nature of sexuality and the meanings that particular sexual behaviors, and identities, may have for African American men" (Bailey 2009, 172).

30. Schechner (2003, 119).

31. The "Realness" concept was made popular in the blockbusting documentary "Paris is Burning" (1989), which examined black and Latino gay Ball culture in the New York area.

32. "House," "(fore)father," and "children/kids" are metaphoric terms of home and kinship used in black gay Ball culture. Marlon Bailey has done an in depth exploration of the use of these terms (Bailey 2009).

33. "Tye Tribbett: The Doctrine of Feeling," YouTube, posted by ShareYourStory, June 18, 2008, https://www.youtube.com/watch?v=uqeIsaXioQk.

34. Bailey (2013, 56).

35. Flunder, October 24, 2014.

36. Jones (2018).

37. McClurkin (2001, 45).

38. Pitt (2010, 44).

39. Pitt (2010, 45).

40. Flunder, October 24, 2014.

41. Jones (2018).

42. Many Catholic churches with parishioners of color adhere to strands of what Peruvian priest Gustavo Gutiérrez coined in 1971 as liberation theology that interprets on the teachings of Jesus Christ as focusing on alleviating the conditions of the oppressed within society.

43. Saint Sabina, "About Us," accessed July 13, 2014 http://www.saintsabina.org/index.php/about-us#sthash.twpLursR.dpuf.

44. Cavan Sieczkowski, "Donnie McClurkin, 'Ex-Gay' Singer, Cut From MLK Concert Over 'Potential Controversy," Huffington Post, August 13, 2013, http://www.huffingtonpost.com/2013/08/13/donnie-mcclurkin-gay-mlk_n_3749861.html.

45. Cleveland (1990); see the introduction and chapter 4.

46. Underwood (2003).

Glossary

altar call. A summons to the altar to acknowledge one's Christian commitment or conversion experience.

Anal play. Various sexual activities that include anal penetration or **anilingus or "rimming"**, the act of licking and/or orally stimulating the anus of a sexual partner.

anointing. A type of performative competence where the performer is perceived as responding to and reflecting interactions with the divine; e.g., "I felt the Spirit. He is anointed!"

Asherah. A Hebrew (Canaanite-derived) female deity who eunuchs worshipped through public self-mutilation. She was represented as a carved cylindrical figurine (made of wood and clay)—a type of pole or tree—with an implanted or flared base. She is described as a wet-nurse to the gods. She is also referred to as Mother of the Gods and the wife of El, the chief God.

bad blood. A catch-all expression in African American vernacular culture for a bevy of blood-related ailments.

bad faith. A term coined by Jean-Paul Sartre that refers to the practice of self-deception. A liar only lies to others, a person of bad faith also lies to her/himself.

ball culture. A predominantly black and Latino subculture in the United States in which participants "walk" or perform various gender identities for trophies and prizes at events called balls.

bareback(ing). Slang for sex without condoms. It is a practice typically associated with gay men.

beats. Recognizable rhythmic patterns and layering.

bel canto. An Italian phrase translated as "beautiful singing." The term emerged in the seventeenth century to refer to an Italian singing style.

the body of Christ. A term that refers to the aggregate of Christian believers.

body theology. To take one's bodily experiences seriously as occasions of theological revelation.

butch. A characterization of men or women as manlike or masculine in appearance or behavior.

cadenza. A sung ornamented passage in a musical performance that is either written or improvised.

castrato. An Italian term referring to a man possessing an altered voice, achieved by a surgery that removed one or both testicles. This form of surgery fell out of practice in the nineteenth century.

celebration moment. Within the structure of traditional African American sermons, it is the height of the message, delivered either intermittently throughout or at the end of the delivery.

children (kids). A euphemism deployed by same-gender loving men for those who are a member of the community.

cisgender. A gender identity in which a person's experiences of their gender match the gender they were assigned at birth.

come out. Conventionally, means to reveal one's queer identity. In African American Pentecostal parlance, it also means to separate oneself from unbelievers.

church family. An immediate cultural cohort or social grouping centered on church participation.

church home. A network of interconnected immediate and extended families

church realness. Black male gospel musicians' expression of gender identity and engage public imagination to defuse rumor and maintain their sense of belonging in their religious community; an attempt to allow the coexistence of religious and queer identities in the primary community of faith; and a signification on an actual category within black and Latino Ballroom culture.

churchy. A term used, sometimes derogatorily, to describe those particularly fixated on church tradition as demonstrated in appropriate speech, gesture, attire, and attendance.

closeted. A person who is not openly homosexual or an individual who is a discreetly same-gender loving.

code-switching. A speaker's alternation between two or more languages while communicating. It is a compartmentalized behavior in which the actor changes gesture in order to identify with the environment.

compartmentalization. A separation of identity expression, such that certain behaviors are withheld or assigned to a particular audience or environment.

competence. The ability to perform within prescribed codes.

compulsory heteronormativity. An environment in which believers are socialized to uncritically assume that their brothers and sisters pursue heterosexual relationships.

contralto. A woman whose rare vocal range and tessitura are the lowest classification. Her rare range extends downward through the range designated for a tenor or baritone.

crank. A Washington, DC go-go music vernacular expression to describe performing good go-go music.

countertenor. A man whose rare vocal range and tessitura are the highest classification. His rare range extends upward through the alto vocal designation.

cultural cohort. A phrase characterizing a peer group.

cultural formation. Terminology for a group of people who have in common a majority of habits that constitute most parts of each individual member's self.

dark play. Richard Schechner's term for a form of play in performance theory in which some of the actors participate and are unaware of their engagement in the game.

delivered. A rhetorical device by which some Christians self-identify as no longer "bound" by certain beliefs, curses, or lifestyle practices; a distancing from perceived faults or sins in a gesture toward spiritual fitness; sometimes used to refer to a deliverance from homosexuality, i.e., "ex-gay."

deep play. Clifford Geertz's performance theory term that was developed by Jeremy Bentham for the games in which the stakes are so high that players are drawn to risk, deception, life and death, and sheer thrill.

defeminization. Doing away with, resisting, or eradicating the display of feminine attributes.

discreet. A person's use of secrecy and privacy.

discrete. A person's selectivity in choosing their sexual partners.

discretionary devices. I propose this term to capture the techniques employed by queer men to distance them from perceived queerness; examples include self-identification, evasion, silence, and suggestion.

down low. A form of perceived social deception or discretion by which homosexual men choose not to disclose sexual preference or are discreetly gay.

drop. Depending on the go-go performance context, the term frequently cues to the musical moment when the groove begins, as in "Let the beat drop."

en travesti. A performance during which a performer is dressed as a person of the opposite sex in an operatic role.

escapism. One's use of imagination or activities to evade problems.

ex-gay. Describes a person who previously had same-gender desire, refrains from engaging in same-sex relationships, and works to replace homosexual their desires with heterosexual desires, perhaps in order to pursue heterosexual relationships; in common Pentecostal parlance, this status is described as being "delivered" from homosexual spirits. (See also **delivered.**)

familiar spirits. Within in Pentecostal theology, familiar spirits are a threat to a believer's maintenance of a pleasing relationship with God. The term conveys one's sense of a spiritual weakness (temptations, habits, associations, bondages, vices, etc.) that may be triggered when a person comes into contact with recognizable people, places, and/or things that resemble involvements that they have left behind to pursue a deeper relationship with God.

fantastic hegemonic imagination. A phrase coined by Emilie Townes that is a portmanteau of Michel Foucault's understanding of the imagination and Antonio Gramsci's use of the hegemony, the fantastic hegemonic imagination—"plays" with history and memory to spawn caricatures and stereotypes.

feminization. The female domination of male submissives in bondage, discipline, submission, and masochism/sadomasochism (BDSM) practices. The term has been adapted to refer to the prevalence of feminine participation in African American. "Feminization" is also code for social and cultural castration.

flaming. A pejorative term to describe a demonstrative, feminine masculinity.

flow. M. Cszikszentmihalyi's concept indicating the state of concentration so focused that it amounts to absolute absorption in an activity. Everyone experiences flow from time to time and will recognize its characteristics: people typically feel strong, alert, in effortless control, unselfconscious, and at the peak of their abilities. Both a sense of time and emotional problems seem to disappear, and there is an exhilarating feeling of transcendence.

forefather. Conventionally, means ancestor. The designation is also a homosexual male leader/mentor; a metaphoric term of paternal kinship in black gay ball culture.

good faith. A term coined by Jean-Paul Sartre to describe one's demonstration of sincerity and candor.

getting ignorant. Elijah Anderson's term for a person's potential or ability to demonstrate their street credibility.

generational curses. In African American Pentecostal church vernacular, it is the manifestation of a pattern of dysfunction stemming from sins or vices that have existed in a family for several generations.

glossolalia. See **speaking in tongues.**

gospel music. Refers to a genre of black sacred music that emerged during the 20th century. Professor Thomas A. Dorsey is called the father of gospel, though he attested that he received musical inspiration from Rev. Charles A. Tindley's ministry. Within the music industrial complex, it is used as a catchall term for black sacred musics.

gospelize. A neologism describing the use of religious, ritual, performance, and aesthetic conventions of gospel music from various periods, regions, and styles frequently to create gospel subgenres such as gospel go-go, gospel house, and gos-pop.

gos-pop. Tonéx's neologism for a musical style that is presumably a fusion of gospel and popular a music.

hegemony. Within a social order, it is the economic, political, and military predominance or control of one state over another.

heteronormative. A worldview that promotes heterosexuality as normal or the preferred sexual orientation.

heteropatriarchal. The dominance of heterosexual males in society.

hetero-presenting. One's performance or presentation of themselves in manner and speech as though they are heterosexual, regardless of their sexual orientation.

homoeroticism. Symbolically same-gender relationships, in which there is desire to unite with the other and it is does not require a sexual enactment.

homomusicoenchantment. A neologism for gender-coded music deployed to charm people who identify with the coded music.

homomusicoenrapture. A neologism for gender-coded music deployed to delight people who identify with the coded music.

homomusicoeroticism. Music-centered same-gender relationships, through which there is desire to unite with the other.

homosociality. Same-gender relationships that are not sensual, romantic, or sexual such as brotherhood or friendship.

homosonoenchantment. A neologism for gender-coded sound deployed to charm people who identify with the coded sound.

homosonoenrapture. A neologism for gender-coded sound deployed to delight people who identify with the coded sound.

homosonoeroticism. A neologism for sound-centered, same-gender relationships, through which there is desire to unite with the other.

homosonority. A neologism for characterizing the production and/or hearing of resonant sound by similar entities, such as perceiving the same gender.

house. A metaphoric term of subgroups in kinship within black gay ball culture, and it is also short for "house music", which is a style of electronic dance music (EDM).

improvisational movement vocabulary. A semiotic and sensuous method of conveying knowledge to other participants.

inscription. The ways the body is socially understood and treated as a discursive text that is read by interactants.

interior disposition. One's demonstration of spiritual discipline.

lavender marriage. A euphemism for a heterosexual marriage perceived as a cover for one or both of the marriage partners' queer sexual orientation.

lead talker (also known as rapper). Similar to a hip-hop rapper, they are lead vocalists in a go-go band who speak during a performance.

liturgical dance. Movement or gesture that is presented during worship.

local theology. Doctrine developed by a local congregation due to their context and history, according to Leonora Tubbs Tisdale.

locked in the pocket. Describes the musical moment or event when a groove is achieved.

mallakhamb. A South Asian gymnastic practice where both men and women master using the pole in gymnastic feats.

masculine-centered. In this research, it is the musicians' use of codes in performance that persistently direct the audiences' focus via the gaze and the hearing toward street credible masculine subjectivity and posture, even when women perform.

mean mugging. A contextual vernacular term for a frowning facial expression; typically signifying the experience of creative intensity and pleasure; infrequently it indicates true displeasure.

mic toss. Impromptu passing or tossing of the microphone during a performance or worship.

microaggressions. Chester Pierce's term used to describe racial assaults as subtle, stunning, often automatic and nonverbal exchanges that are "put downs" by white people.

misandry. The hatred or dislike of men or masculine traits.

misandnoir. A neologism indicating the hatred or dislike of black men or masculine traits.

misogyny. The hatred or dislike of women or feminine traits.

MSMW. An acronym that stands for men who sleep with men and women.

muscular Christianity. The Christian concept of an idealized masculine image that focuses primarily on the place of men in the social order as heads of households.

musical bottom. The musical or sonic assertion of submission or sultriness through the demonstration of facility in lower frequencies, depending on the context.

musical top. The musical or sonic assertion of dominance and transcendence through the demonstration of facility in higher frequencies, depending on the context.

mysticism. Practices that strive toward the direct consciousness of God; the pursuit of oneness with God or an outside force.

ostinato. A phrase or motif that repeats in the same melodic line throughout a musical piece.

peculiar. To be consecrated or set apart; to be socially awkward; or to be sexually queer.

phallocentrism. The privileging of the masculine in understanding social relations.

phallogocentrism. A neologism to account for the privileging of the masculine in the construction of word meaning.

phallomusicocentrism. A neologism to account for the privileging of the masculine in the construction of music meaning.

phallosonocentrism. A neologism to account for the privileging of the masculine in the construction of sound meaning.

post-gay. An ex-gay or formerly gay person.

praise and worship music or songs. A broad term for Christian contemporary music used in worship that is stylistically similar to popular musics. Repertoire conventionally performed during worship services, concerts, and personal devotion.

prima donna. The principal or leading female singer in an opera.

preacher-musician. A person who sings and preaches when they minister.

rapper. See lead talker.

read. A black gay vernacular term for finding a flaw in someone or thing, often done in a performative manner.

real. A black gay vernacular term that may refer to authenticity or the ability to code-switch (speak one or more social language) while performing.

realness. A black gay vernacular term deployed in black and Latino gay ball culture to characterize one's competence in the performance of various gender and sexual identities, according to Marlon Bailey.

reprise. A repeated musical passage or section, often in an impromptu manner.

reprobate mind. A phrase derived from Romans 1:28 that refers to one whose mind is so evil that it is not able stop doing bad things.

ritualization. A strategic *way* of acting; it emerges as a particular cultural strategy of differentiation linked to particular social effects and rooted in a distinctive interplay of a socialized body and the environment it structures.

ruach. Hebrew term for God's omniscience, it is represented as the Holy Spirit or God that indwells.

same-gender loving (SGL). The term is attributed to Cleo Manago in the early 1990s as a black culturally affirming homosexual identity. SGL was adapted as an Afrocentric alternative to what are deemed Eurocentric homosexual identities (e.g., gay and lesbian) which do not culturally affirm or engage the history and cultures of people of African descent.

sermonette. A short and often impromptu sermon that performers may incorporate into their musical performance.

seronegative. A negative result in a blood test for a virus.

seropostive. A positive result in a blood test for a virus.

setting the atmosphere. The ability to readily prepare people to enter the presence of God; a prized skill set of music ministers.

shamanic. Characterizes a person who is an intermediary between the natural and supernatural worlds. They use their powers, gifts, or magic to cure ills, control spiritual forces, tell the future, etc.

social contract. A Rousseauian term for an agreement among members of a group in society.

Shekinah. *Shekinah* is a grammatically feminine Hebrew term that expresses the dwelling or settling of the presence of God in the earth.

signifyin(g). A traditional African artistic mode of psychological self-defense and self-empowerment that historically developed and intensified, while blacks coped with both white oppression and hostilities within African American communities. Signifyin(g) is, in essence, a mode of resistance, coping, commentary, and creative processing to neutralize various inter- and intracultural hostilities.

silent listeners. Silent spectators who gather information, judge, and assert power over those who speak.

sissy. A pejorative term in various US contexts for a man who is perceived to display feminine behavior, attributes, attitudes, and posture.

situational sexuality. Sexual behavior based upon one's social environment that encourages or evokes the activity.

slain in the spirit. Charismatic Christian vernacular for a nonecstatic mode of trancing in which a believer or seeker (presumably) involuntarily falls to or lays on the floor as a result of a move of the Spirit.

social bilingualism or multilingualism. A form of code-switching in which the speaker alternates between two or more social languages. (See **code-switching.**)

sociovisibility. A racial gaze that fixates or frames black subjects within a rigid and limited grid of representational possibilities.

sotto voce. An Italian term for the vocal stylistic approach that is translated as below the voice, in an undertone or barely audible voice (as in an aside).

sounded convergence. Describes the metaphoric sonic clash gospel go-go converts' use to combine modes of shared remembrance with Christian practices of setting themselves apart from their former life.

spatial genitals. Ashon Crawley's neologism that refers to the gendered interpolations of space based on the binary sex system (male/female). Bodies in specific locations are read through spatial genitals and are understood to concede, contest, or contaminate social relationships based on their reflection within the space. Put simply, based on biological constructions of bodies (i.e., "sex"), subjectivities are inculcated (i.e., "gender") with acceptable gestures, stylizations of body, conversation.

speaking in tongues. Vernacular for the ritualizing of a believer's indecipherability while privately or publicly using divinely inspired vocables to communicate through prayer with God in what is called one's "heavenly language." If this practice is enacted publicly, it is believed to be incomplete or invalid if it is done without another believer interpreting, with the help of the Holy Spirit, what is otherwise indiscernible to others gathered.

spoiled identity. Accounts for when the stigma placed upon a person disqualifies them from social acceptance.

STD. Refers to both sexually transmitted diseases or spiritually transmitted disease.

STI. Sexually transmitted infections.

stigma. The mark of disgrace or shame.

tantra. A Buddhist or Hindu ritual text that is dated from the sixth and thirteenth centuries; one's adherence to rituals and practices in the text.

tantric celibacy. May refer to many things within tantra such as conscious celibacy, tantric sublimation, tantric self-love, or solo practice (autoeroticism).

tarrying. A Pentecostal practice similar to the Baptist mourner's bench, where participants enact contemplative prayer.

tessitura. An Italian term for a vocalist's comfortable singing range.

testifying or "giving a testimony." The oral tradition of publicly sharing intimate, favorable stories to amplify God's work in a person's life, with the objective of encouraging others in their Christian faith and prompting exuberant praise.

theopolitics. The intersection of theology and politics that accounts for the flow of knowledge throughout various global structures, as set forth by Corey D. B. Walker.

top. A euphemism for a person who usually engages in the penetrative role in sex. This terms also refers to a person's broader self identity as socially, psychologically, and sexually dominant.

treble timbres. Naomi André's term for vocal designations such as countertenor, contralto, mezzo soprano/alto, and soprano that are conventionally notated on the treble clef.

trickster. African-derived folk figure who are silent in the natural world and were important communicators to God and humans.

turned out. Violent or nonconsensual same-sex sexual encounters.

unspoken. A gestural and rhetorical art of silence, especially in contested spaces and situations. Participants use gesture and silence to communicate something that may not be apparent to all the other participants. It is also refers to those issues that are unutterable in public.

vocalized androgyny. The interpretive processes through which vocal and timbral qualities attributed to one gender are mixed and matched with a body of the another gender.

woman up. Adapted from "man up" to refer to one's ability to be courageous and strong like a mature woman by taking action and accepting responsibility.

womanism. The definition coined by Alice Walker: 1. From *womanish* (opposite of "girlish," i.e., frivolous, irresponsible, not serious). A black feminist or feminist of color. From the black folk expression of mothers to female children, "you acting womanish," i.e., like a woman. Usually referring to outrageous, audacious, courageous or *willful* behavior. Wanting to know more and in greater depth than is considered "good" for one. Interested in grown-up doings. Acting grown-up. Being grown-up. Interchangeable with another black folk expression: "You trying to be grown." Responsible. In charge. *Serious.* 2. *Also:* A woman who loves other women, sexually and/or nonsexually. Appreciates and prefers women's culture, women's emotional flexibility (values tears as natural counterbalance of laughter), and women's strength. Sometimes loves individual men, sexually and/or nonsexually. Committed to survival and wholeness of entire people, male *and* female. Not a separatist, except periodically, for health. Traditionally a universalist, as in: "Mama, why are we brown, pink, and yellow, and our cousins are white, beige, and black?" Reply: "Well, you know the colored race is just like a flower garden, with every color flower represented." Traditionally capable, as in: "Mama, I'm walking to Canada and I'm taking you and a bunch of other slaves with me." Reply: "It wouldn't be the first time." 3. Loves music. Loves dance. Loves the moon. *Loves* the Spirit. Loves love and food and roundness. Loves struggle. *Loves* the Folk. Loves herself. *Regardless.* 4. Womanist is to feminist as purple is to lavender.

xenoglossia. The ability to speak an unfamiliar language. See also **speaking in tongues.**

Bibliography

Abbington, James, ed. *Readings in African American Church Music And Worship.* Chicago: GIA Publications, 2001.

Agawu, Kofi. "Schubert's Sexuality: A Prescription for Analysis?" *19th-Century Music* 17, no. 1 (1993): 79–82.

Allport, Gordon W., and Leo Postman. *The Psychology of Rumor.* New York: Henry Holt and Company, 1947.

Amanpour and Company. "Steven Thrasher on the HIV/AIDS Crisis | Amanpour and Company," posted December 16, 2019. YouTube, https://www.youtube.com/watch?v=N-tdO645qWQ.

Amit, Vered, ed. *Constructing the Field: Ethnographic Fieldwork in the Contemporary World.* London: Routledge, 2000.

Anderson, Elijah. *Streetwise: Race, Class, and Changes in an Urban Community.* Chicago: University of Chicago Press, 1990.

Anderson, Victor. "The Black Church and The Curious Body of the Black Homosexual." In *Loving the Body: Religious Studies and the Erotic.* Edited by Anthony Pinn and Dwight Hopkins, 297–312. New York: Palgrave, 2004.

Anderson, Victor. "Masculinities Beyond Good and Evil: Representations of the Down Low in the Fictional Imagination of Alphonso Morgan's Sons." In *On Manliness: Black American Masculinity.* Edited by W. Whiting and Thabiti Lewis. *AmeriQuests* 6, no. 1, 2 (2008): 1–13.

Anderson, Victor. "The D. L. Phenomenon in the Black Community." *The African American Lectionary,* 2011.

André, Naomi. *Voicing Gender: Castrati, Travesti, and the Second Woman in Early-Nineteenth Century Italian Opera.* Bloomington: Indiana University Press, 2006.

Appadurai, Arjun. *Modernity At Large.* Minneapolis: University of Minnesota Press, 1996.

Arnold, Emily A., and Marlon M. Bailey. "Constructing Home and Family: How the Ballroom Community Supports African American GLBTQ Youth in the Face of HIV/AIDS." *Journal of Gay and Lesbian Social Services* (2009): 171–188.

Atinello, Paul. "Closeness and Distance: Song about AIDS." In *Queering the Popular Pitch.* Edited by Sheila Whiteley and Jennifer Ryecenga. New York: Routledge, 2006.

Awkward, Michael. *Negotiating Difference: Race, Gender and the Politics of Positionality (Black Literature and Culture).* Chicago: University of Chicago Press, 1995.

Bailey, Marlon M. "Gender/Racial Realness: Theorizing the Gender System in Ballroom Culture." *Feminist Studies* 37, no. 2 (Summer 2011): 365–386.

Bailey, Marlon M. "He's My Gay Mother: Ballroom Houses, Parenting, and Housework." *Queers in American Popular Culture* 1 (2013): 169–178.

Bailey, Marlon M. *Butch Queens Up in Pumps: Gender, Performance, and Ballroom Culture in Detroit.* Ann Arbor: University of Michigan Press, 2014.

Baker-Fletcher, G. "Black Bodies, Whose Body?: African American Men in XODUS." In *Men's Bodies, Men's Gods: Male Identities in Post-Christian Culture.* Edited by B. Krondorfer. New York: New York University Press, 1996.

Balch, David L., ed. *Homosexuality, Science and the "Plain Sense" of Scripture*. Grand Rapids, MI: William B. Eerdmans Publishing Company, 2000.

Baldwin, James. *Go Tell it On the Mountain*. New York: Bantum Dell Books, 1953.

Bar Kays. "Holy Ghost." *Money Talks*. Memphis: Stax Records, 1978.

Barton, Bernadette. *Pray the Gay Away: The Extraordinary Lives of Bible Belt Gays*. New York: New University Press, 2012.

Bauman, Richard. "Verbal Art As Performance." *American Anthropologist* 77, no. 2 (1975): 290–311.

Bean, Carl. *I Was Born This Way: A Gay Preacher's Journey Through Gospel Music Disco Stardom and a Ministry in Christ*. New York: Simon Schuster, 2010.

Becker, Judith. *Deep Listening: Music, Emotion, and Trancing*. Bloomington: Indiana University Press, 2004.

Belzen, Jacob A., and Antoon Geels. *Mysticism: A Variety of Psychological Perspectives*. New York: Rodopi, 2003.

Best, Wallace. *Passionately Human, No Less Divine: Religion and Culture in Black Chicago, 1915–1952*. Princeton, NJ: Princeton University Press, 2007.

BET Networks. "'I Am Delivert!' Andrew Caldwell Breaks Down His Come To Jesus Moment | | Went Viral," posted September 5, 2018. YouTube, https://www.youtube.com/watch?v=6v91cp0i35E&frags=pl%2Cwn.

Beynon, John. *Masculinities and Culture*. Buckingham: Open University Press, 2002.

Bhutta, Mahmood F. "Sneezing Induced by Sexual Ideation or Orgasm: An Under-Reported Phenomenon." *Journal of the Royal Society of Medicine* 101, no. 12 (December 2008): 587–591.

Biddle, Ian, and Kirsten Gibson. *Masculinity and Western Musical Practice*. London: Ashgate, 2009.

Bloch, Gregory W. "The Pathological Voice of Gilber-Louis Duprez." *Cambridge Opera Journal* 19, no. 1 (March 2007): 11–31.

Bly, Robert. *Iron John: A Book About Men*. Reading, MA: Addison-Wiley Publishing Group, 1990.

Bogues, Anthony. *Black Heretics, Black Prophets: Radical Intellectuals*. New York: Routledge, 2003.

Boswell, John. *Same-Sex Unions In Premodern Europe*. New York: Villard Books, 1994.

Bourdieu, Pierre. *The Field of Cultural Production*. New York: Columbia University Press, 1993.

Boyd, Robert, Mark W. Muesse, and W. Merle Longwood, eds. *Redeeming Men: Religion and Masculinities*. Louisville, KY: Westminster John Knox Press, 1996.

Boyd, Stacy. *Black Men Worshipping: Intersecting Anxieties of Race, Gender, and Christian Embodiment*. New York: Palgrave Macmillan, 2011.

Boyer, Horace G. "Gospel Music." *Music Educators Journal* 64, no. 9 (1978): 34–43.

Boykin, Keith. *One More River to Cross: Black and Gay in America*. New York: Anchor Books/Doubleday, 1996.

Boykin, Keith. *Beyond the Down Low: Sex, Lies and Denial in Black America*. New York: Carroll & Graf, 2005.

Bowen, C. "Beyond Lisping: Code Switching and Gay Speech Styles," *Speech-language-therapy dot com*, 2002. https://www.speech-language-therapy.com/index.php?option=com_content&view=article&id=62:code&catid=11:admin&Itemid=101.

Bradby, Barbara, ed. "Gender and Sexuality." *Popular Music* 20, no. 3 (2001): 295–300.

Braxton, Greg. "The Black-White Drag Divide: 'White Famous,' Chris Rock and Tyler Perry on Saying Yes to the Dress." *LA Times*, posted December 8, 2017. https://www.latimes.com/entertainment/tv/la-ca-st-humor-men-in-dresses-20171208-story.html.

Brett, Philip. "Musicality, Essentialism and the Closet." In *Queering the Pitch: The New Gay and Lesbian Musicology*. Edited by Philip Brett, Elizabeth Wood, and Gary C. Thomas, 9–26. New York: Routledge, 1994.

Brooks, Daphne A. *Bodies in Dissent: Spectacular Performances of Race and Freedom, 1850–1910*. Durham, NC: Duke University Press, 2006.

Brown, Chuck & The Soul Searchers. *Bustin Loose*. Source Records. Released January 2, 1979.

Brown, Chuck & The Soul Searchers. *Go Go Swing Live*. Future Records & Tapes. Released January 1, 1986.

Brown, Chuck & The Soul Searchers. *The Best of Chuck Brown*. Raw Venture Records & Tapes. Released April 12, 2005.

Brown, Herbert. *Pimps in the Pulpit*. Skippers, VA: InStep, 2012.

Brown, Karen McCarthy. "Mimesis in the Face of Fear: Femme Queens, Butch Queens and Gender Play in the Houses of Greater Newark." In *Religion and Sexuality in Cross-Cultural Perspective*. Edited by Stephen Ellingson and M. Christian Green, 165–186. New York: Routledge, 2002.

Brundidge, Caleb. "About," accessed July 13, 2014, http://www.calebbrundidge.com/About.html.

B.Slade. Interview the author, March 27, 2011.

Burleigh, Glen. "Order My Steps," Burleigh Inspirations Music, BMI, 1994.

Burnim, Mellonee, and Portia K. Maultsby, eds. *African American Music: An Introduction*. New York: Routledge, 2006.

Burt, Ramsay. *The Male Dancer: Bodies, Spectacle, and Sexuality*. New York: Routledge, 2007.

Butler, Anthea. *Women in the Church of God in Christ: Making a Sanctified Church*. Durham, NC: University of North Carolina Press, 2007.

Butler, Judith. *Undoing Gender*. New York: Routledge, 2004.

Butler, Melvin L. "'Nou Kwe nan Sentespri' (We Believe in the Holy Spirit): Music, Ecstasy, and Identity in Haitian Pentecostal Worship." *Black Music Research Journal* 22, no. 1 (2002): 85–125.

Butler, Melvin L. "The Weapons of Our Warfare: Music, Positionality, and Transcendence Among Haitian Pentecostals." *Caribbean Studies. Special Issue: Interrogating Caribbean Music: Power, Dialogue, and Transcendence* 36, no. 2 (2008): 23–64.

Butler, Melvin L. "The Spirit of David: Negotiating Faith and Masculinity in Black Gospel Performance." In *Readings in African American Church Music and Worship, Volume 2*. Compiled and edited by James Abbington, 715–725. Chicago: GIA Publications, Inc., 2014.

Butler, Myron. *Revealed . . . Live in Dallas*. EMI Gospel. Released March 6, 2010.

Byrd, Rudolph P., and Beverly Guy-Shefthall, eds. *African American Men On Gender and Sexuality*. Bloomington: Indiana University Press, 2001.

Cage, Byron. "This Is The Air I Breathe." In *An Invitation To Worship*. Detroit: PAJAM, 2005, compact disc.

Caldwell, Andrew. "I don't have anything else to say about #KimBurrell except sweater dresses are not her friend . . . " Live stream from Facebook on December 31, 2016. Facebook, https://www.facebook.com/executiveandrew.caldwell/videos/vb.100001797325078/1200722389997660/?type=3.

Caldwell, Andrew. "He's spilling all the tea on 'Celebrity Big Kim Burrell." Live stream from Facebook on January 23, 2017. Facebook, https://www.facebook.com/executiveandrew.caldwell/videos/vb.100001797325078/1222200591183173/?type=3.

Camacho, Justin. "Hezekiah Walker Denies Homosexual Allegations." *Christian Post*, March 6, 2006, https://www.christianpost.com/news/hezekiah-walker-denies-homosexual-allegations.html.

Campbell, F. A. K. "Exploring Internalized Ableism Using Critical Race Theory." *Disability & Society* 23, no. 2 (2008): 151–162.

Cane, Clay. *Holler If You Hear Me: Black and Gay in the Church*. BET.com documentary, 2016.

Cannon, Katie Geneva. *Katie's Canon: Womanism and the Soul of the Black Community*. New York: Continuum, 1995.

Carby, Hazel. *Reconstructing Womanhood: The Emergence of the Afro-American Woman Novelist*. New York: Oxford University Press, 1987.

Carpenter, Bill. "Radio Host Reaches Youth Through Rap: She Shows 'It isn't Square to be Saved.'" *Washington Post*, January 2, 1993, E 14.

Cauvin, Henri E. "2 Detectives Indicted on Charges of Misconduct." *Washington Post*, March 22, 2007.

Center for Disease Control and Prevention. "Disclosure of HIV Status." https://www.cdc.gov/hiv/policies/law/states/exposure.html.

Cheatham, Wallace McClain, ed. 1997. *Dialogues on Opera and the African-American Experience*. Lanham, MD: Scarecrow Press.

Church of God in Christ. *Official Manual with the Doctrines and Discipline of the Church of God in Christ*. https://cogicjustice.files.wordpress.com/2012/01/cogic-official-manual.pdf, 1973.

Clair, Robin Patric. *Organizing Silence*. Albany: SUNY Press, 1998.

Clark Sheard, Karen. *All in One*. Karew Records. Released April 2, 2010.

Cleveland, James. *Sings with the World's Greatest Choirs*. Savoy Records. Released June 20, 1985.

Cleveland, James. *It's a New Day*. Savoy Records. Released October 17, 1990.

Clifford, James. *Routes: Travel and Translation in the Late Twentieth Century*. Cambridge, MA: Harvard University Press, 1997.

Clifford, James, and George E. Marcus, eds. *Introduction to Writing in Culture: The Politics and Poetics of Ethnography*. Berkeley: University of California Press, 1986.

Coates, Curtis D., and Hoover, Stewart M. "Meanings and Masculinities." In *Media, Religion, and Gender: Key Issues and New Challenges*. Edited by Mia Lövheim, 141–154. New York: Routledge, 2013.

"COGIC Convocation 'Musical Homosexual and Sissies.'" The Anoited [*sic*] Evangelist Frances Kelly, posted January 25, 2014. YouTube, https://www.youtube.com/watch?v=6qqEClV_K4s.

COGICPR. "Bishop Blake's Official Response To Convocation Incident Regarding Andrew Caldwell," posted November 17, 2014. YouTube, https://www.youtube.com/watch?v=2tQbVAYl9-Y.

Cohen, Judith R. "'This Drum I Play': Women and Square Frame Drums in Portugal and Spain." *Ethnomusicology Forum* 17, no. 1 (2008): 95–124.

Cone, James H. *A Black Theology of Liberation: Twentieth Anniversary Edition*. Maryknoll, NY: Orbis Books, 1990.

Cone, James H. *God of the Oppressed*. Maryknoll, NY: Orbis Books, 1997.

Connell, R. W. *Which Way is Up?: Essays on Sex, Class, and Culture*. Boston: Allen & Unwin, 1983.

Connell, R. W. *Masculinities: Knowledge, Power and Social Change*. Berkeley: University of California Press, 1995.

Connell, R. W. *The Men and the Boys*. Los Angeles: Polity Press, 2000.

Connerton, Paul. *How Societies Remember*. Cambridge: Cambridge University Press, 1989.

Conquergood, Dwight. "Of Caravans and Carnivale: Performance Studies in Motion." *The Drama Review* 39, no. 4 (Winter 1995): 137–141.

Constantine-Simms, Delroy. "Is Homosexuality The Greatest Taboo?" In *Greatest Taboo*. Edited by Delroy Constantine-Simms, 76–87. Los Angeles: Alyson Books, 2001.

Cooley, Timothy, Katherine Meizel, and Nasir Syed. "Virtual Fieldwork: Three Field Cases." In *Shadows of the Field: New Perspectives for Fieldwork in Ethnomusicology*. Edited by Gregory Barz and Timothy J. Cooley, 90–107. New York: Oxford University Press, 2008.

Cooper, Renee. Correspondence with author, January 28, 2015.

Costen, Melva W. *In Spirit and in Truth: The Music of African American Worship*. Louisville, KY: Westminster John Knox Press, 2004.

Crawley, Ashon. "Let's Get It On!' Performance Theory and Black Pentecostalism." *Black Theology* 6, no. 3 (2008): 308–329.

The Crunk Black Feminist Collective. "Birthday Sex." March 1, 2012 http://crunkfeministcollective.wordpress.com/2012/03/01/birthday-sex/.

Cszikszentmihalyi, Mihalyi. *Flow and the Foundations of Positive Psychology: The Collected Works of Mihalyi Cszikszentmihalyi*. Dordrecht: Springer, 2014.

Cszikszentmihalyi, Mihalyi. "The Flow Experience and Its Significance for Human Psychology." In *Optimal Experience: Psychological Studies of Flow on Consciousness*. Edited by Mihalyi Cszikszentmihalyi and Isabella Selega Cszikszentmihalyi, 15–35. Cambridge: Cambridge University Press, 1988.

Culbertson, Philip. *The New Adam: The Future of Male Spirituality*. Minneapolis: Fortress Press, 1992.

Curry, Karen. *Dancing in the Spirit: A Scriptural Study of Liturgical Dance*. Bloomington: Authorhouse, 2004

Cusick, Suzanne. "On a Lesbian Relationship with Music." In *Queering the Pitch: The New Gay and Lesbian Musicology*, 2nd ed. Edited by Philip Brett, Elizabeth Wood, and Gary C. Thomas, 67–84. New York: Routledge, 2006.

Dalton, Harlon. "AIDS in Blackface." In *Black Men on Race, Gender, and Sexuality*. Edited by Devon W. Carbado, 120–127. New York: New York University Press, 1999.

Daly, Mary. *Beyond God the Father: Toward a Philosophy of Women's Liberation*. Boston: Beacon Press, 1993.

Daniels, David, III. "African-American Pentecostalism in the 20th Century." In *The Century of the Holy Spirit*. Edited by Vinson Synan. Nashville, TN: Thomas Nelson, 2001.

Daub, Adrian. "Mother Mime: 'Siegfried', the Fairy Tale, and the Metaphysics of Sexual Difference." *19th-Century Music* 32, no. 2 (2008): 160–177.

Davis, Angela. *Blues Legacies and Black Feminism: Gertrude "Ma" Rainey, Bessie Smith and Billie Holiday*. New York: Pantheon Books, 1998.

Dean, Tim. *Unlimited Intimacy: Reflections on the Subculture of Barebacking*. Chicago: University of Chicago Press, 2009.

DeGruy, Joy. *The Post Traumatic Slave Syndrome: America's Legacy of Enduring Injury & Healing.* Joy DeGruy Publications, Inc., 2017.

Deissmann, Adolf. *Paul, A Study in Social and Religious History.* Translated by William E. Wilson. New York: Harper & Row, 1957.

Dennis, Sheri. "The Gospel Go-Go Review." *Washington Post*, August 21, 2002, 17.

Denoit-Lewis, Benoit. "Double Lives on the Down Low." *New York Times Sunday Magazine*, August 3, 2003, 28–33, 48, 52–53.

Dever, William G. *Did God Have a Wife?: Archaeology and Folk Religion in Ancient Israel.* Grand Rapids, MI: William B. Eerdmans, 2005.

Dillard, Ricky. "Ricky Dillard & New G Worked It Out." Footage from the Stellar Awards performance posted by prophetsgirl on December 23, 2009. YouTube, https://www.youtube.com/watch?v=ONqs-bCsCe4.

Dillard, Ricky. *Amazing.* Light Records, a division of Entertainment One US LP. Released June 10, 2014.

Dixie Chicks. *Dixie Chicks: Shut Up and Sing.* New York: The Weinstein Company, 2006.

Doubleday, Veronica. *What's Faith Got To Do With It?: Black Bodies/Christian Souls.* Maryknoll, NY: Orbis Books, 2005.

Doubleday, Veronica. "Sounds of Power: An Overview of Musical Instruments and Gender." *Ethnomusicology Forum* 17, no. 1 (2008): 3–39.

Douglas, Kelly Brown. *Sexuality and the Black Church: A Womanist Perspective.* Maryknoll, NY: Orbis Books, 1999.

Douglas, Mary. *Purity and Danger: An Analysis of Concept of Pollution and Taboo.* New York: Routledge, 2002.

Downing, Sonja Lynn. "Agency, Leadership, and Gender Negotiation in Balinese Girls' Gamelans." *Ethnomusicology* 54, no. 1 (2010): 54–80.

Duberman, Martin, Marta Vicinus, and George Chauncey Jr., eds. *Hidden From History: Reclaiming the Gay & Lesbian Past.* New York: Meridian, 1989.

DuBois, W. E. B. *The Souls of Black Folk.* New York: Dover Publications, 1944.

Durkheim, Emile. *The Elementary Forms of Religious Life.* London: Oxford University Press, 1912.

Dyson, Michael Eric. *Race Rules: Navigating the Color Line.* Reading, MA: Addison-Wesley, 1996.

Dyson, Michael Eric. "When You Divide Body and Soul, Problems Multiply: The Black Church and Sex." In *Traps: African American Men on Gender and Sexuality.* Edited by Rudolph P. Byrd and Beverly Guy-Sheftall, 308–326. Bloomington: Indiana University Press, 2001.

Dyson, Michael Eric. *Open Mike: Reflections on Philosophy: Race, Sex, Culture, and Religion.* New York: Basic Books, 2003.

Eidsheim, Nina. "Voice as a Technology of Selfhood: Towards an Analysis of Racialized Timbre and Vocal Performance." PhD diss., University of California-San Diego, 2008.

Eilberg-Schwartz, Howard. *God's Phallus and Other Problems for Men and Monotheism.* Boston: Beacon Press, 1994.

Eliade, Mircea. *The Sacred and the Profane: The Nature of Religion.* Orlando, FL: Harcourt, Inc., 1987.

Erlmann, Veit. "The Aesthetics of the Global Imagination: Reflections On World Music in the 1990s." *Public Culture* 8, no. 3 (1996): 467–87.

Evans, James. *We Have Been Believers: An African American Systematic Theology.* Minneapolis: Fortress Press, 1992.

Fanning, Steven. *Mystics of the Christian Tradition*. New York: Routledge, 2001.

Fanon, Franz. *Black Skin White Masks*. New York: Grove Press, 1967.

Fantham, Elaine. "Ancient Sneezing: A Gift from the Gods." NPR, May 27, 2006. http://www.npr.org/templates/story/story.php?storyId=5435812.

Farmer, Paul. "Bad Blood, Spoiled Milk: Bodily Fluids as Moral Barometers in Rural Haiti." *American Ethnologist* 15, no. 1 (1988): 62–83.

Feldman, Martha. *Opera and Sovreignty: Transforming Myths in Eighteenth-Century Italy*. Chicago: University of Chicago Press, 2007.

Feldman, Martha. *The Castrato: Reflections on Natures and Kinds*. Oakland: University of California Press, 2015.

Ferber, A. "The Construction of Black masculinity: White supremacy Now and Then." *Journal of Sport & Social Issues* 31, no. 1 (2007): 11–24.

Ferguson, Roderick. *Aberrations in Black: Toward a Queer of Color Critique*. Minneapolis: University of Minnesota, 2004.

Finley, Stephen. "Homoeroticism and the African-American Heterosexual Male: Quest For Meaning in the Black Church." *Black Theology: An International Journal*, 7, no. 3 (2007a): 305–326.

Finley, Stephen. "'Real Men Love Jesus?': An Overview of Homoeroticism and Issues Related to the Absence of Black Heterosexual Male Participation in African American Churches." *Council of the Society of the Study of Religion (CSSR) Bulletin* 36, no. 1 (2007b): 16–19.

Finley, Stephen. "Masculinity in American Religion." In *Encyclopedia of Religion in America*. Edited by Charles H. Lippy and Peter W. Williams, 1323–1329. Washington, DC: CQ Press, 2010.

Floyd, Samuel A. Jr. *The Power of Black Music: Interpreting Its History and from Africa to the United States*. New York: Oxford University Press, 1995.

Floyd-Thomas, Stacy. *Deeper Shades of Purple: Womanism in Religion and Society*. New York: New York University Press, 2006.

Floyd-Thomas, Stacy, Juan Floyd-Thomas, Carol B. Duncan, Stephen G. Ray Jr., and Nancy Lynn Westfield, eds. *Black Church Studies: An Introduction*. Nashville: Abingdon Press, 2007.

François, Anne-Lise. "Fakin' it/Makin' it: Falsetto's Bid for Transcendence in 1970s Disco Highs." *Perspectives of New Music* 33, no. 1/2 (1995): 442–457.

Franklin, Kirk. *Church Boy: My Music and My Life*. Nashville: Word Publishing, 1998.

Franklin, Kirk. *Hello Fear*. Verity Gospel Music Group, a unit of Sony Music Entertainent. Released March 18, 2011.

Franklin, Kirk. "DC Teaches Kirk Franklin How to Chop {Gospel GoGo}." WHMG TV footage of a March 25, 2011 performance at First Baptist Church of Glenarden posted by GospelGoGo41. posted March 28, 2011. YouTube, https://www.youtube.com/watch?v=XzfKsRu05hw.

Fredrickson, George. *The Black Image in the White Mind: The Debate on Afro-American Character and Destiny, 1817–1914*. New York: Harper and Row, 1971.

Gamson, Joshua. *The Fabulous Sylvester: The Legend, The Music, and The Seventies*. New York: Henry Holt & Co., 2005.

Gaudio, Rudolf P. "Sounding Gay: Pitch Properties in the Speech of Gay and Straight Men." *American Speech* 69, no. 1 (1994): 30–57.

Gaunt, Kyra. *The Games Black Girls Play: Learning the Ropes From Double-Dutch to Hip Hop*. New York: New York University Press, 2006.

Geels, Antoon, and Jacob A. Belzen. *Introduction to Mysticism: A Variety of Psychological Perspectives*. Edited by Jacob A. Belzen and Antoon Geels. Amsterdam: Rodopi, 2003.

Geertz, Clifford. *The Interpretation of Cultures*. New York: Basic Books, 1973.

George, Nelson. *The Death of Rhythm and Blues*. New York: Pantheon Books, 1988.

Gibbs, Geralds. *The Pimp and The Preacher*. Lincoln, NE: iUniverse, 2006.

Giles, Peter. *The Counter Tenor*. London: Frederick Muller Limited, 1982.

Giles, Peter. *The History and Technique of the Counter-Tenor: A Study of the Male High Voice Family*. London: Scolar Press, 1994.

Gilkes, Cheryl Townsend. *If it Wasn't for the Women: Experience and Womanist Culture in Church and Community*. New York: Orbis Books, 2000.

Glenn, Cheryl. *Unspoken: A Rhetoric of Silence*. Carbondale: Southern Illinois Press, 2004.

GMA Dove Awards. "Dr. Bobby Jones GMA Honors Featurette," posted on December 9, 2015. YouTube, https://www.youtube.com/watch?v=fJIohxhH8fc, last accessed December 14, 2019.

Goffman, Erving. *Stigma: Notes on the Management of Spoiled Identity*. New York: Simon & Schuster, 1986.

Gordon, Lewis R. *Bad Faith and Anti-Black Racism*. Atlantic, NJ: Humanities Press, 1995.

Gordon, Lewis R. *Existentia Africana: Understanding Africana Existential Thought*. New York: Routledge, 2000.

Gordon, WyCliffe. *The Gospel Truth*. Criss Cross Jazz. Released October 17, 2000.

Gowen, Annie. "An Introspective New Year's Eve; Many to Stay Close to Family and Friends." *Washington Post*, December 31, 2001, A1.

Greene-Hayes, Ahmad. "Eddie Long And The Black Church's Legacy Of Child Sexual Abuse." News One, January 17, 2017, https://newsone.com/3642647/eddie-long-and-the-black-churchs-legacy-of-child-sexual-abuse/.

Greene-Hayes, Ahmad. "The Reverend James Cleveland: Sexual (In)discretion & Black Church Rumor." Conference presentation on January 9, 2018. New Haven, CT: Yale University.

Greene, Leonard. "Jilted Bishop Launched Scandal Campaign Against Gospel Artist After Romance Was Spurned: Lawsuit." the *New York Daily News*, June 15, 2017. http://www.nydailynews.com/new-york/jilted-bishop-launched-smear-campaign-gospel-artist-suit-article-1.3251360.

Georgia Mass Choir, "He's All Over Me," Zomba Gospell, LLC, 1996.

Griffin, Horace. *Their Own Receive Them Not: African American Lesbians and Gays in Black Churches*. Cleveland: Pilgrim Press, 2006.

Gritten, Anthony, and Elaine King, eds. *Music and Gesture*. New York: Routledge, 2006.

Gross, Larry. *Contested Closets: The Politics and Ethics of Outing*. Minneapolis: University of Minnesota Press, 1993.

Hairston, Teresa "Donnie McClurkin: 50 Years of Life, Ministry, & Music." *Gospel Today*, 2, no. 5, edited by Teresa Hairston (November/December 2009): 22–26.

Hairston, Teresa. "When Scandal Rocks Your World: Bishop Eddie Long Embroiled in Controversy." *Gospel Today* 21, no. 6 (November/December 2010): 18–21.

Hairston, Teresa "The California-Born Gospel Singer Overcoming Homosexuality and Diabetes." Cross Rhythms, February 1, 1995, http://www.crossrhythms.co.uk/articles/music/Daryl_Coley_The_Californiaborn_gospel_singer_overcoming_homosexuality_and_diabetes/40250/p1/.

Hall, Radclyffe. *The Well of Loneliness*. London: Weidenfeld & Nicolson, 1998.

Hall, S. *Representation: Cultural Representations and Signifying Practices (Culture, Media and Identities)*. Thousand Oaks, CA: Sage Publications, 1997.

Hallett, Vicky. "Men Strip Pole Dancing of Another Taboo." *Washington Post*, April 29, 2010. http://www.washingtonpost.com/wp-dyn/content/article/2010/04/26/AR2010042603094.html?wprss=rss_health.

Halperin, David. "Homosexuality's Closet." *Michigan Quarterly Review* 41, no. 1 (2002): 21–55.

Hamessley, Lydia. "Within Sight: Three-Dimensional Perspectives on Women and Banjos in the Late Nineteenth Century." *19th-Century Music* 31, no. 2 (1997): 131–163.

Hammond, Fred. "When the Spirit of The Lord." *Pages of Life* album (Butler 2014).

Harper, Phillip Brian. *Are We Not Men?: Masculine Anxiety and the Problem of African-American Identity*. New York: Oxford University Press, 1996.

Harper, Phillip Brian. *Private Affairs: Critical Ventures in the Culture of Social Relations*. New York: New York University Press, 1999.

Harris, Hamil. "Bringing Easter Out in the Open on the Mall." *Washington Post*, April 5, 1999a, B05.

Harris, Hamil. "Groovin' to the Gospel; Teenagers, Musicians Flock to New Carrolton's Club Jesus." *Washington Post*, May 12, 1999b, M11.

Harris, Hamil. "Making a Joyful Noise Takes on New Meaning." *Washington Post*, April 14, 1999c, M22.

Harris, Hamil. "Putting on a Show for Jesus: Churches Try to Broaden Easter Audience With Stage Spectaculars." *Washington Post*, Mar 30, 2002, B09.

Harris, Hamil. "Donnie McClurkin Does Not Appear at King Memorial Concert." *Washington Post*, August 10, 2013.

Harris, E. Lynn. *Not A Day Goes By*. New York: Doubleday, 2000.

Harris, Michael W. *The Rise of Gospel Blues: The Music of Thomas Andrew Dorsey in the Urban Church*. New York: Oxford University Press, 1992.

Harris-Lacewell, Melissa Victoria. *Barbershops, Bibles, and BET: Everyday Talk and Black Political Thought*. Princeton, NJ: Princeton University Press, 2006.

Haver, William. "Queer Research; or, How to Practice Invention to the Brink of Intelligibility." In *The Eight Technologies of Otherness*. Edited by Sue Golding, 277–292. London: Routledge, 1997.

Havinastroke. "Bishop Moales Leads the War Cry," posted July 18, 2010. YouTube, https://www.youtube.com/watch?v=Me3CWI6iR6U.

Hawkeswood, William G. *One of the Children: Gay Black Men in Harlem*. Berkeley: University of California Press, 1997.

Hawkins, Walter. *Love Alive IV*. Malaco Records. Released June 22, 1990.

Hayes, Eileen M. *Songs in Black and Lavender: Race, Sexual Politics and Women's Music*. Champaign: University of Illinois Press, 2010.

Head, Matthew. "Title: Beethoven Heroine: A Female Allegory of Music and Authorship in Egmont." *19th-Century Music* 30, no. 2 (2006): 97–132.

Hedgeman, Denita. *Guidelines to Starting and Maintaining a Church Dance Ministry*. Mustang, OK: Tate Publishing and Enterprises, 2007

Heilbut, Anthony. *Gospel Sound: Good News and Bad News*. New York: Limelight Editions, 2002.

Hemphill, Essex, and Joseph Beam, eds. *Brother to Brother: Collected Writing by Black Gay Men*. New York: Alyson Books, 1991.

Henderson, Bruce. *Pimp to Preacher: Evangelism 911 With a Former L.A. Pimp.* Fair Oaks, CA: CreateSpace Independent Publishing Platform, 2013.

Henson, Karen. "Victor Capoul, Marguerite Olagnier's 'Le Saïs,' and the Arousing of Female Desire." *Journal of the American Musicological Society* 52, no. 3 (1999): 419–463.

Herman, Judith. Trauma and Recovery: The Aftermath of Violence—From Domestic Abuse to Political Terror. New York: Basic Books, 2015.

Herring, Scott. *Queering the Underworld: Slumming, Literature, and the Undoing Lesbian and Gay History.* Chicago: University of Chicago Press, 2007.

Hibbard, Laura. "Pole Dancing For Jesus." *The Huffington Post*, September 14, 2011. http://www.huffingtonpost.com/2011/09/14/pole- dancing-for-jesus_n_962804.html.

Hill, Renee. "Who Are We for Each Other? Sexism, Sexuality, and Womanist Theology." In *Black Theology: A Documentary History, 1980–1992*, vol. 2. Edited by James Cone and Gavraud Wilmore, 345–346. Maryknoll, NY: Orbis Books, 1993.

Hinson, Glenn. *Fire in My Bones: Transcendence and the Holy Spirit in African American Gospel.* Philadelphia: University of Pennsylvania Press, 2000.

Hodgson, Jay. *Understanding Record: A Field Guide to Recording Practice.* New York: Continuum, 2010.

hooks, bell. "Reconstructing Black Masculinity." In *Black Looks: Race and Representation*, 87–114. Boston: South End Press, 1992.

hooks, bell. *Killing Rage: Ending Racism.* New York: Henry Holt & Co., 1995.

hooks, bell. *The Will to Change: Men, Masculinity and Love.* New York: Simon & Schuster, 2004a.

hooks, bell. *We Real Cool: Black Men and Masculinity.* New York: Routledge, 2004b.

Hopkins, Dwight. "The Construction of the Black Male Body: Eroticism and Religion." In *Loving the Body: Black Religious Studies and the Erotic.* Edited by Anthony B. Pinn and Dwight N. Hopkins, 179–198. New York: Palgrave Macmillan, 2006.

Hopkinson, Natalie. "And Now, Let's Hear it From the Ladies: FAB Disk to Include Stylings of 2 Fans." *Washington Post*, April 4, 2002a, T21.

Hopkinson, Natalie. "Go-Go, and Sin No More: The Gospel Dance Club That Was The Answer to Their Prayers has turned into a Test of Faith." *Washington Post*, August 27, 2002b, C.01.

Hopkinson, Natalie. "New Genre Sets Gospel to a Go-Go Beat: Band Winning Fans in Church, on Street. *Washington Post*, March 14, 2002c, T21.

Hopkinson, Natalie. *Go-Go Live: The Musical Life and Death of Chocolate City.* Durham, NC: Duke University Press, 2012.

Hopkinson, Natalie, and Natalie Y. Moore. *Deconstructing Tyrone: A New Look at Black Masculinity in the Hip-Hop Generation.* San Francisco: Cleis Press, 2006.

Horst, Cindy. "Expanding Sites: The Question of 'Depth' Explored." In *Multi-Sited Ethnography: Theory, Praxis and Locality Contemporary Research.* Edited by Mark-Anthony Falzon, 119–33. Burlington, VT: Ashgate, 2009.

Houghton, Israel & New Breed. *Jesus at the Center.* RGM New Breed/Integrity Music. Released February 12, 2013.

House of Hung Realness. "Mercedez Ellis Loreal Giving the Children Church Realness At Oz!!," posted October 13, 2013. YouTube, https://www.youtube.com/watch?v=pewU7e9whrk.

Hultin, Jeremy. *The Ethics of Obscene Speech in Early Christianity and Its Environment.* Boston: Koninklijke Brill NV, 2008.

Hurd, Stephen. "Undignified." In *A Call to Worship*. East Sussex: Integrity Music, 2004.

Ikard, David. *Breaking the Silence: Toward a Black Feminist Criticism.* Baton Rouge: Louisiana State University Press, 2007.

Jabir, Johari. "On Conjuring Mahalia: Mahalia Jackson, New Orleans, and the Sanctified Swing."*American Quarterly* 61, no. 3 (2009): 649–669.

Jackmizrahi. "Church Cunts," posted June 19, 2009. YouTube, https://www.youtube.com/watch?v=m6OEePySPl4—Mother Leviticus.

Jackson, Jerma. *Singing in My Soul: Black Gospel Music in a Secular Age.* Chapel Hill: University of North Carolina Press, 2004.

Jackson, Ronald L., II. *Scripting the Black Masculine Body: Identity, Discourse, and Racial Politics in Popular Media.* Albany: SUNY Press, 2006.

Jackson, Travis. "Spooning Good, Singing Gum: Meaning, Association and Interpretation in Rock Music." *Current Musicology* 1, no. 69 (2000): 7–41.

Jakes, T. D. *Naked and Not Ashamed.* Shippensburg, PA: Destiny Image Publishers, 1995.

Jamal Bryant Sermons. "Pastor Jamal Bryant Sermons 2016 - These Hoes Ain't Loyal," posted on April 23, 2016. YouTube, https://www.youtube.com/watch?v=yPlX5gQNyk8.

Johnson, E. Patrick. "Feeling the Spirit in the Dark: Expanding Notions of the Sacred in the African American Gay Community." *Callaloo* 21, no. 2 (1998): 399–416.

Johnson, E. Patrick. *Appropriating Blackness: Performance and the Politics of Authenticity.* Durham, NC: Duke University Press, 2003.

Johnson, E. Patrick. *Sweet Tea: Black Gay Men of The South.* Chapel Hill: University of North Carolina Press, 2011.

Johnson, E. Patrick, and Mae Henderson, eds. *Black Queer Studies: A Critical Anthology.* Durham, NC: Duke University Press, 2005.

Jones, Alisha L. "'Playin' Church': Remembering Mama and Questioning Authenticity in Gospel Performance." In *Readings in African American Church Music And Worship, Vole. 2.* Edited by James Abbington, 679–690. Chicago: GIA Publications, 2014.

Jones, Alisha L. "Pole Dancing for Jesus: Negotiating Movement and Gender in Men's Music Praise." In *Esotericism in African American Religious Experience.* Edited by Stephen Finley, Margarita Guillory, and Hugh Page Jr., 314–330. Boston: Brill Academic, 2014.

Jones, Alisha L. "Are All The Choir Directors Gay?: Black Men's Sexuality and Identity in Gospel Performance." In *Issues in African American Music: Power, Gender, Race, Representation.* Edited by Mellonee Burnim and Portia Maultsby, 216–236. New York: Routledge, 2016.

Jones, Alisha L. "'You Are My Dwelling Place': Experiencing Black Male Vocalists' Worship as Aural Eroticism and Autoeroticism in Gospel Performance." *Women and Music Journal* 22 (2018): 3–21.

Jones, Bobby, and Lesley Sussman. *Make A Joyful Noise: My 25 Years in Gospel Music.* New York: St. Martin's Press, 2000.

Jones, Claire. "Shona Women Mbira Players: Gender, Tradition and Nation in Zimbabwe." *Ethnomusicology Forum* 17, no. 1 (2008): 125–149.

Jones, Stanton L., and Mark A. Yarhouse. *Ex-Gays: A Longitudinal Study of Religiously Mediated Change in Sexual Orientation.* Downers Grove, IL: IVP Academic, 2007.

Jordan, Louis. *Saturday Night Fish Fry.* Released 1948.

Jungle Cat. "Guy Does Pole Dancing To Hezekiah Walker's 'I Need You To Survive,'" YouTube, 5:34, footage of an in home performance, posted by "Waddie Grant," posted June 19, 2009. YouTube, http://www.youtube.com/watch?v=v_H5kG9dOoE.

Kalamaras, George. *Reclaiming the Tacit.* Albany: SUNY Press, 1994.

Kaufman, Michael, ed. *Beyond Patriarchy: Essays by Men on Pleasure, Power and Change.* New York: Oxford University Press, 1987.

Keil, Charles. "Motion and Feeling through Music." *Journal of Aesthetic and Art Criticism* 24, no. 3 (1966): 337–349.

Keil, Charles. "Theories of Participatory Discrepancies." *Cultural Anthropology* 2, no. 3 (1987): 275–283.

Keil, Charles. "Theories of Participatory Discrepancies a Progress Report." *Ethnomusicology* 39, no. 1, Special Issue: Participatory Discrepancies (1995): 1–19.

Kemble, Frances Anne. *Journal of a Residence on a Georgian Plantation.* New York: Cosimo, Inc., 1863.

Kernodle, Tammy L. "Work the Works: The Role of African-American Women in the Development of Contemporary." *Black Music Research Journal* 26, no. 1 (2006): 89–109.

Kiki The First Lady, "Donnie McClurkin Is Getting Married . . . To A Woman! Fellow Sanctified Singer Nicole Mullen!." 995theLou.com, https://955thelou.com/1973903/gospel-star-donnie-mcclurkin-is-getting-married-to-a-woman-fellow-sanctified-singer-nicole-mullen/.

Kiki Vidz. "The Red Realness 10s," posted December 4, 2016. YouTube, https://www.youtube.com/watch?v=AlseoiE5oWA.

King, Jason. "Any Love: Silence, Theft, and Rumor in the Work of Luther Vandross." *Callaloo* 23, no. 1 (2000): 422–447.

King, Jason. "Remixing the Closet: The Down-Low Way of Knowledge." *Village Voice*, June 24, 2003.

Kirk-Duggan, Cheryl. "Salome's Veiled Dance and David's Full Monty: A WomanistReading on the Black Erotic in Blues, Rap, R & B and Gospel Blues." In *Loving the Body: Black Religious Studies and the Erotic.* Edited by Anthony B. Pinn and Dwight N. Hopkins, 217–233. New York: Palgrave Macmillan, 2006.

Knapp, Raymond. "Passing: And Failing: In Late-Nineteenth-Century Russia; Or Why We Should Care about the Cuts in Tchaikovsky's Violin Concerto." *19th-Century Music* 26, no. 3 (2003): 195–234.

Koestenbaum, Wayne. *The Queen's Throat: Opera, Homosexuality and the Mystery of Desire.* New York: Poseidon Press, 1993.

Kot, Greg. "His Chicago Sound Was Heard Around the World Chicago House Music Pioneer: Knuckles Was 'Godfather' of House Music—and Much More." *Chicago Tribune.* April 2, 2014, 1.1.

Kripal, Jeffrey J. *Roads of Excess Palaces of Wisdom: Eroticism & Reflexivity in the Study of Mysticism.* Chicago: University of Chicago Press, 2001.

Krondorfer, Björn, ed. *Men's Bodies, Men's Gods: Male Identities in a (Post-) Christian Culture.* New York: New York University Press, 1996.

Kuefler, Mathew. *The Manly Eunich:Masculinity, Gender Ambiguity, and Christian Ideology in Late Antiquity.* Chicago: University of Chicago Press, 2001.

Kunjufu, Jawanza. *Adam! Where Are You? Why Black Men Don't Go to Church.* Chicago: African American Images, 1997.

Kwabata, Maiko. "Virtuoso Codes of Violin Performance: Power, Military Heroism, and Gender (1789—1830)." *19th-Century Music* 28, no. 2 (2004): 89–107.

The Lady Chablis. *Hiding My Candy: The Autobiography of the Grand Empress of Savannah.* New York: Pocket Books, 1996.

Lampley, Tim O. "Exclusive: Luther Vandross Tells Tim Lampley 'Weight' Question Bothers Him," posted August 28, 2012. YouTube.com, https://www.youtube.com/watch?v=-_kJWDBsbGw.

Lang, A. C. "The Creation of Coherence in Coming Out Stories." In *Queerly Phrased: Language, Gender & Sexuality*. Edited by Anna Livia and Kira Hall, 287–309. New York: Oxford University Press, 1997.

Lawless, Elaine J. *God's Peculiar People: Women's Voices and Folk Tradition in a Pentecostal Church*. Lexington: University Press of Kentucky, 1988.

Lawrence, Beverly Hall. *Reviving the Spirit: A Generation of African Americans Goes Home to Church*. New York: Grove Press, 1996.

Leinhardt, Godfrey. "Self: Public, Private. Some African Representations." In *The Category of the Person: Anthropology, Philosophy, History*. Edited by Michael Carrithers, Steven Collins, and Steven Lukes. Cambridge: Cambridge University Press, 1985.

Leonardi, Susan J., and Rebecca A. Pope. *The Diva's Mouth: Body, Voice, and Prima Donna Politics*. New Brunswick, NJ: Rutgers University Press, 1996.

Levine, Martin P. "Bad Blood: The Health Commissioner, the Tuskegee Experiment, and AIDS Policy." In *Gay Macho: The Life and Death of the Homosexual Clone*. Edited by Michael S. Kimmel, 127–137. New York: New York University Press, 1998.

Levy, Claudia. "Eric Torain Dies at Age 39; Brought Gospel, Jazz to WPAS." *Washington Post*, June 15, 2002, B06.

Levy, Leonard W. *Treason Against God*. New York: Schocken Books, 1981.

LexiTelevision. "Lexi Show (Tonex) Part 2," posted September 11, 2009. YouTube, https://www.youtube.com/watch?v=Yg5EhnbZqkA.

LexiTelevision. "Holy Ghost Enforcers Episode 6: The Choir Auditions," posted February 2, 2014. YouTube, https://www.youtube.com/watch?v=k-BiqDWhElk.

Lewin, Ellen. *Filled with the Spirit: Sexuality, Gender, and Radical Inclusivity in a Black Pentecostal Church Coalition*. Chicago: University of Chicago Press, 2018.

Ling, Lisa. "Pray the Gay Away." *America with Lisa Ling OWN*. Televisiosn Network, 2011.

Long, Charles. *Significations*. Philadelphia: Fortress Press, 1986.

Long, Ronald E. *Men, Homosexuality, and the Gods: An Exploration of the Religious Significance of Male Homosexuality in World Perspective*. Binghamton, NY: Harrington Park Press, 2004.

Longobardi, Ruth Sara. "Reading Between the Lines: An Approach to the Musical and Sexual Ambiguities of 'Death in Venice.'" *Journal of Musicology* 22, no. 3 (2005): 327–364.

Lornell, Kip, and Charles C. Stephenson. *The Beat!: Go-Go Music from Washington, DC*. Jackson: University Press of Mississippi, 2009.

Lott, Eric. *Love and Theft: Blackface and Minstrelsy and the American Working Class*. Oxford: Oxford University Press, 1993.

Marcus, George E. "Ethnography in/of the World Systems: The Emergence of Multi-Sited Ethnography." *Annual Review of Anthropology* 24 (1995): 95–117.

Madison, D. Soyini. *Critical Ethnography: Method, Ethics, and Performance*. Thousand Oaks, CA: Sage Publications, 2012.

Madonna. "Vogue." *I'm Breathless: Music from and Inspired by the film Dick Tracy*. Los Angeles: Sire Records, 1990.

Majors, R., and J. M. Billson. *Cool Pose: The Dilemmas of Black Manhood in America*. New York: Lexington Books, 1992.

Manago, Cleo. "Getting the Language Right: HIV & Healing in Young Black America, PART ONE." From a documentary released in 2010, posted by Cleo Manago, posted October 31, 2010. YouTube, https://www.youtube.com/watch?v=JJmu-u8oOhU.

Manigault-Bryant, L., and Lomax, Tamura. *Womanist and Black Feminist Response to Tyler Perry's Productions*. New York: Palgrave, 2014.

Martin, Allie. "Hearing Change in the Chocolate City: Soundwalking as Black Feminist Method," *Sounding Out!*, August 5, 2019, https://soundstudiesblog.com/2019/08/05/hearing-change-in-the-chocolate-city-soundwalking-as-black-feminist-method/?fbclid=IwAR0n2Q2H7f3F_LNOvH3E2psbdmWEQia1PaYC-5pPx69wUvOrvmaeQo1muYo

Martin, John L., and Laura Dean. "Development of a Community Sample of Gay Men for Epidemiologic Study of AIDS." *American Behavioral Scientist* 33 (1990): 546–561.

Martin, Randy. *Critical Moves: Dance Studies in Theory and Politics*. Durham, NC: Duke University Press, 1998.

McClary, Susan. *Feminine Endings: Music, Gender, and Sexuality*. Minneapolis: University of Minnesota, 1991.

McClary, Susan. "Music and Sexuality: On the Steblin/Solomon Debate." *19th-Century Music* 17, no. 1 (1993): 83–88.

McClurkin, Donnie. *Eternal Victim/Eternal Victor*. Lanham, MD: Pneuma Life, 2001.

McCracken, Allison. *Real Men Don't Sing: Crooning in American Culture*. Durham, NC: Duke University Press, 2015.

McCraney, Tarrell A. *Choir Boy*. New York: Dramatists Play Service, 2014.

McCune, Jeffrey Q. Jr. *Sexual Discretion: Black Masculinity and the Politics of Passing*. Chicago: University of Chicago Press, 2014.

McDowell, William. "I Give Myself Away." *As We Worship Live*. London: Integrity Music, 2009.

McGinn, B. *The Foundations of Mysticism*. London: SCM Press, 1992.

McKenzie, Vashti M. *Not Without A Struggle: Leadership Developments for African American Women*. Cleveland: Pilgrim Press, 1996.

Mercer, Kobena, *Welcome to the Jungle: New Positions in Black Cultural Studies*. New York: Routledge, 1994.

Meuth, Elsbeth, and Freddy Zental Weaver. *Sexual Enlightenment: How to Create Lasting Fulfillment in Life, Love, and Intimacy*. Bloomington, IN: Balboa Press, 2013.

Meyers, Leonard B. *Emotion and Meaning*. Chicago: University of Chicago Press, 1956.

Miles, James. "Delivered COGIC Man Speaks Out; MGLCC Weighs In." WMC5, posted November 13, 2014, https://www.wmcactionnews5.com/story/27371057/delivered-cogic-man-speaks-out-mglcc-weighs-in/

Miller, Monica. *Slaves to Fashion: Black Dandyism and the Styling of Black Diasporic Identity*. Durham: Duke University Press, 2014.

Miller, Nancy K. *Getting Personal: Feminist Occasions and Other Autobiographical Acts*. New York: Routledge, 1992.

Miller, Richard. *Training the Tenor Voice*. New York: Schirmer Books, 1993.

Miller, Richard. *The Structure of Singing: System and Art in Vocal Technique*. New York: Schirmer Books, 1996.

Miller, Terry E. "A Myth in the Making: Willie Ruff, Black Gospel and Imagined Gaelic Scottish Origin." *Ethnomusicology forum* 18, no. 2 (2009): 243–259.

Mississippi Children's Choir. *Children of the King*, Malaco Records. Released August 3, 1992.

Mitchell, Henry. *Celebration & Experience in Preaching*, revised edition. Nashville: Abingdon Press, 2008.

Monson, Ingrid. *Saying Something*. Chicago: University of Chicago Press, 1996.

Monson, Ingrid. "Riffs, Repetition and Theories of Globalization." *Ethnomusicology* 43, no.1 (1999): 31–65.

Monteseirin, J., M. J. Camacho, I. Bonilla, C. Sánchez-Hernández, M. Hernández, and J. Conde. "Honeymoon Rhinitis." *Allergy*. 56, no. 4 (2002): 353–354.

Mora, Manolete. "Lutes, Gongs, Women and Men: (En)Gendering Instrumental Music in the Philippines." *Ethnomusicology forum* 17, no. 2 (2008): 225–247.

Morais, Adilson. "My Soul Doth Magnify the Lord" by O'landa Draper, YouTube.com, posted May 13, 2013, https://www.youtube.com/watch?v=EJ23-5PpT_0, last accessed March 25, 2018.

Morris, Gay. "What He Called Himself: Issues of Identity in Early Dances by Bill T.Jones." In *Dancing Desires: Choreographing Sexualities On & Off the Stage*. Edited by Jane C. Desmond, 243–266. Madison: University of Wisconsin Press, 2001.

Mountford, Roxanne. *The Gendered Pulpit: Preaching in American Protestant Spaces*. Carbondale: Southern Illinois University Press, 2003.

Mr Peculiar219 "Peculiar People (Dance in the Rain)." Footage of album release concert at Community of Hope, posted November 19, 2008a. YouTube, http://www.youtube.com/watch?v=9surXatmugU.

MrPeculiar219. "Peculiar People (Peculiar Til I Die)." Footage of album release concert at Community of Hope, posted November 19, 2008b. YouTube, http://www.youtube.com/watch?v=a510K_ycQho.

Muñoz, José Esteban. *Disidentifications: Queers of Color and the Performance of Politics*. Minneapolis: University of Minnesota Press, 1999.

Munson, Benjamin and Molly Babel. "Loose Lips and Silver Tongue, or, Projecting Sexual Orientation through Speech." *Language and Linguistics Compass* 1, no. 5 (2007): 416–449.

Murray, Albert. *Stomping the Blues*. Cambridge, MA: Da Capo Pres, 1976.

Murray, Stephen O., and Will Roscoe. *Boy-Wives and Female-Husbands: Studies in African Homosexuality*. New York: Palgrave, 1998.

Nadolny, Tricia L., and Otterbein, Holly. "The Wildest Things Heard on Philadelphia's Police Scanner during the Eagles Parade." The Philadelphia Inquirer, February 8, 2018. http://www.philly.com/philly/super-bowl-lii/eagles-parade-police-scanner-philadelphia-20180208.html.

Neal, Mark Anthony. *New Black Man*. New York: Routledge, 2005.

Negroponte, Nicholas. *Biti Digitalon*. Zagreb: SysPrint, 2002.

Nelson, James B. *The Intimate Connection: Male Sexuality, Masculine Spirituality*. Philadelphia: Westminster Press, 1988.

Nelson, James B. *Body Theology*. Louisville, KY: Westminster/John Knox Press, 1992.

Nettles, Darryl Glenn. *African American Concert Singers Before 1950*. Jackson, NC: McFarland and Co. Inc. Publishers, 2003.

New Psalmist Baptist Church. "'Some Day' The New Psalmist Baptist Church Mass Choir with Soloist: Patrick Dailey," posted September 15, 2011. YouTube, https://www.youtube.com/watch?v=GKjX7uBJktA&t=385s.

Nketia, J. H. Kwabena. *The Music of Africa*. New York: Norton, 1974.

Noland, Carrie. *Agency and Embodiment: Performing Gestures/Producing Culture*. Cambridge, MA: Harvard University Press, 2009.

Norman, Karin. "Phoning the Field: Meanings of Place and Involvement in Fieldwork at Home." In *Constructing the Field: Ethnographic Fieldwork in the Contemporary World.* Edited by Vared Emit, 71–95. London: Routledge, 2000.

OeauxHaHa. "Carless Hardin—The Pulpit Uncensored," posted November 4, 2011. YouTube, http://www.youtube.com/watch?v=kxDxwS4SmxQ.

Onuora, Adwoa Ntozake. *Anansesem: Telling Stories and Storytelling African Maternal Pedagogies.* Bradford, ON: Demeter Press, 2015.

O'Reilly, Andrea. *Mothers, Education, and Paternal Pedagogies.* Bradford, ON: Demeter Press, 2013.

Parks, Carlton W. "African-American Same-Gender-Loving Youths and Families in Urban Schools." *Journal of Gay & Lesbian Social Services* 13, no. 3 (2001): 41–56.

Patai, Raphael. *The Hebrew Goddess.* Detroit: Wayne State University Press, 1990.

PBS. "Independent Lens | The New Black | Faith Gave Tonéx the Courage to Come Out to His Fans | PBS," posted June 10, 2014. YouTube, https://www.youtube.com/watch?v=rFK38cDKLnI.

Pearson, Carlton. *Live at Azusa 3.* Atlantic Recording Corporation. Released June 6, 1996.

Pearson, Carlton. *The Gospel of Inclusion: Reaching Beyond Religious Fundamentalism to the True Love of God and Self.* New York: Atria Books, 2006.

Pearson, Carlton. "Live Stream with Carlton Pearson: Deliverance from Homosexuality?" posted November 22, 2014. YouTube, https://www.youtube.com/watch?v=escoIRy5BK4.

Peek, Philip. "Re-Sounding Silence." In *Sound.* Edited by Patricia Kruth and Henry Stobart, 16–33. London: Cambridge University Press, 2007.

Penacchi, Gino, and Alessandro Scilitani. *The Heavenly Voices: Legacy of Farinelli.* Italy: Arthaus, 2013.

Perry, Jade. "Tried (It) Again"—Examining Ableism & Homo-antagonism in Burrell's Sermon." Jade Perry, January 6, 2017. https://jadetperry.com/2017/01/06/tried-it-again-examining-ableism-homo-antagonism-in-burrells-sermon/.

Pew Research. "Attendance at Religious Services." https://www.pewforum.org/religious-landscape-study/attendance-at-religious-services/, last accessed November 29, 2019.

"PG Closes 9 Clubs to Halt Violence." *Washington Times,* March 29, 2007.

Pinn, Anthony. *Varieties of African American Religious Experience.* Minneapolis: Fortress Press, 1998.

Pinn, Anthony, ed. *Noise and Spirit: The Religious and Spiritual Sensibilities of Rap Music.* New York: New York University Press, 2008.

Pinn, Anthony B., and Dwight Hopkins. *Loving the Body: Black Religious Studies and the Erotic.* New York: Palgrave McMillan, 2004.

Pitt, Richard N. "'Still Looking for My Jonathan': Gay Black Men's Management of Religious and Sexual Identity Conflicts." *Journal of Homosexuality* 57, no. 1 (2009): 39–53.

Pitt, Richard N. and Sanders, George. "Revisiting Hypermasculinity: Shorthand for Marginalizeed Masculinities?." In *What's Up With the Brothers?: Essays and Studies on African-American Masculinities.* Edited by Whitney Harris and Ronald T. Ferguson. Harriman, TN: Men's Studies Press, LLC, 2010.

Plate, S. Brent. *Blasphemy: Art That Offends.* London: Black Dog Publishing, 2006.

Pollard, Deborah Smith. *When the Church Becomes Your Party: Contemporary Gospel Music.* Detroit: Wayne State University Press, 2008.

Prögler, J. A. "Searching for Swing: Participatory Discrepancies in the Jazz Rhythm Section." *Ethnomusicology* 39, no. 1 (1995): 21–54.

Prince. *Come.* Los Angeles: Warner Bros, 1994.

Ramet, Sabrina P. *Gender Reversals and Gender Cultures: Anthropological and Historical Perspectives*. New York: Routledge, 1996.

Ramnarine, Tina K. "Home in Diaspora." *Beautiful Cosmos: Performance and Belonging in the Caribbean Diaspora*. London: Pluto Press (2007): 18–41.

Ramsey, Guthrie. *Race Music: Black Cultures from Bebop to Hip-Hop*. Berkeley: University of California Press, 2003.

Ramsey, Guthrie. "The Pot Liquor Principle: Developing a Black Music Criticism in American Music Studies." *Journal of Black Studies* 35, no. 2 (2004): 10–23.

Rapport, Nigel. "The Narrative as Fieldwork Technique: Processual Ethnography for a World in Motion." In *Constructing the Field: Ethnographic Fieldwork in the Contemporary World*. Edited by Vared Emit, 71–95. London: Routledge, 2000.

Ravens, Simon. *The Supernatural Voice: A History of High Male Singing*. Woodbridge, UK: Boydell and Brewer, 2014.

Reagon, Bernice Johnson. *We'll Understand It Better By An' By*. Washington, DC: Smithsonian Institution Press, 1992.

Reed, Teresa. *The Holy Profane: Religion in Black Popular Music*. Lexington: University of Kentucky Press, 2002.

Reid, Larry. "Interview w/Tymel Thompson . . . but first . . . ," Facebook, August 5, 2019, https://www.facebook.com/LarryReidLive/videos/2284496634981336/?q=larry%20 reid%20live&epa=SEARCH_BOX.

Reynolds, Simon, and Joy Press. *The Sex Revolts: Gender, Rebellion and Rock 'n' Roll*. Cambridge, MA: Harvard University Press, 1995.

Richen, Yoruba. *The New Black*. New York: Promised Land Films, Inc, 2013. http://www.newblackfilm.com.

"Ricky Dillard & New G Worked It Out." Footage from the Stellar Awards performance posted by prophetsgirl on December 23, 2009. YouTube, https://www.youtube.com/watch?v=ONqs-bCsCe4.

Robinson, Smokey. *A Quiet Storm*. Detroit: Motown, 1975.

Román, David. *Acts of Intervention: Performance, Gay Culture, and AIDS*. Bloomington: Indiana University Press, 1998.

Rommen, Timothy. *Mek' Some Noise: Gospel Music and the Ethics of Style in Trinidad (Music of the African Diaspora)*. Berkeley: University of California Press, 2007.

Rose, Tricia. *Black Noise: Rap Music and Black Culture in Contemporary America*. Middletown, CT: Wesleyan University Press, 1994.

Ross, Alex. *The Rest is Noise: Listening to the Twentieth Century*. New York: Picador, 2008.

Ross, Marlon. "Beyond the Closet as a Raceless Paradigm." In *Black Queer Studies: A Critical Anthology*. Edited by E. Patrick Johnson and Mae G. Henderson, 16–189. Durham, NC: Duke University Press, 2005.

Rouget, Gilbert. *Music and Trance: A Theory of the Relations Between Music and Possession*. Chicago: University of Chicago Press, 1985.

Rousseau, Jean-Jacques. *The Social Contract*. New York: Penguin, 1968.

Rowan, Edward. *Understanding Child Abuse*. Jackson: University of Mississippi Press, 2006.

Sanga, Imani. "Music and Nationalism in Tanzania: Dynamics of National Space in Muzak was Injili in Dar es Salaam." *Ethnomusicology* 52, No. 1 (2008): 52–84.

Sangnam Institute of Indian Martial Arts. "The Topmost Mallakhamb Players Vol. 1," YouTube, https://www.youtube.com/watch?v=6FTBrtifKYQ, last accessed February 24, 2015

Sanneh, Kelefa. "New R&B Sounds, Emanating from One Source." *New York Times*, May 15, 2005.

Sanneh, Kelefa, "Revelations." *The New Yorker*, January 31, 2010. https://www.newyorker.com/magazine/2010/02/08/revelations-3, last accessed November 29, 2019.

Santos, Silvio José dos. "Marriage as Prostitution in Berg's 'Lulu.'" *Journal of Musicology* 25, no. 2 (2008): 143–182.

Sartre, Jean-Paul. *Being and Nothingness*. New York: Philosophical Library, 1956.

Sassen, Sakia. *Sociology of Globalization*. Chicago: University of Chicago Press, 2007. 97–128.

Saville-Troike, Muriel. "The Place of Silence in an Intgrated theory of Communication." In *Perspectives on Silence*. Edited by Deborak Tannen and Muriel Saville-Troike, 3–8. Norwood: Abex, 1985.

Schechner, Richard. *The Future of Ritual: Writings on Culture and Performance*. New York: Routledge, 1993.

Schechner, Richard. *Performance Studies: An Introduction*. New York: Routledge, 2006.

Scholz, Piotr. *Eunuchs and Castrati: A Cultural History*. Translated by John A. Broadwin and Shelley L. Frisch. Princeton, NJ: Markus Wiener Publishers, 2000.

Sedgwick, Eve Kosofsky. *Epistemology of the Closet*. Berkeley: University of California Press, 1990.

ShareYourStory. "Tye Tribbett: The Doctrine of Feeling," posted June 18, 2008. YouTube, https://www.youtube.com/watch?v=uqeIsaXioQk.

Shirley, George. "Il Rodolfo Nero, or The Masque of Blackness." In *Blackness in Opera*. Edited by Naomi M. Andre, Karen Bryan, and Eric Saylor, 260–274. Champaign: University of Illinois Press, 2012.

Slobin, Mark. "Micromusics of the West: A Comparative Approach." *Ethnomusicology* 36, no. 1 (1992): 1–87.

Smallwood, Richard. "Total Praise." From On *Adoration: Live in Atlanta*. Zomba Recording, LLC. Released April 30, 1996.

Smallwood, Richard. *Total Praise: The Autobiography of Richard Smallwood*. Newark: Godzchild Publications, 2019.

Smith, Eric Ledell. *Blacks in Opera: An Encyclopedia of People and Companies, 1873–1993*. Jefferson, NC: McFarland & Company, Inc., 1995.

Smith, Thérèse. *Let the Church Sing! Music and Worship in a Black Mississippi Community*. Rochester, NY: University of Rochester Press, 2004.

Snethen, Worthington. *The Black Code of the District of Columbia*. New York: The A. & F. Anti-Slavery Society, 1848.

Snorton, C. Riley. *Nobody is Supposed to Know: Black Sexuality on the Down Low*. Minneapolis: University of Minnesota Press, 2014.

Soft Cell. *Non-Stop Erotic Cabaret*. Mercury Records Unlimited. Released 1981.

Solie, Ruth A., ed. *Musicology and Difference: Gender and Sexuality in Music Scholarship*. Berkeley: University of California Press, 1993.

Southern, Eileen. *The Music of Black Americans: A History*, 3rd ed. New York: Norton, 1997.

Sovatsky, Stuart. *Eros, Consciousness, and Kundalini: Deepening Sensuality Through Tantric Celibacy and Spiritual Intimacy*. Rochester, VT: Rock Street Press, 1999.

Spargo, Chris. "Formerly Gay Minister Donnie McClurkin Revealed to Be Dating Female Gospel Singer After God Cured Him of 'the Curse of Homosexuality,'" *Daily Mail*, August 16, 2016, http://www.dailymail.co.uk/news/article-3743877/

Formerly-gay-minister-Donnie-McClurkin-revealed-dating-female-gospel-singer-god-cured-curse-homosexuality.html.

Spencer, Jon Michael. *Sacred Music in the Secular City From Blues to Rap*. Durham, NC: Duke University Press, 1992.

Spencer, Jon Michael. *Blues and Evil*. Knoxville: University of Tennessee Press, 1993.

Spencer, Jon Michael. *Theomusicology: A Special Issue Of Black Sacred Music* 8, No. 1. Durham, NC: Duke University Press, 1994.

Spiller, Henry. *Erotic Triangles: Sundanese Dance and Masculinity in West Java*. Chicago: University of Chicago Press, 2010.

Staples, R. Black. *Masculinity: The Black Male's Role in American Society*. San Francisco: Black Scholars Press, 1982.

Stecopoulos, Harry, and Michael Uebel, eds. *Race and the Subject of Masculinities*. Durham, NC: Duke University Press, 1997.

Steele, Claude M. *Whistling Vivaldi: And Other Clues to How Stereotypes Affect Us*. New York: Norton, 2010.

Stein, Sade. "Meet the Pole Dancing Man." Jezebel. April 27, 2010. http://jezebel.com/5525636/meet-the-pole+dancing-men.

Stenseng, Frode. *A Dualistic Approach to Leisure Activity Engagement—On the Dynamics of Passion, Escapism, and Life Satisfaction*. PhD Dissertation., University of Oslo, 2009.

Stephens, Charles. "The Risk of Loneliness." Huffington Post. October 16, 2013. http://www.huffingtonpost.com/charles-stephens/the-risk-of-loneliness_b_4100018.html.

Stephens, Vincent. "Pop Goes the Rapper: A Close Reading of Eminem's Genderphobia." *Popular Music* 24, no.1 (2005): 21–36.

Stobart, Henry. "In Touch with the Earth? Musical Instruments, Gender and Fertility in the Bolivian Andes." *Ethnomusicology Forum* 17, no. 1 (2008): 67–94.

Story, Rosalyn M. 1993. *And So I Sing: African-American Divas of Opera and Concert*. New York: Amistad.

Strine, Mary, Beverly Long, and Mary Frances Hopkins. "Research in Interpretation and Performance Studies: Trends, Issues, Priorities." In *Speech Communication: Essays to Commemorate the Seventy-Fifth Anniversary of the Speech Communication Association*. Edited by Gerald Phillips and Julia Woods, 181–204. Carbondale: Southern Illinois University Press, 1990.

Tatum, Beverly Daniel. *"Why Are All The Black Kids Sitting Together in the Cafeteria?": And Other Conversations About Race*. New York: Perseus, 1997.

Taylor, Barry. *Entertainment Theology: New-Edge Spirituality in a Digital Democracy*. Grand Rapids, MI: Baker Academic, 2008.

Tenney, Tommy. *The God Chaser: My Soul Follows Hard After Thee*. Shippensburg, PA: Destiny Image Publishers, 1998.

Tenney, Tommy. *The God Catcher: Experiencing the Manifest Presence God*. Nashville: Thomas Nelson, Inc., 2000.

TheOriginalMalehogany The LeroneBakerStory. "COGIC Convocation 'Musical Homosexual and Sissies.'" The Anoited [sic] Evangelist Frances Kelly, posted January 25, 2014. YouTube, https://www.youtube.com/watch?v=6qqEClV_K4s.

Thrasher, Steven. *"War, Crime, and HIV: An Accounting on AIDS and Racism in the United States."* Research presentation at Indiana University, October 24, 2019 Indiana Memorial Union State Room.

Timolampley. "Exclusive: Luther Vandross Tells Tim Lampley 'Weight' Question Bothers Him," posted August 12, 2012. YouTube, https://www.youtube.com/watch?v=-_kJWDBsbGw.

Tisdale, Lenora Tubbs. *Preaching as Local Theology and Folk Art*. Minneapolis: Fortress Press, 1997.

Tonéx. *O2*. Zomba Recording, LLC. Released July 10, 2002.

Tonéx. *Out the Box*. Zomba Recording, LLC. Released May 18, 2004.

Tonéx. *The Naked Truth*. Nureau Inc. Released August 29, 2008a.

Tonéx. *Rainbow*. Nureau Inc. Released September 16, 2008b.

Tonéx. *Unspoken*. Zomba Recording, LLC. Released March 13, 2009.

Townes, Emilie Maureen. *Womanist Ethics and the Cultural Production of Evil*. New York: Palgrave, 2006.

Tribbett, Tye. *Victory Live!* Sony SMB Music Entertainment. Released May 23, 2006.

Tujillo, Alicia. "Lap Dancing Nun Performs for Church," *BBC News*, July 13, 2014, http://news.bbc.co.uk/2/hi/7988322.stm.

Turino, Thomas. *Music as Social Life: The Politics of Participation*. Chicago: University of Chicago Press, 2008.

Turkle, Sherry. *Life on the Screen: Identity in the Age of the Internet*. London: Phoenix, 1997.

Turner, Kathleen S. *And We Shall Learn Through the Dance*. Oregon: Pickwick Publications, forthcoming.

Turner, Patricia. *I Heard It Through the Grapevine: Rumor in African-African Culture*. Berkeley: University of California Press, 1993.

Underwood, Steven Gregory. *Gay Men and Anal Eroticism: Tops, Bottoms, and Versatiles*. New York: Routledge, 2003.

Vandross, Luther. *Live in Wembley*. BBC 1987. https://www.youtube.com/watch?v=NR2v9xll2o0, last accessed December 14, 2019.

Viljoen, Martina. "'Wrapped Up': Ideological Setting and Figurative Meaning in African-American Gospel Rap." *Popular Music* 25, no. 2 (2006): 265–282.

Wald, Gayle F. "'Have a Little Talk': Listening to the B-side of History." *Popular Music* 24, no. 3 (2005): 323–337.

Walker, Alice. *In Search of Our Mother's Gardens: Womanist Prose*. Orlando: Harcourt, Inc., 1983.

Walker, Corey D. B. "On (The) Word and Flesh: The Theopolitics of Knowledge in Black Heretics, Black Prophets: Radical Political Intellectuals." *The C.L.R. James Journal* 12, no. 1 (Spring 2006): 193–206.

Walker, Hezekiah & The Love Fellowship Crusade Choir. *Live in London*. Benson Music Group. Released May 20, 1997.

Walker, Hezekiah & The Love Fellowship Crusade Choir. *Family Affair II: Live at Radio City Music Hall*. Zomba Recording, LLC. Released August 20, 2002.

Walker, Wyatt Tee. *Somebody's Calling My Name*. Valley Forge, PA: Judson Press, 1982.

Walser, Robert. *Running With The Devil: Power, Gender, and Madness in Heavy Music*. Middletown, CT: Wesleyan University Press, 1993.

Walton, Jonathan. *Watch This!: This Ethics and Aesthetics of Black Televangelism*. New York: New York University Press, 2009.

Ward, Brian. *Just My Soul Responding: Rhythm and Blues, Black Consciousness, and Race Relations*. London: University of California Press, 2004.

Wartofsky, Alona. "What Go-Goes Around . . .: The funk Genre that Brought DC to Its Feet 20 years Ago is back With A Joyous Refrain—The Party's Not Over." *Washington Post*, June 1, 2001.

Watson, Nick J. "Muscular Christianity in the Modern Age: Winning for Christ or Playing for Glory." In *Sport and Spirituality: An Introduction*. Edited by Jim Parry, Mark Nesti, Simon Robinson, and Nick Watson, 80–94. New York: Routledge, 2007.

Webster, James. "Music, Pathology, Sexuality, Beethoven, Schubert." *19th-Century Music* 17, no. 1 (1993): 89–93.

Weeks, Jeffrey. *Sex, Politics & Society: The Regulations of Sexuality Since 1800*. New York: Longman, 1989.

Weekes, Melinda E. "This House, This Music: Exploring the Interdependent Interpretive Relationship Between the Contemporary Black Church and Contemporary Gospel Music." *Black Music Research Journal* 25, no. 1/2 (2005): 43–72.

Weheliye. Alexander G. *Habeas Viscus: Racializing Assemblages, Biopolitics, and Black Feminist Theories of the Human*, Durham, NC: Duke University Press, 2014.

Werner, Craig H. *Higher Ground: Stevie Wonder, Aretha Franklin, Curtis Mayfield, and the Rise and Fall of American Soul*. New York: Crown, 2004.

West, Cornel. "Black Sexuality: The Taboo Subject." In *Traps: African American Men on Gender and Sexuality*. Edited by Rudolph P. Byrd and Beverly Guy-Sheftall, 301–307. Bloomington: Indiana University Press, 2001.

White, Calvin. *The Rise of Respectability: Race, Religion, and the Church of God in Christ*. Fayetteville: University of Arkansas Press, 2012.

Williamson, Reginald. "Defeminizing the Church: Will This Encourage More Men to Attend?" 2011.

Williamson, Reginald. "Defeminizing the Church: Will This Encourage More Men to Attend?." Designed by Paul Davis. April 2016.

williamstempleCOGIC. "Donnie McClurkin & Evangelist Joyce Rodgers Talks to the Youth COGIC," posted January 8, 2011. YouTube, https://www.youtube.com/watch?v=gJEonFztD0w&t=144s.

Wilson, David. *Inventing Black on Black Violence: Discourse, Space, and Representation*. New York: Syracuse University Press, 2005.

Wilson, Olly. "The Heterogeneous Sound Ideal." *Black Music Research Journal* 3 (1983): 1–22.

"Woman Offers 'Christian Pole Dancing Class' in Houston." *The Urban Daily*. March 22, 2011. http://theurbandaily.com/special-features/wtf-special- features/theurbandailystaff2/christian-pole-dancing-class-houston-video.

Woodard, Vincent. *The Delectable Negro: Human Consumption and Homoeroticism within U.S. Slave Culture*. New York: New York University Press, 2014.

Woods, DeWayne. *Introducing DeWayne Woods & When Singers Meet*. Zomba Recording, LLC. Released 2006.

Young, Tamara. "Is Travis Greene the Future of Gospel Music?" Jetmag.com. posted May 20, 2016. https://www.jetmag.com/entertainment/is-travis-greene-the-future-of-gospel-music/.

Zak, Albin J. *The Poetics of Rock: Cutting Tracks, Making Records*. Berkeley: University of California Press, 2001.

Zhang, Jane Hongjuan. "Of Mother and Teachers: Roles in a Pedagogy of Caring." *Journal of Moral Education* 36, no. 4 (December 2007): 515–526.

Index

For the benefit of digital users, indexed terms that span two pages (e.g., 52–53) may, on occasion, appear on only one of those pages.

@ChurchFunny, 83
1999 (Prince), 192
  "How Come You Don't Call Me" (Prince), 192

absenteeism, 3–4, 5–6, 28, 54–55, 96–97
  black male, 99–100, 115, 147–48, 207–08, 221
Adam! Where Are You?: Why Most Black Men Don't Go To Church (1997), 99–100
Adams, Yolanda, 47–8, 43–4n.24
Adda, Ben, 125
adult male soprano soloists, 71, 75–76
advertisement
  of queer possibility, 66, 100–1
aesthetic
  African-derived music styles, 75, 76, 123, 128
  amplified-muffled speech, 130–1
  music, 8
African-American Christian masculinity, 4, 28–29, 31, 82, 84–85, 103, 136, 174–5, 176
  Black progressive, 32–33
  hegemonic gospel, 99, 104
  muscular Christianity, 4, 19, 103, 104, 113, 116, 123, 123n.25, 139, 156, 172–173n.2, 222
  "nonchurchy", 139
  Pentecostal, 16
African-American countertenor
  African-derived oral and European-derived concert music, 75
  formal training and performance in Western art music performance, 75
  "gendered sound", 34
  lineage, 75
  navigating racial and gender bias in white opera industry, 76–77
  perceived as peculiar, 34, 72
  sonic castration and whitening, 74–75
  unconventional, 73
  Western opera and gospel music, 79
  worship traditions black congregations, 72, 75

African-American gospel
  orality, 117–18, 132, 152–53, 206, 209
  rhetoric as orality, 152–53
African-American gospel Music, 75–76
  sonic "safe place", 33
  See also gospel music
African-American men
  contributions to contemporary concert and opera performance, 76–77
African-American Protestant congregation
  anxieties of countertenors in, 75
African-American worship, 18–19, 72–73, 91
  decline in black men's participation, 4, 6, 16
  "meaningful worship leadership", 25–26
  peculiar pleasure, 24–25
African- and European-derived heritages, 75
African culture
  no distinctions of, the sacred and the profane realms of life or between the spiritual and the material worlds, 90–91
  talking drums, 124
African Methodist Episcopal (A.M.E), 97, 154
  Community of Hope A.M.E., 115, 146, 147
  Ebenezer A.M.E., 115, 140, 147, 176n.7
African religious rites, 75–76
African worship, 90–91, 123, 124
  religious and nonreligious realms were not distinguishable, 91–92
African-American Christian churches, 87
  as dainty, 3
African-American Christian praise dance, 90, 104
African-American Christianity
  body theology, 168–9
  body theology through music, 153–54, 155
  Pentecostalism, 61, 205–6
African-American congregants:
  conservative, 5–6, 31
African-American man
  using the pole to worship, 97
African-American religiosity
  profane concept, 90–91

African-American worship, 24–25, 29,
    32–33, 99–100
  engineered, 3
  Pentecostal, 1
African-American worship services, 90–91
African-derived music styles
  African-American quartet music, 76
  Go-go music, 123
  in the United States, 76
  rhythm and blues (R&B), 76
Afro-Caribbean instrumentation and musical
    elements, 118–119
agential self, 93
  dangerous modes of power and authority of
    the, 93
air, 96–97
  a fresh wind, 96–97
  as God's omniscience, 96–97
  Holy Spirit that indwells the believer and
    seeker, 96–97
Allen, Fernando, 80
Allport, Gordon, 201n.9
American Academy of Religion (AAR)
    conference, 189n.35
American Pole Fitness Association, 96
Amplified Noise Act of 2018
  criminalizes black musicians, 125
anatomical metaphors, 77
  The Diva's Mouth, 77
  the Queen's Throat, 77
And We Shall Learn Through the
    Dance: Liturgical Dance as Religious
    Education, 91–92
Anderson, Elijah, 89, 141–42
Anderson, Victor, 109
André, Naomi, 73, 74–75n.8, 77
androgyny, 78, 153, 176–77
  hermaphrodite, intersex, third sex,
    transvestite, transsexual, and
    effeminate, 77–78
  Piotr Scholz define, 77–78n.29
  symbolically united in a being, 77–78
  vocalized, 77–78
angelic, 76, 77–78
anointed, 8–9
  music that is from and for God, 72–73
  queer, 188
anointing, 11, 173, 188, 196
anti-homosexuality sermons, 17, 206–9
  homo-antagonistic, 202–3
anxiety
  about men's dance in worship, 97, 100
  being transparent, 151

black masculine, black male identity, 33,
    87–88, 213
choir director leadership competency, 13
deliverance from homosexuality, 202–6
  Donnie McClurkin's, 36, 37–38, 203, 205
  gospel go-go, 116–17
  HIV/AIDS, 17, 17–18n.51, 59
  homoerotic haze, 107
  "letting slip show," 186, 186n.25
  queer potential, 13, 85, 176
  separation from church family, 176
  testimony, 209–210
  in worship, 97
Apostolic Pentecostal, 94, 152
appearance of evil
  in the Holy Bible, 12n.40, 99
art of silence, 174, 181
Asherah
  Hebrew goddess, 112, 222
assumptions about identity, 6–7, 171
  high-singing male performances, 72
Atlanta, 28, 157
  "Hotlanta", 157
Attinello, Paul, 169
attire ambiguous style, 153–54
  audience interpretation, 153
  extramusical elements, 154
  form of communication, 153
  gendered materials, 153
  performance, 153
attraction of, 82
  Patrick Dailey, 82
  Donnie McClurkin, 82
Atwater, Larry "Stomp" 133–34, 144
audience's expectations, 79
aural-visual philosophy, 87
aural-visual qualities, 34, 80
authenticity
  interior disposition, 187
Awkward, Michael, 21–22
Azusa Street Revival, 181n.13

B.Slade, 15–16, 17, 34
  code performance, 15–16
  name change, 15, 15n.48
Babel, Molly, 42– 43n.16
Backyard Band
  go-go bands, 115, 128, 119, 133–34, 124, 125,
    128, 140, 147
bad blood, 164–165,
  Bailey, Marlon, 156–57, 156–57n.25, 198–9n.3,
    183–184, 198–199, 200, 209, 210 n.29,
    211n.32

Butch Queens up in Pumps: Gender, Performance, and Ballroom Culture, 156–57n.25
  on gender system categories, 156–57, 156–57n.25
  "men," 156–57n.25
  "trade" gays, 156–57, 156–57n.25
Baldwin, James, 104
  Go Tell It on The Mountain, 104, 181n.14
Bangles, The, 149n.4
bareback(ing), 162–63, 164, 166, 167, 184–85
Barnwell, Ysaye, 117–118
Bar Kays, The, 194n.48
barriers of gender conformity, 73–74
Barron, Charisse, 189n.35
"Beams of Heaven" (Some Day) by Charles A. Tindley, 71
  arranged-composed by Nathan Carter, Jr., 71
Bean, Carl, 202–3n.11
"Before I Die" (Kirk Franklin), 126–7
bel canto, 81
believers
  Queer, Pentecostal, same-gender loving, 172
Bell-Armstrong, Vanessa, 44n.24
Belzen, Jacob A., 87–88n.2, 94
"Beyond the Veil" (Daryl Coley), 194–95n.50
bilingualism, 54, 210
"Bi Our Love" from *The Children* album (B.Slade) 223–24
Black and Latino Gay Ballroom, 43–44, 156–57, 156–57n.25, 163–64n.50, 198, 199, 200, 198–99n.3, 209, 211–12,
Black Code, 124–25, 142–43
Black dandyism, 158, 158n.35
Black Entertainment Television (BET) Network, 29, 47, 53, 66, 216–17
  Daniel Moore, 216–17
  Sunday Best, 216–17
Black gay vernacular
  read, 19, 195, 211, 212
  realness, 156–57n.25, 195, 200, 210, 211n.31, 212
  "slayed," 158n.34
  "sweet tea", 157
"top", 217
black gospel. *See* sacred music
  on gender expression of men, 20
  participants, 91
  on sexual orientation of men, 20
black gospel music, 1, 152–53
  masculinities constituted, 88
  queer identities performed, 88
  as sonic safe place, 35

styles, 71
symbols constructed, 88
unconventional, 73
Western opera and, 79
black gospel participants, 30, 91
Black male
  absenteeism, 28, 100, 123, 147–48, 221
  sacred identity, 11
  spirituality, 121
  worship, 97
black masculine anxiety, 12–13, 28, 87–88
  absenteeism, 28, 59, 96–97
  dance in worship, 100
  decline in church participation, 4, 147–48
  ideal masculinity, 84
  mannerisms, 84
  in worship, 97
black men
  absenteeism, 3, 100, 146–47, 221
  as platform for black men, 93–94
  decline in church participation 4, 115
  imagined as evil, 103
  in church leadership, 3
  in the economy, 5
  sexuality and Identity in Gospel Performance, 5–6
Black Men Voices white observers characterized, 75–76
black men's bodies
  black beast, 32
  demonic, 31
  white supremacist, 31–32
black men's worship
  real or imagined surveillance, 93
black Pentecostal tradition
  multivocal, 93
black Protestant audiences'
  receptiveness to countertenors' vocal performance, 80
black religiosity and multimedia engagement, 79–80
black sacred music
  public arts interventions, 71
  See also black gospel
Black Skin White Masks (Frantz Fanon), 104
Black vocalists underrepresented in predominantly white institutions, 73
Black Vocality symposium in Chicago, 74
black worship
  "heathenish" and profane, 90–91
Body Count (punk band), 119
body language, 88, 97–98, 104
  Gaze, 157–58

body language (*cont.*)
  "gos-pop," 157
  misunderstanding of, 97–98
  misunderstood, 96
  unspokenness, 184
  uses to manage perceptions about identity, 49, 72, 84
Body Theology, 153–55, 168–69
  in church performances, 80
  feminized male, 187
  in heteronormative African-American Context, 154–55
  uses to manage perceptions about identity, 84
body of Christ, the, 90, 110–11, 154n.16, 168–69, 216
  crucified, 33, 111n.66, 113–14
  metaphoric, 216
Bogues, Anthony, 10
Bonds, Samuel L. E., 13–14, 71
Bonnerfide radio, 195
Boogie Down Productions, 146n.75
Booth, Tiffany, 111
born again, 149–50, 176
"born this way," 202–3, 202–3n.11
Boston University, 102
boy soprani, 73
Boyd, Stacy C., 14–15, 27–28, 33, 60
broadcast television networks, 29, 36, 47, 51–52, 53, 66, 70, 70n.2, 71–72, 79–80n.35, 79–80, 216–17
  Black Entertainment Television (BET), 29, 47, 53, 66, 216–17
  The Dream Network, 70, 70n.2, 152
  The Word Network, 29, 51–52, 71–72, 71n.3, 79–80n.35, 79–80, 158
  Trinity Broadcasting Network (TBN), 29, 36,
Brooks, Daphne, 24
Brown, Chuck, 118–19
  "Bustin' Loose," 118–119
  "Go-Go Swing," 118–119
Brown Douglas, Kelly, 22, 23
Brundidge, Caleb, 105
Bryant, Charles Anthony, 66–67, 194n.47
Bryant, Jamal, 3, 3n.16, 18
Buggy "The General," 127, 133–34, 143
Burleigh, Glen, 90
Burrell, Kim, 39, 44–45, 61–62, 81, 202, 206–7, 206–7n.20
Burton, Rorie, 186–87n.29
Butler, Melvin L., 10, 29–30, 92
Butler, Myron
  "covered," 126
Bynum, Juanita, 20–21

cadenza, 81
Caesar, Shirley
  "Hold My Mule," 159–60n.38,
  "I Remember Mama," 8–9n.29
Cage, Byron, 2, 18, 79–80n.35, 96–97
Caldwell, Andrew, 39, 46, 49–50n.33, 50n.38, 59, 62n.71, 69, 101, 221
Callahan, Daniel, 162n.46
"Can you sing us?," 81
Caravans, 43n.18
Carter, Earl, 44–45, 46, 47, 50–51, 211
  homo-antaganoistic sermon, 60
  "homosexual spirit", 62
Carter, Jr., Nathan Mitchell, 71, 72, 72n.6, 80, 85–86
  "Some Day," 71, 72–73
  intervention for, 77
Castrato/i, 74–75, 74–75n.8, 77–78, 82–83, 85–86
  castrato performances, 85–86
  and eunuchs, 77–78
castration, 74–75, 74–75n.8
Cathedral of the Holy Spirit (Bridgeport, CT), 120n.21
Center for Black Music Research (CBMR)
  Black Vocality symposium, 74–75, 77
Chapman, Morris, 52–53
charismatic Christian, 1n.3, 9, 38, 87, 92, 93, 123, 202, 218
  aesthetics, 123
  "church mothers", 56–57, 70, 138, 203
  faith tradition, 29–30, 38, 39, 87, 137, 138, 193, 202
  go-go musicians approach, 123
  models of, 120
  slain in the spirit, 173, 173–74n.4
Cheers (television show), 224
Cheng, William, 36n.2
Chicago, 27, 28, 72–73, 99–100, 101–02
  University of Chicago, 25, 53, 162n.46, 186n.29,
Children of the Gospel (COTG), 13–14
chocolate cities, 27–28
choirboy, 139, 139n.60, 174–75
  diminished manhood, 174–75
choir director
  flamboyant stereotype, 12–13, 16, 115–116, 115–116n.2
  focal point, 13
  humor, 12
  leadership competency, 13
  masculinities paradigm, 32–33
  privileging of men's employment, 5
  trope, 12–13, 16–17, 102, 148
Christian embodiment, 33

Christian worship, 1n.3, 10, 16, 19, 23, 26, 27–
    33, 44, 91–92, 99, 103, 105, 107, 113n.69,
    138, 147, 148, 155, 178, 179, 185, 216,
  Africanisms, 123–24,
  black male participation, 3, 95, 96,
    103, 221-2
  black worship, 24, 85–86, 90–91
  competence, 9,
  deliverance, 38–9
  distraction, 154
  groove theory, 132,
  homoeroticism, 109–14,
  interiority, 175
  message, 134–9,
  not partying, 145
  Pentecostal, 1–4, 23, 38, 51, 215
  poles in, 90–91, 96
  private, 93, 96, 104
  pulpit, 49
  rituals, 174
  sounded convergence, 130
  transparency, 141, 143, 150-2, 188
  undignified praise, 108, 115–6, 121
  unspoken, 179
  vitality, 178
  worship (adage), 87
Christianity
  muscular, 4, 18–19, 103–4, 113–14, 116,
    122–3, 122–3n.25, 139, 148, 173n.2,
    222, 282
church, 91–92, 207–8
  anti-homosexuality, 41
  attendance, 2
  black church fragility, 213
  Catholic, 74, 216, 216n.42
  church boy, 132–133, 136–139, 174–75,
    176, 173n.1
  church entertainers, 206n.19
  "church family," 174–175
  "church girl," 128
  church homesickness/home longing,
    95, 96–97
  comedy, 198
  convergence, 129
  Council of Toledo, fifth-century, 32
  church home, 215, 216, 218
  early Church, 181n.13
  feminized, 2, 2n.11, 3, 100, 103–4, 106,
    109–110, 121, 173n.2, 222
  folklore, 198, 6n.27
  fundamentalist, 178
  defeminized, 3n.12, 139
  "invisible church," 125

  leadership, 5, 7, 18, 25, 26, 34, 58, 60, 69,
    100–101, 115, 116–17, 124–25, 133–134,
    143, 168, 207, 220
  men's involvement, 4, 31, 99–100
  "mockery," 61–62
  multimedia, 29
  "playin'," 42–43
  predatory, 63
  protocol, 82
  public square and religious sanctuary, 113
  random, 95
  roles, 18–19
  salutation, 82
  sex, 177
  sexual violation, 52–53, 164, 168, 191, 207
  storefront, 163
  "the church," 52
  "unchurched," 140, 154
  underworld (subculture), 64, 68, 214
  Western church music repertoire, 77
  women, 20, 23–24, 56–57, 70, 138, 176, 200,
    219, 220
church boy, 136, 139, 176
  use for diminished manhood, 138–39,
    172–173n.1
church music ministry, 7, 16, 19, 25, 60, 68,
    73–74, 147, 175, 202n.10
  bilingualism, 210
  boyish, 103
  "Can LGBT People Be Active in My
    Church, 169
  church, 73, 143, 221
  comfort zone, 215
  countertenor, 72.
  Donnie McClurkin, 53, 178
  escapism, 178
  feminizing, 43
  gay, 24, 26, 208
  gestures, 103
  gospel music is gay music, 205
  HIV/AiDS, 170
  Kim Burrell, 61
  manly, 103
  men, 5, 26, 33, 100, 219
  queer, 103
  preacher-musician, 152, 170, 171, 221
  predators, 207
  safe space, 179
  shamanic role, 183
  terms for male participation in, 139
  Tonéx, 152
  vocal participation, 205, 220
  women, 3, 4, 20, 24

Church of Gays in Christ, 44
Church of God in Christ (COGIC), 44–45, 46,
    47, 49, 103, 201, 202, 206, 206n.20, 207–
    209, 211, 215, 216
  absenteeism, 54–55
  Carlton Pearson, 49, 63, 204–5
  Charles Blake, 50–51
  Charles Anthony Bryant, 66–7
  convocation, 39, 44, 45, 51, 55, 58, 60,
    68, 101, 201, 202, 203, 206, 206n.20,
    207–209, 211–2
  convocation script, 211
  deliverance teaching, 50, 51, 206
  female pastors/preacher, 20, 39, 61n.67
  heteropatriarchal system, 60
  homo-antagonistic and
    anti-feminzation, 202–3
  John Hannah, 101
  love ethic, 50–51
  preacher-musician, 202
  raised, 20, 49, 61, 63, 66, 101, 170, 205
  spiritual affliction of queer and
    gender-nonconforming, 51–52
  struggle, 52, 52n.40
  theology, 53, 62n.69
  Walter Hawkins, 170
church worship domain
  choir loft, 24, 150, 152–53
  musicians' pit, 116n.2, 152–53, 152–53n.9
  pulpit, 152–53
churchy, 132–33, 138
  non-, 139
circus arts, 94–95, 94–95n.25. See also pole
    fitness
  cis-gender/cisgender, 3, 20, 21, 59n.60,
    116n.2, 186n.25, 218–19
  Ballroom culture, 209
  Pentecostal, 209
  Word of Faith movement, 218–19
Clark Sisters, 44–5, 47–8, 81, 149, 202
Clark-Sheard, Karen
  "If I Can't Say a Word, I'll Just Wave My
    Hands," 184
  2nd Chance album, 184
  "Prayed Up," 126
class and gender
  African American male idenity, 26–7
  heavy metal music, 21
  Cleveland, James, 14–5, 17, 43n.18, 48–9, 59,
    70, 169, 216n.45
closet, 54
  white masculinity setting standard, 54
  "glass closet", 54

"Homosexuality's Closet" (Halperin), 77–8
"in the closet", 171
  oppressive, 185
  out of, 167, 183–4, 208–9
closeted, 14–15, 183–84, 186
  Donnie McClurkin, 168
  "hidden" in sanctuaries, 156, 188n.34
  James Cleveland, 14–5
Coates, Curtis, 105n.42
code
  attire, 45–46, 51–52, 55, 56, 84–85
  feminine, 63, 69, 84, 203
  feminine masculine, 102
  flamboyance is, 29–30
  performance in, 15–16
  gendered, 11, 16, 19, 72, 123, 153, 154, 203
  HIV/AIDS, 14–15, 165
  masculine, 19, 114, 117, 121, 123, 124
  moral, 25–26
  orality, 19, 38
  perform in, 16
  queer, 54, 148, 154–5, 162–64, 169, 175, 180
  sensual, 45, 51
  "spiritual son(s), 18n.53
  Victorian, 91, 103n.35
  code-switching, 141–42, 210
coded performance
  in Pentecostal worship, 40, 51–52
codes of conduct
  in worship performance, 72
codes of respectability, 91, 106
  Victorian, 90–91
code-switching, 141, 210
COGIC, 40, 50, 52, 53, 55, 57, 58, 59, 61n.67,
    61–62, 62n.69, 66, 102–3
  convocation, 39, 40, 202, 203, 206n.19
Coley, Daryl, 13–14, 17, 38, 40, 41n.11, 41n.12,
    42n.13, 42n.14, 42n.15, 43n.18, 43n.19,
    43n.20, 43n.21, 43n.22, 44n.23, 44n.24, 49,
    51, 61, 68, 88–89, 202, 194n.50
Coley, Jenelle, 88–89
Collins, Patricia Hill, 27, 27n.82
Columbia University 67
  "Are the Gods Afraid of Black Sexuality?"
    Conference, 43n.22, 67, 104, 106, 170n.66,
    183n.19, 183n.17
Come album (Prince), 193
  "Come"(Prince), 193
come out, 8–9, 39, 52n.40, 172–73
Comforter, 2, 43, 42n.15, 43n.20
  See also Holy Spirit
"Comforter has Come, The," (Daryl Coley)
    42n.15, 43

coming out, 104, 156, 181, 184, 186
commoditization, 13
  of gendered sound production, 74
communication modes, 34, 54–5, 94, 96, 155,
    182, 202, 207, 210, 215
  rhetorical device semantic snowballing
    define, 155–56
communication style
  non-verbalized rhetorical art, 154–55
  queer performers, 154–55
  recognized by LGBTQ and "straight"
    ally, 154–55
  unspoken, 154–55
Community of Hope AME Church
    (Hillcrest Heights/Temple Hills, MD),
    115, 147
compartmentalization, 183
the Complex (Temple Hills, MD), 121, 122
complexity
  of conceptualizing gendered vocal
    sound, 77
compulsory heterosexuality, 38, 55, 202, 222
  heteronormativity, 69
congregational gaze, 103
Conquergood, Dwight, 161–62
Constructions of Black Masculine Sacred
    Dance, 90
constructions of masculinity, 24, 43, 101,
contralto, 77
  Ysaye Barnwell, 117
Cooper, Renee, 25–26
"Cop Killer" (Ice T), 119
Corbiau, Gérard
  virtual voice, 74–75
Cosmopolitan Church of Prayer Choir
    (Chicago, IL), 198–99
Coulter, Tadhi, 186n.29
Council of Toledo, 32
countertenor, 73, 74, 75n.12, 78, 79, 221
  aesthetics, 73–74
  casted as submissive, 73–74
  gendered sound embodiment, 34
  homoeroticism of, 82–83
  lineage, 75, 85–86
  orality, 152–53
  peculiar vocal qualities, 34
  pedagogues, 74–75
  personae, 77
  queer potential, 82–83
  sexuality, 85–86
  sonic castration and whitening, 74–75
  sound, 73–75
  worship leader, 80

countertenor designation
  embodied negotiation between feminine
    sound and masculine vocal power, 77–78
countertenor singing
  skepticism in vocal designation, 78–79
  soloist, 71
  sound attraction, 82–83
  sounding like women, 70
  sound straight, 82–83
  style rather than a vocal designation, 78–79
countertenor vocal technique, 72, 79, 81–82
  gendered sound, 78–79
countertenors and castrati, 61n.68, 74–75, 85
"Covered" (Myron Butler), 126
Crawley, Ashon, 24–25, 93–94
Crawley, Y'anna, 119, 127
cross-cultural performance
  African American churches, 85–86
Crouch, Andraé
  "Can't Nobody Do Me Like Jesus," 119
Csikszentmihalyi, Mihál, 205n.17
cultural accessibility, 81
cultural competence
  gauging, 81
cultural contexts
  African-derived and European-derived, 85
cultural familiarity
  worship leader and trained artist, 72–73
Cummings, Benny, 43n.18
curfew laws, 125–26n.34
  Black Codes, 125–26n.34
  Jim and Jane Crow, 125–26n.34
  The Juvenile Curfew Act of 1995, 125–26n.34
Curry, Karen, 91–92
Cusick, Suzanne, 10, 11

D'Angelo, 194
Dailey, Patrick, 71, 72–73, 74, 79–80, 81, 82,
    83–86, 186n.25
  melismas, 81
  performance practice choices, 71–72
  sociocultural strategies of gendered
    sound, 79
dance, 1n.3, 11, 27, 39, 34, 40n.10, 69, 84, 85, 87–
    112, 103n.35, 122n.24, 123, 126, 127, 124,
    144–8, 149, 149n.4, 157, 159–60, 162n.46,
    175, 183, 194, 196, 198, 199, 220, 221
  construction of masculine sacred
    dance, 90–94
  danced devotion, 94
  masculine representations, 105
  non-religious styles, 90–91
  Patrick Dailey on "masculine posture," 84

dance (*cont.*)
  praise, 88, 90, 95, 103–4
  praise pole dance, 90, 95, 96
  queer dance styles, 90–91
  research, 104 (*see* liturgical dance;
    praise dance)
dancers, 92, 98, 99, 103, 106, 111, 116n.4,
    103n.35
  ballet, 98
dancing, 87, 88, 92, 94, 99, 105, 111n.66, 199
  like David, 105n.43
  pole dancing, 96, 11
  regulations and belief, 91
  reverence or irreverence, 97
  with grace, 85, 103
Daniels, David, 78,
Daniels, David III, 181n.13
Daniels, Tim, 186n.29
dark play, 162–63
*Daryl Coley Live: Live at the Bobby Jones Gospel
    Explosion VII,* 194n.50
David (of the Bible), 18, 30, 87–88, 91, 199
  David's Full Monty, 93, 93n.18
  Davidic model of undignified praise/worship,
    30, 103–5, 108, 113, 115, 115n.1, 116, 123,
    139, 141, 111n.66
  as a model for masculine movement, 93
Dean, Crystal, 111
Dean, Tim, 162, 166
decoding, 155
  attire, 153
  Pentecostal homosexual men's
    practice, 154–55
  re-code, 154–55, 180
  STD/STI status, 165
defeminization, 3n.12, 5–6, 139
  muscular Christianity, 4
  of worship, 3, 3n.12
  deliverance, 15, 15n.49, 36, 39n.7, 38, 39, 40,
    52n.40, 59n.60, 62n.69, 63, 168, 170n.64,
    172, 182, 191, 201, 203, 204–210, 205n.17,
    213, 217
  addictions, 39
  change, 15
  Chicago as a site, 27–28n.84
  from homosexuality, 38, 39
  ministry for, 15n.49
  narratives, 34
  Pentecostal beliefs, 42
  physical ailments, 39, 41
  process of, 41
  rituals, 32, 38, 39, 39n.7, 40–5, 52n.40,
    52–60, 63–7

spiritual afflictions, 39
  in values, 63
"Deliverer" (Daryl Coley), 41n.11, 44
demonic, 38n.6, 31, 32, 38, 40, 52n.40, 62n.69,
    62, 158n.33, 206n.20
Dennis, Sheri, 121n.22
DeVaughn, Raheem, 133–34
Dillard, Ricky, 102
  "Higher," 126
  "Worked it Out" 198–200
discordia concors, 78
discreet
  arrangement, 89
  believers' fears, 144, 176
  Communication, 27, 162–63, 207, 210
  Deceptive practice, 182–183
  gay men, 15, 15n.49, 151, 213–14
  gay preachers, 15
  HIV/AIDS, 169–70
  In worship, 182, 184
  intimate bonds, 182
  Marriage arrangment, 88–89
  Music composed by, 205
  Overrepresenation, 67, 204
  preachers, 15
  same-gender loving, 67, 183–84
  sex, 150–51, 157–58
  sexual identity, 177, 180, 182–83
  social navigations, 197
  solidarity, 186
discrete, 52n.39, 53, 56, 179, 210
discretionary devices, 173, 198, 202,
    210–11, 217
distinction between
  gospel go-go and go-go, 117, 121, 126, 133, 140,
    142, 145–46
Dixie Chicks, 184n.23
  Dixie Chicks: Shut Up and Sing, 184n.23
  expectations of queer musicians, 184
  "Shut Up and Sing" term, 184n.23
Dixon, Thomas Tyler, 13–14
Dodson, Antoine, 48n.28
Do the Right Thing (movie), 119
domain of nonblack musicians, 73
"Don't Ask, don't tell," 12, 19, 38, 49, 53–54, 64,
    150–51, 165, 183, 199
  stigmatization of queer believers, 150–51
Dorsey, Thomas, 70n.1, 120n.21
Double Door club, Chicago, IL, 224
Douglas, Kelly Brown, 22
down low, 6, 21, 42, 53–54, 58, 171, 203,
    210, 213–14
  deceptive, 219

Jeffery McCune characterizes, 57–58
  social media, 212
  Tonéx, 159–60
Draper, O'landa , 43–44, 43–44n.23
Dream Network, The, 70, 70n.2, 152
dress code, 154, 154n.16
  as a way to relate to audience, 154
DuBois, W. E. B., 7, 8, 174–75
  double consciousness, 54, 54n.47
  The Souls of Black Folk, 7, 176
Duke Ellington School for the Arts (DESA)
  (Washington, DC), 71
Durkheim, Emile, 40n.10, 185
Dyson, Michael Eric, 29–30, 29n.90, 44, 107,
  108–109, 177, 185, 186n.29, 194

E., Sheila, 42n.13
Easter Sunday, 95–6
  See also Resurrection Day
Ebenezer A.M.E. Church (Ft. Washington,
  MD), 115, 140, 147, 176n.7
Eilberg-Schwartz, Howard
  *God's Phallus: And Other Problems For Men
    and Monotheism*, 109, 110n.63,
Eliade, Mircea
  *The Sacred and the Profane: The Nature of
    Religion*, 90–91n.9
embodying the woman's soul, 77–78
en travesti, 61n.68, 72–73, 84–85
erotic, 1, 2n.11, 10, 16, 18, 31–32 , 43, 65–68,
  77–78, 88, 90–91, 93, 95, 106, 108–11, 118,
  156, 174, 179, 185, 189, 219, 220
  -ism, 31, 43–44, 108, 179, 185
  appetite, 65,
  autoeroticism, 77–78, 95, 189
  contemplation, 32
  "David's Full Monty", 92–3
  deliverance ritual, 67
  homoerotic, 18, 68, 104, 107, 109–10, 111,
    189, 192, 214, 215
  homomusicoerotics, 11
  "male gaze", 106
  pole dancing, 88
  seasoning, 65
escapism, 203
Escovedo, Pete, 42n.13
ethic of care, 27, 27n.82, 99, 207–8
  Patricia Hill Collins, 27
ethnic identity, refer, 20–21
ethnography, 21, 26–28, 31, 72, 201
  live performance, 72–73
  multisited, 21, 26, 27
  participatory, 29

ethnomusicological research, 13, 46, 76, 80, 131
  contributions of black high-singing male solo
    vocalists, 76
Eurocentrism of the content, 20n.62, 100
European Americans, 31–32, 39n.7, 64, 65,
  184n.23, 91
  adhered to Victorian codes of respectability,
    90–91, 103n.35
European concert music, 71, 75, 76, 77
ex-gay, 34, 105, 113, 132–3, 140, 167, 168,
  168n.57, 197, 202–3, 210–11, 213–215,
  217, 216n.44, 220
  term, 168n.57. *see also* formerly gay
euphemism,
  "eye," 157–58n.31
Experience Unlimited Band (E.U.), 126, 128
  "Da Butt," 126– 127
Extramusical elements, 154
  attire, 154
  audience interpretation, 154
  fashion-forward image, 154

"F@ce Down" (B.Slade)
  connotations, 188, 194, 194n.51
face down, 194
falsetto, 77n.21, 170
  D'Angelo, 194
  Prince, 75n.12, 77n.20, 78n.33, 193, 194,
    register, 78–79, 78n.33,
  tones, 75–76, 75n. 12,
  "una voce falsa," 78–79, 78n.33
familiar spirits, 211
  Biblical term, 133–34, 211
Fanon, Frantz, 103
Fantasia, 149
fantastic hegemonic imagination, 107, 107n.54
  neologism conceptualized, 107n.54
Farinelli, 74–75
Fausto-Sterling, Anne, 24
Feldman, Martha, 81
Fellowship of Affirming Churches, 20
female homosociality
  of prayer, 101–2
female-coded, 46, 63, 84
  feminine, 84
  gendered materials, 153
feminine masculinity, 4, 6, 13, 36, 50, 101, 139,
  186n.25, 191, 204, 206n.20, 209, 221
  choir director, 139
  "effeminacy," 191
  inappropriate touch, 195
  presenting, 24
feminine-presenting, 24, 60, 186, 197

femininity, 76, 102
  church space, 100–1
  domain, 175
  male femininity, 104,
  music ministry, 45
  weakness, 175
Fenton, Kevin, 186n.29
Ferguson, Roderick, 52, 52n.39, 54n.48
Finley, Stephen, 4n.18, 87n.1, 110n.60, 113n.69
  maleness of God, 109
fire, 1, 8–10
  as encounter, 1
  New Testament Bible symbolic, 1–2
  Pentecost, 2
  quick fire, 160
  wildfire, 15, 89, 225
fire and desire, 1–10, 39, 115
First Baptist Church of Glenarden, MD, 126
First Corinthian Baptist Church in Harlem, NY,
  170n.66
flamboyance, 12–13, 16, 30, 33–4, 39, 60, 102,
  114, 116, 116n.2, 148, 151, 198, 218
  choir director, 97, 150–51
  performers, 104
flaming, 5–6, 8–9, 13, 39, 47, 54
  divine purification, 8–9
  feminine masculinity, 8–9
  human homophobic, 8–9
  Insiders use of, 5–6
  Pentecostal worship, 8–9
  speaking in tongues, 8–9, 46n.26, 47n.27
flow, 27, 179, 203, 204, 205n.17
  airflow, 50
  emotion, 113
  global flows, 10
  money, 219
  musical and rhetorical performance, 6,
    48, 186,
  vocal aesthetics, 48
Floyd, Jr, Samuel A.,
  sacred and secular, 91
  signifyin, 154–55, 160
  song, dance, and drum, 34
  talking drums, 124
fluidity of
  bar, 98
  gender, 71, 77
  gesture, 102
  identity, 210
  sexuality, 53
  vocal designation, 71–72
Flunder, Yvette, 5, 5n.22, 17, 20–21, 67–8, 104,
  168, 168n.58, 170, 170n.66, 183, 183n.17,

186n.29, 191, 202, 203, 205, 212, 212n.35,
  214, 214n.40
"Jesus is my boyfriend," 5
shaman, 67, 183, 183n.17, 188, 203
formerly gay, 34, 38, 50–1, 203, 206–7. see
  also ex-gay
formerly lesbian, 20
Fortune, James, 158–59
Foster the People, 163–64
Foucault, Michel, 107n.54
Fraizer, David, 88–89
Franklin, Gertrude (Mother), 175
  Franklin, Kirk, 49, 70n.1, 79n.35, 126,
    126n.40, 138–39, 156n.24, 158–59, 173,
    126n.40, 156n.24, 173n.1, 178
  "choir boy," 174
  "church boy," 174
  The Fight of My Life, 156–57n.24
  "mama's boy," 174
  Kirk Smith, 174
Funk, 115, 120, 128
  Bar-Kays, The, 132n.48
  go-go is percussive, 115, 118–19, 120, 127–8,
    194.n48

gates, 189n.36, 189
Garrett, Joyce, 14
Gates Jr., Henry Louis, 154–55
Gaunt, Kyra, 131, 132n.49
gay Ballroom culture, 43, 156–57, 156–57n.25,
  196–200, 199n.3, 209, 210–12,
  Butch Queens, 156–57n.25
  "children/kids," 211, 211n.33
  construct homes, 210n.29
  Femme Queens, 156–57n.25
  "(fore)father," 211, 211n.33
  gender system, 156–57, 156–57n.25
  "house," 211, 211n.33
  realness, 156–57n.25, 211n.32
  "tipping," 90, 196
gay designations
  "post," 156–57
  "T" or "tea," 156–57
  "trade," 156–57
Gay Speech Style, 50, 50n.33, 50n.35
  speech impediment, 62
Gaye, Marvin, 10n.34, 189n.36
  sexual healing, 189, 189n.36
Geels, Antoon, 87–88n.2, 94
Geertz, Clifford, 27, 163
gender, 2–13
  decline in black men's participation, 2–21
  equality, 4

feminization, 2, 3, 30, 103, 110, 112, 222, 2n.11
male absenteeism in black churches, 4–5
male dominated, 4–5
social construction in church worship, 2–3
gender expression, 2, 6, 8, 9, 12, 12n.40, 13, 15, 20, 26, 38, 40, 49, 50, 53, 55–6, 58, 60–63, 66, 67, 73, 84, 101, 102, 108, 116, 160, 169, 176, 178, 182, 198, 203, 206–11
nurtured by women, 103
questions about, 82
gender identity, 5, 6, 8–12, 14, 15, 18, 48, 62, 87, 153–54, 179, 206–7n.19, 217
gender-inclusive, 71–72
programming, 71–72
language, 111
gender roles, 5, 13, 26, 30–31, 200
gender-bending traditions
en travesti production, 72–73
gendered
in Church Worship Domain, 18–19, 151–53, 200
preacher-vocalist, 49
gendered characterizations
bodily queering, 77
countertenor, 77
gendered materials, 153
ambiguous style, 153–4
gendered paradigms, 94
gendered performance
higher vocal ranges as feminine, 72, 75–76
lower vocal ranges as masculine, 75–76
gendered sound, 4, 34, 40, 72, 75, 79
commoditization of, 74
Dailey's sociocultural strategies of, 85–86
embodied symbol, 74–75
heteronormative frameworks, 72–73
male high-singing, 69, 70–72, 75–77, 75n.12, 77n.21, 79–81, 85, 170, 221
sociocultural strategies, 79
vocal technique, 85–86
gendered voice in gospel
complications of sonically ambiguous presentations of, 72–73
gender intertwine and compete, 72–73
long-standing heteronormative frameworks, 72–73
Gendering Gospel Music (Charisse Barron, Cory Hunter, Cheryl Townsend Gilkes and Alisha Lola Jones), 189n.35
genitals, 190–1
cultural, 24
spatial, 24, 152–53, 177

gestural heteropresentation, 84, 89, 138–43
as a competent and appropriate minister, 84
and mannerisms, 84, 87
"getting ignorant" 89, 138, 141–42, 143
Gilkes, Cheryl Townsend, 189n.35
Glenn, Cheryl, 4n.19, 174, 179, 179n.11
notion of silence, 174, 179n.11, 181n.13
GMA Dove Awards, 1n.1, 43–4n.23
GmagazineNow, 97
God, 1–10
as air, 96–97
closeness to/with, 94, 96, 111, 111n.66, 112–13, 140–141,
constructed as male, 88, 93, 111, 205–6
decent and proper expression, 91–92
experience, 93
as male Bridegroom, 110, 111
male demonstration of intimacy with, 94
seek, 3, 40, 93
symbolically more congruent for women to embody, 96
Goffman, Erving, 215
go-go, 34, 115, 116–17, 118–19, 120, 124, 127–8, 130–1, 132, 136
aesthetics of vocal techniques, 123
"beat ya' feet" Dance Style, 122, 122n.24,
"bounce beat", 121, 126, 144
Chuck Brown, 118–19
co-opting, 127
"crank," 143
DC music tropes, 137–8
development of, 116, 120
inaccurate portrayal, 119
Masculinities described as, 132–33
musical party, 118–19
musicians origins, 142
perceived male tastes, 117
tradition of remembrance, 120
youth victimization and drug-related crimes, 119
Go-Go Report
Prince George's County Maryland, 124–25
Google, 98
Gordon, Lewis, 109, 112–13, 188
gospel. Also see gospel music
gospel choir directors, 8, 11–17, 30, 33, 34, 76, 87, 97, 102, 105, 116, 123, 139, 148, 151, 198, 44n.23
continuum of sexual orientation and gender identity, 87
male vocal worship leaders, 6, 7, 11–13, 16, 36, 40, 48, 49, 60, 61, 69, 76, 80, 86, 102, 116, 117, 151, 189

gospel go-go, 34, 113–114, 115–148
 aesthetics, 123, 146
 African American preaching
  tradition, 120–21
 condemnation, 124–25
 emotive qualities, 123
 established tensions, 124, 125–26
 events function as services, 143
 "Gospel Go-Go Music Lineage," 120n.16
 historic phases, 120n.19
 masculine domains, 134
 muscular Christian interpretation of the
  Davidic undignified praise model, 123
 negotiation of identities, 143, 143n.69
 "peculiar" vocalized interjections, 123
 practices comparable to, 120
 "shout out," 134–35
gospel go-go band
 Peculiar People, 130–47
 Submission Band, 144–45, Appendix A
gospel go-go music, 34, 113–15, 116–47
 admission price in comparison, 120
 anxiety, 117, 161
 evangelistic tool, 120
 groove theory literature, 132
 Kirk Franklin resemblance, 173
 masculine-centered approach, 220–21
 response to their trauma, 120
 The Complex (venue), 121
 signified, 125
gospel music guild:
 Gospel Music Workshop of America
  (GMWA), 17, 41n.12, 70, 71, 152,
  152n.8, 212
 Hawkins Music and Arts Conference, 50
 National Convention of Gospel Choirs and
  Choruses (NCGCC), 120n.21
"Gospel music is gay music", 205
Gospel Music Workshop of America (GMWA),
 17, 41n.12, 70, 71, 152, 152n.8, 212 See also
 gospel music guild
gospel singing, 1, 49, 68, 88, 114, 117, 130, 149,
 152, 164, 176, 198, 204, 215, 217, 222, 224
 as erotic and sensual, 10, 189
 continuum, 47
 gender framework, 72–73, 222
 singing high, 69, 70–72, 75–77, 75n.12,
  77n.21, 79–81, 85, 170, 221
 singing low, 118, 121
Gospel Today, 17, 37–38, 40, 41
gospelized mysticism, 87–88
Grammy, 1, 36, 40, 48, 59, 68, 88, 150, 158,
 158n.35, 198

Gramsci, Antonio, 107n.54
Grant, Waddie, 97
Gray, John, 18
"Grease Pole Climbing Competition," 95n.25
Greene, Leonard, 102n.33
Greene, Travis, 59, 191n.43
Guillory, Margarita, 87n.1

Haddon, Deitrick, 79–80n.35, 158–59
Hairston, Teresa, 17, 37, 40, 41n.12, 42n.13,
 42n.14, 43n.18, 57, 61
Hall, Daniebelle, 41n.12
Hall, James, 102, 198,
Halle, Germany, 71
Halperin, David, 77–78, 154–55
Hammond B 3, 45
Hammond, Fred, 87n.1, 92, 92n.15, 149, 158–59
Handel Festival, 71
Hannah, John, 101–02
Hardin, Carless, 167, 167n.56, 168
Hargett, Tavon, 94–95
Harper, Philip Brian, 12, 28n.85
Harris-Lacewell, Melissa Victoria, 28, 28n.87
Harris, Larnelle, 52–53
Hawkeswood, William, 30–31
Hawkins, 20, 45
Hawkins Music and Arts Conference, 50
Hawkins, Edwin, 42n.14, 70n.1, 119, 202,
 "Oh, Happy Day," 119
Shirley Miller, 20, 168n.58
Hawkins, Tramaine, 42n.14, 88–89, 170n.66
Hawkins, Walter, 17, 42n.14, 70n.1, 88–89, 170,
 168n.58, 170n.66, 202
 Love Alive IV, 170
Hawks, Annie Sherwood, 149
"The Heavenly Voice," 77–78
Hebrew Bible, 1–2n.5, 18, 30, 87, 91, 189–90
 See also Old Testament
Hedgeman, Denita, 91–92
"He Delivered Me" (Daryl Coley), 39,
 41n.11, 41–42,
hegemonic, 32–33, 113–14, 148, 179
 of black masculine movement, 97–98
 gestural masculinity, 84, 113
 gospel masculinity, 84–85, 99, 113
 imagination, 107
 perceptions, 72, 84–85
Hello Fear (Kirk Franklin), 126
heteronormative, 14–15, 26, 50, 80
 closeness to God, 96, 111–12
 construct, 30, 96, 105
 contradictions of manhood, 26
 effeminate, 106

ideal, 34, 84
identification, 150–51
performance, 84–85
resisting feminization, 112
sexual attraction to, 53–54
sexual overtures from, 53–54
terms, 110
heteropatriarchal, 5, 6–7, 11, 13, 103–4, 173,
    173–74n.4, 205–6
allowing daughters to attend, 100–1
distance from perception of socially
    feminized/castrated, 176
double consciousness, 53–4n.48
God imagery, 32–33
humiliation, 56
incendiary language, 206–7
Jungle Cat disrupts, 106
Kirk Franklin, 173
leadership, 25, 55
metanarratives, 173
power structure, 218–19
protecting church leadership, 34
sermons, 174, 197
Tye Tribbett, 172
upholding male, 60
vision of worship, 103
heteropresentation, 5, 7, 11, 13, 18, 25, 37, 50–
    51, 55, 61, 70, 84, 151, 159–60, 173n.2, 174,
    201, 202, 209, 210, 218–19
hetero-presenting. See heteropresentation
Hill, Renee, 23
Hinds, André "Dré" 129–30, 131, 134–42, 145
Hinson, Glenn Fire In My Bones, 8–9.n29, 143
historically black college and university
    (HBCU), 73
HIV/AIDS, 14–15, 16–17, 18n.53, 39, 41, 55,
    147, 162–3, 165, 166, 167, 169, 170, 186–7,
    186–7n.29, 225, See also STDs/STIs
anxiety, 17–18n.51
Dewayne Woods, 169–70n.64
Luther Vandross, 43–44n.21
Seronegative, 162
Seropositive, 165, 166
TRUVADA aka PrEP, 161–62, 161–62n.45
Washington, DC, 27–28n.84
Hobbs, Darwin, 17–18
Holley, W. A, 42n.14
Holy Bible, 31, 87, 90, 92, 111, 133, 161, 182,
    194n.46
holy hip-hop, 133
Jesus's body, 90
nonage parishioners expect, 31
protesters, 111

Holy Convocation, 44,
Holy Ghost, 8, 43, 62n.69, 104, 187, 12n.38, 194,
    194n.48
workout, 120
Holy Ghost Enforcers, 12
"Holy Ghost" song from Money Talks album
    (The Bar Kays), 194n.48
Holy Spirit, 1–2, 8, 41–3, 53, 87–88, 96, 113,
    120, 174n.4, 181n.12, 187, 192, 194n.46,
    194n.47, 194n.48, 213, 9n.29, 43n.20,
    46n.26, 62n.69, 120n.21, 150n.7, 173n.3
"Comforter," 42n.15, 43n.20
erotic, 193–94
tarrying for, 181n.15
homoantagonistic, 3, 8–9, 43–4, 47, 48, 59–60,
    62, 172, 199, 202–3, 206–7, 206–7n.20
homoeroticism, 104, 109, 110
of countertenor sound, 82–83
homomusicoenrapture, 116
homophobia, 23, 28, 173n.2, 174
homophobic, 9, 11, 18, 29, 31, 45, 63, 100, 103,
    104, 174, 180, 185, 197, 200,
    anti-homophobic, 215–7
    music ministers' sexuality, 99–100
    sermon styles, 15, 18n.51, 29, 31, 45, 174, 180,
    185, 197
homophone, 157
"Eye Call", 157
"Bi," 223–24
homosexual, 9, 12, 17, 20, 22, 34, 36, 38–58,
    61–3, 66–9, 83, 88–89, 100, 106, 155,
    157, 160–71, 172–8, 182, 184–6, 188,
    197, 201–19
men as conserative and
    fundamentalist, 175–76
queer identity, 17, 19
homosexual socialization, 54, 155
homosexual spirit, 61, 62, 206–7n.20
"Homosexuality's Closet", 77–78
homosocial, , 18n.52, 18, 40, 101, 111, 115–16,
    191, 217, 220–21
attributing queerness, 195
in the Catholic Church, 111n.66
homosonoenrapture, 116
honeymoon rhinitis, 190–191n.40
Hood, Robert E., 31–32
Hoover, Stewart, 105n.42
Hope, Aaron, 129, 129n.45, 131, 144–45
Hopkins, Dwight, 31–3, 107–8,
Hopkinson, Natalie, 119–20, 121n.22
Horst, Cindy, 27
"Hotlanta", 157
Houghton, Israel, 126, 194n.49

Houston, Whitney, 193
Howard Gospel Choir, 118–119
Howard Theater, 149
Howard University, 22, 149
Huck-A-Bucks, 128
Huffington Post, 97, 166–7
Hughes, Thomas, 103
Hunter, Cory, 189n.35
Hurd, Stephen, 115n.1
Hylton, Roberto L., 125
hypermasculine, 17–18, 17–18n.51, 19, 114,
        204, 124, 221
    Bishop Eddie Long, 17–18n.51
    media portrayal, 221
hypermasculinity, 139–40
    go-go lead talker, 204
    in gospel go-go, 113–14, 204
    Richard Pitt, 97n.28
    George Sanders, 97n.28

"I am delivered," 46, 47–48, 49, 51–58, 213
"I Give You Praise" (Richard Smallwood),
        194n.47
"I Need You to Survive" (Hezekiah Walker),
        88–90, 94, 223
Ice T, 119
    "Cop Killer," 119
ideal masculine communication, 85–86
ideal masculinity
    Patrick Dailey, 84–85
identities, 20n.62, 22, 33, 54n.48, 87, 143,
        154n.16, 160, 170, 188, 199n.3, 204,
        210n.29, 219
    beyond Christianity, 9, 19,
    binary, 24, 26
    in black Christianity, 15, 19,
    insider-outsider, 21
    LGBTQ, 52, 62
    performers', 16, 72
    queer, 88, 155–56, 168
    sexual and gender, 155–56, 197, 200, 212, 217
illegibility of men's gendered performance, 71
Impact Ministries International
        (Detroit), 191–92
In Living Color
    "Men on Film," 50n.33
Israel Houghton & New Breed, 194n.49
    "No Turning Back," 126
Iverson Mall, Temple Hills, MD, 146

Jackson 5, 149
Jackson, Mahalia, 12
Jackson, Michael, 160, 193, 195–6

Jackson, Wayne, 191–2
Jamaican dancehall, 8–9, 8–9n.30
Jamaican dancehall songs
    "Boom Bye Bye" (Buju Banton), 8–9, 8–9n.30
    "Mr. Chi Chi Man" (T.O.K.), 8–9
Jamaican terms:
    proposes aggression toward gay men,
        8–9n.30
    "batty man, batman, batty boy, batty bwoy",
        8–9n.30
Jericho City of Praise (Landover, MD), 149–50
Jesus at the Center (Aaron Lindsey), 126
Jesus, 2, 5, 42, 49, 60, 90, 94, 108, 111, 113, 119,
        120, 126, 168, 178, 195, 196, 198, 206, 208
    is boyfriend, 5
    blood, 168–9, 196
    body, 90
    body theology, 168–9
    Christians believe, 120
    resurrection, 195
    sheep, 178
    "tarrying", 181n.13
    tradition, 167–68
Johnson, Donnie, 172–3, 176
    "Are All the God's Afraid of Black Sexuality?"
        symposium, 172
Johnson, E. Patrick, 11, 29–30, 47–8, 101n.31,
        104, 157, 159–60, 159n.38, 183–184,
Jones, Alisha Lola, 84, 95, 136, 141, 144, 189n.35
    "Are All the Choir Directors Gay?," 5–6,
        12–13, 29–30
Jones, Alvin Augustus, 14n.44, 70n.2, 152
Jones, Bill T. 103, 103n.35
Jones, Bobby, 44, 44n.23, 102
Jones, James H., 164
Jones, Martha Butler, 14n.44, 70n.2
Jongintaba, Yahya (formally Jon Michael
        Spencer), 90–91
Jordan, Louis
    "Run Joe," 118–19
Judeo-Christian faith, 9–10
    roots of gospel, 222
Judeo-Christian heteronormative
    patricarchal resisting feminization, 112
Jungle Cat, 29, 87–88, 89, 90, 91–92, 93–99,
        102–11, 113, 220, 221, 223
Juvenile Curfew Act of 1995, The, 125–26n.34

Kabbalistic literature, 194
Kaepernick, Colin, 184n.23
Keil, Charles, 131–32
Kelly, Frances, 206–7, 206–7n.19, 211
Kemble, Francis A., 75–76

kinesthetic knowledge, 93
    corporate practice, 93
King, Jr., Martin Luther, 28n.84, 118, 202
    2013 Memorial concert, 202–3
    "I Have a Dream", 28n.84
King Tut aka Pharoah Tutankhamun,
    149, 149n.4
Kingsley, Charles, 103–4
Kirk-Duggan, Cheryl, 93–94
Kripal, Jeffrey, 109–10
KRS-One, 146n.75
Kuefler, Matthew, 112
Kunjufu, Jawanza, 99–101, 103, 109 Appendix C
    musical men diminishing their
        masculinity, 104–5

laryngeal
    countertenors, 78–79
    phonology and the use of articulators,
        42–3n.16
    self-control, 90
lavender marriage, 36–7
Lawless, Elaine, 23
Lawrence, Donald, 1
Lee, Spike, 119
    Do The Right Thing, 119
    School Daze soundtrack, 126
Lee, Tony, 133, 146, 147
"Letting slip" or "let slip," 186, 186n.25
Levine, Martin, 164–65
Lewis, Ned, 14
Lexi (Lexi Allen), 12, 57, 158, 186
    The Lexi Show, 52, 158, 186–87
Lindsey, Aaron
    Jesus at the Center, 126
listeners, 1, 10, 43, 50, 72–7, 77n.20, 80, 82, 83,
    90, 129, 137, 145, 157, 158, 160, 161, 163,
    175, 188, 189, 192, 203
    silent, 82, 187
Little Richard, 76–77n.20
liturgical dance, 87, 90–2, 94, 96–7, 194–5
    meaning, 90–92
    praise dance, 94, 95
    relationship with music, spoken word, and
        silence, 91–92
liturgical dancer, 91–92
liturgical practice
    substitution of corporate, 96–97
Live in Wembley, 43–4
Lloyd, Jeremy, 149
Long, Eddie, 17–18, 17–18n.51
Lornell, Kip, 119
Los Angeles, 41, 83, 181n.13

Louis Vuitton, 12, 12n.38
Love Alive IV (Walter Hawkins), 170
Lynn, Gloria, 43n.18

Madison, D. Soyini, 27
Madonna, 163–64n.50, 198–199
Malas-Godlewska, Ewa, 74–75
male absenteeism, 3–4, 5–6, 28, 54–55, 59,
    96, 100, 115, 148, 207–208, 221
Malebranche, David, 186–7n.29
male coded elements, 121, 123
male falsettists, 76–77n.20, 78–79
male femininity, 102, 103–4, 103–4n.39, 105
male high-singing, 43, 69, 71, 72, 75–9, 88, 118,
    198, 221, 75–6n.12
    aesthetic, 76
male movement, 90–1, 93, 96–113, 123
    being emblematic of a gay or ambiguous
        sexual orientation, 104
male participation, 3–5, 8, 24–25, 30–1, 38,
    101, 174–5
    in prayer or intercession ministry, 102–3
male privilege, 23
male singer's identity
    positive reception, 72
male soprano, 70
    E. Patrick Johnson, 47–8, 54–55
Mallakhamb, 94–95, 94–95n.24
mama's boy, 139, 172–73n.1, 174–5, 203
    use for diminished manhood, 174
man physically worshipping, 97–98, 107–9
    complex imagery of, 97–98
Manago, Cleo, 20–1n.62
manufactured voice as a metaphor, 74–75
Maroon 5, 224
Marrow, Mari, 186–7n.29
Martin, Allie, 125
Martin, Steve, 149n.4
Mary Mary, 79–80n.35
masculine vocality, 175
masculinities, 29, 132, 146, 221
    constituted in gospel music, 88
    gay ballroom culture, 156–57
    gospel go-go, 113–14
    in worship, 22, 29–30, 32–33
    Sacred Dance, 90
Masonic Temple, 119
maternal pedagogies, 70
Mays, Vickie M., 186–7n.29
McClurkin, Donnie, 29, 70, 79–80n.35, 87,
    158–59, 165n.53, 168, 178, 187n.30, 191,
    197, 201–17, 202n.11, 220,
    critiques, 69,

Mays, Vickie M. (*cont.*)
  delivered from homosexuality, 17–18, 36–40,
    36n.1, 44–45, 51–9, 54n.48, 63–4, 68–69
  heteropatriarchal scripts, 34,
  on deflection, 198
  public script, 68
  stopping the music, 202–6
McDowell, Amy, 123n.25
McDowell, William, 192
  "I Give Myself Away," 192
McGinn, Bernard, 93–94
"mean mugging" or "mean mug", 142, 142n.64
media, 18, 44, 47, 56, 72, 74, 79, 80, 83n.42, 89,
    106, 107, 110, 111n.66, 119, 142n.66, 149,
    214, 221, 222
  blame for youth victimization, 119
  emotionally expressive, 27–8
  male leadership, 3
  representations of African American, 3
  social media, 29, 36, 48n.28, 50, 61, 62,
    83, 83n.42, 93, 127n.42, 159n.38, 167,
    186n.28, 212
  streaming, 79
  technologies of communication, 29
medieval Western music tradition
  dominance of high voices, 77
Melchor-Barz, Gregory, 36n.2
Messiah, 2, 47
  Blue-eyed, 158n.33
metaphoric
  angelic and gender nonconforming sound, 76
Metropolitan Museum of Art, 149n.4
Meuth, Elsbeth, 94–95, 94–95n.23
mezzo-soprani, 73
microaggressions, 137–38, 137–38n.57, 184
migration scenarios, 96–97
Miller, Monica, 158n.35
  *Slaves to Fashion: Black Dandyism and the
    Styling of Black Diasporic Identity*, 158n.35
Miller, Nancy K., 21–22
Miller, Richard, 75–76n.12, 78–79 ,
Mills, Stephanie, 13–14
  ministers, 3, 36, 37, 56, 69, 74, 80, 82, 138,
    143, 152, 177, 186, 187, 189, 192, 208, 215,
    219. *See* worship leaders
  music, 26, 31, 40, 52n.40, 73, 80, 100, 167,
    198, 204
misandnoir, 45–46, 60
misandry, 45–46
Mitchell, Henry H, 152–53
Mitchell, Jr, Luke, 118–119
Mitchell, VaShawn, 79–80n.35
Moales, Kenneth H., 120n.21

molestation narratives, 156
Moore, James, 1
morality clauses, 25–26
Morgan State University, 72, 72n.6, 80
Morgan, Wess, 79–80n.35
Morris, Gay, 103
Morton, Paul, 224
Morton, PJ, 224
Moss Clark, Mattie, 101–102, 202
Moss, J., 79–80n.35, 158–59
Mountford, Roxanne, 152–53
Mt. Zion Baptist Church in Oakland, 42n.14
Mullen, Nicole C., 36, 36n.1, 214
multilingualism, 53–54, 208–209, 210–11
multimedia, 3, 71–72, 79–80, 106
  and worship, 29
Munoz, José Esteban, 53–54, 55
Munson, Benjamin, 42–43n.16
muscular Christianity, 4, 19, 103, 104, 113, 116,
    123, 123n.25, 139, 156, 172–173n.2, 222
  Amy McDowell on, 123n.25
  growing feminization, 103–104
music and movement, 35, 40, 85, 87, 100, 106,
    113, 123, 142, 143
  early conceptualization of, 90–91
music conferences
  Gospel Music Workshop of America
    (GMWA), 152n.8, 212
  Hawkins Music and Arts Conference, 1, 70n.1
  National Convention of Gospel Choirs and
    Choruses (NCGCC), 70n.1, 120n.21, 212
music ministers, 26, 31, 40, 52n.40, 73, 80, 100,
    167, 198, 204
  ethnomusicological research, 79–80
  flamboyant, 198
  homophobic belief, 99–100
  informed as gay, 30–31
  STD/STIs, 167
music ministry
  as feminine, 44–5, 153–54
  Black countertenor, 73–74
  feminizing or queering act, 43
  form of eunuchoidism to handle women, 220
  instrumental as masculine, 152–53
  manhood, 99–100
  most prized musical competency, 1
  musical and rhetorical devices
  queerness association, 67–68, 103
  "semantic snowballing" 155–56
  shamanic role, 183
  word play, 154–55
musical and social performance
  gender ambiguity, 77–78

musical gesture
  masculine representations, 104
musical performance
  as celebration, 120n.21, 153–54, 164, 215,
    dual process, 72–73
  as an intervention, 77, 153–54, 162–3, 167
  to share a story, 153–54
  uncover and celebrate scandalous
    topics, 153–54
Music of Black Americans, The, (Eileen
  Southern), 90–91
"My Soul Doth Magnify the Lord" (O'landa
  Draper), 43– 44n.23
mystic, 94, 108, 111, 111n.66, 205
  Christian, 110
  Jungle Cat, 94, 108
  Kabbalistic, 194
  realm, 96
  Tiffany Booth, 111
mysticism, 87–88n.2, 93–94, 110, 111–13
  in African-American Pentecostal worship, 94
  distinction between homoeroticism and
    homosexuality, 111–13
  five dimensions within, 87–88n.2
  gospelized, 87–88
  intellectual dimension, 94
  Jeffery Kripal, 110
  Jungle Cat's, 93–94

Naked Truth mixtape songs, *The* (Tonéx),
  156, 157
  "Eye Call," 157
  "Gone" (Dedicated to Corey Hampton)," 157
  "Gotta Love Me," 157
  "Standing In Truth" 157
  "Sweet Tea," 157
National Council of Negro Women, Inc.'s
  (NCNW) annual Black Family Reunion,
  The, 142
Nelson, James, 153–54
New Birth Missionary Baptist Church (Atlanta,
  GA), 17–18
New Black documentary, The, 157, 204
"New G" (aka New Generation), 198–99
New Jack Swing-era, 160, 181
New Life Covenant Church (Chicago, IL), 101
New Olive Baptist Church, The (Washington,
  DC) 118–119
New Orleans, 7, 28, 70, 152, 224
New Psalmist Baptist Church (Baltimore, MD),
  71, 71n.3, 72–73, 74, 79–80, 81,
New York Times, The, 97
Nobili, Anna, 111n.66

"La ballerina del Signore (the ballerina for
  God)," 111n.66
North Carolina, 94, 99, 143, 147
  sanctified music events, 143

Obama, Barack, 28
Oberlin College, 70, 128
observer, 108, 183
  gaze, 13
Odhiambo, Franklin Owino, 105
"oftener"
  soprano, 82
"oftener tenor," 75–76, 82, 88–89
Old Testament, 87, 91
  "when the Spirit of the Lord moves," 87n.1
one's spirituality, sexual orientation, and
  attractiveness, 85–86
open secret, 19, 222
openly gay man, 15–16, 50, 51, 67, 69, 149, 150,
  156, 162–63, 173, 208–9, 218–19
  music ministry colleagues, 208–9
  critics, 214
opera, 71, 72–73, 75, 76–77, 79, 81, 82–3, 84–5
  Farinelli, 74–75
  gender-bending traditions, 73
opera and concert performance Black men
  careers, 76
opera seria, 81
operatic and gospel performance
  use of stylized melisma, 81, 81n.37
"Order My Steps" (Glen Burleigh), 90
Out of the Box Album, 156

Pace, Dejuaii, 20–21, 168n.58
Page, Hugh Jr, 258
"Paris is Burning" documentary, 199, 209,
  211n.31
participant-observers of audience or
  congregation, 150
Patai, Raphael, 193–194
Paul, Jason, 149
peculiar, 8–9, 10, 11, 15, 18, 19, 21–22, 23, 24–25,
  26–27, 188n.34
  aesthetics, 15
  appropriate minister, 84, 84n.45
  aspect of being a believer, 133–34
  audible (and visible), 188n.34
  biblical vision, 137
  constructing peculiarity, 18
  countertenor embodiment, 34, 77
  countertenors as, 72
  go-go, 116, 123, 135
  gospel performances, 19

peculiar (*cont.*)
Holy Spirit peculiarizes, 8–9
"I am delivered," 44, 51, 213–14
message of, 135
physical responses, 87
racial and gendered digitalized
   mixture, 74–75
Peculiar People (band), 129–130, 135–38,
   139–140, 144–145, 204
Bandmembers: MayDay, Warchild, Deborah
   "Jlyrical", Brandon "Chavo", Ronald "Trae"
   Saunders, Aaron Hope, Nate Rhodes, and
   Jay Julien, 135n.55
"Peculiar People Sound Requirement List,"
   146n.74
Peculiar People and Tonéx, The, 156
peculiarity, 9, 23, 24, 45, 83, 84n.45, 126–27,
   130, 135–8, 178, 188, 188n.34, 192,
   221, 222
Peirce, Charles, 155–56, 199
Pentecost, Day of, 1–2
Pentecostal Assemblies of the World (PAW),
   152, 168–69, 178, 208
Pentecostal beliefs, 1–2, 10, 39n.7, 40n.10,
   171, 193
Pentecostal African-American, 105, 116,
   151, 153–54
"cultural genitals," 24
deliverance, 42
ex-gay, 167, 168n.58
Holy Spirit, 42–43
homosexuality, 20–21, 40
peculiar believer, 10, 21–22
"struggle" term, 39, 52, 52n.40
Pentecostal Church of Jesus Christ, 120n.21
Pentecostal Communities, 65–66, 150–51, 163
Pentecostal congregations
heteropatriarchal scripts, 148
male-centered theologies, 4–5, 13, 24
reestablish borders, 24–25
women, 3, 4–4, 13, 20–21, 23–25
Pentecostal worship, 1–2, 8, 105
musical telos, 51
telos, 1, 204
percussion, 88, 116, 12, 123, 124, 129–36, 144–
   46, 192, Appendix B
body percussion, 123–24
in go-go, 34, 123–24
registers as masculine, 135
signifies, 129
strategic attraction, 133
performance, 11, 27, 29, 30
aural-visual, 8

black sacred music, 11
castrati and eunuchs, 77–78
castrato performances, 85–86
demonstrative, 30
of irony, 88–89
Morgan State University repertoire, 80–81
peculiar, 26
performance competence, 9, 15–16,
   72–73, 79
performance venue context, 80–81
queer, 16, 19
rhetorical, 6
ritual, 40n.10
seven functions, 38n.6
signifiers, 15
social familiarity in the "black church," 82
"sound like women", 79
Performance domain of the African-American
   Church worship
instrumental of the musician, 150
performance theory, 4, 54, 170, 201
dark play, 162–63, 170, 210–12, 212, 217
deep play, 162–63
performative possibility
of bodily orifices, 100–1
performer's incompetence, 84–85
persona, 78, 210
artist, 35
black Baptist man, 83–84
choir director, 12
Christianity, 116
countertenor, 77
international, 158
public, 39, 44, 215
sonic, 118
unspoken, 197
phallic symbols, 94, 111, 112, 162
phallogocentric, 201
-ism, 18
"Pheremone"(Prince), 193
Phipps, Wintley, 52
phobic, 45–6, 55
Pitt, Richard, 97n.28, 174–5, 182, 186, 214
pleasure, 10–1, 18, 19, 25, 37, 42–3, 60, 63, 108,
   117, 123,
in musical services, 19, 205
pain and pleasure, 127–8, 130, 140,
   148, 190–1
pleasure derived from pain, 100–1
Sex and transcendence, 11n.36, 108
Tantra, 94–5
pole, 88–96, 94–5n.24
Asherah, 112

as cross, 94, 108–9
circus arts, 94–5
Jesus Christ's body, 108
khamba, 94–5n.24
phallic, 111
symbolic barriers, 111–12
symbolism appropriating, 99
worshipping on, 94
white women's use, 110–11
see also, pole fitness
pole dance, 88–96, 107, 194–5, 220–1
as blasphemous, 107
US male, 94–5n.25
pole dancer
male, praise body language, 88
pole dancing, 34, 90–91, 104, 108
incorporation into worship, 91–92
praise pole dance, 90–91, 95, 96, 98
unconventional, 87–88
see also, Jungle Cat
pole fitness, 94–95, 94–95n.25, 96, 97–98,
99, 103–4
instructor, 94
Pollard, Deborah Smith, 133, 154, 154n.16
Pope, 111n.66
Postman, Leo, 201n.9
prostration, 192, 194–95
body-on-body, 191–92,
Pot, The (Radio), 127
praise dance, 30, 88, 90–6, 99, 102–5, 107–9,
111, 115, 122, 220
dancer, 88n.2
masculine representations, 105
praise pole dance, 87–8, 95–96
hegemonic notions of dancing, 113
prayer, 101, 181n.12
contemplative, 181n.13
female homosociality of, 101
"ritual dimension", 87–8n.3
"Prayed Up" (Karen Clark-Sheard), 126
prayer room, 46, 101
"Praying gay Christian men," 182
preachers. 4, 13, 15, 17, 29, 31, 40, 51, 79, 138,
153, 167, 174, 177, 197, 206, 211, 215, 217,
219, 220, 221
expectations, 30–31
get a pass, 174
male role, 30–31, 32–33, 60
paradigmatic facilitator, 6
same-sex desire as demonic, 62
visible masculinities, 29–30
preacher-musician, 6–7, 148, 151–52, 154, 176–
77, 203, 204, 215, 221

androgynous, 221
queer, 34, 158–59, 171
role, 151–52
self-pleasure, 18n.57
worship leader role, 151
Preachers of L.A., 158–59
preacher-vocalist, 48–9
aesthetics as vocal style, 48–49
preaching in African-American
Tradition, 152–53
"celebration moment," 152–53
gender identification, 152–53
in mainline Christian
denominations, 152–53
performance, 152–53
speech fluctuation, 152–53
voice modulations, 152–53
preferences, 36, 37, 71, 76, 84, 89, 162, 177
congregation perspectives, 27–9
queer sexual, 15
"present like a man", 84
prima donna, 76–77, 81
Primm, Beny J., 186–87n.29
Prince, 76–77n.20, 160, 192, 193
Prince of Praise, 17–18, 96,
private devotion, 4, 93, 182
profane gestural connotation, 91–92
progressive sexuality, 25–26, 171
Promise Keepers, 103–4
protocol, 82, 200
in the black church, 82
performed, 200
public arts interventions, 71
Public Broadcast Station (PBS), 205n.16
Public Enemy, 146n.75
public expectations influence African American
vocalities, 72–73
pulpit ministry, 3, 6n.27, 24, 60
gendered, 152–53, 215
queering of, 25, 151
"Pumped up Kicks" (Foster the People), 163–64
Puritanism the Second Great Awakening, 90–91

Queens, 47–8, 208
Butch, 156–57n.25
Femme, 156–57n.25
queer body theologies, 151
queer euphemisms, 43–44
"deliverance", 44
"eye call", 157–8
"Eye Call" (Tonéx), 157–58
love interest designations, 43–44
"sweet tea" 157, 157n.30

queer euphemisms (*cont.*)
  "T", 158
  "top," 217
  "twirl," 105, 105n.46
queer gaze, 158
  in heated worship, 104
queer identities performed
  in gospel music, 19, 26, 88, 156, 179
queer idiom, 213
  (fore)father, 211, 211n.32
  house, 211, 211n.32
  kids or children as, 163–64, 211n.32
  turned (out), 211, 211n.32
queer perspectives of Tonéx, 150–51
queer potential, 4, 8, 12, 13, 18n.51, 26, 30, 34,
    53–4, 58–60, 66, 83, 85, 99, 103, 107, 118,
    158, 180, 211, 220
  anxiety, 85
  Dance, 107
  of countertenors, 82–83, 85
  "pathological", 214
queer sexuality, 100, 104, 171
  counting the cost, 173
queer theory, 25
queering of
  pulpit ministry, 151
queerness, 2n.8, 12, 17, 19, 20, 30, 38, 40, 47,
    50, 52n.40, 55, 58, 67–9, 148, 160, 171,
    174, 176, 182, 188, 201, 210, 211, 213, 217,
    220, 222
  African-American identity, 150
  facility, 205
  gospel music social networks, 150
  musical, 16
  practices and intimacies in Pentecostal
    Christianity, 150
  shamanistic trait, 203–4
  social, 191
  unmarking, 209
  worship, 116

racial and gendered biases, 74–75
  African American men, 76–77
  disparity in casting in, 76–77
racial/phenotypic attributes, 20–21
radio, 9, 14, 29, 70, 131, 169, 193, 219, 14n.44
  event, 195
  interview, 20
  personalities, 128
Ragin, Derek Lee, 74–75, 76–7, 77n.20
"Rainbow" (Tonéx), 157, 157n.28
rainbow, 12
  biblical, 157

LGBT, 157
Ralph, Sheryl Lee, 186–7, 186n.29
Rare Essence, 128
read, 19, 49–50n.33, 195, 209, 211. *See also* black
    gay vernacular
realness, 156–57n.25, 195, 200, 210, 211n.31,
    212. *See also* black gay vernacular
reappropriating gestures, 104
re-code
  heterosexual codes, 154–55
Redman, Matthew, 115n.1
religious pluralism, 4, 87–88
restrictions, 22, 34
  ecclesial, denominational, and
    organizational, 87–88
  "masculine", 34
Resurrection Day, 1–2, 87–88, 95, 146
rhetoric
  -centered emphasis, 133
  African American worship, 6–7
  conventional, 26–26
  deliverance, 61
  gospel, 152
  heterosexist, 175–76
  of the pulpit, 25, 49, 150
  other rhetorics, 220–21
  Pentecostal, 19
  "unmanly" or boyish, 175–76
rhetorical, 29, 58
  art of silence, 174
  congregants' perception, 49
  Daryl Coley, 43–44
  Donnie McClurkin, 168, 206–7, 217
  denote the male role, 6n.27
  deliverance, 52n.40, 213
  devices, 43–4, 151
  domain, 150
  "effeminate," 50
  heterosexuality, 202
  indelicate, 50–1
  Peculiar People, 135–6
  preachers, 40
  Tonéx, 151, 154–5, 161, 171
  unspoken, 174, 179, 186, 197
Rich, Adrienne, 38
Richen, Yoruba, 157
  The New Black (2013), 157
ritual, 9, 183
  African aesthetics, 131
  approaches, 1–2n.5
  aural-visual dynamics, 11
  aspects, 40
  Ballroom culture, 199n.3

body-to-body, 188, 189–90, 191–92
coed, 111n.66
cultivates solidarity, 186
Catherine Bell, 186
distraction, 204
deliverance ritual, 32, 38, 39, 40, 43, 44–45,
    52, 52n.40, 60, 63, 67
dominate symbols, 168–69
expanded, 145
feminine-presenting men targets, 60
gospelized mysticism, 87–88
house music, 159–60
impromptu, 61
initiation, 183
musical, 39, 40
outside culturally relevant, 142
Pentecostal holiness, 66
performer, 221
"pomp and circumstance", 192
praying, 181
prestige, 19
preacher-musicians, 151–52
monitoring, 125
outcomes, 41
Richard Schechner (four perspectives), 38n.5
"speaking in tongues", 173–4n.3
welcoming and affirming to LGBTQ
    expression, 159
ritual dimension, 87–88, 88n.3
ritual of unspokenness, 17, 174, 179, 180–81,
    182, 183, 186
Cheryl Glenn, 174
empower/disempower for homosexual
    men, 182
ministry of presence, 171, 173, 220
moving from, 174
performance of sung, 182
on silence, 179, 179n.11
roles in worship 5, 6, 11, 13, 49, 60, 151
preacher, 6, 26, 30–31, 209
vocal musician, 6, 30–31, 215
Roman Catholic Church
manipulated and violated men's sexuality and
    castrating, 74
Ross III, Clifton, 149
Rousseau, Jean-Jaques, 66n.84
rumor, 8, 12n.40, 12–13, 14–16, 17, 37, 208–9,
    cautionary repertoire, 90
defuse, 201
Donnie McClurkin, 51–52, 56, 213–14
Hezekiah Walker, 88–89
life of their own, 201n.9
queer sexual, 12–13

Tymel Thompson, 36–37
Walter Hawkins, 170n.66
Run DMC, 119
    Raising Hell Tour, 119

sacred expression, 96, 108
sacred performance
since middle 16th century Europe, 76
safe place, 223
    LGBT, 223
    party, 119–20,
    sacred, 159–60,
    term, 116–117n.5
St. Louis, MO, 101
St. Patrick's Day, 96
"Salome's Veiled Dance and David's Full Monty"
    (Cheryl Kirk-Duggan), 93
same sex relationships, 17, 19
same-gender desire, 5, 6, 8, 49, 53, 54, 62, 65,
    67, 156, 159, 167, 183, 251
same-gender loving, 20–21, 20n.62, 34,
    36–37, 40, 43, 67–68, 151, 171, 178, 180,
    188, 195, 202, 212, 214, 217, 39n.8
association as "big problem," 172–73
Cleo Manago, 20–1n.62
never been sexually violated, 156
"spiritually transmitted diseases," 167
Sanders, George, 97n.28
Sartre, Jean-Paul
    "bad faith," 188
    Tonéx differs, 188n.33
Saturday Night Live, 149n.4
Schechner, Richard, 38, 38n.5, 162–63, 210–11
    dark play, 162–63
Scholte, Peter, 223–24
    "We Are One in the Spirit," 223–24
Scholz, Piotr, 77–78, 77–78n.29
Scott La Rock, 146n.75
self-deception, 181–82, 187, 188,
    188n.33, 192
self-disclosure, 16–17, 39–51, 56, 57–58, 68,
    150, 158, 159, 188, 201–2, 208, 222
self-identify, 39n.8, 69, 173
    David Coley, 17
    consequences, 69, 176
    "I am delivered", 49
    preserve livelihood, 30
    Tymel Thompson, 37
self-pleasure, 18, 18n.57, 94–95, 104, 189
    masturbation, 189
semantic associations, 94
"semantic snowballing" 155–56
Semiotics, 199, 205–6

sensual, 10, 58, 87–88, 93, 105
  exotic and sex work, 105
  Song of Solomon, 105n.41
sensual conveyance
  in public sacred space, 93
sensuousness and erotic suggestiveness, 90
  Kirk Franklin, 156–57n.24
sermonettes, 151–52, 176
sermonic selection, 18–19, 80
sermons, 4, 23, 40, 62, 174, 187, 206–7, 217
  African American Pentecostal, 189
  alter call, 217
  antagonistic, 60
  anti-homosexual, 15, 17, 29–30, 31, 39, 50–51,
    57, 63, 65, 186
  anti-feminization, 202–3
  COGIC, 202–3
  deliverance, 44–45
  death knell, 174
  defuse, 180
  heteropatriarchal, 197
  Holy-Bible based, 31
  homo-antagonistic, 202–3
  homophobic, 29–30, 174, 180
  "homosexual spirit, 62
  impromptu, 151–52
  sexual abstinence, 189
  social justice, 216
  socially silent, 186
sex therapy, 94–95
sexual ambiguity, 21, 88
sexual and gendered vocal sound, 85
  social and theological navigation, 72–73
"Sexual Healing" (Marvin Gaye), 188n.34
sexual healing, 43–4, 44, 167–68, 189, 188.34
sexual proclivities of men, 88
  sexual violation, 52n.42, 53, 55, 156,
    164, 190–1
  queer, 53
  spectrum, 52n.42
  stereotype, 156
  theme of youth, 164
  sexuality, 5–6, 8, 10, 11, 11n.36, 12, 13, 15–17,
    17–8n.51, 18, 19, 22–23, 25, 32, 35, 41, 47,
    52n.39, 54, 68, 69, 80, 85–6, 88–9, 100,
    104–105, 108–112, 153–154, 159–60, 163,
    165, 167, 167–69, 184–185, 197, 198, 205,
    206, 206–7n.19, 206–7.n20, 207, 208, 213,
    221, 225,
  abusive discourse, 93
  African American Christianity, 39n.7, 108,
    139, 153–54, 156, 173n.1, 221, 222,

bareback, 166
black men's, 27–28
castration, 74
confusing and abusive discourse about, 93
conflation of, 62–63, 175
deacons and elders, 49
delivered, 66
discreet, 182–183
down low, 54
fearful of Black, 32–33
in religious studies, 23–24
intervention, 161–162,
misandnoir, 60
misuse of, 195
molestation, 207–8
monitored, 213
queer, 59, 99–100, 171, 173, 204
registers as feminine or queer, 5–6
situational, 156–57,
surrogates, 58–59
Tantra, 94–95
terms to question manhood, 139
Torain's death, 14
unethical and reprobate, 178
unspoken, 205–206
sexualized symbols and signifiers
  mixing of, 97
Shekinah, 193–94n.45, 194, 194n.46, 222
Shirley, George, 76–77, 84–85, 101
"shut up and sing," 184, 184.23
signifier, 2, 10, 21–2, 29, 35, 155
  androgyny and sexual impotency, 77–78
  castrati, 77–78
  Donnie McClurkin, 211
  female seduction, 97
  God, 10, 151–52
  homosexuality concealment, 88–89
  human martyrdom, 178
  "minister", 84n.45
  smoke, 1–2n.8
  Tonéx, 15
signifyin(g), 8–9n.30, 10n.33, 17–18n.51, 43–44,
    81, 154–56, 159–60, 162–63, 165, 171, 180,
    182, 188–89, 198–99, 210–11, 215
Simpson-Currenton, Evelyn, 13–14
"sings us," 81
sissy, 60, 61, 63, 175, 206–7
  "sissified," 101
situational sexuality. 17–18n.52, 40–41,
    53, 156–57
"slain in the Spirit," 173–74, 173–74n.4
Slaughter, Alvin, 52–53

Slominski, Tes, 36n.2

Smallwood, Richard, 5n.23, 13–14, 59, 76–77n.20, 118–119, 149, 193–94n.47

Smith, Horace, 168–69, 168–69n.59

Smith, Michael W., 96–97

Smith, Rend, 125n.31

Smitherman, Geneva, 154–55

Smokey Robinson
   A Quiet Storm album, 193

sneezing
   euphemism and symbolism, 190–91, 190–91n.40

Snorton, C. Riley, 12–13, 53–54, 103

social and theological, 31, 72–73, 79, 84n.45, 85, 109–110, 120–121, 168–169, 171, 184–185, 186,
   issues, 85–86
   Jungle Cat, 99
   naviagation, 72
   Peculiar People's, 135–136

social bilingualism or multilingualism, 54, 208–9, 210
   McClurkin's, 53–54
   also code-switching, 141, 210

social change, 35

social contract, 12–13, 66, 66n.84, 150–51
   "don't ask, don't tell," 12, 150–51

society's expectations
   gendered bodies make sound, 73–74

sociovisbility, 183–84

"Some Day" (Nathan Carter, Jr), 71, 72–3, 77, 79–80, 81, 85–86
   treble timbres, 77

Song of Solomon, 90, 105n.41

sonic and visual stereotypes, 71

sonic patriarchal construct, 32–33, 74–75

sonic symbolism
   of male high-singing, 77

Sorrett, Josef, 5n.22

sotto voce, 181, 181n.15, 182

sounded convergence, 129, 130–31, 132

Southern, Eileen, 75–77, 90–91, 124

spatial-genitalia, 24, 152–53, 177

speaking in tongues, 8, 40, 42n.16, 43, 46n.26, 173–74, 181n.15, 203
   speaking in other tongues, 2, 46, 50
   speech and sexual orientation, 42n.16
   xenoglossia, 46n.26, 173–74n.3
   See also Holy Spirit
   speech, 6–7, 9, 12, 42–3n.16, 49–50n.33, 123, 134–5, 138, 155, 183, 186, 187, 197, 179n.11

amplifed-muffled, 130–1

Barack Obama, 28

censored, 182

continuum between speech and singing, 47

defect from or advertise queer possibility, 66

gendered male, 179

manuscript preaching, 152–3

mimicking, 124

phallogocentric, 201

queered, 100–1

"talking drums," 124

speech pathology
   assessing deliverance, 63
   gender expression, 59
   impediment, 50, 62
   rhetorical technique, 57

Spiller, Henry, 36n.2, 111–112

spirit, 9, 93–94, 96, 113, 140, 167–68, 204, 206
   catch, 48
   David, 92, 198–99
   demons, 52n.40
   European and American colonizers, 65
   "familiar spirits", 133–34, 211
   -filled, 10, 11
   homosexual, 61, 62
   "in Sprit and in truth", 20, 156, 171, 180, 184, 186–87, 188
   -inspired, 205
   masculine, 3
   perverted, 61–62
   of the lord, 7–8, 13, 41n.12, 39, 41, 42–43, 66, 81, 87, 88, 200,
   "slain in the Spirit", 173–74
   taboo, 194–95
   "thrill", 42 , 43–44
   "warrior chants and unquiet spirits", 196, *see also* Holy Spirit, spirt of God

The Spirit of David album (Fred Hammond), 92

spiritual interiority, 87, 151

spiritual warfare, 31, 120, 123, 130, 142–43

spiritually transmitted diseases, 168

spoiled identity, 215

SSAATTBB choir, 71, 71n.4

"Stand" (Donnie McClurkin), 186–87n.30

standing imagery, 186–97, 186–87n.30

Standing-n-Truth: Breaking the Silence Documentary, 186–187, 186–187n.29

"Standing in the Need of Prayer", 181–82
   ("It's me, it's me, oh Lord"), traditional Negro spiritual, 180–1, 181n.12, 181n.14

"standing in (one's) truth", 151, 186–187, 188
   motivation for, 174

"Standing in Truth" (Tonéx), 157
STD/STI, 161, 162, 164, 165, 166, 167, 168,
    169, 170
    See also HIV/AIDS
Stellar Awards, The, 1, 1.n1, 36, 40, 48–49, 59,
    88–89, 195, 198–99
Stephens, Helen, 43n.18
Stephenson, Charles, 119
Stereotype, 7, 32, 43, 53–4, 60, 71, 102
    African-derived physical and spiritual, 31
    choir director, 6, 8, 12, 16–17, 115–16,
        198, 218
    bodily, musical participation, 102
    catalyst for same gender desire, 156
    male choir directors or vocal worship leaders
        are gay, 29–30, 75–76
    men's worship, 35, 140–41
    Men on Film sketch of *In Living Color*,
        49–50n.33
    male vocal participation as queer, 38
    sexual vioaltion, 156
    "sing high like a woman", 75–77
    spoken queerness phonetically, 50,
stigma, 17, 58, 186–7n.29
    black men together, 147–48, 153–54
    black male absenteeism, 54–55
    euphoria, 193
    homosexuality, 17, 49, 58, 68, 88–89
    queerness, 58
    victims of imbalanced, sexualized same-
        gender power, 215
Stonewall, 154–55
"Stop the Violence," 146–147, 146n.75
*The Structure of Singing: System and Art in Vocal
    Technique* by Richard Miller, 78–79
style, 2, 16–17, 48–49, 72
    African American singing, 81
    African-derived, 76, 123–124
    ambiguous attire, 153–54
    Andrew Caldwell, 50, 51
    aural-visual, 43–44
    Caleb Brundidge, 105
    call and response, 71
    castrato, 74–75
    communal remembrance, 120–121
    Richard Miller, 78–79
    concert and opera performance, 76–77
    D'Angelo, 194
    Daryl Coley, 42
    David, 92
    Donnie McClurkin, 56–57
    gender expression, 39
    go-go, 126, 127–29, 133–35, 138, 147

gospel go-go, 124–125, 132, 141, 147
    Kirk Franklin, 175
    lead vocalist, 48–49
    masculine style of worship, 9
    non-religious dance, 90–1
    Olly Wilson, 130–31
    Prince, 193
    Ricky Dillard, 198, 200
    sermon, 15
    SGL, 148
    The Holy Ghost Enforcers, 12
    Tonéx, 152–53, 160–2, 170, 171, 195
    vocals, 6, 146
    worship, 32–33
"The Supernatural Voice," 77–78
surveillance, 13, 53–54, 66, 102–04, 107, 124,
    184, 217
    real or imagined, 93
    police, 118–19
Sweet Holy Spirit Church (Chicago), 192
Sweet Tea (E. Patrick Johnson), 30, 47, 101n.31,
    157n.30
symbol, 10–3, 29, 33, 35, 45, 46, 75, 88, 90, 94,
    97, 104n.39, 109, 111, 113, 157, 162, 163,
    168, 196, 199, 200
    constructed in gospel music, 88
    impurity of women's menstrual cycle and
        men's semen 45–46n.25
    of the pole, 87–88, 94

"Tainted Love" (Soft Cell), 189
"talking drums", 124
    US colonial prohibitions, 124
Talmudic sages, 193–194
tantra, 94–95
    celibacy, 94–95, 95n.23
    yoga philosophy, 94–95
Tatum, Beverly Daniel, 117n.5
"Taxation Without Representation," 119n.16
television and Internet domains, 79–80
Tennessee, 46, 72, 203
tensions
    social and theological, 79, 185
tessitura, 71–72, 217
testimony, 39, 41–2, 41n.12, 50n.38, 46–66, 106,
    155, 164, 187–8, 201, 210, 105n.44, 170n.64
    becoming heterosexual, 39, 41, 48
    biblical phrase, 87n.1
    biblical reference, 53–54
    delivered testimony template, 51, 58
    musical, 41
    pathological perception, 59–60
    sung, 48

theopolitical principle
standing in one's truth, 173
theopolitics, 8, 10, 39, 213
of fire and desire, 40
of knowledge is, 10
"This Is The Air I Breathe" (Byron Cage) 96–97
Thomas, Jeffrey, 102
Thomas, Walter, 80, 175–76
Tindley, Charles A.
"Beams of Heaven" (Some Day), 71
Tisdale, Lenora Tubbs, 202n.10
Tonéx, 15–16, 18, 21–22, 29, 34, 51–52, 57–
58, 68, 88–89, 104, 149, 150–52, 153–58,
160–74, 177n.8, 178–97, 199, 203–5, 208,
213, 221, 223, 15n.48
"Am I Post? Am I Trade?" 156–57
attire, 153–54
"B 13ND, " 188, 192
"Believer," 196
creative process, 151
"Eye Call," 157–58
"F@ce Down," 188–89, 194, 194n.51
"GLOR 3X, " 193–94
on gospel music scene, 68
"Make Me Over," 196
muscular body, 156–57n.24
musical and rhetorical devices, 154
name changes, 15n.48
not repenting, 176
Out of the Box album, 156
as a preacher-musician, 151–52
radical heterogeneity, 188n.34
Rainbow EP, 157
rejecting deliverance, 172 (see also Anthony
C. Williams; B.Slade)
"reprobate mind," 208, 213
shamanic role, 183
"Sneeze," 188–95
"Standing In Truth," 157
Standing-N-Truth Documentary, 186,
186n.29
The Naked Truth mixtape, 156
The New Black documentary, 157, 176, 178,
204, 205n.16
"Unspoken", 188, 195
Unspoken Album, 150, 151, 154–55, 157–58,
160, 164, 171, 173, 179, 180, 181, 183, 184,
186, 187
"Work On Me," 149, 196
Torain, Eric, 13–4, 16, 21
Townes, Emilie, 107, 107n.54, 196
transparent, 41, 93, 140
appears, 184

implications of queer identity, 151
kinesthetic knowledge to private devotion, 93
not transparent, 187
treble timbres, 43, 61, 77, 198–99
"aural genealogy," 77
sounded embodiment, 77
Tribbett, Tye, 126, 172–73, 176n.7, 211
cheating, 158–59
come out expression, 172–73
"Victory", 126
trickster, 183
Trinity, 91–92
Trinity Broadcasting Network (TBN), 29, 36
Trinity United Church of Christ, 215–16
Truth Apostolic Community Church (San
Diego, CA) 152
Truth, D.A., 158–59
TRUVADA aka PrEP, 161–62, 161–62n.45
Turino, Thomas, 155–56
"turned out," 53, 206–207, 211,
Turner, Kathleen S., 91–92
Tweed, Thomas, 111

unchurched, 140, 154
undignified praise, 30, 103, 105, 113, 115n.1,
115–16, 123, 139, 141
"Getting ignorant," 89–88, 137–38, 139,
141–42, 143
"Undignified" (Matthew Redman), 115n.1
United States, 76, 104
African-derived music styles, 76
Black men's dance performance, 106
colonialism, 31, 123–24
forms of terror, 65
gaze upon black men's bodies, 103
HIV/AIDS pandemic, 17
media, 44–45
stigmatization of STD/STI, 164–65
theologically conservative, 216
White supremacy, 103
University of California–Los Angeles, 82–83
University of Chicago, 15, 53, 162n.46, 186n.29
Ethnoise!, 162n.46
unspeakable, 50, 171, 173–74, 176, 180
unspoken, 34, 64, 150–51, 153–55, 174, 177,
179, 180, 181, 182, 185, 187, 196, 219–23
within African-American contexts,
156–57, 176–77
culture of unspokenness, 65–66
through gestures, 182
as rhetoric of silence, 176–77, 179
taboo, 64
in worship leadership, 173

Unspoken album (Tonéx), 149–51, 153–55, 157–59, 160, 164, 170–171, 173, 177, 179–80, 180–181, 182, 183–184, 186–87
gestural responses to God, 182
"Wired," 150–51, 159–61, 163, 164, 166, 169

Vandross, Luther, 43–4, 43n.21
Vaughn, Sarah, 43n.18
Verizon Center (Washington, DC), 149
vertical dance, 98
Victorianism, 32, 65, 91, 103, 103n.35
vocal classification or designation, 71-2
    absence of, 71–72
    European-derived concert music composer, 71–72
    fluidity between conventional, 71–72
    gender-inclusive and imaginative casting, 71–72
    rare, 71–72
    traditional prerogative and progressiveness, 71–72
    Western classical music, 73
vocal music ministers, 1
    choir directors, 5, 13, 16, 29
    worship leader, 12–13
vocal worship leadership, 189, transdenominational, 80
"Vogue" (Madonna), 163–64n.50, 199
Voguing, 163–64, 163–64n.50, 199
Voice Studies Now Conference at UCLA, 82–83n.41

"Walk Like an Egyptian" (The Bangles), 149n.4
Walker, Alice, 23, 23n.71
Walker, Corey D.B. 10
Walker, Hezekiah, 48–49, 79n.35, 88n.5, 88–89, 223
Walker, Monique, 88–89
Walser, Robert, 21
Walton, Jonathan, 29, 79–80
"War Cry," 120, 123
    pentecostal motif, 120n.21
Warchild (rapper), 136
Wartofsky, Alona, 119
Washington City Paper, 125
Washington Performing Arts Society (WPAS; now Washington Performing Arts), 14
Washington Post, The, 14, 97
Washington, DC, 14–6, 14n.44, 26–8, 28n.84, 34, 71, 79, 94, 115, 116, 118–19, 119n.16, 121, 124–9, 126n.34, 135, 138, 139, 142, 146, 147, 149, 163, 176n.7, 202

Duke Ellington School for the Arts (DESA), 71
Mt. Calvary Holy Church, 60
Mt. Sinai Church, 2n.7, 15n.49
1968 uprisings, 118
1990s crack cocaine epidemic, 14
Washington, DC–Baltimore, 79–80
Washington National Opera (WNO)
    The Educational Department, 81
Watch This!: The Ethics and Aesthetics of Black Televangelism (Jonathan Walton), 79–80
Waters, Maxine, 186n.29
Watson, Nick, 103
"We Are One in the Spirit" (Peter Sholte), 223–24
Weeks, Thomas, 20
West, Cornel, 32–33
Western art music
    African American novices, 81
    conventions, 85–86
    unconventional gospel music, 73
Western art music pedagogues
    of black voices as inadequate instruments, 74–75
    countertenor voice, 74–75
    gimmick, 74–75
Western church music repertoire, 77
White supremacist, 32, 107
    gaze upon black men's bodies, 103
Whitfield, Thomas, 43n.18
Whitley, Kym, 186n.29
Whitman, Walt, 13–14, 216
Wilkins, Kimberly "Sweet Brown," 48–49.28
Williams, Anthony C. or Tonéx, 15, 15n.48, 51, 57, 149–51
Williams, Anthony Sr, 178
Williams, Nolan, 13–14
Williams, Pamela, 186n.29
Williams, Yvette (née Graham), 153
Williamson, Reginald, 2–3, 100, 139
Wills, Denise Kersten, 118n.9
Wilson, Nancy, 43n.18
Wilson, Olly
    heterogeneous sound ideal, 130–31
Winans, The, 45, 202
Winans, CeCe, 79–80n.35
Winans, Vicki, 14
"Wired" 150–51, 159–63, 168–69
"With Long Life (He Will Satisfy Me)" (Israel Houghton), 194n.49
WKYS 93.9 FM, 128
womanism, 23, 23n.71
    "womanish," 23n.71, 23

womanist, 21, 22, 23, 23n.71, 93
  biblical interpretation of David dancing, 93
women contralti, 73
Wood, Dewayne, 169–70, 169–70n.64
  "God Still Heals" 169–70
  "Let Go, Let God" 169–70n.64
Word Network, The, 29, 52, 70n.2, 71–72, 79,
    79n.35, 158, 186–87
"Worked it Out" (Ricky Dillard and New
    Generation), 198–99
Worship
  aesthetics, 1, 8, 11, 30, 72–3
  African- American Pentecostal, 1
  black Pentecostal Christian, 155–56
  connotations of deliverance rituals in, 67–68
  embodied worship, 87
  erotic, 10
  explores sensuality, 97
  heathenish and profane, 90–91
  homomusicoerotics, 11
  iconicity, 10, 105, 160, 199, 205, 222
  leaders role, 1
  peculiar masculine, 97
  performance, 1
  physical pleasure, 8, 11, 108

queer believers equipped, 67–68
queer gaze, 104, 105
queering act, 43
restrictions for black men, 34
roles in, 30–31
"setting the atmosphere" 1
singing, 1
subordinate position, 64
transdenominational worship leader,
    80, 85–86
and women, 23
worship leader, 1
worship leader, 1, 2, 11, 13, 16, 80
  competency, 85–86
  preacher-musician, 151
worship practices
  Baptist and Pentecostal, 96–97
  governmental policies, 125–26
worth the wait movement, 189, 189n.36
Wyatt, Gail E., 186–87n.29

Yale Divinity School, 105n.41
Yale Institute of Sacred Music, 117–18
YouTube, 11, 29, 36, 93, 95, 97, 98–99,
    104–105